W9-DDI-669

ARCHITECTURAL METAL SURFACES

ARCHITECTURAL METAL SURFACES

L. William Zahner

WILEY

JOHN WILEY & SONS, INC.

Library of Congress Cataloging-in-Publication Data:
Zahner, L. William.
   Architectural metal surfaces / by L. William Zahner.
      p. cm.
   Includes bibliographical references and index.
   ISBN 0-471-26335-4 (cloth)
   1. Metals—Surfaces. 2. Architectural metal-work. I. Title.
   TA459.Z23 2004
   721'.0447—dc22

                                             2004011438

Printed in the United States of America
10 9 8 7 6 5 4 3 2 1

To Meg, Katy, Claire, and Liam

CONTENTS

PREFACE

> *"Many persons hold the opinion that the metal industries are fortuitous and that the occupation is one of sordid toil, and altogether a kind of business requiring not so much skill as labour. But as for myself, when I reflect carefully upon its special points one by one, it appears to be far otherwise."*
>
> —BERMANNUS, Burgomaster of Chemnitz, Saxony, 1550

Bermannus was around in the days when working with metal consisted of mining, smelting, casting and hammering. Most metals were used as armaments created by blacksmithing. Blacksmithing was hot, dirty, and grimy work, very physically demanding. Metal was cast into strips and hammered repeatedly, folding, bending, heating, and quenching until the right stiffness and hardness were obtained. These guys had to be brutes.

They were also the most skilled individuals in the area. They were in high demand. Some of these early metal smiths experimented in different surfacing textures. Imagine the first knight to show up for battle adorned with hammered and polished armor. Armor made of etched iron and inlaid with brass. Or the acclaim the first damascene sword would receive. It was probably an honor to get whacked with it.

It would have required weeks, perhaps months to create one set of elaborate armor, and the task would require someone of particular skill. In a lifetime only a few sets of armor could be produced by the same individual. Metal sheet and plate was surely in short supply, so experimenting with the finish would have been of particular consequence.

A damascene sword required incredible skill and knowledge to produce. The texture and character of these ancient blades is an art difficult to match today, centuries later. The artistry of the surface was thought to possess mystical properties, adding to the emotional desire of these fine metal surfaces.

In the past 25 years, I have had the opportunity to work on projects of fascinating and challenging architecture, architecture that challenged the very limits of current metal manufacture. Some of the projects have been sordid toils, but many have expanded the current knowledge of the art of surfacing in metal.

A renaissance of sorts is occurring today, a renaissance that has expanded the realm of metal like no time before. There have never been such a variety of metals, finishes, and textures. Coupled with digital definition and computer-controlled design and manufacturing, the full benefit of metal is available to the designer. Structural characteristics such as tension and compression behaviors can be intertwined with economy, aesthetics, and fabrication techniques.

Like the early metalsmiths, working on metal surfaces would become nothing but toil if we simply repeated the same color, tone, and finish over and over. Certainly, there is a place for mass-produced blandness. The early model T designs offered a choice—black. After some time, the demand changes. Do we wish to be unique, or do we have a subconscious desire to veer away from bland uniformity?

The attributes of all surfaces are similar, governed by physical constraints dictated by the interface with the ambient. All surfaces must relate with the surroundings. Sometimes this is an intimate relationship, an exchange of electrons, a mix of atoms, an ever-so-slow transition to another form as the metal transforms back to the surrounding environment. Other times, surfaces must act as a barrier: a bipolar relationship, a relationship having opposing attitudes toward the environment. Metal is often thought of in this way, an unmoving, unchanging, impenetrable skin.

The trick of good metal design is to achieve a level of elegance. Textural tones of softness, like the elegant stainless steel "curtain" of the Chicago Millennium band shell or the soft glasslike color of the Cleveland Planetarium, place metal in the realm of fine jewelry. These surfaces become the "jewels" of our cities.

Producing these large metal surfaces requires a clear understanding of the relationship of metal to the physical world. Metal moves slowly and quietly, like the inhalation and exhalation of the human body. Like our skin, the geometry of the surface of metal must change, very slightly but with incredible force. Elements must be assembled from smaller portions known as panels, or sometimes even referred to as skins. These panels create patterns on the surface and accommodate the physical requirements the ambient imposes.

The book is assembled in three parts. The first deals with the initial view of the surface as we approach from a distance of approximately 1,000 meters. Colors of the surface are apparent as the overall geometry of the building takes form. Metal possesses certain characteristics of absorption and reflection as the surface interacts with the light wave. This interaction is like no other material known. The subtle changes in light intensities that our planet experiences from hour to hour and day to day will greatly influence the perception we have of metal surfaces. These characteristics are dependent on the particular metal. Each metal possesses slightly different characteristics as it interrelates to light.

For metals to possess an interest as a surfacing material, they must have the capacity for beauty—what we see, the way light and shadow play across the surface, define the shape, color, and detail. Light, with its extraordinary complexities, dual behaviors of particle and wavelength, its components of color, lack of mass, and its capability to influence our mood and behavior—when light is diminished, detail and color are lacking.

Metal surfaces interplay well with light. They possess color and exhibit a reflective behavior known as metallic luster. Surfaces of metal can have subtle shades that vary with angle of view, time of day, and the disposition of the ambient. Surfaces of metal are intended to weather pleasantly with the passage of time. As oxygen and other compounds in the atmosphere join in with the surface of metals, the interplay with light changes. Instead of the bright reflective surface of new metal, a more refined reflection of experience and age occurs.

As we approach the surface, details and shadows are more prevalent. The second part of the book deals with the view of a surface from a distance of approximately 100 meters. The patterns made on the surface become visible as soft shadowing or as bold reveal lines separating the continuum like farm fields seen from high in the air. Patterns on the surface create a new layer of detail and complexity.

Patterns are such an intrinsic part of our world. As infants we stack blocks and sketch patterns with crayons. We create patterns in woven rugs and tapestries. Subtle patterns are created by the cloth of the suits men wear—not to mention their neckties. Many patterns reflect what occurs in the natural world.

Human nature often strives for symmetry, a balanced and consistent predicable surface. In nature, this is rarely the case. That Christmas tree, no matter how we rotate it in our living room, never quite arrives at a "perfect" symmetry. We place objects on our mantles in such a manner to give a "balanced" appearance. The "feng shui" of our world is ingrained by some odd measure of balance within our minds.

When looking closely at the branches of that Christmas tree, we see a regular pattern of unique but similar features. The similarity is in appearance and color; the regular is in predictability and consistency. However, there are subtle differences. Breaks in symmetry occur to provide uniqueness to each branch. Our approach to surfacing objects often follows similar parameters. Elements are similar if not exact, in appearance and color, and follow a predictable path. Every surface will have an apparent edge, if not a real one, and most surfaces will have an abrupt transition in plane, a hole or slice set into it. It is how these are handled that provides interest and intrinsic beauty to a surface.

Surfaces have criteria relating to functional requirements. Requirements can be as effortless as standing, or they can have arduous demands of resisting changes in temperature, pressure, radiation, and impact, while confronting the insidious presence of moisture. A discussion of the performance requirements of the surface and the various components involved with making a surface are examined. The seams that form an integral part of all surfaces must perform in ways equaling the body of the surface itself. These joints in the armor must function to remove stresses that develop and still provide a pleasant appearance to the surface. Herein lies the main functional challenge of all surfaces.

Moving in closer still, we arrive at the basic makeup of the surface. This final part discusses processes of producing colors, textures, and finishes that impart reflective characteristics to the metal. This is the "fabric" of the metal itself.

Metals fall into two groups, those that are intended to remain unchanged through the life of the surface and those that are intended to change with time and exposure. The desire of those first blacksmiths to create unique and interesting surfaces on metal continues today in a robust and growing industry. Techniques and processes used on metals for one industry are refined and intertwined in the artistic and architectural use of metals.

The fortuitous aspect may still be involved in much of what is created, but changes are in the making. We are moving to produce the surfaces in more consistent, regular, and predictable forms…until, of course, we explore the next branch of the tree.

ACKNOWLEDGMENTS AND CREDITS

The following individuals assisted in the preparation of the details and images within the book.

Roger Reed
Ed Huels
Julia Ng
Jacqueline Lichty

Nuvonyx Corporation of St. Louis, Missouri

Veeco Instruments Inc.; "Solutions for a Nanoscale World." Optical Profile equipment and information.

Deborah Bigelow and Bill Gauthier—American Burnish

Photographs:
Linda Staats—Photography—"Museum of Glass Sunrise"
J. Scott Smith—Photography—Private residence—interior fireplace surround
Lara Swimmer—Photography of EMP
Rimex—photos of EMP
J. Scott Smitt—"Residence" photo
Rheinzink America, Inc.—Photo of Ministry of Information
Follansbie Steel
VM Zinc
Paul Clausen—Image of Millennium Park
SFS Architects—Michael L. Christianer AIA
Paul Martin
Greg Chambers

PART 1
THE INTERACTION OF LIGHT WITH GEOMETRY

"He will sit as a refiner and purifier of silver."
—MALACHI 3.3

At 10^3 meters—1,000 meters—building outline, color, and shape become apparent. Color at this distance is influenced by surface alterations and by surrounding colors. The reflected accumulation of colors from the various surfaces combine. Shadows darken while reflected sunlight brightens. The view is homogeneous. Edges of the building are distinct, but detail on the surface is less apparent.

At 10^2 meters—100 meters—distinctive color and major aspects of the surface detail become apparent as shadows begin to define edges. From this distance, laps and shadows are nonexistent. The edges and geometric shape are apparent against a contrasting background. The color of the surface is reflected but still heavily influenced by the surrounding colors and light-scattering effects of the surface texture and atmosphere. Slight contrasts can be seen, but they are more ghostlike. Their existence is arbitrary and subjective.

Exterior surfaces viewed at this distance are heavily influenced by how they receive light. White light from an overcast sky "washes out" the color, making it paler. Scattering effects of the clouds can inhibit certain wavelengths, allowing other wavelengths to dominate the reflection off of metal surfaces.

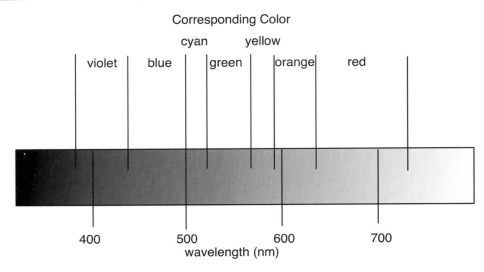

FIGURE I.1. Colors and their corresponding wavelength.

The color can be inherent tones of the metal itself or it can be enhanced by the reflection of the surroundings. The portion of the light wave that makes up the visible spectrum is shown in Figure I.1. The reflective appearance is dependent on several properties all surfaces possess. The reflective nature of the material, the gloss of the surface, will determine the intensity of the reflective image. A surface's texture can be enhanced by the degree of saturation of its color. Consider a lightly wetted surface of coarse stone. The moisture enhances the gloss level of the stone surface. The richness of the color of the stone is increased. Light scattering from the coarse surface is muted by the moisture. The moisture darkens the surface and the color is more saturated. Colors reflecting from a glossy surface are more saturated than those reflecting from matte surfaces. Some thin film interference also may be occurring. For metal surfaces, particularly finely textured surfaces, the condition is similar. Gloss will increase due to the layer of moisture, and the base color of the material will appear.

Approaching a surface from a distance, the eye quickly defines the geometry of buildings wrapped in metal. On bright sunlit days, variations of plane appear as different colors or shades. Light-scattering effects from coarse finishes scatter the light, while specular surfaces reflect the light and image of surrounding structures. Specular reflections are defined as "clear, well-defined images." For metal surfaces, there are degrees of specular reflectivity. Metals can be highly polished to develop mirrorlike reflectivity. Stainless steel and aluminum can be polished to reflect images with little distortion or muting of the reflection. Other surfaces can receive textures with various degrees of specular reflectivity. Satin-finish stainless, glass-bead stainless, and many textured stainless surfaces can reflect intense levels at their angle of

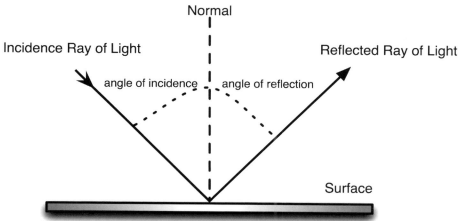

The law of reflection : Angle of incidence = Angle of reflection
The law of reflection holds on a point basis for all types of metal
surfaces - smooth or rough

FIGURE I.2. Law of reflection.

reflection. The law of reflection is depicted in Figure I.2. The law holds
that a reflection back to the observer is a point-by-point basis. That is
why mild dents and imperfections in reflective surfaces can only be
seen when the precise angle of view is achieved.

Specular surfaces will reflect colors from surrounding surfaces and
light originating from these surfaces, sometimes producing an altered
appearance (see Figure I.2). This is important to note: Metal surfaces
will reflect the shadows and colors of trees, cloud shadows, and the
color of other objects depending on the level of reflectivity of the specular surface.

Surfaces of metals can be made to possess diffused reflectivity as
well. Diffused reflectivity is created by a rough or coarse surface. The
reflectivity from a diffused surface is low. Essentially, very little, if any,
of an image is reflected back to the viewer. For example, if the surface
of the pages of this book were specular, it would be difficult to read.

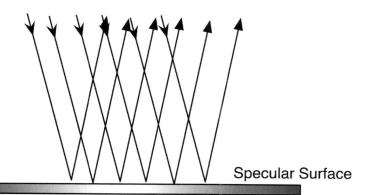

Specular Surface

FIGURE I.3. Mirror specular reflectivity.

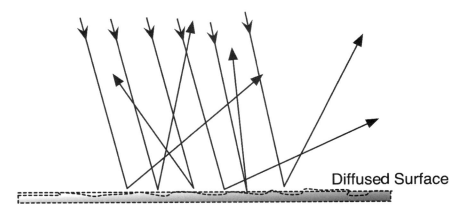

FIGURE I.4. Diffused reflectivity.

Incident light hitting the pages and reflecting off the specular surface would make it difficult to perceive the contrasting text (see Figure I.3).

Diffused surfaces scatter the light in different directions (see Figure I.4). This reduces the intensity and glare from the light source. Metal surfaces can be provided with various textures that achieve this behavior. The roughness of the microscopic surface will determine how diffused the reflection will be. With many metals, leaving them to weather creates a coarse surface as the oxides develop and thicken. Thus, the surface grows more and more diffused with time.

Lights interplay with all surfaces, whether they are stone, glass, or metal, and determine much of our opinion of the object. Metals have a special intimacy with light that changes with conditions throughout the day, and are influenced by shadows and reflections of other objects, as well as the contrast and brightness of the surface itself. The color and tone of the sky, perhaps, is the most influential of all when it comes to exterior surfaces of metals.

The color of the sky and the intensity of light reaching the earth obviously influence all exterior appearances. Trees and grass often appear a deeper green in certain overcast conditions.

The sea will sparkle in the sun as light strikes the tops of waves and reflects back to the viewer. The same sea will appear deep purple and blue when the sky is overcast. Metal will also exhibit similar variations in different lighting conditions.

There are several metals used in architectural and ornamental construction (see Table I.1). The available forms vary depending on the metal type. All of the metals classified as architectural are available in sheet, wire, and cast forms. When considering structural shapes, the available metals are limited.

It is significant to note that the form a metal takes also limits or directs the type of finish that the metal surface can possess. All metal

TABLE P1.1

Architectural Metal and Available Forms

Metal	Available Forms
Aluminum	Sheet, plate, foil, wire, castings, extrusion, pipe, tube, bar, rod, structural shapes, coating on other metals
Copper	Sheet, plate, foil, wire, castings, extrusion, pipe, tube, bar, rod, small structural forms, coating on other metals
Copper alloys	Sheet, plate, foil, wire, castings, extrusion, pipe, tube, bar, rod, small structural forms
Gold	Foil, leaf, bar, coating on other metals
Iron	Sheet, plate, wire, castings, pipe, tube, bar, rod, structural forms
Iron alloys—steels and stainless steels	Sheet, plate, wire, castings, extrusion, pipe, tube, bar, rod, structural forms
Lead	Sheet, plate, wire, castings, extrusion, pipe, tube, bar, rod, coating on other metals
Magnesium	Sheet, wire, casting, extrusion, bar, rod
Nickel	Sheet, plate, wire, casting, pipe, tube, bar, coating on other metals
Tin	Sheet, foil, wire, castings, extrusion, pipe, tube, bar, rod, small structural forms
Titanium	Sheet, plate, foil, wire, casting, coating on other metals
Zinc	Sheet, foil, wire, casting, extrusion, pipe, tube, bar, rod, coating on other metals

forms are created from scrap or ore material at a mill source. The mill source melts down the scrap and ore, then adds various compounds and elements to purify or alloy the metal. The metal typically is poured hot and cast into a large block of material. From here the initial, early form takes shape. For example, foils, sheets, and plates are created from large rectangular cross sections. Extrusions and wire are created from large circular cross sections.

The finish, when produced in the hot form, regardless of the metal, is rough. The surfaces have scale, grain marks, and generally a rough texture. Secondary processes of cleaning the scale and oxides, then passing the surface through more finished rolls or dies, imparts a surface that is smoother and more receptive to postfinishing processes.

Postfinishing processes are typical to what is used in the final product form. These are the finishes that are intended for long-term exposure to the ambient environment. They impart surface quality and behavior to the metal. The postfinishes and textures are what we interface with and formulate our opinions on. There are significantly more metal finishes and textures available to the design community today than at any other time in history.

Metal surfaces do change. Each metal has particular expectations as it undergoes aging. Some are expected to change in a prescribed way, while others are not expected to change for the life of the surface. Weathering of the various metals is dependent on exposure. Exposure to certain elements in the atmosphere will have significant impact on the weathering character of a metal, regardless of expectations. For metal intended to weather, the compounds that develop on the surface change in color and appearance as they gradually develop thick oxide coatings. The interplay with light is altered as the interplay with the environment stabilizes. What was once a shiny surface often changes to a diffused darkening patina.

As we approach the surface from a distance, features that define the character of the metal shell begin to take form. Shadow lines become visible and seams become a mosaic of elements.

CHAPTER 1
EXPECTATIONS OF VARIOUS METAL SURFACE FINISHES

"*Blue skies*
Smiling at me.
Nothing but blue skies
Do I see."
—IRVING BERLIN

Light from the surrounding sky reflecting off of a metal surface provides an ever-changing mosaic. Depending on the reflective nature of the metal surface and the light from the atmosphere, the effect will change. Metals have an intimate relationship with light. For example, the No. 2D finish in stainless is a relatively dull surface, but it possesses a gloss level higher than many other metal surfaces. On an overcast day, the metal appears as if it were painted flat white. On a bright sunny day, the surface takes on the color and appearance of still water.

The surface of stainless steel will reflect approximately 49 percent of visible light. The wavelength reflected by stainless steel tends toward the blue scale. Cloudy, overcast skies scatter the sunlight. This phenomenon, known as *molecular scattering*,[1] would suggest that the blue scale of the spectral wavelength is scattered by scattering the blue wavelength; the color blue has less of an impact on the color reflected from the surface of objects. This explains why the sky loses the blue color during overcast and twilight conditions. It also explains why the

---

[1] Sunlight contains the full spectrum of visible light. It possesses all colors. As the light from the sun enters our atmosphere, it causes the air molecules to oscillate. The oscillation is caused by the electromagnetic behavior of the light wave. This oscillation causes the electrons and protons in air to produce electromagnetic radiation at the same frequency as the incoming sunlight. This radiation is emitted or scattered in all directions. The blue component of the visible spectrum has shorter wavelengths and higher frequencies than the other colors, particularly red. The electrons and protons oscillate faster from this shorter blue wavelength. This scattered blue light is significantly more prevalent than the red. Violet light is even more scattered than blue, but less violet passes through the atmosphere. Thus, we have a blue sky.

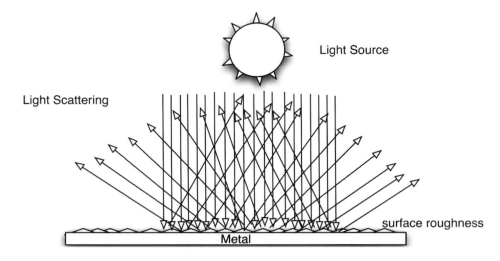

FIGURE 1.1. Light-scattering behavior.

TABLE 1.1

Reflective Metal Surfaces—Higher Reflectivity

Metal	Finish	Degree of Reflectivity—New	Degree of Reflectivity—Aged
Stainless steel	Mirror polish #9, #8, #7	Specular—mirror	Specular—mirror
Stainless steel	#2BA	Specular—mirror	Specular—mirror
Aluminum	Mirror polish	Specular—mirror	Depends on alloy and exposure-dulls down
Monel	Mill- finish	Specular—mirror	Reduced from oxide
Stainless steel	#2B	Specular	Specular
Aluminum	Mill—cold rolled	Specular	Depends on alloy and exposure
Stainless steel	#4	Specular—scattering in one direction	Specular—scattering in one direction
Copper alloys	Mirror polish	Specular—red/yellow	Diffused
Stainless steel	Glass bead	Specular—diffused in all but angle of reflectivity	Specular—diffused in all but angle of reflectivity
Gold	Leaf	Specular—bright yellow	Specular—bright yellow
Stainless steel	Angel hair	Specular—significant scattering	Specular—significant scattering
Copper	Cold rolled	Specular	Diffused
Zinc/zinc coated	Mill—unweathered	Specular	Diffused
Aluminum	Angel hair	Specular	Diffused
Brass—lacquered	Satin finish	Diffused—slight specular	Diffused—slight specular
Titanium	Mill—cold rolled	Diffused—slight specular	Diffused—slight specular

color of stainless takes on the appearance of a white painted surface. The blue color is less prominent, and the other colors wash across the surface. Under direct bright sunlight, sunlight possessing the full spectrum of wavelengths, such as the midday overhead sun, the surface of the metal will look brilliant and consistent (see Figure 1.1). Scattering the full spectrum light of the overhead sun by the rough, diffused surface of the metal will provide the most intense full color.

With metals, it is often desired to have a reflective surface—not necessarily blindingly bright but one that catches the eye (see Table 1.1). Its relative reflectivity is much greater than surrounding surfaces. Human nature, and that of some animals, for that matter, is attracted to gleaming and glittering objects. A gold leaf surface shimmers in the sunlight like a beacon when seen from a distance. As if the light is generated from the metal itself, gold will appear remarkably bright even on overcast days. A zinc surface by contrast, dulled by oxide, reflects a blue-gray tone in bright light and looks the color of pewter in overcast sky.

With all metals you have the ability to adjust the reflective nature of the surface (see Table 1.2). The ability changes with exposure time; and with some metal surfaces, the choices are limited. However, if desired, you can achieve a dull, flat, black appearance, devoid of the slightest visual sheen of any kind. Blackened by oxide, copper, zinc, and aluminum can have grainy, black, mottled surfaces. The mottling has degrees of black, some with a reddish tint, others with a gray tint.

TABLE 1.2

Reflective Metal Surfaces—Lower Reflectivity

Metal	Finish	Degree of Reflectivity—New	Degree of Reflectivity—Aged
Stainless steel	Mirror polish #9, #8, #7	Specular—mirror	Specular—mirror
Stainless steel	#2BA	Specular—mirror	Specular—mirror
Aluminum	Mirror polish	Specular—mirror	Depends on alloy and exposure-dulls down
Monel	Mill- finish	Specular—mirror	Reduced from oxide
Stainless steel	#2B	Specular	Specular
Aluminum	Mill-cold rolled	Specular	Depends on alloy and exposure
Stainless steel	#4	Specular—scattering in one direction	Specular—scattering in one direction
Copper alloys	Mirror polish	Specular—red/yellow	Diffused
Stainless steel	Glass bead	Specular—diffused in all but angle of reflectivity	Specular—diffused in all but angle of reflectivity
Gold	Leaf	Specular—bright yellow	Specular—bright yellow
Stainless steel	Angel hair	Specular—significant scattering	Specular—significant scattering
Copper	Cold rolled	Specular	Diffused
Zinc/zinc coated	Mill—unweathered	Specular	Diffused
Aluminum	Angel hair	Specular	Diffused
Brass—lacquered	Satin finish	Diffused—slight specular	Diffused—slight specular
Titanium	Mill—cold rolled	Diffused—slight specular	Diffused—slight specular

Other metal surfaces can have a low reflectivity generated by layering a light-scattering texture over a dull coarse grain. These finishes, such as glass-bead titanium or shadow stainless steel, have a metallic feel but a diffused reflectivity. Anodized aluminum has a coarse grain created by the hexagonal cell growth of its oxide. This reduces the reflectivity sufficiently, yet the surface still possesses a metallic quality.

Weathering steel develops a very coarse surface, as does blackened aluminum. The darkened surface of weathering steel does not reflect light well and appears dark reddish-brown. Blackened aluminum appears mottled flat black with streaks of occasional whitish deposits.

THE COLORS OF METALS

Theory and Behavior

Solar radiation that reaches the earth's surface occupies a small portion of the complete electromagnetic band. Radiation is caused by vibrations and is characterized by wavelengths rather than mass. This portion includes some ultraviolet, all visible light wavelengths, and approximately half of the infrared (see Figure 1.2). Light is an electromagnetic wave.

All metals are sensitive to particular light waves and emit electrons when these electromagnetic waves interact with the surface. The electromagnetic wave

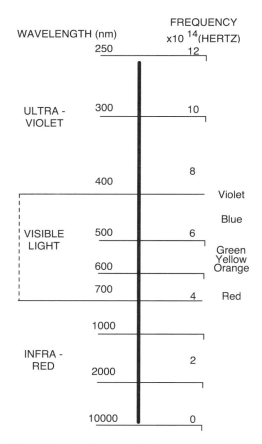

FIGURE 1.2. Solar radiation portion of the electromagnetic band.

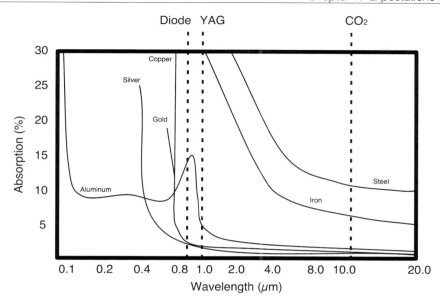

FIGURE 1.3. Wavelength and the corresponding absorption percentage of various metals.

excites the electrons in one energy level and moves it to higher energy level. Due to the atomic makeup of metal atoms, one would expect that light falling on a metal surface would be fully absorbed. Metals readily and strongly absorb electromagnetic radiation from light. But the light wave is absorbed only to a level a few molecules thick. Because of this very strong absorption characteristic at the surface, further absorption is inhibited. This behavior is also why certain metals can be efficiently cut with a laser while others cannot. Lasers produce high energy light at various wavelengths, depending on the energy source.

Figure 1.3 shows a CO_2 laser emitting a high-energy beam at a wavelength of 10.6 μm. Steel and iron absorb light at this wavelength, steel at about 12 percent, and iron more around 6 percent. The light energy is quickly absorbed and the molecules of steel are energized to the point at which the molecular bonds break down and allow the laser beam to cut through the metal. However, using the same beam with the same energy level that just cut through 3 mm steel on copper, the result has no effect. Copper absorbs a different wavelength while reflecting the others.

With most other materials, the reflectivity of the surface is defined by how much of the light is transmitted through it and how much is reflected from it. Defined as a percent reflectivity, R, for a beam of light hitting or reflecting off a surface at an angle perpendicular to the surface, known as normal incidence, is defined by the equation:

$$R = 100 \times (n - 1)^2 / (n + 1)^2$$

where n is the refractive index[2] of the material (see Table 1.3).

---

[2] The refractive index is a constant used to describe the relationship of the speed of light through two materials. The value n is defined as the ratio of:

$$\frac{\text{Speed of light in material 1}}{\text{Speed of light in material 2}}$$

The incident light is in material 1 and the refracted light is in material 2.

TABLE 1.3

Refractive Index of Various Materials When Compared to a Vacuum

Material	Refractive Index
Vacuum	1
Air	1.0005
Water	1.33
Glass	1.5
Diamond	2.417

For instance, glass with a refractive index of 1.5 gives an *R* of 4 percent. This would mean that 96 percent of the visible light is transmitted into the glass. However, for metals, the equation changes. A more rigorous algorithm goes further by replacing the refractive index with what is known as the *complex refractive index*. $N = n + ik$, where k is the coefficient of absorption and i is given the value of $\sqrt{-1}$. Thus, for metals:

$$R = 100 \times (n - 1)^2 + k^2 / (n + 1)^2 + k^2$$

With metal, light is intensely absorbed only to a depth of a portion of the light wavelength—a few hundred atoms thick. The light causes slight electrical currents on the surface of the metal, exciting more electrons, which emit light out from the surface. This creates a very strong reflection. The very intense absorption on a polished metal surface free of oxides and foreign substances will cause an equally intense reflection. From the surface, this enhanced reflective characteristic creates the bright intense tones know as *metallic luster*.

The metals are selective in what they reflect in visible light (see Table 1.4). Likewise, they are selective in what other wavelengths they will transmit or absorb. This is because of the ariations in their coefficient of absorption values, k.

TABLE 1.4

Light Reflected from Metal

Metal	Visible Light Reflected from a Polished Surface
Silver	95%
Aluminum	90%
Tin	70%
Gold	61%
Chromium	61%
Iron	58%
Nickel	50%
Stainless steel	49%

Lead, for example, will block short wavelengths such as X-rays and gamma rays; it also blocks low-frequency sound waves. Zinc, on the other hand, is very sensitive to very short wavelengths and will emit electrons when these waves interact with the surface. Aluminum hampers radio waves. Gold has the capability to reflect radiation above 500 nm, which is the region of infrared. Thus, gold is often used as a thin coating on glass and protective gear used by firefighters.

The phenomenon of metals appearing different shades or tones in different lighting conditions is directly related to the wavelength absorbed and reflected (see Figure 1.4).

Additionally, light-scattering behavior of the finish can influence the surface color of various panels. For example, satin-finish stainless steels with small, tight finish grit lines or tiny lapping indentations are excellent light-scattering surfaces. On bright sunny days, the metal has a bluish cast because of the reflection of the blue wavelength of the sky. Hot spots of reflectivity are diffused, softening the intensity. If circular polishing with overlapping grits creates the satin finish, the reflected light is more polarized (similarly with the glass bead finish), so much so that on overcast days, or when the sun is low in the sky, distinct differences are apparent. These differences are the result of the stainless-steel surface not reflecting consistently in the 500 nm and below wavelength. In bright sunlight, all parts of the stainless-steel surface reflect well in the 500 to 600 nm range. The overcast sky and the twilight sky scatter the blue wavelength so that the surface of the stainless steel, which reflects this wavelength well, appears flatter, washed out in color. Variations appear that are not apparent in bright light. Sometimes even an opposite characteristic occurs where dark contrasting spots appear in the sunlit surface but appear light in the twilight, blue wave-

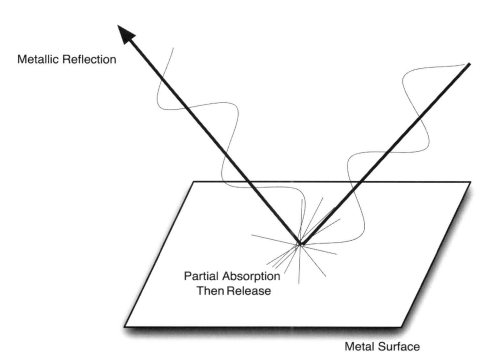

Metallic Reflection

Partial Absorption
Then Release

Metal Surface

FIGURE 1.4 Light reflected off of a metal surface is partially absorbed, then reemitted, creating the intense metallic reflection.

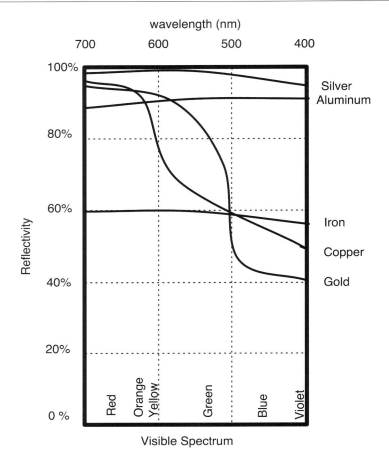

FIGURE 1.5. Color and wavelength reflected by various metals.

length-deficient glow. Figure 1.5 shows a variety of metals and the percent reflectivity of various wavelengths of the light spectrum.

Other metals have similar characteristics. Aluminum reflects a whitish-gray tone. The more intense the sun, the fuller the spectrum and the greater the white intensity will be. Overcast or twilight, and the metal is more silver gray. Anodized aluminum surfaces are composed of aluminum oxide. Clear anodized is aluminum oxide with a seal applied within the pores of the metal, the seal being deionized water or nickel. Colored anodized aluminum utilizes metal dyes impregnated into the pores or chemical reactions of the impurities in the alloy. The aluminum oxide is a crystalline surface, glasslike in nature. It has extremely poor formability and fractures when impacted, heated excessively, or formed. Light reflecting off of the surface is scattered by the many tiny pores on the surface and the microscopic roughened surface created by the etching prior to the oxide growth. There is an added depth in thick oxide coatings, which is created by light passing through the surface and reflecting back off of the base metal. Sometimes a slight rainbow effect can be seen created by light interference.

New copper can look as if it is on fire in low twilight, when the red wavelength of light is more prevalent. The surface of new copper is specular, moderately polished from the cold rolling process, imparting a burnishing effect on the copper. This polished surface will show minor distortions in and out of plane. In the light of the low sun, the surface comes alive with variable distortions across the surface. The copper looks as if it's a flaming vertical pool of water as the strong red tones are reflected. Eventually, the surface oxidizes and reflectivity gives way to earthy tones of a dull, darker, surface. Oil-canning distortions on the surface are no longer apparent because there is such a drop-off of reflectivity.

COLORS OF METAL SURFACES

The color of a metal surface as one approaches from a distance is influenced by several factors: the reflective nature of the metal surface, the context of the color, the position of the sun in the sky, overcast or haze conditions, and shadow effects created by surface alterations such as fenestration, relief and intaglio (see Table 1.5).

Brightness and Context

The perceived color in any surface is dependent on *brightness* and *context*. Brightness is considered the overall intensity of the reflection and is quantified as such: 100 percent brightness would be brilliant white; 0 percent brightness would be dark black. Context is considered to be the color hue and saturation, where hue is defined as the dominant wavelength that best matches the perceived color. For example, you might describe a color as more red than blue or more green than yellow. The red or green in this example would be the hue.

Saturation is the purity of the color. It is defined as the intensity nearest the dominant wavelength. Saturation is further distinguished as *chroma*, *tint*, and *shade*. Chroma is the color intensity, tint is the color modified toward white, and shade is the color modified toward black. Saturation can also be described as vividness, dull or sharp. Using these criteria, you could arrive at the values indicated in Table 1.6 for the various metals used in architecture.

Various colors can be imparted to surfaces, colors other than the typical gray-silver tones or the soft reddish tones of copper. The colors are imparted to metal surfaces by means other than pigmented coatings. Light interference or alloying attributes can introduce various color tones into metal surfaces with remarkable results. Metallic salts can be impregnated into the pores of anodized

TABLE 1.5

Color Influences

Color Influence	General Effect	Specific Influence
Surface texture	Brightness/dullness	Reflective nature of the surface
Surface color	Context	Hue and saturation
Sun position	Light wavelength	Full or partial spectrum reaching the surface depending on position of the sun in the sky
Overcast/haze	Light wavelength	Scattering of wavelength—partial spectrum reaching the surface
Fenestration, relief and intaglio	Shadow contrasts	Darkens surface or creates banding
Angularity of reflection	Color contrast	Light and dark tones

TABLE 1.6

Colors of Metal

Metal	Lighting Condition	Brightness	Hue	Saturation: Dull or Sharp
Aluminum—natural	Noon sun	90 to 100	White	Sharp
Aluminum—clear anodized	Noon sun	70 to 80	White	Sharp
Aluminum—clear anodized	Overcast	40 to 60	White	Dull
Aluminum—blackened	Noon sun	0	Black	Sharp
#2D stainless	Noon sun	80 to 90	Blue	Sharp
Titanium	Noon sun	50 to 60	Yellow	Sharp
Zinc—preweathered	Noon sun	40 to 50	Blue	Sharp
Copper	Overcast	20 to 40	Red	Dull
Lead	Overcast	10 to 20	Blue	Dull
Gold leaf	Noon sun	80 to 90	Yellow	Sharp

aluminum to produce an amazing array of colors that still maintain the metallic sheen of the base metals (see Table 1.7).

The colors listed in Table 1.6 all have a degree of metallic luster. With the exception of the patinas and weathering steel, the colors are glossy or specular in their reflective levels. Matching specific colors—that is, matching, say, a specific green tone—is not practical. These metals achieve their color from the interplay of light off their surface and the character of the oxide growth on their surface. If you want specific colors, then consider pigments and dyes.

REFLECTIONS OF SKY: SUN POSITION AND LIGHT SCATTERING

Very few materials reflect the natural beauty of the sky the way metal surfaces will. As described earlier, metals absorb particular wavelengths of light and then reemit them with a heightened energy level, producing the metallic luster we associate with metal. This is a property unique to metals (and semiconductors).

The smoother the surface, the more this effect will be apparent. The surface texture of the metal will affect the appearance significantly when viewed from a distance. Similarly, the atmospheric conditions—cloudy, sunny, smog-covered, and sun position in the sky—all affect the light the metal receives. The position of the sun in the sky will determine the intensity of various wavelengths of light that are delivered to the metal surface. Scattering effects of cloud cover will alter the wavelength reflected off of the metal.

Angle of view is another condition that can create alterations in the surface appearance of metals. Depending on the nature of the finish, light-scattering effects will be different when viewed from different angles. The physics involved are not unlike light reflecting off of a rippled surface of water.

TABLE 1.7

Colors of Metals

Color	Metal Type
Violet	Anodized aluminum with metallic salt Titanium with interference coloring Stainless steel with interference color Titanium-coated stainless steel—interference Copper—initial oxide interference
Blue	Anodized aluminum with metallic salt Titanium with interference coloring Stainless steel with interference color Titanium-coated stainless steel—interference Zinc—slight bluish tint Steel—oxide tinting
Green	Anodized aluminum with metallic salt Titanium with interference coloring Stainless steel with interference color Titanium-coated stainless steel—interference Gold alloy—greenish yellow tint Copper patina Copper alloy patinas
Yellow	Gold Copper alloys—brass Anodized aluminum with metallic salt Titanium with interference coloring Stainless steel with interference color Titanium-coated stainless steel—interference Nickel silver—silver-gold color Zinc patina—custom yellow-white oxide
Orange	Weathering steel Copper alloys—high copper content Copper patinas Anodized aluminum with metallic salt
Red	Anodized aluminum with metallic salt Titanium-coated stainless steel—interference Copper alloys—high copper content

Finishes that are made of small scratches on the metal surface or of microscopic indentations will scatter light. The angle of view, as well as the angle of reflection, will influence the appearance of the surface. Scattered light is partially polarized. When the light beam reflects off the surface, the wavelength is shifted. Under polarized light, hues of relative light and darkness appear. The reflected light seen by the viewer is coming not from a single point on the surface of the metal, but from several points arriving at different angles.

Light-scattering effects occur on cloud-covered days as well. Under light scattering, the longer wavelengths, the blues, tend to be muted. For metals that absorb and reflect more on the blue wavelength, you would expect them to appear darker. Stainless steel is one of the metals that reflect more on the blue scale. Copper and gold absorb most strongly on the red region of the light spectrum, hence reflect more intensely on the red scale. Thus, cloudy days have only a minor effect on the reflected light from gold and copper surfaces.

Blue light is a higher energy level and tends to scatter more readily off of small particles or small surface scratches. The atmosphere is full of small, microscopic particles, as are the fluids in the eye. Light scattering in the atmosphere not only gives the sky its blue color but also can create haze or glare in the case of the fluids within the eye. This is why pilots and hunters use amber-colored lens. The amber color filters out the blue wavelength and provides greater sharpness to the image reaching the eye.

Full sunlight during the middle of the day contributes nearly the full intensity of the light spectrum. Metals look most brilliant in such light, even if they are not in direct reflection such as north-facing surfaces or sunlit interiors. When the sun is near the horizon, again the shift of the wavelength is to the red side. The sky is darker, less blue, and has more red or purple tones. Metals respond to this change according to the wavelength they absorb and reemit.

Different metals absorb and reflect different wavelengths of light, and light conditions change constantly throughout the day, as diagrammed in Figure 1.6. Therefore, in conditions where light-scattering effects and polarization occur, you should expect variations in surface appearances at different times of the day and under different cloud covers. This is precisely what occurs.

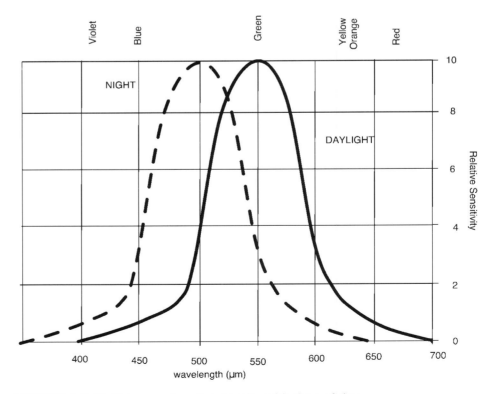

FIGURE 1.6. Shift in wavelength intensity with time of day.

A metal surface with the sun directly behind the viewer creates a relative bright spot. Shadows are diminished or eliminated, and the bright spot moves as the viewer moves around the surface. This effect is known as the *opposition effect*. The bright spot is white in color because of the intensity of the sun's reflection. All other colors are washed out by the intense whiteness. "Angel hair" finishes and satin finishes show this opposition effect. A bright, white circle of light moves across the surface, tracking with the viewer as he or she moves.

The brightness of all exterior surfaces is compared to the brightness of the sky. When discussing contrast in brightness, David Lynch and William Livingston, in their book *Color and Light in Nature*, Cambridge University Press, 2001 state: "The only difference between black, gray and white is their brightness for which the surrounding background provides the standard of comparison."

This is true in particular for low reflective surfaces. A dull stainless-steel surface in overcast light can appear as if it is flat white paint next to the brightness of the sky. By altering the reflectivity of the surface by glass-bead blasting, the diffused nature of the finish as it reflects the diffused light from the overcast turns the appearance to pewter gray. Apply an angel hair finish, and the surface takes on a brown-gray cast. Seams and reveals appear muted. Sensory relationships of dimension are reduced.

REFLECTIONS AND WATER

Light from water arrives via three regions: (1) the surface of the water, refracted through the top section of the water and scattered from the water volume and suspended particles; (2) refracted through the water as light is reflected from the bottom of the pool surface; then (3) refracted a second time from the water to air interface.

The reflected light is polarized from the scattering nature of the waves and from the effects of the refractions through the water from the bottom and intermediate regions. This reflected light plays off of the waves at different times of the day. The effect, known as *glitter*, produces shimmering reflections on metal surfaces, creating a fabriclike flow of contrasting color.

At high sun (Figure 1.7), the waves roll under the light beam and scatter at an angle approximately four times that of the wave angle. When the sun is low in

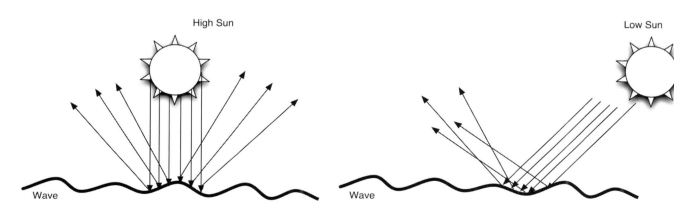

FIGURE 1.7. Reflection off the surface of water at high noon.

FIGURE 1.8. Reflection off the surface of water at sunset or sunrise.

FIGURE 1.9. Glitter from the overhead sun.

FIGURE 1.10. Dark zones from overcast sky.

the sky, the effects are markedly different. As the sun moves lower in the sky (Figure 1.8), the angle of incidence changes with each wave pulse.

On overcast days, the opposite of glitter occurs. Each wave top, instead of being a bright light is now dark. Blue color is toned down and water takes on a purplish color.

Metal and water in their relationship with light have similar behaviors. Just as the wavelength of light reaching the surface changes in intensity, like the waves rolling over a beach, the appearance of a metal surface changes as it interacts and reflects these varying intensities created by changing light and angle of incidence (see Figures 1.9 and 1.10).

The deciding factor of whether to use metal or not for a particular surface is dependent on the way light interplays off the surface and back to the viewer. The light coming from the surrounding environment changes, as does the metal surface itself. The interplay is far more dynamic and interesting. Metal is unique among surfacing materials in this regard. Each metal has its own peculiar way of interacting with the light striking it. Look the other way for a moment and something new may appear.

CHAPTER 2
SPECIFIC METALS AND EXPECTATIONS OF APPEARANCE

"Colors answer feeling in man, shape answers thought, and motion answers will."

—JOHN STERLING, POET 1884

Various metals are used in architectural and ornament applications, and the list of metals and the finish surfaces available continues to grow. Each metal has unique attributes—in the way they interact with their environment, in the way they are finished and treated, and in the way they perform as they interact. For architectural and ornamental applications, Table 2.1 contains the current list of common and some uncommon metals.

ALUMINUM

Nearly all uses of aluminum have some degree of additional surface enhancement (see Table 2.2). Most applications utilize the formability, strength, and lightweight characteristics of the metal, preferring to coat the aluminum with enamel to add color to the surface. This way, painted aluminum surfaces can take advantage of the excellent corrosion resistance developed at edges and scratches.

Aluminum is very reactive, far from noble. It immediately forms a layer of oxide approximately 0.1 μm in thickness when exposed to air. This very adherent amorphous oxide layer offers significant corrosion protection to the metal under most circumstances. However, the color this oxide layer develops, particularly when combined with various pollutants from the environment, is not always pleasing. Depending on the surface finish, blotchiness, dark stains, and fuzzy deposits can develop. A maintenance program that periodically removes deposits from the surface can reduce these occurrences.

TABLE 2.1

Elements and the Metal Form

Element	Metal Form
Aluminum	Aluminum alloys
Copper	Commercial pure copper
	Copper alloys—brass
	Copper alloys—bronzes
	Copper alloys—silicon bronzes
	Copper alloys—nickel alloys
Gold	Gold alloys
Iron	Cast irons
	Steels
	Stainless steels
Lead	Lead alloys
	Terne
Magnesium	Magnesium alloys
Nickel	Nickel plating
	Monel—nickel/copper alloys
Tin	Tin alloys
	Tin plating
Titanium	Titanium alloys
Zinc	Zinc alloys
	Galvanizing
	Zinc/tin alloy coatings

If the aluminum surface is well drained and kept free of deposits from other metals, it will develop an even gray-white color. The surface will still retain a metallic appearance dulled slightly from the oxide growth on the surface.

The higher the polish on the aluminum surface, thus the smoother the surface, the better it will drain and resist deposits collecting. Specular mill finishes are smooth and lack a true mirror appearance. These surfaces when left to weather will perform well if used where they are naturally washed or when they are maintained by a periodic scrubbing to remove the particles that collect.

There are several surface treatments used on aluminum to draw on the metallic tones of the metal. The most common treatment is anodizing. Anodizing utilizes the unique oxidation of the surface when accelerated under the influence of a strong electrolyte and an electrical current. The aluminum oxide that forms is a semiconductor of electricity, while the base aluminum material is a strong conductor of electricity. The current running through the electrolyte develops a deep pore through the less conductive material all the way to the more conductive base aluminum. The pore is microscopic and very consistent across the surface. Color tones can be imparted to the oxide, retaining the distinctive metallic feature of aluminum.

TABLE 2.2

Aluminum Finishes

Aluminum Finishes	Relative Reflective Levels
Mill finish	Specular
Alclad-coated	Mirror specular
Satin finish	Diffused specular
Angel hair finish	Diffused
Ground finish	Diffused
Embossed	Specular
Mirror polish	Mirror specular
Clear anodized	Diffused
Champagne anodized	Diffused
Light bronze anodized	Diffused
Medium bronze anodized	Diffused
Dark bronze anodized	Diffused
Color anodized—metal salts, yellow, green, blue, gold, red	Diffused
Gray anodized	Diffused
Dye anodized	Specular and diffused
Brightened—chemically	Mirror specular
Blackened	Diffused
Bead blast	Diffused
Shot blast	Diffused
Cast surface	Diffused
Etched	Diffused—mottled

Other less common means of imparting color to aluminum can produce mottled flat black, dull gray, and a dark mottled red-black. These processes combine aluminum's reactive nature with its stable oxide growth. Somewhat difficult to control, these processes develop a course surface on the metal.

Different alloys of aluminum can be coated onto the surface of aluminum sheet and plate to develop specific properties. Known as alclad, this process coats one alloy of aluminum with another, usually a higher purity aluminum alloy. The higher-purity alloy protects the stronger, less-pure alloying material from atmospheric attack. In this manner, you can use a higher-strength alloy aluminum with poor corrosion resistance. The pure sheet provides excellent barrier coating and a decent galvanic protection.

ANODIZING

A common form of protection, one that utilizes the more metallic nature of the surface, is anodizing, that is, anodic oxidation of the metal surface. The oxide layer produced on the surface of aluminum during anodic oxidation can be as much as 30 μm in thickness—300 times thicker than the oxide layer that develops on aluminum naturally.

Anodizing provides an aluminum surface with a significant reduction in reflectivity. Polishing the aluminum prior to anodizing, whether mirror or satin, will not produce a more reflective anodized surface. The etching process that prepares aluminum for anodizing imparts a grainy texture to the metal and would turn a reflective surface into a dull grainy surface. Polishing after the anodizing process will damage the oxide film.

Matching Sheet to Sheet

It is not uncommon to have slight variations from one sheet to the next when anodized, regardless of whether color is imparted or not. This is not the case with dye-dipping processes; but for most exterior anodizing processes, this is a drawback to the use of anodized aluminum on a surface. The color difference is difficult to overcome mainly because of the subtlety in the behavior of the anodized surface. Unless the color and tone are significant, it is difficult to see the variations when the anodized sheets or parts are in the fabrication process. It is not until the parts are set side by side that the contrast in color is apparent. To make matters more difficult, this contrast in color may be apparent only in certain lighting conditions.

The variations in color tone are due to several factors. The surface of the aluminum must first be etched. The etching process dissolves the oxide from the surface. Variations in the alloy, grain structure, and smoothness of the surface affect the rate of dissolution. The sheets or parts are assembled on racks and immersed into the acid bath to begin the anodizing process. Current is applied and the porous oxide grows. The process is timed to achieve the desired thickness. Unfortunately, slight variations begin to occur in the electrolyte tank as the process is undertaken. Aluminum dissolves from the surface into the acid tank, altering its effect slightly. The longer the process, the more variations will occur. Thus, the thick hard-coat oxide coatings desired for exterior applications tend to vary the most. Coil anodizing processes, which utilize a shorter time period and thus a thinner oxide, result in a better color match.

BEGIN WITH THE MILL SOURCE

Controlling the casting is another way to achieve good color control, even with the thick anodized surfaces. When aluminum is cast into the large ingots, or blocks, to be rolled into sheet or plate, the impurities in the mix rise to the top. Removing the top quarter or third of the block will eliminate these impurities. As the block is reduced to plate or sheet thickness by further rolling, you arrive at a very high-quality, homogeneous material. The cost is higher but the results are significant. The aluminum when anodized will be more consistent.

Bead blasting the aluminum plate with glass beads prior to the anodizing process will also aid in achieving a superior surface for anodizing. The soft aluminum surface will take the bead blasting well. Pressure used to drive the beads into the aluminum can be reduced, thus shaping from the bead-blasting process is reduced. Flattening still is necessary. The result is a very consistent surface that will take surface etching and achieve a consistent final anodizing. The addition to the Modern Art Museum of Fort Worth, Texas, Figure 2.1, utilized anodized glass-bead-blasted aluminum plates as wall panel elements. The remarkable

FIGURE 2.1. Modern Art Museum of Fort Worth, Texas. Glass-bead-blasted and anodized aluminum surface. Designed by Tadao Ando.

surface achieved by this finish possesses a visual depth unlike other anodized finishes when viewed in bright light.

Matching Extrusion to Sheet or Plate

When matching extruded aluminum to sheet or plate, additional variables come into place, not least of which is the alloy used to extrude. Extrusions and wrought products are made from different castings and thus will have different alloying mixes. Extrusions are usually made from aluminum alloy 96061. Clear anodized, non-colored finishes can be matched up with sheet and plate alloys of the A95000 and A96000 series. The process requires that the extrusion batch anodizing occur at the same facility and follow the same processing.

Developing an Acceptable Range

When colors are introduced, you should confer with the anodizing facility. Usually one will have to arrive at a range acceptance. Developing an acceptable range for the final product is only possible with the final product in hand. Until the metal is cast and sitting ready to receive the anodizing process, any range is only a representation of what the final metal will potentially be. The only way to be certain is to develop the range after the casting is performed.

FIGURE 2.2. Contemporary Art Museum in Cincinnati, Ohio. Black oxide aluminum surface. Designed by Zaha Hadid.

Once the metal is cast and rolled or extruded to the profile, desired range samples can be established. This is really the only time to achieve accurate range samples. Unfortunately, there is no turning back at this stage. The metal is cast and payment is due as long as the metal meets the alloy grade within the standards established by the industry. Nevertheless, it is still desirable to create samples on similar alloy runs to narrow down the possibilities. The range samples should be large enough to provide a clear comparison: 900 mm square for sheet (36 inches) or 900 mm in length for extrusions is an adequate size.

View the anodized surface from different angles and in different lights. You will be surprised how the position of the sun and the degree of overcast can affect the color of anodized aluminum. Usually, overcast conditions will show the most significant variations. Full-spectrum, overhead sunlight will often produce a more homogeneous surface appearance. Therefore, establish the range in the light in which the surface is to be judged.

Blackening of Aluminum

There are several methods of producing a flat black, mottled surface on aluminum sheet. Alloys with higher zinc content seem to work the best, but other alloys can be used. The black color obtained is flat and mottled due to the variable coarse nature of the aluminum surface achieved. The roughened surface is sealed with an acrylic lacquer or other such clear coating that resists ultraviolet and heat.

Black is a great absorber of the infrared wavelength. It does not take long for a blackened surface to reach temperatures that are painful to the touch. Using blackened aluminum of this form requires recognition of the thermal characteristics the aluminum will undergo, as well as accessibility to the public.

This form of blackening involves, first, thoroughly cleaning the surface of the aluminum of all foreign particles, oils, and grease. The surface is then etched in a mild acid or strong alkaline to remove the oxide. Adding a level of "tooth" to the surface by sanding or coarse blasting with aluminum oxide also helps. Immediately after the oxide is removed in the etching process, the aluminum sheet or part must be immersed in the coloring solution. The coloring solution used on aluminum to produce the mottled flat black color is usually proprietary. Always follow safety and environmental procedures when working with chemical treatments on metal.

The resulting surface is leatherlike in texture, with a flat, black sheen. The surface appears different when viewed from different angles. The finish obtained is not unlike a photographic negative of a smooth concrete surface with all the subtle variations that give concrete its unique attributes. The Rosenthal Contemporary Art Museum in Cincinnati, Ohio, Figure 2.2, has a portion of the exterior and interior wall surfaces clad in large blackened aluminum plates.

Like all black surfaces, particularly coarse, grainy façades, deposits of dirt and other substances contrast against the dark background. Rain does not aid in the cleaning of such shells because of the considerable roughness. Evaporation patterns develop on black coarse surfaces, leaving behind irregular deposits that can be difficult to clean, particularly if they have been left on for long periods of time.

Gray tones can also be created using similar processes. Rubbing down the blackened aluminum surface will leave a mottled dark gray, pewterlike color. The gray color obtained is very adherent and stable.

Alclad

Alclad is the term given to coating one aluminum alloy over another aluminum alloy. The coating is applied by passing aluminum sheet or plate of one alloy through a molten spray of another aluminum alloy. The plate of aluminum is then passed through high-pressure rolls to further bond the alloys together. The result is a metallurgic bond of two different alloys. Typically, the clad alloy has improved corrosion resistance or provides cathodic protection to the base metal. The clad alloy adds only a mere 0.0002 to 0010 mm in thickness. The alclad coating is available on most aluminum alloys. Minimum quantities apply due to the nature of the process.

High purity coatings of aluminum are soft and very bright. Cold rolling of the alclad sheet or plate burnishes the surface, creating a high-polished, highly reflective, appearance. This can be adjusted by postapplying a satin polish, bead blast, or clear anodized finish. Exposed to the atmosphere, these finishes hold their luster longer than nonalclad aluminum. The drawback to the alclad coatings is that they are soft in their high purity state, so soft they can be scratched with a fingernail. Anodizing will harden the surface. Glass-bead blasting will also harden the surface slightly.

Aluminum Coatings on Other Metals

Aluminum is often used as a coating on other metals. It affords a bright, shiny, corrosion-resistant barrier. Unlike the zinc of galvanizing, aluminum coatings do not provide galvanic protection to the underlying metal. It is a hot-dipping process, whereby metal sheet or plate is passed through a bath of molten aluminum or aluminum alloyed with zinc or silicon. The surface is a white-gray color with a fairly high reflectance initially. The surfaces weather to a lower reflective, gray tone.

Aluminum–zinc alloys are in common use as a cladding for steel. Their performance has been found to be superior to that of galvanized coatings over steel. The surface is brighter and has a distinctive light spangle.

Aluminum is also coated on stainless steel. The coating is an alloy of aluminum and silicon. The coating is applied over 409 and 439 stainless steel. This provides a bright reflective coating and affords some additional protection to these alloys of stainless steel.

COPPER AND COPPER ALLOYS

When these metals are first installed, they are generally free of surface oxides. Newly installed copper often arrives in the standard mill specular surface. This is a somewhat reflective surface, not to the level of a mirror but bright to the view under direct reflection.

In sunlight, particularly when the sun is low on the horizon and surrounding shadows are lengthened, the copper surface will reflect the light and appear as if it were ablaze with fire, due to the fact that copper absorbs and reflects on the red side of the spectrum, and sunlight on the horizon is richer in this wavelength. The result can be a very bright, flamelike appearance, seeming brighter than the light it is reflecting.

Whether used for exterior or interior purposes, the metal can be expected to develop a tarnish. The surface of clean, oxide-free copper will fingerprint immediately. Copper will react with the slightly acidic moisture from human skin and develop a copper oxide that can be rather tenacious. Cotton gloves are, therefore, recommended, and a quick wipedown with commercial oxide cleaners will work temporarily. But keeping copper bright and shiny is an art in itself. Removing the oxide can be achieved, but the surface is sensitive to further oxide development; and the more humid the air, the quicker the oxide develops.

Copper alloys perform similar to copper. *Brass* is the term given to cover the various alloys of copper, with the main alloying element being zinc. More yellowish and golden tones are apparent with the brass alloys. As zinc is added to the alloy mix, the color becomes more and more yellow. This occurs to the point of metallurgical phase change. This is important to note from a forming standpoint. As zinc is added to copper beyond the 40 percent level, a metallurgical alteration of the grain or crystal structure occurs, making the resulting alloy less ductile. The color also begins to change and the golden hue becomes less apparent. See Table 2.3.

Mirror polishing copper and copper alloys is a simple process. Clean the surface to eliminate all foreign matter. Buff the surface using fine polishing wheels. Avoid contact with other metals. The copper and copper alloys are softer than most other metals. The metals polish easily because of their softness.

TABLE 2.3

Colors of Copper Alloys

Common Name	Alloying Elements—Nominal	Color
Copper—99.9%	None	Salmon red
Gilding metal	5% Zinc	Reddish-orange
Commercial bronze	10% Zinc	Salmon red with gold tint
Red brass	15% Zinc	Golden red
Cartridge brass	30% Zinc	Yellow
Yellow brass	35% Zinc	Yellow
Muntz metal	40% Zinc	Golden yellow
Architectural bronze	40% Zinc, 3% Lead	Golden yellow
Nickel silver	25% Zinc, 10% Nickel	Silver with gold tint
Nordic Brass™	5% Aluminum, 1% Zinc	Yellow with slight green tint
Aluminum bronze	8 to 10% Aluminum	Light yellow color
Silicon bronze	3% Silicon	Red color
Phosphor bronze	3 to 9% tin, .03 to .35 Phosphorus	Dirty yellow color
Manganese brass	1.2% Manganese, 29% Zinc	Golden brown

Copper alloys can be brightened chemically by applying phosphoric acid. Rinsing and neutralizing the surface is critical after brightening (see Table 2.4). Other chemical-brightening methods can be used on copper alloys. Essentially, they remove the oxide layer, leaving a bright, reflective surface, but one that will quickly tarnish if not coated.

TABLE 2.4

Copper Alloy Surface Finishes

Copper Alloy Finishes	Relative Reflective Level
Coppermill finish	Specular
Satin finish	Diffused
Angel hair finish	Diffused
Bead blast	Diffused
Cast	Diffused
Mirror polish	Mirror specular
Embossed	Diffused
Prepatinated	Diffused
Blackened	Diffused
Hammered	Diffused
Etched	Diffused

The bright, reflective colors of copper alloy surfaces that are exposed to air will oxidize similar to that of pure copper. The oxides develop and darken the surface, capturing the sunlight in nonresponsive sulfates and carbonates. The reflections are dull and often spotty. From a distance they are dark, somewhat reddish-brown to black.

Weathering of Copper Alloys

Copper is a fascinating metal to use when considering color. No other metal comes close to offering the variety of color that copper can develop. Copper seeks other elements to develop compounds that possess unique color attributes. Essentially, the copper surface, like most metal surfaces, seeks components in the atmosphere and surroundings to combine with. Over long periods of time, the metal surface develops compounds that resemble closely their mineral equivalent. Once this occurs, the copper compounds are defiant and stubborn. Further change is inhibited.

For instance, copper roofing, exposed for a century or more, develops a thick, beautiful green patina. This patina is typically the result of sulfur and oxygen from the air combining with the surface copper atoms. Water intermixes the reaction, and, over time, the surface develops a hydrated copper sulfate not unlike that of the mineral bronchantite. Today, the development of these green copper sulfate patinas has greatly diminished. The reason is that the atmosphere is cleaner and less polluted with sulfur compounds necessary to form the green patina. Thus, it takes considerably longer today to develop the green patina in many areas of Europe and the United States. In dry climates, the green patina may never develop; and in coastal regions, chlorine is added to the surface of copper alloys to develop a blue-green patina of copper chloride. This will appear more rapidly, first as a very pale green across a darkening surface.

Many chemical techniques can be used to color copper and copper alloys. Among them are proprietary techniques that prepatinate copper sheets with deep, rich green patinas not unlike those that formerly took several decades to develop naturally. Some of these proprietary techniques can develop the rich brown tones of cupric oxide on the copper surface. There are also techniques that can develop browns, yellows, and oranges, in various hues, to create beautiful colors from the chemical combination with copper oxide. These processes are called *artificial patination*. Some take hours to develop while others occur rapidly. Black and dark brown oxides can be readily developed on copper and copper alloy surfaces. These dark colors can be made to appear almost instantaneously on the surface.

The process of patination is an art more than a science. The effects on color development are highly dependent on ambient conditions and surface preparation processes. The metal surface must be thoroughly cleaned. All grease, oils, and oxidation-retardant compounds must be removed from the surface. This can be achieved by dipping copper product in concentrated phosphoric acid or a heated bath of sodium hydroxide (caustic soda). Only people experienced with working with acids and strong bases should perform these pretreatments, as extreme caution must be exercised when working with such chemical treatments. The use of proper safety equipment, eye protection, rubber gloves, and a respirator is essential; and the work must be performed in a well-ventilated space.

A slight "tooth" can be added before or after this stage by lightly sanding the surface or bead-blasting the surface. This will help the coloring solutions develop and bind into the copper surface.

Once the surface of the metal is thoroughly clean and dry, waste little time in applying the patina solutions. The copper alloy surface is very receptive at this point and will react rapidly to develop colors. By waiting, copper oxide will develop, inhibiting the receptivity of the surface.

Adding *blackening solutions*, and building on this as a base, can sometimes aid in the development of rich green patinas. Blackening solutions are strong reagents that cause the copper alloy to become very chemically active when first applied. Coat the patina with Incralac or wax to "freeze" the surface and help hold the chemical reaction onto the surface. It proceeds slowly under the coating, and the lacquer resists moisture, allowing the patina to bond with the base metal.

There are numerous patina solutions available for use on copper alloys. Applied both hot and cold, these solutions have various degrees of success. The most critical part of the procedure is to begin with a clean, oxide-free surface. The surface must be receptive to the particular solution. The available processes, and the formulas and techniques, are too numerous to cover here, but, in brief, the best approach is as follows: Determine the color and tones desired. Experiment on a small representative sample until the desired results are achieved. Or, better yet, consider working with an expert in the process, or use one of the prepatinated sheets. Using the prepatinated sheets is an excellent method of creating a large patina surface.

Field-applying patina to a surface is extremely difficult. Success is fleeting and rare. There are just too many variables to control, and the necessary solutions can be quite hazardous. What looks successful one moment on a field-applied patina can deteriorate quickly as the weather conditions change or as the oxide unzips from the copper and washes off the surface.

Copper alloy surfaces, whether they are prepatinated or not, continue to age. The aging occurs at a progressively slower rate as the copper surface reaches a chemical equilibrium. For example, bronze statues, exposed to the weather for centuries, often develop a darkish "bloom" in the form of a spot or streak. These localized changes are the product of natural pollutants and the further aging of the surface.

The predominant oxide to develop on the surface of copper alloys exposed to the atmosphere is cuprous oxide, Cu_2O. This oxide is essentially the mineral cuprite. The color is reddish brown, but often exhibits a range of color from orange to yellow, even purple. These are "interference colors" created by the thin oxide layer over the reflective base material. Cuprous oxide is insoluble in water. It is a semiconductor of electricity, which is part of the reason why copper continues to oxidize further beyond the basic oxide. Cuprous oxide forms readily on copper alloy surfaces in the presence of moist air. The minerals of copper undergo a very slow aging process, though the process is somewhat faster when near the sea. Chlorine combines with the cuprous oxide surface layer to develop a pale green mineral, paratacamite, $Cu_2(OH_3)Cl$.

Another somewhat common mineral formation on copper alloys combines carbon dioxide and forms carbonates over the initial cuprous oxide layer. The carbonate mineral forms are malachite and azurite. These relatively uniform corrosion products are difficult to artificially create. The mineral forms of copper are shown in Table 2.5; and the copper surface color expectations are listed in Table 2.6.

All copper and copper alloy surfaces exposed to the atmosphere undergo changes. On a molecular level they seek various compounds from the atmosphere

TABLE 2.5

Minerals of Copper

Mineral Form	Equation	Classification	Color
Enargite	Cu_3AsS_4	Sulfide	Gray-black with violet
Bornite	Cu_5FeS_4	Sulfide	Reddish, tarnish
Cuprite	Cu_2O	Oxide	Deep red to red-gray
Aurichalcite	$(ZnCu)_5[(OH)_3CO_3]_2$	Carbonate	Pale green, blue
Chalcopyrite	$CuFeS_2$	Sulfide	Brassy yellow with green tinge
Covellite	CuS	Sulfide	Blue-black
Chalcocite	Cu_2S	Sulfide	Lead gray
Variscite	$Al(PO_4)2H_2O$	Phosphate	Yellow green with blue tinge
Chrysocolla	$CuSiO_3$	Silicate	Green blue
Azurite	$2Cu\,CO_3 \cdot Cu(OH)_2$	Carbonate	Deep blue
Dioptase	$Cu[Si_6O_{16}]6H_2O$	Silicate	Emerald green
Turquoise	$CuAl_6[OH_2/PO_4]4H_2O$	Phosphate	Sky blue, blue-green
Malachite	$Cu\,CO_3 \cdot Cu(OH)_2$	Carbonate	Light green, blue-green
Bronchantite	$Cu_4SO_4(OH)_6$	Sulfate	Bright emerald green
Atacamite	$Cu_2Cl(OH)_3$	Halide	Dark green
Antlerite	$Cu_3SO_4(OH)_4$	Sulfate	Green to dark green, black
Tenorite	CuO	Oxide	Metallic gray-black
Spertinite	$Cu(OH)_2$	Hydroxide	Blue-green
Georgeite	$CuCO_3 \cdot Cu(OH)_2$	Carbonate	Translucent blue
Rosasite	$(CuZn)_3(CO_3)(OH)_4 \cdot H_2O$	Carbonate	Blue green
Nantokite	$CuCl$	Chloride	Pale green color
Atacamite	$Cu_2(OH)_3Cl$	Chloride	Green, glossy tone
Paratacamite	$Cu_2(OH)_3Cl$	Chloride	Pale green color
Clinoatacamite	$Cu_2(OH)_3Cl$	Chloride	Pale green color
Botallackite	$Cu_2(OH)_3Cl$	Chloride	Bluish green

and readily combine with them. They actually remove pollutants from the air, albeit very slowly, by combining with sulfur dioxide and carbon monoxide to form mineral compounds that effectively trap the pollutants.

Copper Coating on Other Metals

Occasionally, copper is used as a coating on other metals. Typically, it is plated over steel or stainless steel with a thin-plated coating of nickel sandwiched between. Copper plate is used on decorative interior and exterior fixtures. The plating will, if not coated with Incralac or other oxide-inhibiting lacquer, tarnish and weather similar to solid copper. Stainless-steel sheets with copper plating are available as well for use as an exterior cladding material.

TABLE 2.6

Copper Surface Color Expectations

Compound	Color	Approximate Time
Copper oxide (CuO)	Black streaks	Matter of weeks; loses its sheen and reverts to the brown oxide
Copper oxide (Cu2O)	Spotty brown	Copper loses its sheen after several weeks, quicker if humid, wet ambient
Copper oxide	Rich brown	6 to 12 months
Copper sulfate or Copper chloride	Light green tint over dark brown	5 to 10 years, depending on the intensity of the environment
Copper sulfate or copper chloride	Deep green	20 to 50 years

GOLD

Gold is one of the oldest metals known to humankind. It is the most malleable and ductile of all metals. Gold applied as a thin strip, square leaf, or plating interacts with light with intensity unmatched by other metals. It can be hammered thin to the point at which it is partially transparent, 0.01 mm thick. Gold is very soft in its purified state. Cold working has no effect on the stiffness of gold as it does with most other metals. Only when alloyed with other metals, usually copper and silver, does gold improve hardness. Gold is also very dense and has good conductivity of electricity and heat. It is a powerful infrared reflector, thus it stays cool and is used where surfaces must reflect intense heat.

This beautiful metal is highly corrosion-resistant. It will not be affected by normal exposure to the environment. That is why it stays so shiny and reflective. Sulfur, the usurper of copper and silver, has no effect on gold, nor do chlorine and carbon dioxide. Water will not corrode gold, and most organic salts have little effect.

Gilding

Gold is typically applied using a technique known as *gilding*. Gilding, an ancient skill, involves applying a thin layer of gold foil in the form of strips or small squares onto the surface of another material. The term gilding describes a process that encompasses a range of applications whereby a thin layer of gold is applied to a substrate material. The ancient process utilized mercury, where gold would be applied as an amalgam with mercury. The mercury would be removed as a vapor by heating the substrate, leaving the gold behind to adhere to the surface.

But because mercury vapor is a very toxic substance, today, gilding processes include vacuum deposition, electroplating, sputtering, as well as several other application methods. Generally, on exterior architectural and ornamental gilding, the base material is usually metal. Copper or copper alloys are the metal of choice but lead-coated copper, cast iron, and tin have also been gilded.

Deterioration of Gold Surfaces

The discoloration or tarnish seen on pure gold is the product of the underlying metal corroding, not the gold itself. The gilding is porous, and if a separating

TABLE 2.7

Reduction Potential

	E^o
$Au^+ + 1^{e^-} \approx Au$	1.69
$Au^{3+} + 3^{e^-} \approx Au$	1.50
$Cu^+ + 1^{e^-} \approx Cu$	0.52

barrier between the gold and the base metal has been breached, the underlying metal will corrode if moisture is present.

Gold is very noble, and most other metals will be sacrificial when in proximity to gold. Gold has a very high reduction potential. In equilibrium, it will cause most other metals to undergo galvanic attack.

Table 2.7 shows the equilibrium of gold and the reduction potential, E^o, which corresponds to the voltage potential of the metal in solution. Note how much more positive the value is than copper. This indicates that when these two metals are in contact via an electrolyte such as water with a slight acidic character, the copper will corrode. Of the many metals in architecture, gold is considered to be nobler in relationship to other metals such as iron, aluminum, and zinc (see Table 2.8). This being the case, it is a good practice to separate zinc and aluminum from gold.

Gold is often gilded onto other metals in one of its many alloy forms. As just stated, gold typically does not tarnish or corrode, but the underlying metal does via the porosity of the gilding. If the gilding layer is not pure gold, however, it will develop a slight oxide or tarnish.

Alloying of Gold Coatings

Gold coatings and jewelry are often designated by their level of purity (see Table 2.9). This system, called the Caret System, was derived from an ancient weight comparison system using the kirat, or seed, from the locust tree. Arab and African traders of the metal used the system in antiquity. Apparently, 24 beans corresponded to a certain volume of gold, thus 24-kirat gold. Today, the purity of gold as described by the Carat System is based on parts per 24. Additionally, the fineness of gold is described as the weight fraction in parts per 1000. Thus, pure gold is considered 24 carat with a fineness of 1000.

Gold alloys greater than 18-carat gold become progressively softer and will easily abrade. They are used as decorative surfaces, for the color they possess; and, in the case of exterior applications, these higher-purity alloys resist oxidation and maintain the beautiful luster. Maintaining and restoring gold-leaf surfaces will need to be undertaken in all exterior applications of the metal.

Colors of Gold Alloys

The color of gold alloys depends on the mix of three elements: gold, silver, and copper. Increase the silver content in relation to gold and the color changes from yellow to yellow-green and then to white with a yellow tint. Copper, on the other hand, changes the gold alloy progressively redder in color. Gold and silver are miscible into each other; that is, molten gold and silver will dissolve completely

TABLE 2.8

Electromotive Scale of Various Metals

	Voltage Potential	Metal
Least Noble	−1.03	Zinc
	−0.79	Aluminum
	−0.61	Cast iron
	−0.53	Active stainless steel
	−0.36	Copper
	−0.31	Bronze
	−0.29	Brass
	−0.28	Tin
	−0.27	Lead
	−0.25	Monel
	−0.15	400 Series Stainless—passive
	−0.10	Titanium
	−0.08	300 Series Stainless—passive
Most Noble	+1.29	Gold

TABLE 2.9

Carat Purities

Carat	Alloy	Fineness
24 carat	99.99% Au	1000 thousandths
22 carat	92% Au	920 thousandths
	5% Ag	
	3% Cu	
20 carat	84% Au	840 thousandths
	8–10% Ag	
	3–5% Cu	

into each other and form a homogeneous solid material. Gold and copper will as well. This will occur under all ratios of the two metals. However, silver and copper will not; they are miscible only within a very tight range of ratios of the two. Mixing all three metals will create an alloy that is much harder and less malleable than alloys of gold–silver or gold–copper. Color depends on the ratio of these three elements:

Au–gold—yellow color

Ag–silver—white color

Cu–Copper—red color

The color of the gold alloy is dependent on the amount of copper or silver in the alloy mix. Figure 2.3 describes the colors that are obtained as various proportions of the three elements are alloyed together. As silver is introduced to the alloy, the color tends toward the white scale. As copper is added, the color moves toward the red scale.

The process of leafing should be undertaken by those experienced in the art of gilding, as it is not simple; and, due to the high cost of the material, it is not a process one wants to master by trial and error. In any event, as with all metal-finishing applications, starting with a clean surface is required. The general steps used in the gilding process are:

1. Thoroughly clean the metal surface of all foreign matter.

2. Slightly roughen the surface by light blasting with glass or abrasion wheels.

3. Remove the oxides from the surface by using a mild etching solution or deoxidizing agent.

4. Apply an oxidation inhibitor. In the case of copper alloys, sodium benzotriazole works well.

5. Seal the surface. Today, a good epoxy primer, zinc chromate, or good acrylic will perform best.

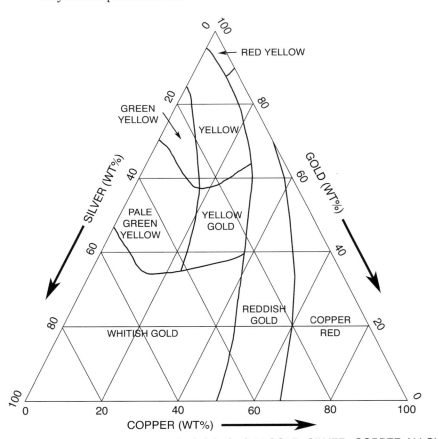

COMPOSITION RANGE FOR VARIOUS COLORS IN GOLD–SILVER–COPPER ALLOYS

FIGURE 2.3. Color behavior and the relationship to alloying of gold–silver–copper.

6. Apply the sizing and the leaf or foil to the surface while brushing down with a very fine application brush.

Electrodeposition of Gold

Plating of gold by electrodeposition is another means of applying a thin layer of gold onto the surface of a metal. Electrodeposition can be selectively applied by using resistive material. In selective electrodeposition, a portion of the surface is plated. The gold coating is very thin with a very fine grain. Thus, it matches closely the underlying surface being plated and provides a deep reflective luster. The color obtained is the very yellow color of 24-carat gold.

Texturing of Gold Surfaces

Adding texture to the surface prior to applying the gilding or electroplating can enhance the reflective nature of the gold finish. Texture can be induced into the sealing layer of acrylic or epoxy; or it can also be developed in the base metal. By adding texture to the surface, the intensity of the reflection can be enhanced by the scattering effect of the roughened surface. Light-scattering brings out the color of the metal. Even a slight coarseness will enhance the appearance of the gilding and further brighten the surface, particularly when viewed from a low angle of incidence. The drawback is, the coarse surface collects and holds dirt, requiring more frequent cleaning.

IRON, STEEL, AND STAINLESS STEEL

Stainless Steels

Stainless steels are naturally reflective. Oxidation does not develop very rapidly and the surface remains very smooth. Having a tight, smooth surface enhances the corrosion resistance of stainless steel. The more the surface is polished, the better the long-term performance.

During the production of stainless steels, the mill surface of the thick plate is cleaned of scale using strong acids. This process, known as *pickling,* dissolves the heavy oxides and free iron carbides that rise to the surface of the hot plate.

Further reduction of the stainless-steel thickness is performed on cold semipolished rolls. These rolls impart a smooth, reflective sheen on the surface of the metal. This initial sheen is the base for all subsequent finishes. The surface is designated as a No. 2B finish. Dull sheens can also be developed using rolls that have a dull surface. These initial finishes are known as No. 2D. See Figure 2.4.

The more specular No. 2B finish can be further enhanced by special annealing processes. Annealing the stainless steel in a controlled atmosphere will create a mirrorlike surface known as Bright Annealed, designated as No. 2BA. The No. 2BA can be the base surface for glass bead, No. 8 and No. 9 mirror surfaces, as well as fine satin finishes. The No. 2BA will provide a consistent color and surface for the more refined surfaces.

The reflective character of the various stainless-steel finishes can be divided into three categories as shown in Figure 2.4. The Reflective Finishes can be described as those that reflect light similar to a mirror. A bright light will reflect as a "hot spot." The angle of incidence equals the angle of reflection. Very little scattering of light occurs. The No. 9 finish is the equivalent to a mirror on one scale while the No. 2B finish is somewhat smoky.

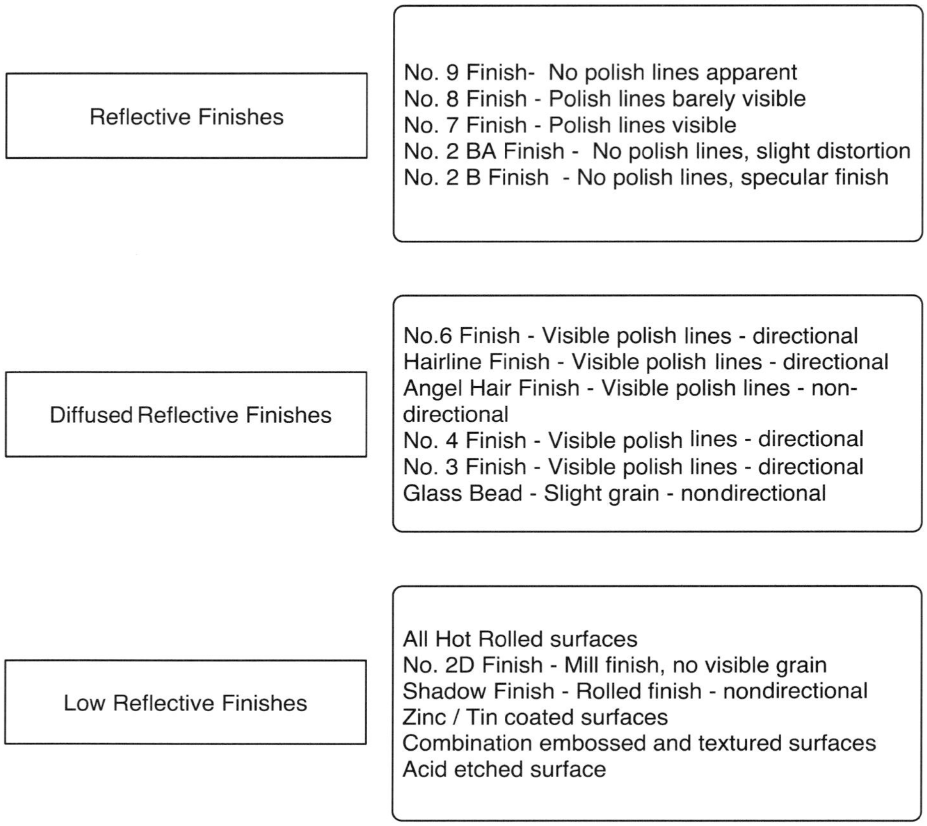

| Reflective Finishes | No. 9 Finish- No polish lines apparent
No. 8 Finish - Polish lines barely visible
No. 7 Finish - Polish lines visible
No. 2 BA Finish - No polish lines, slight distortion
No. 2 B Finish - No polish lines, specular finish |

| Diffused Reflective Finishes | No.6 Finish - Visible polish lines - directional
Hairline Finish - Visible polish lines - directional
Angel Hair Finish - Visible polish lines - non-directional
No. 4 Finish - Visible polish lines - directional
No. 3 Finish - Visible polish lines - directional
Glass Bead - Slight grain - nondirectional |

| Low Reflective Finishes | All Hot Rolled surfaces
No. 2D Finish - Mill finish, no visible grain
Shadow Finish - Rolled finish - nondirectional
Zinc / Tin coated surfaces
Combination embossed and textured surfaces
Acid etched surface |

FIGURE 2.4. Stainless-steel finishes and the corresponding level of reflectivity.

Disturbing the even reflective surfaces with minute surface fractures or indentations, which scatter the reflected light slightly, produces the Diffused Reflective Finishes. Because these finishes are typically applied over the Reflective Finishes, they possess a brightness, an almost glowing behavior when in strong light.

The Low Reflective Finishes possess a dull reflection. Light is effectively scattered by the rough surface. and these surfaces appear flat in most light.

Because of the chrome content, 18 percent on average for most architectural alloys, stainless steel reflects 49 percent of the visible wavelength of light (see Table 2.10). It is much more heavily weighted toward the blue wavelength and captures well the tone of the sky. As stated earlier, on cloudy days, stainless steel will appear very dull and lusterless. This is due in part to the scattering effect of the clouds, which reduces the blue segment of the wavelength of light reaching the stainless-steel surface.

Because of the specular nature of stainless-steel surfaces, slight variations in plane can affect the relative color. Moving around the surface changes the angle of view from one surface of a plate or panel relative to another. The more direct the reflection, the lighter the color. The panel that is slightly askew will appear darker in strong light. A stainless-steel surface can look dark from one angle of view, then light in color from a different angle of view. The difference can

TABLE 2.10

Stainless-Steel Finishes

Stainless-Steel Finishes	Relative Reflectivity
Shadow	Diffused
No. 2D	Diffused
Angel Hair on No. 2D	Diffused
Angel Hair on No. 2B	Diffused—bright
No. 2D with matte coined surfaces—proprietary finishes	Diffused
No. 2B with matte coined surfaces—proprietary finishes	Diffused—bright
No. 2B	Specular—nonmirror
No. 2BA (bright annealed)	Mirror specular
No. 3	Diffused—bright
No. 4	Diffused—bright
Hairline	Diffused—bright
Glass bead	Diffused—bright
No. 7	Mirror pecular
No. 8	Mirror Specular
Embossed over No. 2B	Diffused—bright
Interference coloring on the above	Black, green, bronze, gold, red, blue
Zinc-coated	Diffused

be only a few degrees out of plane (see Figure 2.5). This faceted reflection is common in stainless steel thin-plate surfaces. This is also why "oil-canning" tendencies are greater in stainless steel. The relative high and low points in a stainless-steel surface reflect light back to the viewer at varying angles, which create apparent visual distortions in the surface.

When fabricated and installed correctly, as shown in Figure 2.6, the reflection is not distorted by the undulating surface. Light washes over the diffused reflective surface in straight lines. The mirror reflective surfaces show straight lines as straight images and not curved images.

Stainless-steel surfaces, particularly the diffused finishes such as No. 4 satin, angel hair, and glass-bead-blast surfaces, reflect the colors and shadows of the surrounding environment, but in a more scattered, subdued fashion.[1]

---

[1] The author was involved with a rather large curtainwall surface of glass bead stainless steel. The building was situated in a very wooded region. The trees came within a few meters of the building surface. The author received an excited call from the contractor saying that the panels he supplied were different colors and that he better get to the project immediately to see for himself. The author caught a flight and arrived at the project the following morning. The contractor pointed at the pristine walls and said they were all blotchy and mottled the afternoon before but now they appeared even and beautiful. The next day, the contractor contacted the author again saying the mottling had returned. As it turned out, what he was seeing was the reflections of the trees in the afternoon sun.

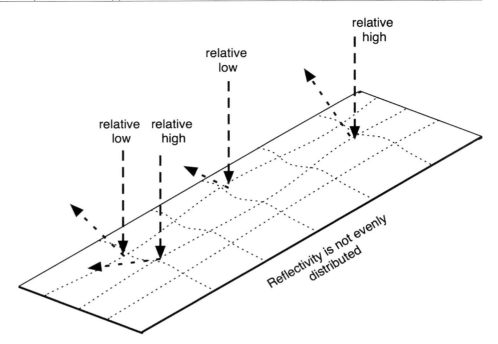

FIGURE 2.5. Graphic depiction of "oil-canning" reflective behavior.

FIGURE 2.6. Mobile Oil Headquarters in Lenexa, Kansas. Hairline-finish stainless steel overlaid onto No. 9 finish stainless steel.

So-called oil-canning characteristics can be concealed in some views with the scattering effect of satin finishes. Other views, and the deflections, appear to pop out visually. This is due to the localized reflectivity of the surface and the viewer's precise position.

Visual defects such as *chatter* are more visible in reflective stainless-steel surfaces than in most other materials. Chatter defects are caused when the polishing belts slip during the application of the finish. Whether the finish is a linear satin finish, such as a No. 4 or No. 3, or a mirror finish, slight reflective differences caused by the slipping of the polishing belts will create a series of visual lines of distorted reflection. The viewer cannot feel the distortion, but it is apparent when viewing the surface at an acute angle. These distortions are not repairable.

Chatter is distinguished from *coil stop lines* in that they are in the finish and not in the metal. That is, chatter defects are on the surface, whereas coil stop defects go through the metal. Figure 2.7A shows the mirror-polished face of a 4-mm-thick plate of stainless. Figure 2.7B shows the reverse side of the same plate. The visible line is a coil stop line. Coil stops occur when the ribbon of metal at the mill is undergoing cold rolling processes. The cold rolling process moves the metal at high speed from one tensioned roll to another. When the ribbon of metal stops during the process, a line is imparted to the metal. This is a single line versus multiple chatter lines. The metal is not appropriate for architectural applications where appearance plays an important part.

Steel

Steel is usually considered a utilitarian material, better used as a skeleton, hidden from view by the beauty of another material. But steel can be a very intriguing surfacing material. The color of steel is a greenish blue to blue-gray material. The surface can be polished, oiled, stained, and enhanced in ways many other metals only try to duplicate. Essentially, there are two distinct forms of the plate and sheet: hot rolled and cold rolled. Hot rolled has a courser, grainy surface with some darkish streaks, and often it is coated with mill oil. Hot rolled is available in thicknesses as thin as 1.5 mm (0.063 inches) up to heavier plate sec-

FIGURE 2.7A. Coil stop barely visible on the mirror-polished face.

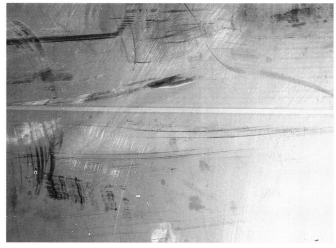

FIGURE 2.7B. Coil stop clearly visible on the reverse side of the polished stainless steel.

tions of 50 mm. Cold rolled has a smoother surface and is available in thinner sheet. Cold rolled steel is generated by the rolling of hot rolled product through subsequent cold rolls. Steel can be polished, blackened, blued, reddened, distressed, and hammered. The tones can be industrial or elegant. Steels, if exposed to moisture in liquid or gaseous state, will develop the characteristic red rust. Steel can be treated with wax or oils or they can be coated to maintain the surface finish and resist corrosion. Table 2.11 lists some common steel finishes.

Steel possesses a unique color and surface characteristic that immediately connotes a feeling of strength and substance. The problem to overcome with steel is its ever-changing, ever-deteriorating nature. Its natural oxide is soluble and thus it continues to seek oxygen and water until only dust remains. This characteristic, however, can be used to produce some interesting surface and appearance effects.

The color of steel is a dark blue-gray to gray-black. The surface, when heated, develops various interference colors, which quickly gives way to a deep blue-black tone as it cools. Hot rolled steel surfaces have a grainy texture, the result of removing the deep scale during the pickling process. Scale is a hard, glassylike substance that forms on hot rolled steel. Pickling baths of sulfuric and hydrochloric acid remove the scale and the surface oxides. When this occurs, small textural rivulets are left on the surface.

Heating the steel surface in the presence of steam creates a blue tone. This process, known as *bluing*, will create a more corrosion-resistant surface, at least for interior exposures. Other bluing processes using proprietary chemistries are available. It is possible to seal the surface with clear coatings or wax to maintain the color and resist further oxidation.

Cast steel, or cast iron, has a very grainy surface created by the sand cast form used to create the part. Other methods of casting steel are available that can provide a smoother finish, but the sand cast method is predominantly used for ornamental steel parts. The surface produced is generally a dark gray-black. It is possible to grind and wire-brush the surface, creating decorative reflective behaviors. Adding heat, the color goes from shiny silver-gray to a blue-gray with tints of other colors.

Steel is typically coated with an oxide-inhibiting coating. Because of the level of porosity of steel surfaces, signs of corrosion will often appear as red spots beneath the surface coating. It is very difficult to get all the moisture out before

TABLE 2.11

Steel Finishes

Steel Finishes	Relative Reflectivity
Angel Hair —sealed, waxed, or coated	Diffused
Glass bead—sealed, waxed, or coated	Diffused
Darkened—sealed	Diffused—dull
Galvanized	Diffused—dull
Aluminum/zinc-coated	Diffused—bright
Weathering steel	Diffused—reddish brown
Terne-coated	Diffused—dull

coating. Heating the surface is one method, but this can alter the surface color, unless low heat is applied.

Chemically darkening the surface and then sealing with a good lacquer can capture the unique color and feel of steel plates. Figure 2.8 shows an interior project that incorporated steel plates and steel castings that had been chemically darkened and sealed. The surface has required very little maintenance after more than seven years.

Weathering Steel

Weathering steel is a steel alloy that contains copper. Known also as copper-bearing steel, this alloy readily develops an oxide in the presence of moisture. The oxide is a red iron oxide. The mineral form approaches that of *hematite*. Typically hydrated, this course oxide forms on the surface very rapidly. Often, soot, pollutants, and imperfections within the steel become trapped in the quickly forming course oxide, creating streaks and dark spots.

Acceleration of the surface can be achieved by using an oxidizing agent such as diluted hydrochloric acid, ammonium chloride solution, or even industrial hydrogen peroxide. The color achieved by acceleration is dark reddish orange. Lightly sanding the surface between applications will remove the loose particles that tend to rub off or wash off and deposit as stains on surrounding material. Continuing to work the surface in this manner will create a thick adherent, leatherlike oxide film. The color is a dark rich red.

Weathering steel is susceptible to chloride attack. Deicing salts will attack the surface and prevent the formation of the dense iron oxide, causing further erosion of the surface and eventual perforation.

When using weathering steel, it is very wise to paint the reverse concealed side to prevent the oxidation surface from occurring on both sides and thinning

FIGURE 2.8. Oakley World Headquarters, in Foothills Ranch, California. Darkened and oxidized steel plate interior.

out the metal. Thicker gauges, thicknesses greater than 1.5 mm (0.063 inches), do not need the back coating.

MORPHOLOGY OF THE WEATHERED STEEL SURFACE

Weathering steel arrives from the mill source like other steels. It typically has a thin coating of mill oil. The mill oil is placed on the surface as a lubricant during cold rolling operations and to resist oxidation while the metal is stored. Oil-free surfaces of steel, weathering versions or not, will oxidize when exposed to humid air.

To start the process of oxidation, the weathering steel should be free of surface oils, fingerprints, and grease. Degreasing the surface or exposing the surface to the weather can achieve this. Once degreased, water can be misted on the surface and allowed to dry, a process repeated for several days. This will cause the surface to develop a fine layer of orange-colored iron oxide. It is important to evenly mist the surface, avoiding pooling or channeling of the water, as these tend to make the surface streaky.

Applying a stronger oxidizing agent in between water applications will create a dark red to reddish brown surface. Further wetting creates a deeper, coarse reddish brown oxide.

During the wetting and drying cycle, some of the oxidation thickens rapidly. As the oxidation moves deeper into the steel, this surface may flake off. Some blackish streaks of carbonlike rust can develop as the oxidation moves further into the metal. Eventually, the oxide coating becomes very dense and hard. This can be expected to take several years. Even with the accelerated procedures, the real dense surface develops over time, slowly, with oxygen from the air joining with the iron oxide to form the hard mineral hematite.

LEAD

There are two ways lead is used as a surfacing material in architecture. One is as heavy sheets, the other as a coating over another metal. The sheets are manufactured from commercially pure lead. Both conditions have unique surface attributes. Lead sheets are smooth, grainy, and very malleable. Lead coatings are applied in the hot dipping method, usually over copper; or in the case of terne, the lead–tin coating, over stainless steel and steel. A small amount of antimony or tin is usually present in the hot bath. The cooling of the lead coating on the metal surface of copper creates variations in thickness and a heavy spangle of lead crystal formation. The characteristics of lead are summarized in Table 2.12.

Lead Sheet

When first applied, the lead sheet is dark gray with a slight blue appearance. The surface is almost always mottled with dark streaks and splotches contrasting with lighter gray regions. The appearance is that of a gray hide of some very tough animal. Interference colors appear as very subtle variations across the surface, the result of the very thin clear lead oxide that develops on the surface. In certain lights, the lead has an almost wetted look, as some regions are glossy while other regions appear flat. Up close, the effects of the interference are diminished but the character of the lead surface is almost organic in appearance.

Eventually, on exposure to the surrounding atmosphere, the lead oxide grows thicker and absorbs other compounds. Lead carbonate forms in cleaner

TABLE 2.12

Characteristics of Lead

High Density	Low Tensile Strength
Excellent cast ability	Low creep strength
Excellent formability	Low hardness
Good conductor of electricity	Poor elasticity
High thermal expansion	Low melting point
Excellent corrosion resistance	Toxic when consumed

exposures. Lead sulfide forms in more industrial exposures where sulfur is present.

All soluble compounds of lead are toxic, thus the material should be used where it cannot be touched. Runoff moisture should not go directly back into natural waters. Filtering through soil would be preferred.

Another characteristic of the lead sheet is the product of its low tensile strength. Sculptures or cladding made from the metal appear as if a dull gray cloth has been draped over them (see Figure 2.9). The edges are soft in appearance and tend to undulate across the object.

Lead sheets come in various thicknesses and weights (see Table 2.13). The thicker sheets have a slightly coarser surface. Thin sheets, in thicknesses less than 1 mm, are easily folded by hand. Thicker sheets can be hammered along the seams. The low creep strength and low tensile strength result in the lead slowly moving and sagging over time. With each thermal cycle of expansion and contraction, the heavy, dense lead sheet moves and sags to conform to the support surface.

Lead is available in cast and extruded forms, as well as sheet lead. The surface of lead scratches easily, exposing bright lead within the scratch, but this soon darkens as the lead oxide quickly develops. Lead does not polish out; it is simply too soft. You can burnish the surface, which will produce a temporarily

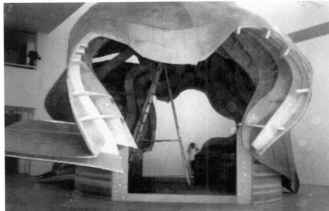

FIGURE 2.9. Lead clad sculpture, "The Horsehead," designed by Frank Gehry.

TABLE 2.13

Standard Lead Sheet Thicknesses and Weights

Pounds per Square Foot	Approximate Thickness (in.)	Approximate Thickness (mm)
2.0	0.031	0.79
2.5	0.039	1.00
3.0	0.047	1.19
3.5	0.055	1.39
4.0	0.063	1.60
5.0	0.078	2.00
6.0	0.094	2.38
8.0	0.125	3.18
10.0	0.156	4.00
12.0	0.188	4.76
14.0	0.219	5.56
16.0	0.250	6.35

shiny appearance, but it will not last. Lead will, over time, darken to an even dark gray to gray-black appearance. It will lose reflectivity, and all interference films will disappear.

Pewter is not lead. The appearance pewter has is brighter, more silver in tone. Pewter at one time in history had significant lead content, but, today, pewter is a tin–antimony alloy. (See the discussion of tin later in this chapter.)

Lead-Coated Metals

Lead is predominantly used as a coating of other metals (see Table 2.14). Lead or a lead–tin alloy is applied to other metals by dipping them into a molten bath of lead alloy. Terne is an alloy coating that is approximately 80 percent lead and 20 percent tin. Terne-coated steel has been in use for over 200 years as a metal skin. Typically, terne-coated steel was painted, often with the red lead oxide paint. Left exposed to the atmosphere, terne would eventually disintegrate. Terne is a good barrier coating, but affords the base steel little galvanic protection.

TABLE 2.14

Typical Lead-Coated Metal Surfaces

Base Metal	Coating	Initial Color	Aged Color
Copper	Lead	Spangled blue gray	Very dark gray
Steel	Terne—75 to 93% Lead, 25 to 7% Tin	Mottled brown-gray appearance	Rust red unless painted
Stainless steel	Terne—75 to 93% Lead, 25 to 7% Tin	Mottled blue-gray; somewhat reflective	Dark gray; low reflectivity

Terne-coated stainless steel is, however, used as a surfacing material, both exposed to weather naturally and as a substrate for paint. Terne-coated stainless steel, lead-coated copper, and terne-coated steel are used as thin sheet metal skins. Formed into standing and batten seam roofs, flat seam roofs, fascias, and, on occasion, wall cladding, these materials have performed well throughout the past century as an economic, corrosion-resistant surface material.

LEAD-COATED COPPER

Lead-coated copper has a similar appearance to lead sheet, with the following exceptions. Because the lead coating is applied by dipping a sheet of copper into molten lead and then allowing it to cool, the texture of the metal takes on an added character. The molten lead tends to pool in small rivulets on the surface of the copper. The lead cools in large crystals on the surface, creating a slight spangle appearance, not unlike galvanized steel. This imparts a unique texture to the surface, giving the lead a unique texture with slight contrasting gray shades of color.

As the metal sheets are stacked and transported, a slight burnishing effect occurs on the lead surface, which tends to brighten the high parts of the small rivulet. As the metal weathers, the clear lead oxide develops on the surface, creating interference color effects. The brightened tops of the texture enhance these interference color effects. This effect will remain for approximately three to five years. After this time, lead-coated copper darkens to an even dark gray tone.

TERNE-COATED STAINLESS

Terne-coated stainless steel lacks the "molten metal" texture of lead-coated copper and is slightly lighter in appearance. The approximate 20 percent of tin creates a lighter gray-blue color on new material. Stainless steel will not transfer and dissipate the heat as rapidly as copper sheet does when removed from the hot baths. The texture is smoother and lacks a spangle. The tin creates a finer grain and causes the molten metal on the surface to cool at a different rate than lead alone.

Terne-coated stainless steel when first installed is more reflective than lead-coated copper. Interference films do not develop as readily on terne-coated stainless steel. Weathering darkens the surface to an even gray, slightly lighter than lead-coated copper.

In some parts of the United States, lead carbonate or lead hydroxide forms on lead and terne surfaces. These lead compounds do not have the intended dark gray color. Lead carbonate is a chalky white formation on the surface. Lead hydroxide is a reddish formation, almost like rust. Both are becoming more common on lead surfaces because of the improved air quality, particularly the lack of sulfur.

Because of the lead content, there is no easy corrective action to surfaces that develop the lead carbonate or lead hydroxide. Cleaning will remove lead and require containment and proper removal. Most likely, the compounds will return to the lead surface.

NICKEL

This silver-gray metal is very tough and malleable. Not considered for architectural uses in the pure metal form, nickel is more expensive in comparison to other metals, thus it is used typically as plating or as an alloy constituent with other metals. Nickel is a common alloying constituent in stainless steel, particularly those used for architectural cladding. Nickel today finds its greatest use in austenitic stainless-steel alloys rather than as a stand-alone metal cladding or plating.

Along with its toughness and formability, nickel is very corrosion-resistant. Nickel is used in industrial applications where high temperature and high stress conditions are subjected to corrosive environments.

Nickel can be polished to a bright, high, lustrous appearance, or it can be given a fine satin or "angel hair" finish. It will, however, dull out on exposure to the atmosphere as the oxide grows on the surface. Over time, nickel will develop a greenish gray patina.

In China, and later in Europe, an alloy of nickel, copper, and zinc was in use for several centuries. This alloy is known today as German silver or nickel silver. Nickel silver contains from 20 to 25 percent nickel, which gives it a beautiful golden silver appearance. Nickel is commonly used in conjunction with copper. The two metals are soluble in any proportion.

Monel

Monel is an alloy of copper and nickel. This silver-gray metal was the predecessor of stainless steel. When new, it resembles stainless steel in appearance. Monel contains 63 percent nickel and from 25 to 32 percent copper. The balance is iron and manganese. Nickel and copper will dissolve into one another at various proportions when in the molten liquid form.

In sheet and plate, the monel surface takes on the quality of the cold rolls similar to stainless steel. Polished rolls produce a specular finish; dull rolls produce a low reflective surface. Monel can have a grain applied to the surface similar to the ubiquitous No. 4 finish provided on stainless steel, or it can be custom-finished with glass beads, embossed, or lightly grained with the angel hair finish or other custom finishing (see Table 2.15).

Monel is malleable. Sheets of monel are formed into thin cladding surfaces such as metal roofing, fascia, and surfacing. However, monel will rapidly work-harden when cold-worked. This will require annealing for subsequent forming. Monel is highly corrosion-resistant, thus it performs well in industrial, coastal, and urban environments. The ratio of nickel to copper is very similar to the natural mineral form found in the earth, hence its stability when exposed to corrosive environments.

TABLE 2.15

Monel and Nickel Finishes

Monel and Nickel Finishes	Relative Reflectivity
Mill	Diffused
Angel Hair	Diffused
Mirror Polish	Mirror specular
Hairline or No. 4	Diffused

When new, the appearance of monel is similar, if not indistinguishable from, stainless steel. Stainless steel has a slight bluish cast imparted by chromium. Polished monel reflects the color of the sky, but in an overcast sky, the surface appears slightly darker than stainless steel. Monel gets its initial color from the significant nickel content in the alloying mix. The reflective index of nickel when polished is 0.63, which actually is greater than stainless steel. Over time, monel develops tarnish with a brown-green cast. It loses its luster with time but still retains a silver-gray metallic cast with a green-brown patina. It owes its weathered appearance to the large amount of copper in the alloying mix.

Nickel Plating

Other significant uses of nickel are as a plating material. Nickel is used as an intermediate plating under chromium or brass to provide corrosion protection to the base metal. Nickel can be plated alone as well. It does not offer galvanic protection, but provides a barrier against corrosion. Nickel plating is often used on forged and cast hardware and on fixtures for the furniture and decorative plumbing industry.

Plating is the electrodeposition of one metal onto another. The nickel is taken out of solution and thinly applied to the electrically charged surface of another body. Electrodeposition of nickel can occur in layers to a significant thickness. To produce a satin texture, fine inert particles are suspended in the plating bath and deposited with the nickel plate.

Nickel Cladding

Thin nickel sheet can be clad under high pressure to low carbon steel, stainless steels, and copper. Nickel cladding of stainless steel has been used in Japan as a cladding material for some years now. The nickel-clad stainless-steel sheet is annealed at very high temperatures. The annealing takes place in a chamber fed by outside air to create a nickel oxide. The oxide mutes the reflective level of the surface. The color is a greenish gray. The oxide develops interference colors when viewed at various angles. Nickel-clad stainless steel has superior corrosion resistance, but the relative cost created by the nickel limits its usage.

Other Nickel Alloys

Other nickel alloys of interest, but of little use to date in architecture, are the nickel–iron alloys and the nickel–titanium alloys. An alloy of nickel–iron known as invar has a coefficient of expansion of zero for temperatures between –50°C and 100°C. The alloy has wide uses in clock devices because of this characteristic.

A nickel–titanium alloy known as nitinol has shape memory characteristics. When the metal is heated, the crystal structure of the metal undergoes a shift, and the form of the metal changes. As the heat is released, the metal returns to the original shape. The metal does not undergo strain hardening but actually has a characteristic of strain relieving as it returns to the original shape.

MAGNESIUM

Magnesium is a silvery white metal, which quickly oxidizes on exposure to form a thin gray patina. This lightweight metal, the lightest of all commercially available metals, weighs in at one-third less than aluminum. It has good formability and excellent corrosion resistance in the high-purity form.

Magnesium is usually alloyed with other metals such as aluminum and zinc. Alloying improves the strength, but corrosion resistance is decreased. Sheet and plate are rolled from alloys containing approximately 3 percent aluminum and 1 to 2 percent zinc.

Magnesium may have a place in architectural cladding due to its lightweight nature and formability. However, certain inherent characteristics will limit its use. Magnesium will be attacked by seawater. Magnesium is at the extreme end of the galvanic metal scale; hence it will sacrifice itself when in a galvanic couple with all other metals. When heated to 550°C, it bursts into an intense bright flame as it rapidly combines with oxygen. Shavings and dust from fabrication processes will have to be controlled. It was once used in flashbulbs because of its rapid and bright burn.

Another architectural use of magnesium is as a base metal for acid etching and engraving. Magnesium can be easily etched. It responds to photoengraving techniques better than many other metals.

SILVER

Silver, the metallic white metal when polished, acts as the standard of comparative appearance for all other metals, with the exception of gold and copper. Silver has been around since the first early coins were produced. The Egyptians used the metal as a currency around 5000 BCE.

Silver has the highest electrical conductivity of any metal, nearly 8 percent higher conductivity than copper. Additionally, silver has the highest thermal conductivity among metals. Silver is more malleable than copper but less than gold. In alloy forms involving copper, silver is considered for jewelry and silverware. Rarely used as an architectural metal, silver is sometimes used as an ornamental metal or metal plating. Silver is a high-maintenance material because of its rapid tarnish. Silver has extremely good corrosion-resistant properties, however; it absorbs sulfur readily from the air, tarnishing to a black silver sulfide.

Silver can be readily electroplated onto other metals. Silver salts impregnated onto the surface of other metals via vacuum deposition and as free ions in clear coatings are finding more uses today because of their antibactericidal behavior. Steel and stainless steel can be purchased with the silver ion coatings applied to the surface. The ions in the coating act as excellent antimicrobial films.

ZINC

Zinc has been in use as an architectural cladding material for many decades. Either in the commercially pure sheet form or as the ubiquitous coating on steel, typically referred to as galvanized, zinc is a bluish gray metal. In the commercially pure form, zinc is available in various sheet sizes, castings, and small cross-section extrusions. Zinc sheet is currently available in mill finish, preweathered finish, and darkened finish (see Table 2.16). The mill surface is a bright, tinlike appearance. It has a silver color. Mill-finish zinc quickly weathers to a dull blue-gray color as it develops zinc hydroxide over the surface. In most instances, the zinc hydroxide quickly forms a surface of zinc carbonate. Zinc carbonate offers excellent corrosion protection to the base metal. The pleasing color

TABLE 2.16

Zinc Finishes

Zinc Finishes	Relative Reflectivity
Natural	Specular
Preweathered	Diffused
Darkened gray	Diffused—dull
Blackened	Diffused—flat black

develops quickly in most exposures. Coastal exposures develop a chlorinated hydroxide with a slightly lighter cast.

More often, zinc is used in the preweathered form. The preweathered surface is developed at the mill source. The surface arrives with a dull gray to greenish gray coating of zinc carbonate on both sides of the sheet. Zinc sheet is also available in black and gray-black colors. The colors are developed by oxidation processes and are successfully used in exterior applications. These flat, dark colors have very low reflective levels. They absorb heat like all black metals, so caution should be exercised when used where they are accessible to touching.

Other colors are possible on zinc as well. Zinc is a reactive metal and accepts influences of chemical oxidation processes on the surfaces. Whites, pale yellows, and various tones of gray can be developed on zinc surfaces. The development of various patination colors on zinc are in their infancy as far as the architectural and ornamental industry.

Zinc Coatings

GALVANIZED

There are two predominant types of galvanized steel: hot-dipped galvanized and electroplate galvanized (see Table 2.17). The hot-dipped forms are steel surfaces

TABLE 2.17

Galvanized Coating Thicknesses

Coating Designation	Minimum Thickness (oz/sf)	Minimum Thickness (kg/m^2)	Federal Specification QQ-S-775E
G235	2.35	0.72	Class A
G210	2.10	0.64	Class B
G185	1.85	0.56	
G165	1.65	0.50	Class C
G140	1.40	0,43	
G115	1.15	0.35	
G90	0.90	0.28	Class D
G60	0.60	0.18	Class E
G30	0.30	0.09	

dipped in molten pure zinc. The duration of immersion in the hot molten bath determines the thickness obtained. A metallurgical bond is formed between the zinc surface and the steel. Highly pure zinc is at the surface with an intermediate alloy layer at the steel/zinc interface. This intermediate layer provides a significant amount of the corrosion protection to the steel base material. The outer, pure zinc layer acts as a barrier to protect the steel and gives the metal its characteristic color and spangle appearance. The inner layer provides a transition zone that resists attack on the base steel by sacrificial action.

GALVANIZED SPANGLE

The spangle is a unique and interesting formation on the galvanized surface. It is created by the slow cooling of the zinc surface on the steel. The process involves running a sheet, plate, structural shape, or constructed shape into a molten bath of high-purity zinc. Additional trace metals are put into the molten zinc to assist in the formation of the zinc crystal on the surface. As the hot, coated steel exits the bath of zinc, it is blasted with air to remove excess zinc from the surface. The zinc surface cools with the steel base material. As the surface cools, crystals of zinc develop across the surface.

The electroplated galvanized steels have the pure zinc outer layer but lack the intermediate alloy layer that mixes the steel and zinc. Galvanized surfaces will lose the spangle and form a gray zinc oxide film with a slight tooth or fuzziness to them. Sometimes, streaks of red rust will develop on galvanized steel surfaces where the steel is no longer getting the benefit of the galvanic protection.

Zinc Coatings on Other Metals

Zinc–tin alloy coatings are being applied to other metals such as copper and stainless steel. These coatings are applied by hot dipping the sheet into the molten metal. The surface is then smoothed by a blast of air across the surface. Because of the rate of cooling, tin within the mixture, and the air blast across the surface, a very light, almost indiscernible spangle develops. Contrasting light and dark grains create the spangle. They appear almost as small smears on the surface.

The initial color of the metal is a low reflective whitish gray color. The minute light zones on the surface influence the color. These are created by a more reflective metal grain intermixed with dark, low reflective grains. Reflectivity is muted by the coarseness of the dark low reflective surface, but the surface is still bright in intense sunlight. As it weathers, the surface develops a gray patina. Reflectivity is conquered by a roughened surface that develops as the zinc–tin alloy combines with carbon and oxygen in the surrounding atmosphere. The tone is darker in urban environments when other pollutants combine on the surface.

TIN

Tin is used more often as a coating on metals rather than as a sheet or casting. As a coating, tin does not oxidize at room temperatures or in water. It is nontoxic. Pure, unalloyed tin sheets and castings will oxidize and darken when cooled below 13°C. The crystalline lattice of the element becomes rearranged and the surface blisters. Adding other elements such as lead, copper, or bismuth prevents this occurrence. The ubiquitous tin can is a very thin coating, about one micron thick, of pure tin over steel. The coating is applied by electroplating onto the surface. Tin does not provide galvanic protection as does zinc. It is essentially the coating that protects the underlying metal.

One significant use of tin sheets is for organ pipes. Desired for their resonance quality, organ pipes are constructed from rolled and welded tin sheets. The tin sheets are actually tin–lead alloys formed from cast strips. The tin–lead alloys vary from approximately 20 to 90 percent tin, depending on the tone desired. Another interesting characteristic of these cast strip alloys is the surface, which has a texture of spots, like the hide of an animal.

The surface finishes obtainable on the tin-plated alloys are limited to the shiny plated smooth appearance. The surface is rarely, if ever, mechanically abraded due to the need to keep the coating sound and thick. For tin sheet, the finish is usually a mill surface created by passing the sheet through dull cold rolls. The surface can be polished either with a satin finish or buffed to a specular finish. Textures can also be applied to the surface by means of embossing or coining rolls. The soft metal will take embossing quite readily. Refer to Table 2.18 for the initial color and eventual color of various tin alloy surfaces.

Terne coatings are a tin–lead alloy. Hot dipping steel or stainless steel into molten baths of the material applies terne coatings. Terne coatings were addressed earlier, in the discussion on lead.

TIN-COATED COPPER

Tin coatings on copper are available in sheet form. Tin applied by hot dipping copper sheet or by plating copper sheet is used as a cladding material in both Europe and the United States. Tin-coated copper appears initially very silver-white in color, the color of sand-cast aluminum. The surface is grainy and soon loses its sheen as it weathers to a thin tin oxide. Over time and exposure, some of the copper bleeds through, creating a slight greenish tint to the surface.

Pewter

Pewter is a tin-based alloy containing antimony, copper, and sometimes silver. Pewter sheets and castings are used more in small decorative features. Pewter is very malleable. The color is a silver-white tone. The following are the universal alloying designations for cast and wrought forms of pewter.

Pewter Cast Alloy	L13911
Pewter Wrought Alloy	L13912

TABLE 2.18

Tin Alloy Color

Tin Alloy Form	Initial Color	Exposure to Ambient
Tin plating	White-gray	Unaffected
Tin Sheet—alloyed	Light gray	Unaffected
Pewter	Silver-white	Darkens slightly
Tin-coated copper	Grainy silver-white	Darkens with green tint
Speculum	Bright silver-white	Brown tint—dull tarnish

Speculum

Speculum, a silver-brown tin–copper alloy once used as mirrors, is rarely used today. Tin is alloyed with between 51 and 67 percent copper. The optimum range for decorative work is 57 to 58 percent copper. Beyond this, it more readily tarnishes. Below this, the image is cloudy. Speculum can be polished to a high reflectivity. Interior uses resist tarnish well.

TITANIUM

Thanks in large part to the famous architect Frank Gehry, the metal titanium has undergone a transformation into one of the most formidable architectural metal surfaces. The soft gray color with a hint of gold provides, in Mr. Gehry's words, "an old-world appearance." Titanium is almost always provided with the surface obtained at the mill. This surface can be a smooth, slightly glossy gray tone or it can be moderately coarse from glass-bead blasting or shot peening. The stiffness of the surface resists deep embossing but can receive many of the same patterns available on stainless steel. Mechanical finishes are rarely applied because of the strange reactive nature of the metal. Titanium has an explosive characteristic when it comes to oxygen. Scratching the surface using sanding belts causes sparks as the minute particles are abraded from the surface. Abrading the surface under oil is dangerous and can cause explosive reactions as the dust finds oxygen. Thus, titanium almost always comes in the mill annealed and pickled state or with a glass bead texture.

Titanium needs to be viewed in the full spectrum of light. On close examination, the surface looks gray; but at a distance of a few meters, when viewed in the full spectrum, it has a very slight golden cast. On overcast days, the metal looks medium gray with a slight golden tone. On bright sunny days, the gold tone shimmers like nickel silver.

Titanium is corrosive-resistant and does not react with oxygen or moisture when used as a cladding in rural, urban, or seaside exposures. Of all the metals, titanium is the most inert. Few natural atmospheres will have any permanent effect on the metal. Whether utilized as a cladding near the sea or the industrial center of a city, the metal will stand unaffected and unchanged.

Titanium develops a tight, impervious oxide layer immediately on exposure to air. This oxide layer is very thin, less than $10\,\mu m$, and will not react with chlorides and sulfides under normal atmospheric conditions.

For architectural and ornamental uses, commercially pure, Grade one titanium sheet is used. Titanium sheet is produced by initially hot rolling to reduce the thickness, followed with annealing and pickling to remove the scale that develops during cooling. The next step is an initial cold rolling pass. The sheet is then degreased in an alkaline solution. Another annealing process is performed to remove the stresses from the cold rolling operation. This time the annealing is performed in a vacuum to control the surface finish. Following this, the final finish is imparted to the sheet. There are basically three finish surfaces available for titanium.

■ Shot blast and acid-cleaned sheet
■ Cold roll on roughened rolls
■ Cold roll on smooth rolls

Each of these finishes imparts a slightly different reflectance to the titanium surface. The shot blast provides an even texture of a fine grainlike surface. This grainlike texture induces a diffused reflectivity and affords a beautiful, unique surface on the metal, similar to a fine casting.

The cold roll on roughened rolls is similar to a No. 2D stainless. This provides a dull, low reflective surface that is smooth and darker in appearance. The cold roll on smooth rolls imparts a more reflective surface. Still low in reflectivity in relation to other metals, this surface has a glossy sheet to it.

Coloring of Titanium

Titanium has the capability to develop a very thin, transparent and stable oxide film immediately on exposure to oxygen. This oxide layer can be thickened to develop interference films that produce vibrant colors. Interference colors are unique for titanium and differ significantly from the colors produced from stainless-steel interference coloring.

Titanium, when subjected to a voltage of sufficient order while immersed in a strong electrolyte, will grow a thick, transparent oxide film. As the film thickens by just a few molecules, colors are generated by light interference. For instance, at 10 volts, a 18-μm-thick film develops. This is nearly twice the oxide thickness that develops on the surface of titanium sheet. The interference color is a pale gold. At 30 volts, the oxide thickens to 61 μm and the interference color perceived is a light blue.

Colors obtained are vast and quite beautiful. Further, the color is enhanced by the surface texture provided on the titanium sheet. The soft, low reflective nature of the titanium surface imparts this same character to the color. The colors obtained are pastel. They do not possess the deep metallic reflectance seen with polished stainless steel. Table 2.19 lists these characteristics of titanium.

Titanium can be expected to remain consistent in color for decades, as it has a high resistance to compounds in the atmosphere that can discolor the surface. Discolored titanium, when it occurs, is usually due to the formation of titanium carbide, TiC, below the surface of the oxide. This should not occur under most applications. It can, however, be generated from the mill process. The appearance is a dull, blotchy reflectance in relation to surrounding surfaces of titanium.

Concerns of color changes of the titanium sheets used on the Guggenheim Museum in Bilbao, Spain are unfounded. The titanium surface, as with all reflective metal surfaces, will show soot and dirt. Additionally, substances such as thin sprays of silicon sealers, disintegrating bituminous compounds, and other construction-related substances could adhere to the surface of metals because of the slight difference in polarity of the materials. If not removed quickly, they can accumulate into more significant and adherent films.

Another factor that influenced some of the color differences of the Guggenheim titanium surface is a reflectivity difference from one side of the sheet to the other. It is difficult to get protective coatings to adhere to the titanium surface. Coatings using adhesives will work, but they apply films to the surface of metals, which can be difficult to remove. Electrostatic films just do not want to adhere to titanium. The manufacture of the thin titanium plates involved a simple shingle form. Geometrically, the shingle, when flipped, has essentially the same appearance as the opposite side.

The titanium when cold rolled has a smooth texture on both sides, but one set of rolls, usually the top one, is the prime side. The prime side has a superior

TABLE 2.19

Voltage, Film Thickness, and Corresponding Color of Titanium

Voltage	Film Thickness (Å)	Color Obtained
0	15	Silver-gray
2	25	Silver-gray
4–6	105–132	Slight gold tint
8–10	160–180	Pale gold
12	270	Gold
14	242	Dark gold
16	254	Dark gold with tint of purple
18–20	260–272	Purple with gold tint
22	349	Blue/purple
24	364	Dark blue
28	469	Medium blue
30–32	610–715	Pale blue

surface, clean and free of imperfections. If a protective film is not placed on the prime side, then people working with the material could easily mix the prime with the nonprime side, particularly when the finish is a mill cold rolled surface. Their relative reflective level must be viewed to determine which side is prime. It is good practice to avoid this by marking the nonprime side with an indicator mark. Sometimes, even the direction off the coil is important.

TITANIUM COATINGS ON OTHER METALS

Thin films of titanium can be coated on other metals such as stainless steel and steel. The coatings are applied by vapor deposition. Vapor deposition is a process whereby a metallic film is created on the surface of the metal by vaporizing an alloy of one metal while under vacuum.

Several approaches are used. Many of the processes were refined in the microelectronics industry. On ornamental and architectural metalwork, physical vapor deposition (PVD), chemical vapor deposition (CVD), and sputtering are the processes that are used. Physical vapor deposition is the technique used most frequently on large-scale sheet projects (see Table 2.20). (The techniques of vapor deposition are discussed more thoroughly in Chapter 8.) But, in general, the reflective nature of the base surface, the level of abrasion, polish or bead blast, is reflected through the thin deposition.

Titanium coatings applied via the deposition process create vivid colors. The colors are interference colors and thus have an enhanced reflectance. Interference colors are created from the interplay of the light wave with two closely positioned surfaces. Figure 2.10 depicts how one wave reflects off of the oxide to air surface and the other wave reflects off of the base metal to oxide layer interface. As they reflect back to the viewer's eye, a portion of each wave interacts. The interaction,

Light Angle of Incidence

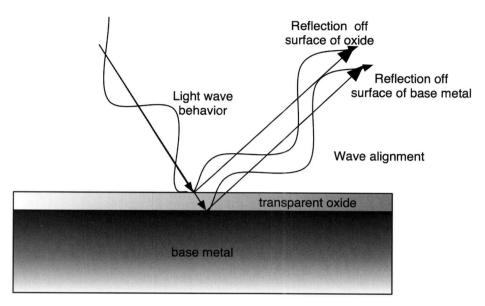

FIGURE 2.10. Graphic depiction of the interference phenomenon.

known as light interference, either reinforces a portion of the wavelength or opposes a portion of the wavelength, canceling it out. The result is color.

Colors obtained from the application of vapor deposition are very stable. The titanium coating is hard and abrasion-resistant. Many tool steels used to pierce metal are coated with a thick titanium nitride. This characteristic gold coating provides a superior surface, with improved hardness and wear resistance. The gold color in this instance is not an interference color but the color of the alloy created by the combination of titanium and nitrogen. The colors used for decorative purposes are created by thinner depositions. Table 2.20 lists the colors that can be achieved with thin film titanium coatings.

Metal coated with this process can be formed without damaging the thin film. Color changes slightly along the bend. The coating is a thin layer of transparent titanium oxide. Stainless steel is the base metal used when achieving the interference colors. The polish on the stainless steel is mirror, satin, angel hair, or

TABLE 2.20

Colors Achieved from Vapor Deposition

Colors
Black
Bronze
Light gold
Dark gold
Rose gold
Silver
Gray

any number of mechanically created finishes. The combination of the polish on the base stainless-steel surface with the color achieved by the phenomena of light interference creates different tones, from bright metallic colors to softer, satin finishes.

Each metal has its own vocabulary of finishes and colors. Surfaces made from any of these metals, regardless of the finish applied, must interact with the surrounding environment. The ever-changing environment continually applies forces to the finish surface, requiring it to interact and adapt. As surfacing materials, each metal follows similar rules. Many of the joining methods and seaming methods that join panel elements together can be similarly applied, regardless of the metal used.

PART II
THE SURFACE MOSAIC

...in which I call architecture..."petrified music."

—GOETHE

At approximately 10^2 meters—100 meters—the edges and surface boundaries become visible. Depending on the nature of the seam, distinct surface elements start to appear. Details are generated from the seams and edges that establish the boundaries between thin plates. Additionally, details appear from changes in material or geometric planes. The edges of the surface are defined by contrasting shading effects and light reflecting at different angles, creating relative dark and light zones.

As you approach to within 10^1 meters—10 meters—patterns and shadows created from offset lines or overlapping plates become apparent. Contrasting patterns created by color or reflectivity enhance the beauty of large open surfaces throughout time and culture. Consider the patterns created from the variation in size and color of stone walls, even those that do not have adornment of stature and elaborate antefixes (see Figure II.1). Patterns develop as one stone element is placed onto another, creating a texture that is both functional and attractive.

Or consider the contrasting patterns created by the mosaic applied to a Persian door. The texture adds character; it draws the eye like a flower attracting a butterfly (see Figures II.2 and II.3). Woven fabric

FIGURE II.1. Main Temple at Machu Picchu, Peru.

rugs from the Middle Eastern culture or the Native American culture all are adorned with colorful patterns of contrast. Many of the images are astonishingly similar across cultural and temporal chasms. The purpose is the same: create beauty and interest out of the simplest of forms— the flat plane, the open expanse that makes up the surface of an object, building form, or even an open field.

FIGURE II.2. Moroccan doors.

FIGURE II.3. Moroccan doors.

Douglas Hofstadter, in his book *Godel, Escher and Bach: An Eternal Golden Braid* (Basic Books, 1979), describes patterns derived in algorithms, music, and art as follows: "The elusive sense for patterns which we humans inherit from our genes involves all the mechanisms of representation of knowledge, including nested contexts, conceptual skeletons and conceptual mapping, slip ability, descriptions and meta-descriptions and their interactions, fission and fusion of symbols, multiple representations, default expectations and more." The patterns created on surfaces are generated from these same mechanisms. They are the expression of our knowledge of the materials, limited by the constraints of current manufacture. Patterns are mapped across the surface, using a priority established for both functional behavior and visual context. Patterns relieve the banal.

Patterns are common in nature. When we create something—a painting a fabric, or even a shading cabana on a beach—we develop patterns, which are either a product of function or a way the mind naturally falls to order. Many aspects of nature show similar forms: spherical shapes such as the atom, water drops, fruit on trees, planets, and stars. The spiral shapes such as snail shells, flowers, draining water, tornados, and galaxies. Or the honeycomb shape, which is a series of hexagons, as are certain crystal formations, and the microscopic pores developed from the electrochemical action of anodizing. One might consider why we have any differentiation in nature at all since all the components are very similar. Ian Stewart, in his book *Nature's Numbers* (Basic Books, 1995), asks, "If the laws of physics are the same at all places at all times, why is there any 'interesting' structure in the uni-

FIGURE II.4. Madagascar chameleon.

FIGURE II.5. Reformed Latter Day Saints temple roof, Independence, Missouri, designed by Hellmuth, Obata, and Kassabaum.

verse at all?" Over time, one might expect the rules that drive these patterns to induce certain blandness to the landscape where every part is essentially interchangeable. What reason exists for the symmetry to vary? What is the cause?

The same could be said for the surface structure of our built world. The drive for standardization can often be viewed as having dominion over creativity. It really is a simplistic view on the world. But it is pervasive. Look at the city of Berlin: while undergoing a renaissance of fascinating architecture after the fall of the Wall, the city is taking on a texture unlike no other. Building walls set on curves, contrasting surfaces of metal and glass—this all counterposed to the mundane, dull, and boxy façades of the Soviet utility. Developers in the suburbs of the United States prefer to bulldoze into oblivion everything nature developed before they rebuild the environment into a controlled, sterile world, void of creativity, eventually boring those who choose to live there until they move on to the next natural setting to bulldoze. The cycle continues.

Surfaces created by metal can establish patterns over a wide range of functional purpose. Limited by the manufacturing technology of the raw stock form, patterns created from metal sheets and plates are highly variable. It is unfortunate that, often, these constraints of manufacture establish a foothold in the mind of the designer. It is necessary to understand the constraint and develop them in concert with the functional and aesthetic nature of the material.

All metal surfaces must move and, to some extent, breathe. Surfaces made of metal move from thermal effects as their atoms are excited by the changes in temperature. This movement must occur without the accumulation of stress. Each design must understand this movement and account for it. The seams, joints, and edges have to account for this movement while still inhibiting the passage of the outside world into the inside world.

The surface must interact with the environment. All surfaces are interface layers between one set of criteria and another. Ezio Manzini, in his book *The Materials of Invention* (Arcadia srl, Milano, 1986) put it this way: "The idea of a mute and static border to matter is thus replaced by an idea of the surface as an interface between two ambients, with a role including an exchange of energy and information between the substances put into contact."

Surfaces used as exterior skins of buildings and structures perform as barriers to the changing environment of our world. They must take up and stave off the changing conditions encountered, all the while keeping the environment on the interior of the surface static. Moisture, wind, and radiation all must be detoured by the exterior surface of a structure, for what appears as passive deterrence with little change in the surface appearance, in reality, is active. The metal expands and contracts within the seam as temperatures change throughout the day. The joint collects moisture arriving on the surface, removes the energy, and redirects it out. Metal surfaces intercept the energy of the wind, distribute the energy in the form of imposed loads across the surface, and redirect it to the supporting structure.

All surfaces have terminations or changes in visual plane. The edges subconsciously attract the eye: how large or small an object is, where one element starts and the other ends. Such information is gleaned almost immediately when viewing most surfaces. Edges define whether something is neat or ragged. Wear and tear on a surface is usually indicative of the condition of an edge. For metal surfaces, the quality is determined by the edge. The skill level, the overall feel of a surface, is derived by how the edges finish. The edges are the most visually important parts of any surface. They impart emotional attributes to the overall body of the work. Feelings of softness or hardness, quality or low skill, old or new, are derived from the appearance of an object's edge.

A termination point on a surface establishes transitions from one surface character to another. The termination must often contend with variations in material behavior from one surface to the next. The termination must be an edge of the surface. Terminations are the places where loads and stresses are not passed from one surface to the next. Movements such as thermal and seismic may be taken up within the termination, but they are not typically passed across to the next surface.

Metal surfaces are anything but petrified. They are like a skin and must interact with their surroundings as well as define the appearance of what they are covering. They must be assembled well or they fail in their purpose.

CHAPTER 3
FUNCTIONAL REQUIREMENTS OF A METAL SURFACE

"Resistance is futile."
—THE BORG

The functional aspects of a metal surface are critical as to how it interfaces with the surrounding ambient conditions. The surface interplay with light is but one aspect, and is dependent both on the physical characteristics of the surface and on the way light arrives to the surface.

The surface is where "the rubber meets the road," where the ambient conditions and the set of points making up an object meet and interface. On most objects, the outer surface is very different from the inside materials, both in purpose and in behavior. The exterior side is required to encounter operational conditions that are significantly different from those intended for the inner side of the surface. Failure of the outer surface is defined by its inability to restrict the ambient from reaching the interior of the object.

All metal surfaces must interact with the surroundings. For architectural projects the surface must function to protect the interior from the ever-changing conditions of the environment. Table 3.1 lists the functional requirements of metal surfaces that act as the skin of a building.

PROTECTIVE BARRIER

One of the key purposes of a surface is to act as a barrier to the ambient. The outer layer must inhibit the operational influences of the environment on the internal parts. Nature deals with this characteristic on its higher organisms by providing a specialized layer to interface with the outside world. Metal surfaces must also offer a specialized skin that protects the inner, more delicate, core materials and spaces.

TABLE 3.1

Functional Requirements of Metal Skins

Functional Requirements
Protective barrier to internal structures
➤ Radiation inhibition
➤ Biological inhibition
➤ Chemical inhibition
Moisture control
Wind pressure dynamics/transfer to surface structure
Stress conditions under thermal changes
Resilient nature when confronted mechanically
Time stability

Time capsules, seamed and sealed, then buried or entombed, are made of metal. Metals such as copper, stainless steel, titanium and lead that offer a corrosion-resistant skin are the materials of choice for such capsules because of their capability to resist the effects of time. Metals, even thin envelopes, can offer significant protection against the exposures time brings forth on the materials of this earth.

Radiation Protection

One of the first capabilities afforded by metal surfaces is protection from radiation. This is why radios do not perform well in metal-clad buildings: Most architectural metals inhibit their wavelength. Ultraviolet radiation is reflected from metal surfaces as well as infrared radiation. Lead, as anyone knows who has had his or her teeth examined, is an excellent radiation shielding material. Due to the high density of lead, X-rays and gamma rays are shielded from passing through.

The reflective aspect of some metal finishes, such as aluminum, stainless steel, and aluminum–zinc-alloy-coated steel, deflects back significant amounts of the radiant heat. Roof surfaces covered with reflective, light-colored metal have been shown to reduce heat gain in vented attic spaces by as much as 47 percent. This translates to lower cooling costs.[1] Alternately, in Scandinavia, dark-colored roofing is often used. The dark surfaces absorb solar energy, particularly on the infrared. This heats the surface and aids in snow melting. Thin reflective metal coatings of aluminum applied to fiberglass will reflect heat and enhance the insulating properties.

Biological Protection

Metals also are good at inhibiting biological infiltration. Copper works especially well in preventing mold and fungus from growing. Copper is used as a surfacing material on boat hulls to resist the fouling of the surface by barnacles and algae. The alloys of copper, brass, and bronze do not diminish this capability.

---

[1] According to tests performed by Parker, Sonne, Sherwin at the Florida Solar Energy Center, Flexible Roofing Facility, Summer 2002. Tests were performed on six types of roof systems.

Metals do not absorb water like other building materials, and their tendency to heat up under solar exposures is not the most conducive environment for mold or fungus growth. Fungus and mold can form on zinc, steel, and aluminum but the foundation is not there. Metals do not store water or provide water to mold. Metal oxides do not make an environment conducive to mold spores. Some metal oxides are even ecotoxic.

Silver ion implantation onto metal surfaces is being utilized to act as a biological-resistant surface capable of inhibiting the growth of spores and molds. This relatively economic process offers some interesting potential for combating concerns of biological contamination. Copper, tin, silver, and iron oxides from weathering steel (copper-bearing) appear to be the most resistive to biological contamination. Other metal surfaces such as zinc and stainless steel do not support bacterial growth and can be easily sanitized.

Chemical Protection

Resistance to chemical attack is another characteristic of metals. The resistance of metals to oxidation is in proportion to a metal's chemical resistivity. Additionally, the rate at which a metal joins with other elements to develop compounds through the transfer of electrons in electrochemical reactions is a measure of a metal's chemical resistivity.

Metals resist most chemical attacks, particularly those somewhat natural attacks from sulfur and carbon-based contaminants (see Table 3.2). Acids can cause metals to become more reactive. Staining can occur, but metals perform well in providing resistance to chemical attack. Metal cladding is used as housings in power plants, chemical plants, and other industrial complexes.

All metals react with oxygen and moisture. Oxygen combines to form the characteristic thin metal oxide film. Moisture from the atmosphere combines with the oxide to form a hydrated oxide. The oxide and hydrated oxides are extremely important to resisting further chemical attack. These oxides are necessary to form the impervious barrier that will extend the life of a metal surface.

TABLE 3.2

Chemical Agents Found in the Environment

Chemical Agent	Major Source	Metal Affected	Result of Exposure
Sulfur	Combustion	Copper	Green patina
		Monel	Green/brown patina
		Lead	Dark patina
		Silver	Dark tarnish
Carbon	Carbon dioxide	Lead	Whitish oxide
		Zinc	Dark blue-gray patina
Chlorine	Sea	Aluminum	Pitting
	Deicing salts	Copper	Green-blue patina
		Stainless steel	Red spots
Silicon	Airborne blast particles and sealers	Stainless steel	Discolor
		Titanium	Discolor

MOISTURE CONTROL

Moisture control is a demand of any exterior surface. It must keep moisture from infiltrating and damaging the subsurface framing and finishes. This must occur while the surface undergoes the action of the predicted extremes of the ambient conditions. Not only the surface of the material itself but also those parts of the surface such as seams and edges must perform the same function as conditions change and as materials age. The skin is only as good as its weakest part. If the joint between panels is sealed, then the sealant must be developed and applied to provide the same levels of moisture protection over time and under expected loading criteria as that of the metal.

Metal performs better than all other materials in this regard when correctly applied. There is not a plastic, bituminous, rubber, silicone, or mortar system known to exist that can perform as well as metal in keeping moisture at bay. Look at boat construction. Wood boats require constant maintenance. They are gorgeous, but not dependable. Or consider plastic and fiberglass. They are temporary. They can be easily molded and fitted, but they have a limited life—there's no way around it. As to plastics, they must yield to the environment and are inherently fragile. Ultraviolet, photooxidation, and thermal energy affects all work to destroy the organic polymer bond that holds plastic together. Coat them with metal and they last longer, but not as long as metal.

Give me a metal boat. In architecture, metal surfaces must shed water. They shed moisture by lapping to allow gravity to move water off the surface, or they have additional seals at their joints, which resist the infiltration of moisture. Metal surfaces can also be decorative, and they allow water to enter behind them to another barrier zone. In this way they simply shed some moisture and provide protection against radiation.

Rainscreen

To effectively shed moisture, metal surfaces must act as a rainscreen. For a surface to leak from water infiltration, there must be three conditions in place:

- ▦ Water
- ▦ Opening
- ▦ Force to move the water through the opening

Water can also occur within a surface by condensation. Condensation is introduced by way of another mechanism. For metals, this can be of particular concern because of the thermal transfer characteristic of metals. Metals are poor insulators. They conduct heat and cold through enclosures if they form an unbroken connection from one side of the wall to the other. The ends of fasteners passing from the outside to the interior side of a well-insulated wall will breach the insulation and offer cold points for moisture to condense. Steel purlins, spanning on top of the structural steel, often compress the insulation that surrounds them. This compression breaks the metal-to-metal connection, but the compressed nature at the purlin reduces the insulating capability.

Water, of course, is present at some time or other everywhere on earth. Openings are difficult or impossible to completely eliminate, in particular from metal surfaces. As discussed in subsequent chapters, seams are an integral part of all metal surfaces. Seams, by their very nature, are breaches in a surface.

The third category, the force needed to move moisture through a surface, can be controlled through good design practices and the use of the Rainscreen Principle. Although this principle has been used successfully for centuries, its physics have only been explained of late. It is an intuitive principle, involving an understanding of the actions of moisture delivery systems. The Rainscreen Principle involves an understanding of the vehicles of moving moisture through an exterior surface and designing barriers to address these forces.

FORCES THAT MOVE WATER THROUGH A SURFACE

Consider that on a metal surface, or any surface for that matter, there are five means of delivering the force needed to move moisture from one side of a surface to another through an opening:

1. *Gravity.* Moisture moves downward from its weight.
2. *Kinetic energy.* Wind drives moisture against a surface.
3. *Surface tension.* Moisture sticks to a surface and follows it until gravity overcomes it.
4. *Capillary action.* Moisture will move between two surfaces in close proximity by a surface tension developed between the moisture and the surfaces.
5. *Differential pressure.* Moisture will move through the smallest of openings through a surface when the pressure on the wet side is greater than on the opposite side.

The gravitational force is overcome by good detailing. Lapping so that moisture moves down and over surfaces is the most direct way. Sometimes referred to as "positive lapping," metal surfaces should never be lapped such that moisture traveling down one surface will pass behind another. Additionally, it is good practice to develop a slope to shed moisture from horizontal surfaces.

Kinetic energy is delivered from windblown rains. Gravity can also add to the kinetic energy on sloped surfaces that collect and move the moisture rapidly. For example, on a valley flashing, the upturned "V" in the middle of the flashing is there to take the energy out of water flowing down a roof, thus preventing it from being driven up and under the opposite side of the roof (see Figure 3.1).

For most surfaces, the wind is the greatest source for kinetic energy. Eliminating this as a source for moisture infiltration requires a barrier to deflect the moisture and take the energy out of the water, similar to the upturned "V" on a valley flashing.

Metal edges can be folded to occur behind seams and offer a physical obstruction to moisture. Discontinuity of the folded edge at the corners of the folded panel is where moisture can enter and should be avoided. Simply put,

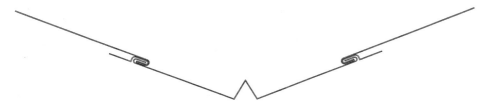

FIGURE 3.1. V-fold in valley flashing is required to remove energy from flowing moisture.

physical barriers are out-turned extensions of the metal surface. Once the force behind the moisture is deterred, gravity is allowed to pull the moisture out. Such restrictions can also track moisture. Figure 3.2 shows two examples of metal barriers at the open joints between panels. Ends or barriers should also be in place to prevent the tracking along the seam and deflect it out onto the face of the surface.

Nonmetal physical restrictions can also be used. Gasketing can remove the energy of windblown moisture. Water may get through an outer layer of gasketing, but the energy has been removed and the force of gravity takes hold, drawing the water down. Figure 3.3 shows gaskets being placed in front of the upturned metal return legs on the panel.

Surface tension and capillary action are similar forces created by the molecular attraction of a liquid to a surface it is in contact with. In regard to surface tension, this would describe the way water running down a vertical surface can then change its direction and run horizontally. As depicted in Figure 3.4, drops of water will move horizontally a certain distance due to the attraction of a liquid to a solid surface.

Capillary action is the force used to describe the behavior of a liquid being drawn through a space between two surfaces or through a tubular surface. The

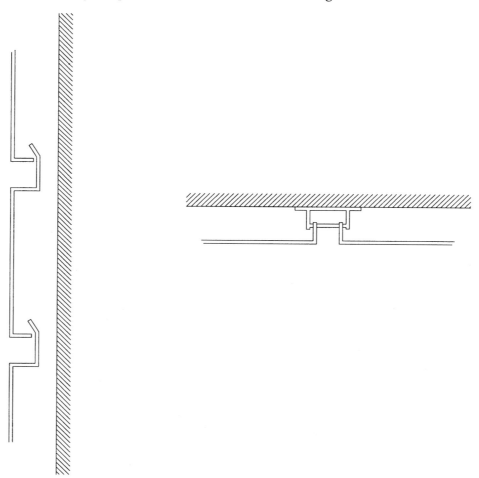

FIGURE 3.2. Returns folds at surface element seams are designed to remove wind energy from moisture.

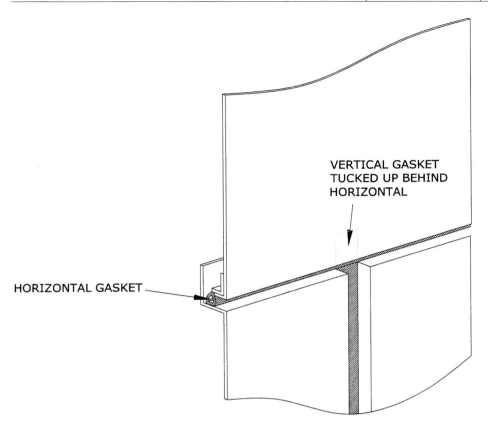

FIGURE 3.3. Gasketing in seams remove wind energy behind moisture.

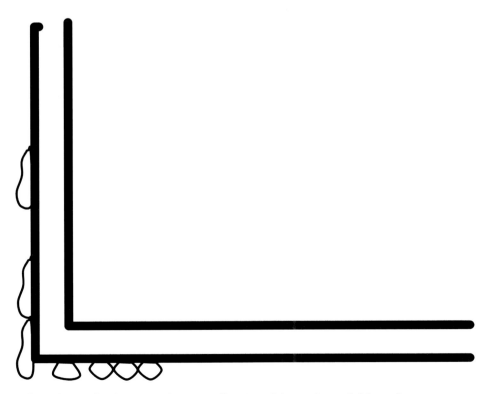

FIGURE 3.4. Surface tension can direct moisture along right angles.

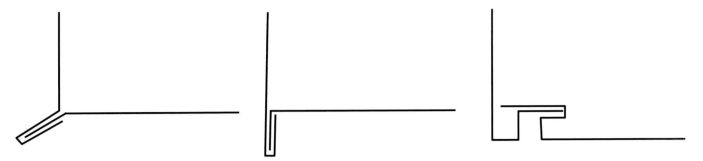

FIGURE 3.5. Examples of drip edges designed to break surface tension.

molecules of water adhere to the walls of the adjoining surface and are drawn into the space by the phenomenon of surface tension. Developing capillary breaks into the detail can thwart these forces. For example, on vertical surfaces, it is recommended to add drip edges and kicks at transitions from vertical to horizontal. Water tracking by surface tension will be released when it confronts a change in direction that forces it upward. Refer to Figure 3.5 for examples of some surface tension breaks that can be formed into metal.

Capillary action requires the development of a release chamber. Capillary action draws water through a constricted space. The space has to be small enough for the surface tension of the liquid-to-solid interface to pull the weight of water through. Figure 3.6 depicts how capillary forces can draw moisture up above the level of a reservoir. If the constricted space changes in geometry by

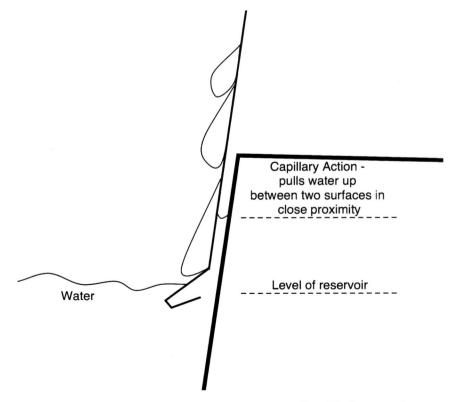

Capillary Action -
pulls water up
between two surfaces in
close proximity

Level of reservoir

Water

FIGURE 3.6. Capillary action drawing moisture uphill behind two surfaces.

enlarging, it will effectively release the force, and the capillary movement will cease.

Capillary breaks can be created in metal-to-metal constructs by developing ribs or offsets perpendicular to the capillary flow. As moisture moves in between two surfaces of metal, it arrives at the enlarged chamber. Capillary forces fall off and the water is subjected to gravity. (Refer to Chapter 6, Figure 6.18, for various capillary breaks.)

Differential pressures are a significant force to overcome in designing a surface to be a moisture barrier. If there is a differential across a surface, water will be drawn through even a pin-sized hole. Differential pressures develop when there are localized high-pressure zones and low-pressure zones. All surfaces experience these variations in pressure. On a building structure, pressures can vary on the outside surface. In a windy condition, pressures at the edges and at the top of a structure are greater than those on other regions.

Pressures on the inside of the building can be lower than on exterior surfaces if the air systems are not balanced. Doors can be difficult to open in spaces where the pressure is low in relation to the outside spaces. Fans pushing air out of a space must have an adequate supply of replacement air; otherwise a local pressure drop will result. This will bring water and air into the space from any breach, no matter how small. Even fastener threads can, if the pressure is great enough, allow water to enter a structure.

One solution, as it relates to the Rainscreen Principle, is known as the "pressure-equalized wall." As mentioned, the differential of pressures from the outside surface to the inside surface of a structure result in a majority of water infiltration issues. Eliminate this pressure differential and you eliminate moisture infiltration.

Pressure Equalization: The Rainscreen Principle

Assuming you are able to address each of the other force mechanisms for bringing water into a system, you still must address the major culprit of pressure differential. To develop a pressure-equalized surface, you need to provide an airspace behind the exterior surface but within the wall cavity. This airspace must be limited and restricted. In other words, the airspace must be chambered to divide off sections. This is necessary to limit the development of significant differential within the airspace itself. One way this can be accomplished is by setting up baffles that restrict the air movement between confined spaces. It is not necessary to completely seal the spaces, but they should restrict the passage of air from one chamber to the other.

You need to minimize the entry into this airspace. Ideally, there should be only one entry point of sufficient size that it will not be covered completely by water during a heavy rainstorm. As pressure builds up on the outside surface, it also builds up on the inner side of this surface, essentially equalizing the pressure between both sides. This takes away the pressure differential, which would force water through this outer layer.

The inner wall surface must still resist moisture but it sees far less than its outer covering. The dynamic force behind the moisture has been removed by the outer wall, if designed correctly. Condensation within this space should be minimal because the space is vented to the outside air.

Figure 3.7 shows the vertical joint used on the Modern Art Museum of Fort Worth, Texas. The museum was designed by Tadao Ando. The patented system

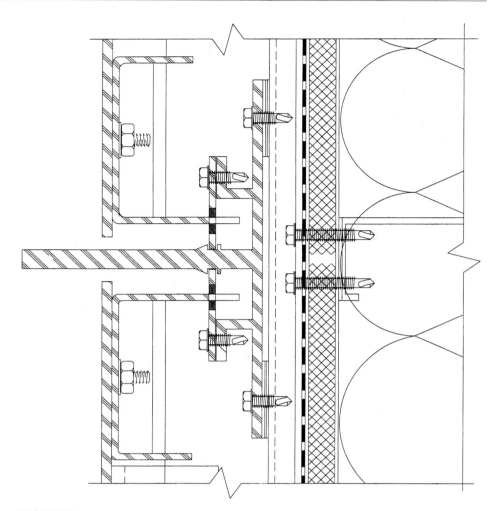

FIGURE 3.7. Pressure equalized vertical joint system used on the Modern Art Museum of Fort Worth, Texas.

incorporates many of the principles of pressure equalization. The joint is open, but narrow and restricted. Air can pass to the reverse side; however, water is restricted by the continuous baffles in the joint. The backup system is studs and a rigid backing material.

INNER SURFACE REQUIREMENTS

Pressure-equalized walls need the inner surface to be the air barrier. The outer surface takes out most of the moisture but air is still free to access the inner wall. This can be performed by membranes or seals that wrap the inner surface. The outer wall will provide the radiation protection for these membranes and seals. This will drastically improve the life of these materials.

The inner surface must be designed to support the outer wall system as well. Herein lies one of the most difficult design issues to overcome by rainscreen systems or, for that matter, all metal surfacing systems. Table 3.3 discusses the functional issues that must be developed by this connecting system.

TABLE 3.3

Functional Issues of Inner Wall Connection

Functional Issues to Be Established by Connection to Inner Wall
Penetrate the air barrier.
Accommodate thermal movement.
Penetrate the interior moisture barrier.
Overcome thermal connection—outside to inside.
Support the dead load of the wall.
Transfer all loads to the inner structure.

There are, in general, three types of structural backup walls used on exterior enclosures that support rainscreen wall systems. First are the continuous supporting walls, such as metal decks, plywood-backed surfaces, concrete, and concrete block-backed surfaces. These surfaces provide support attachment points virtually anywhere. Metal roof surfaces often fall in this category of backup support. The second surface is the point/distributed load wall. Wood and metal studs fall into this category. These walls, often covered with lightweight gypsum board or rigid insulation board, are designed to have the load distributed to each stud. Thus the attachment must be made at each stud along the wall or roof surface, regardless of the spanning capability of the outer surface. If the studs are spaced 12 inches (300 mm) or 18 inches (450 mm) apart, it does not matter; they must be attached even when the exterior skin is capable of spanning several times this distance. These walls are designed to take a distributed load across them. Skipping attachments can overstress regions where the load becomes concentrated. The third type of structural backup wall is the point-loaded wall. A curtainwall frame system would fall within this category. Framing members are positioned at various points along a structure to receive the concentrated point loads developed by the outer skin. Purlin-supported roofs and girt support walls also fall within this backup wall support system. Examples of these backup support categories are delineated in Table 3.4.

Each of these wall support systems must be able to accommodate the connection between the outer and inner surface. There are various mechanisms to accommodate thermal transfer. Since many of the support structures are metal, separating these with a nonconductive material will usually suffice. Materials

TABLE 3.4

Backup Support Categories

Category	Examples
Continuous backup	Metal decking, plywood backing, concrete block
Point/distributed load backup	Metal studs, wood studs
Point load backup	Curtainwall framing, girts, purlins

such as durable plastic, rubber, and rigid synthetic spacers capable of compression and offering rigidity when subjected to load are required.

Seals of silicone or gasketing material placed around the connection often handle air and water. Gasketing material can also benefit the thermal breach concerns. They must have a long-term life potential because they are not accessible. They should be tested selectively before the final surface is applied, either in development of the system or in as-built condition.

WIND PRESSURE DYNAMICS

Wind pressure dynamics can alter the geometry of the panel, drive moisture through a seam, and overstress the attachment system. Typically, wind pressure concerns are negative pressures, away from the surface. Certain areas on a surface undergo varying degrees of pressure. Corners, edges, and overhangs usually are exposed to more significant negative pressure. The pressure on the outside face of a metal skin is lower in relation to that on the inside face of the skin. This occurs as air passes over the surface rapidly, decreasing the pressure on the surface. This is essentially how an airplane wing develops lift.[2] The air on the topside of the wing has to move faster than the underside due to the wing curvature. This creates a differential pressure where the pressure on the top surface of the wing is lower than that on the bottom surface. This difference causes the plane to rise. High winds have a similar effect on a metal surface. The fast wind moving over a surface creates a lower pressure at the metal surface than behind it. Corners and edges of surfaces create wind eddies and pulsating pressures that can create larger differential wind pressures.

Metal skins are unique in their capability to transfer wind loads to the structure of a building. Metal surfaces fall into one of the structural categories listed in Table 3.5.

Pressure-Equalized Systems: Structural Aspects

A pressure-equalized system is firmly held onto a structure but allows the pressure on the inside surface to match the outside surface, refer to Figure 3.8. As the negative pressure develops on the surface of the metal, the air allowed to pass through joints in the system equalizes the pressure on the back side of the surface. Imagine if there were significant holes in the wings of an airplane, the differential pressure would never develop because the high pressure below the wing

TABLE 3.5

Structural Categories of Metal Surfaces

Surface Structural Categories
Pressure-equalized
Nonpressure-equalized—structural skin
Nonpressure-equalized—overlay membrane skin

---

[2] Bernoulli's Principle states that as the speed of a moving fluid, in this case air, increases, the pressure within the fluid decreases.

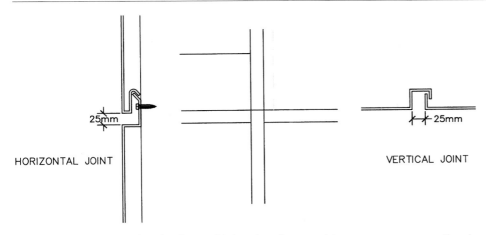

FIGURE 3.8. Vertical to horizontal joint development in a pressure-equalized wall.

would be allowed to get to the low pressure above the wind. The seams in a pressure-equalized wall allow air to freely move from one face to the other. The air path must be baffled to prevent localized increases in pressure and resist driving rain from entering. Pressure-equalized systems, in theory, do not see the negative pressure load on the metal surface because the pressure is equalized on the opposite side of the metal surface. This load, however, is seen on the surface behind the metal rainscreen.

These systems require a heavy thickness sheet or plate with a developed section and stiffness around the perimeter. Because they require an airspace on the back side, the pressure-equalized panels must be of sufficient strength to resist positive pressures imparted on their surfaces, and they must be sufficient to hold their form. The changing pressures from the outside surface to the inside surface could make the panel flutter. This could overwhelm the connections and the metal with fatigue. Thus, it is critical to understand the stress and movement the metal skin is demanded to take. Think of a flag in the wind. The force of the wind pressure moves the flag to the point of least resistance. The panel must be stiff enough to resist the instantaneous loads and transfer the load to the attachment points without excessive deflection.

Nonpressure-Equalized Structural Skin System

The nonpressure-equalized panel is a rigid surface capable of transferring the dynamics of the ambient through to the structure of the building. The external forces are applied to the skin, and either through direct connection or diaphragm the load is applied back to the supporting structure. Interlocking seams, gaskets, or other seals created along the boundaries of the panels deter moisture. The nonpressure-equalized panel is of sufficient section and stiffness to take the full force of wind or physical pressure without permanently deforming.

Joint systems are typically closed as shown in Figures 3.9 and 3.10. Air may be allowed to pass through the joint but not freely. Thus pressure will not quickly equalize. The panel's elements are held firmly to the structure with expansion and contraction allowances incorporated at the panel-to-panel junctions.

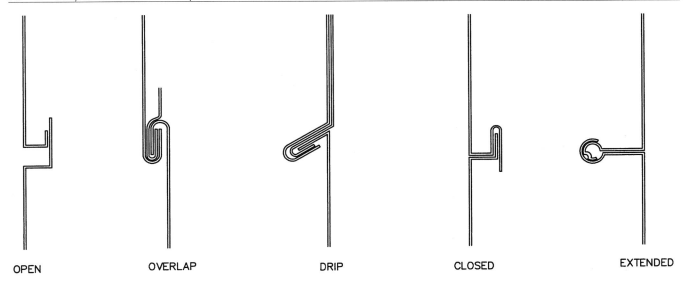

OPEN   OVERLAP   DRIP   CLOSED   EXTENDED

FIGURE 3.9. Examples of nonpressure-equalized seams.

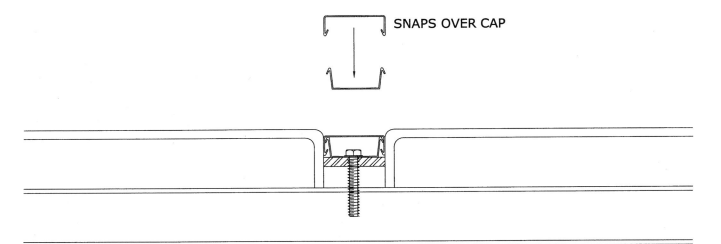

SNAPS OVER CAP

FIGURE 3.10. Vertical joint with snap over cap. Nonpressure-equalized joint.

Nonpressure-Equalized Overlay Membrane Skin

The nonpressure-equalized overlay membrane skin at first appears to overcome physics. Thin metal surfaces have been used for centuries as cladding surfaces. For instance, the copper roof is typically manufactured from 0.7 mm (0.024 inch) copper sheet. Constructed into a standing seam of anywhere from 24.5 mm (1 inch) to 36 mm (1.5 inch) in height over a pan width of 500 mm (15 inches), one would think that this near-paper-thin form could not withstand any significant loading. Copper roofs, and for that matter all the overlay membrane skins, require a rigid backing placed continuously behind the surface. The airspace behind the metal should be no more than that created by the rise of an interlocking lap, similar to flat seam metal walls; refer to Figure 3.11. As pressure is applied in the positive direction, the solid substrate takes up the resistance. As negative pressure is applied, a phenomenon of load transfer occurs. Under a dynamic loading

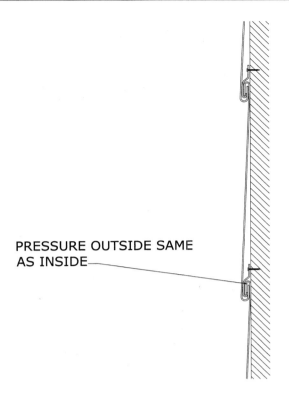

PRESSURE OUTSIDE SAME
AS INSIDE

FIGURE 3.11. Flat seam interlocking joint is
pressure equalized at the seam.

condition, high negative pressure on the surface of the metal, the metal skin tries
to move away from the structural surface. But to do so requires displacement. No
air displacement is allowed through the seam, and immediately an equal pressure is applied to the structural wall. This is difficult to simulate.

Apply the load slowly and the metal deforms (see Figure 3.12). Time allows
air to move in and displace the metal. Engineering calculations often do not
factor in the phenomenon, but ignore the concept of pressure equalization that
occurs in rainscreen designs.

These systems are centuries old. The performance has been proven; engineering must follow suit.[3] Observations conducted following the damage caused
by Hurricane Andrew, in 1992, to various roof surfaces found that such thin skin
overlays on a rigid surface performed better than more rigid panels acting as
nonpressurized structural panels.

During a windstorm, air is rapidly moving over a surface, creating eddies
and vortexes that pulse differential loads. Because of the nature of the seams
used on thin metal, single-lock, double-lock, and other similar seaming methods,
albeit not airtight, are restrictive to air movement. The rapid loads on the thin
metal surface create a localized vacuum on the back side of the thin skin. This
immediately transfers the load to the backup surface structure.

---

[3] Engineering calculations deal with static loading applied to thin metal surface at localized points of
support.

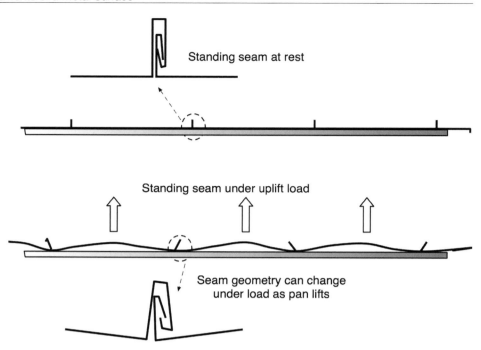

Standing seam at rest

Standing seam under uplift load

Seam geometry can change
under load as pan lifts

FIGURE 3.12. Geometry change of a seam when presented with sufficient uplift loading.

A variation on this phenomenon is experienced in sheet metal fabrication facilities. To remove the top sheet from the stack of metal, air must be first allowed underneath the sheet. Lifting an edge and "rolling" air under the sheet allows air to move under the metal. Without doing this, the sheet cannot be removed from the surface. A vacuum develops as one attempts to lift the sheet above the surface of the sheet below. Leaving the sheet on the stack after rolling air below it will shortly return it to its previous behavior as the air is slowly displaced by the weight of the sheet.

Occurrences of an entire roof being removed by a tornado have been observed, yet the walls of the building are still partially in place. The roof was constructed of thin 26-gauge terne-coated steel roof, clipped and nailed to a plywood decking at 12-inch centers. The thin metal roof, plywood, and insulation board were found fully assembled to the metal decking, and the decking in turn to the steel joists.[4] The entire assembly had been lifted and set down approximately 300 yards away. For this to occur, the entire assembly would have to have been pushed from below, which is unlikely because the building walls were still intact. Or the negative pressure developed from the extreme wind speed would have to have been applied to the thin roofing, which in turn would need to transfer the load to the underlayment and eventually the decking.

---

[4] In the late 1980s, a tornado passed over a church in south Kansas City. The roof of the church was constructed of 26-gauge terne-coated steel in a batten seam configuration. All the seams had been machine-seamed tight into a double-lock configuration. The tornado lifted nearly the entire roof up and set it down several hundred yards away. The thin steel roofing was attached over the insulation board and fastened into a 22-gauge metal decking. The decking was attached to the steel joists. The roof was found still intact with the joists underneath.

The point is that thin metal skins can resist significant negative loads when they are constructed well and when they are fully backed by a substrate that develops an air barrier. Essentially, they never see these loads. If there is no way for air to travel under the metal rapidly enough to displace the metal, then it simply will not move.

Tests being performed on metal skins apply static loads to develop the equivalent negative pressure differential. These tests apply the loading very slowly, often to the back side of the sheet. The sheet deforms. The deformation simply alters the panel geometry, and thus conditions are not indicative of reality. Few thin metal systems can withstand the imposed static loads. Place a sheet of paper in a glass container and apply a vacuum to the container: the paper will not move. The pressure below the paper, on the edges of the paper, and the top of the paper is the same. Allow air to the back side and the paper is pushed around the container.

STRESS UNDER THERMAL CONDITIONS

Every metal surface must be able to deal with the stress and buildup of stress generated by thermal changes (see Table 3.6). Metal surfaces on external structures absorb energy from the sun. This absorption can be significant. Alternately, metals give up energy to their surroundings more rapidly than other materials when the energy source is removed. Metal surfaces must be able to accommodate the changes created by these thermal effects. The absorption of energy, and the subsequent heating of the surface, causes the metal surface to expand; conversely, the cooling of the metal causes the metal to contract or shrink slightly. Unlike other materials, with the exception of plastics, most metals change in dimensional characteristics when heated or cooled.

The metal surface must respond to this constant change in dimension. The change is predictable and is more pronounced in the direction of the grain alignment. That is, rolled product such as sheet, plate, tubing, and bar have their grains stretched and aligned along their length. Cast and forged metal products have grains that are in various alignments. Powder metal assemblies do not possess directional grain behavior.

Metal surfaces respond to the dimensional changes by absorbing them into their geometry and changing the overall form, such as a boat hull or an airplane fuselage. Metal decking and exposed fastener wall panels are also hard fixed surfaces. The plates that make up these surfaces are hard-joined so that the surfaces act as a single unit. Fastenings must be able to allow this movement without restriction. If fasteners restrict the surface, tremendous shear stresses develop, which can overwhelm the surface at the fastener point or shear the fastener. Reducing the distance between fasteners will fix components of the surface and reduce the accumulation. Bowing, surface distortion, commonly known as oil canning, can occur between fixed points.

MECHANICAL IMPACT

Crushing a can is quite simple; denting a car body is not so simple—at least not on most. Thin metal offers very little resistance to denting. What thin material does? Plastic perhaps, until it fractures from ultraviolet exposure or thermal

TABLE 3.6

Expansion Coefficient of Various Metals

Metal/Alloy	Coefficient of Thermal Expansion μ in/in °C	Expected Expansion (inches) of a 120-inch Metal Segment	Expected Expansion (mm) of a 3-meter Metal Segment
Lead	29.3	0.13	3.30
Zinc	24.9	0.11	2.79
Aluminum	23.2	0.11	2.79
Tin	23.0	0.10	2.54
Architectural bronze	20.9	0.10	2.54
Muntz metal	20.8	0.09	2.29
Yellow brass	20.3	0.09	2.29
Red brass	18.7	0.09	2.29
Commercial bronze	18.4	0.08	2.03
Silicon bronze	18.0	0.08	2.03
Copper	16.8	0.08	2.03
Aluminum bronze	16.8	0.08	2.03
Stainless steel	16.5	0.08	2.03
Nickel silver	16.2	0.07	1.78
Gold	14.2	0.05	1.27
Monel	14.0	0.06	1.52
Iron	11.7	0.05	1.27
Steel	11.7	0.05	1.27
Titanium	8.4	0.04	1.02

Expansion and contraction direction
away from fixed points

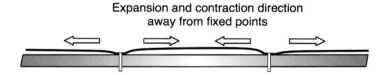

FIGURE 3.13. Expansion and contraction can distort metal surfaces between fasteners.

impact. The cultural sense of metal is established by its capability to be produced thin. Only plastic, and perhaps wood in the basis of paper, can be rolled so thin. Metal resists impact like no other material known to humankind. Make it thin and hit it with a (metal) hammer. It will dent, but the dent can often be reversed. The metal yields but stays in existence. Hit any other material, of matching thickness, with the same hammer—stone, glass, ceramic, wood, plastic, rubber—and see what happens. Rubber works; it absorbs the impact. Metal does as well, but differently. Metals move; they yield to the energy transfer. If the energy is sufficient to overcome the internal structure of the material, then a permanent deformation will occur. For most metals, it must be substantial.

There are three common potential sources capable of providing the necessary energy to deform most metal surfaces.

- ▨ Hail
- ▨ Foot traffic
- ▨ Service-related impacts

Exterior metal surfaces are subject to potential damage from hail impact (see Table 3.7). Hail can carry a surprising amount of energy, particularly when it groups into large hail ice formations. The shape of hail can concentrate the impact load as well. Typically, hail takes the form of round ice balls or grouped ice balls into larger round shapes. It has, however, been seen to take disc-shaped forms. The more common pea-size hail ice, up to perhaps 15 mm in diameter, do not carry the necessary energy to overcome the yield strength of metal and produce an impact dent on a metal surface. Figure 3.14 shows hail dents in a copper roof with a rigid backing. The hail was approximately 3 inches (75 mm) in diameter. Smaller hailstones did not dent the surface.

TABLE 3.7

Hail Impact Potential

Metal (Cold Rold Temper)	Thickness	Damage Due to Impact 12-mm Hail Ice	Damage Due to Impact 25-mm Hail Ice
Weathering steel	1.6 mm (16 gauge)	None	None
Aluminum (rigid backing)	1.5 mm (0.063)	Minor	Medium
Stainless steel	1.0 mm (20 gauge)	Minor	Minor
Titanium (fully backed)	0.7 mm	Minor	Minor
Zinc (fully backed)	0.7 mm	Minor	Medium
Copper (fully backed)	0.7 mm (20 ounce)	Minor	Medium
Steel (fully backed)	0.6 mm (24 gauge)	None	Minor

FIGURE 3.14. Dents in a copper roof from large, baseball sized, hail impacts.

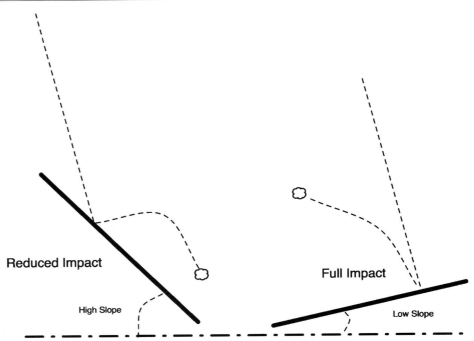

FIGURE 3.15. Hail impact forces are dependent on angle of impact.

Surfaces that are perpendicular to hail take the impact energy most directly. Vertical surfaces and sloping surfaces can deflect some of this impact. But surfaces perpendicular to the direction of force take the full-impact load. Automobile damage occurs on the flat surfaces, which are perpendicular to the direction of impact.

The softer metals are more inclined to yield to the force of hail ice and permanently deform. Thin copper and aluminum surfaces fall within this category. Interestingly, both of these can sometimes be repaired—if you are so inclined. Both of these metals have a high thermal expansion coefficient. You can heat the surface at the point of impact and then quickly cool them with dry ice. The temperature change pops out the impact crater.

Stainless steel, titanium, and weathering steel are stiffer materials. Stainless steel and titanium are often provided in thin coverings and thus can be dented by impact from hail. Weathering steel is used as a thicker cladding material. It would require a significant energy source to dent weathering steel cladding.

Impact from hail ice is dependent more on the size of the hail ice and on the direction of impact. Hail ice 25 mm and greater in diameter harnesses a significant amount of energy. Such storms producing those hail sizes are rare, fortunately.

Damage to the service life of a metal roof from hail ice is rare, if it ever occurs. It is usually the winds that accompany such storms that do the damage. Visual appearance is all that is affected by the hail impact. The more reflective the surface, the more apparent the indentations will be.

Foot traffic on low-slope metal surfaces, ledges, and other access regions can do more damage than hailstorms, particularly if tools or ferrous parts are

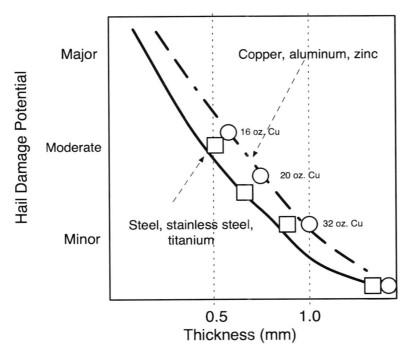

FIGURE 3.16. Hail damage potential of various metal thicknesses.

dragged against the surface and imbed steel particle. Designs should consider maintenance traffic and access. Maintenance personnel should protect metal surfaces when they are accessing them. Under traffic areas, rigid surfaces can be included to stiffen and take the impact from traffic.

Service-related impacts are a significant problem to metal surfaces used on the interior of buildings or that occur near ground level. Such service impacts as lawn care equipment, baggage-handling equipment, and access ladders can scratch, dent, or otherwise mar metal surfaces.

One of the embossed surface finishes will help to conceal many impacts and stiffen the surface of metals that receive the embossing, but the appearance of the surface may not suit the design.

Consider removable panels or surface skins of metal at the lower locations. This may require some "attic" stock be kept on hand to ensure finish matching. The best approach is to design in protective treatments that direct impacts away, such as curbs, bollards, and corner guards.

TIME EFFECTS

We still expect our concrete assets to last beyond the wink of an eye or the cycle of the season. Metal has always held the characteristic of time value. An entire industry is devoted to recycling metals—all metals. No other material known has the inherent value of metal. All metal has value. Some would argue that all material has value, whether wood, glass, ceramic, or plastic. Metal is king in this realm. But most building owners or their designers do not think about recycling their surfaces. They want to know what they have to do to the surface to maintain it, to keep it performing as planned. Maintaining may relate to keeping it as originally constructed for some time in the future, preferably the useful life of the building. Or maintaining may require controlling its behavior as it ages—not unlike a child. We want to have a predictable outcome, somewhat general but predictable all the same.

Aesthetic issues aside, metals can perform their functions quite well for significant durations of time if designed and constructed correctly. The key is to handle the stress buildup within the surfacing system. Stress cycles are common in all surfacing systems. The induced loads that are applied, released, and then applied again create stress cycles. Distribute the loads; make the loads small in comparison to the sectional capacities, and the fatigue conditions will be kept in control.

Stress cycles are also created from expansion and contraction of the surface. If the surface is allowed to "float," essentially frictionless over the supporting surface, stress again is kept very small, virtually nonexistent. If, however, fasteners bind the surfaces because no allowances were made for slotted holes to accommodate movement, or if interlocking joints restrict the movement because they inadequately accommodate the elongation or shrinkage of the material, then significant overstressing conditions can develop and create fatigue in the metal element.

Of the functional aspects of metal skins, several stand out as challenges for long-term performance. Those are listed in Table 3.8.

Chemical attack over time will change the components of the metals, rendering them nonfunctioning remnants of their past strength. Metals that have been subjected to chemical attack develop compounds that can dissolve in moisture or lack structure to resist the dynamic impacts of wind. Resiliency gives way to fracturing. Metal, particularly at regions of cyclical stress buildup, will fracture. This condition is accelerated by chemical exposure.

All metals will dissolve in some solution, even titanium and bronze. But the environment would have to get very dicey to have any measurable effects on these metals (see Table 3.9). Other metals are more susceptible to changes in the environment that generate corrosive compounds. Zinc, for instance, is not "fond" of acidic waters; nor is stainless steel the best for chlorinated environments. Metals do not give way immediately; it is the repeated exposure that breaks down the metal into soluble compounds. Copper, it is warned, should be kept away from cedar shake shingles. The tannic acid from the shingle brightens the surface and thus keeps the oxide from developing. However, the amount of tannic acid in

TABLE 3.8

Functional Aspects of Metal Skins

Functional Aspects That Deteriorate over Time	Effect on Metal
Chemical inhibition	Moisture control
	Wind pressure resistance
	Resilient nature
Stress conditions under thermal changes	Moisture control
	Wind pressure resistance
	Resilient nature

TABLE 3.9

Environmental Exposures and Preventive Measures

Metal	Deteriorating Environment	Preventive Measures
Aluminum—natural	Seacoast	Thick anodize or paint.
Copper alloys	Ammonium compounds	Coat surface with an impervious barrier.
Iron, steel	Humidity	Keep coated with oxide-inhibiting coating. Remove all signs of corrosion and protect.
Stainless steel	Seacoast, road salt, other high-chloride exposure	Use corrosion-resistant alloy forms.
Weathering steel	Moisture on both sides; standing moisture	Vent back side. Paint the back side. Eliminate all places of potential standing moisture.
Zinc	Moisture on both sides; standing moisture	Vent back side. Paint the back side. Eliminate all places of potential standing moisture.

a shingle roof is insignificant when it comes to the long-term performance of the copper. Copper gutters have been shown to carry away moisture draining from cedar shake roofs for decades with little apparent deterioration.

The corrosion behavior that overwhelms a metal's resiliency is known as *stress corrosion cracking*. Metals subjected to constant chemical attack lose their ability to overcome internal stresses. Small cracks spontaneously begin to appear at regions where stress is the most intense. Few metals are completely immune to stress corrosion cracking, but designing movement allowances in connections so stress buildup is very small can thwart the behavior. Stress corrosion cracking is a granular corrosive behavior. It begins around the microstructure of the metal grains and propagates outward.

All metals used as external surfacing must be able to expand and contract as thermal conditions change. If they are exposed to corrosive environments, like the seacoast or industrial regions, the capability to move and slip along edges and folds is critical. If you can eliminate stress buildup, particularly stresses that repeat and approach the yield point of the material, this corrosion condition can be kept under check (see Table 3.10).

TABLE 3.10

Stress Concentrations on Surfaces

Regions on Metal Surfaces Where Stress Cycles Occur	Indications of Stress Buildup
Corners, particularly welded, soldered, or pinned	Cracks in welds or solder joints; seam openings
Fastener locations	Oil canning between fasteners; elongated holes; fastener heads shearing off
Standing ribs and seams	Buckling; seams splitting at base
Ends of panels	Excessive oil canning; buckling; warping along the ridge
Penetrations	Oil canning around penetration; elongated hole
Plane of wall	Oil canning; shearing of clips; bowing

Most of these conditions can be corrected. They almost always require an allowance for expansion and contraction to occur without buildup of stress. If they are not corrected, it is most likely the surface will require premature replacement at some point.

Metal as a protective covering or skin must be able to separate and resist the various assaults the environment has to offer. This utility must be incorporated into a visually appealing surface. There are innumerable ways of creating the metal skin. The techniques of assembling the various elements to create the surface have similar parametric relationships. These relationships must incorporate these functional requirements if the surface is to perform over time.

CHAPTER 4
THE SURFACE MOSAIC

"Symmetric is a mathematic concept.
Symmetric is an aesthetic concept."

Few surfaces can be as smooth and even as the shell of an unbroken egg. Dimension and scale effects of our physical world are influenced by constant changes as energy is absorbed and released. Finite elements have dimensional limitations, which are created not only by manufacturing and handling restrictions, but also by the physical properties of matter.

Certainly it is possible to manufacture long ribbons of metal or extruded shapes that extend for great distances, but their practical use has diminishing capabilities as external forces begin to accumulate. Frictional forces and internal stresses from thermal expansion, among others, begin to overwhelm the sectional strength of the material and, for that matter, the aptitude of those who must handle these large elements. One solution is to generate seams and joints within the body of the surface. These seams and joints create patterns.

Patterns can be created by the arrangement of the seams and contrasting colors placed strategically across a surface. Patterns created out of metal used as a surfacing material typically refer to a regular, repeating system; a system that is replicated across a plane like shingles on a wall or the pans created by upturned seams on a metal roof. The viewer subconsciously interprets the rules of symmetry being employed to create the pattern.

Patterns can also be constructed by voids in the metal surface placed in regular rows or sequences. When the holes in the surface are small and spaced in close proximity to one another, they form a surface texture. *Perforated metal* is the term used to describe the piercing of metal.

When spaced irregularly, they can form contrasting patterns as light and dark zones are generated on the metal surface. They can also be cut irregularly to produce unique shapes that influence light behavior on the surface.

Developing surfaces from elemental features whose seams and reflective tones impart a perception of harmony and order is a human conditioning, sometimes taken to extreme context.

More complex surfacing can involve patterns whose symmetry is not easily identified.

BREAKING SYMMETRY

Another concept that is being employed is derived more naturally: breaks in the symmetry where essentially one pattern overcomes or is derived out of another. The employment of broken symmetry and irregular patterns developing from other patterns is a very natural concept. Chaos theory describes the natural tendency for symmetrical patterns to be broken, re-established and broken again. Irregular patterns are much more accepted and usual when depicted in pictures. Regularity appears out of place or posed.

Many aspects of nature show similar tendencies to pattern development.

■ Spheres: stars, planets, oranges, raindrops

■ Spirals: flowers, snail shells, whirlpools, galaxies

■ Hexagons: stone formations, honeycombs

There are general principles that underlie these natural pattern formations. Initially, broken patterns or unpredictable patterns lacking a strict symmetry at first can appear undisciplined or sloppy. However, considering the opposite, is stated by Ezio Manzini in the fascinating book, *The Materials of Invention* (Arcadia srl, Milano, 1986), "A world of significant forms but of homogeneous and commonplace surfaces would completely lack a dimension of sensory relationships."

For symmetry to break it must exist in the first place. Small departures cause the real symmetric system to select states from the range available to the idealized perfect system. This is the general principle of pattern formations. Certain physical constraints including those at atomic levels and those occurring from the interaction with the specific environment, both natural and man-made, lead to these small departures from symmetric systems. Pattern formations become the "fabric" that defines the surface.

PATTERN GENERATION

Patterns are assembled from elements. Interconnecting or overlapping boundaries define each element. Elemental boundaries overlap, often creating a circular relationship, without end and with no beginning. Overlapping elements do, however, possess a priority.

Metal surface patterns are often the product of a complex interaction of several variables. The designer wishes to create a surface pattern that works with the overall geometry of the building. This pattern creates the first order of texture on the building surface. How the pattern relates to the building edges, openings, and transition points is crucial to the overall appearance. Performed correctly, the outcome is visual music. Done incorrectly, the appearance is as if an accident or afterthought. The craftsperson who takes care in the layout, combined with the engineering of the interface of materials, can achieve a grace and composure that is almost natural in effect.

David Wade, in his book *LI: Dynamic Form in Nature* (Walker and Co., 2003), describes 24 patterns that show ". . . a sense of overall order, showing clear repetitive features but lacking a strict periodicity." These are patterns that develop, break symmetry, and develop further (see Table 4.1). They are found throughout nature, and they all possess "an imprint of the forces working upon them."

Surfaces of metal can lead to certain families of the 24 dynamic forms of nature. At a basic metallurgic level, the formation of crystal structures fall into several LI formations. Surface patterns created from metal elements have differing constraints. The principles that generate the various LI formations are perhaps "manifestations of the gestalt," inherent through the forces of physics that are responsible for the things around us. For metals used to clad architectural and ornamental surfaces, the inherent principles include those constraints in the manufacturing and installation processes. Figure 4.1A shows a somewhat cel-

TABLE 4.1

LI-Dynamic Forms in Nature as Described by David Wade

Dynamic Form	Description	Natural Form
Aggregation	Clustering	Moldlike
Anfractuous	Mazelike, winding and turning	Fingerprints
Angulated	Formed with angles	Layering of stick forms
Brancha	Branching	Fan coral
Brechia	Breaking, separating	Fractured stone
Cellular	Cells, sharing boundaries	Cells
Concentra	Propagation around centers	Polished geode
Contornare	Physiologic formations	Branching lake
Crackle	Shrinkage patterns	Crazing networks in plastic; cracks in dry mud
Filices	Fernlike formation	Fern plant forms
Fracture	Cracks in elastic material	Wood bark
Labyrinthine	Maze pattern	Microscopic grain of metals
Licheniform	Lichenlike growth patterns	Lichen and moss
Nubilous	Cloudlike	Clouds
Phyllotaxy	Dynamic spirality	Leaf formation in plants
Polygonal	Geometric quasiregularity	Soap bubbles
Retiform	Netlike formation	The wing of an insect
Rivas	River drainage system	Stream formation as seen from the air
Ripples and dunes	Wind and current patterns	Sand dunes
Trigons	Triangular formation	Patterns on some seashells
Variegatus	Tendency to form clusters	Coloration on some bird eggs
Vasculum	Leaf vascular system	Leaf patterns
Vermiculate	Wormlike, mutually repellant	Pattern some insect larvae make under bark; intestinal pattern
Viscous Maculae	Flamelike	Instantaneous flame pattern

FIGURE 4.1A. Stainless-steel shingles at the Weatherhead, Case Western Reserve University, Cleveland, Ohio. Designed by Frank Gehry.

FIGURE 4.1B. Bermuda seams constructed from weathering steel.

lular pattern snaking across the geometry of the Case Western Reserve Roof. Figure 4.1B is a weathering steel angulated pattern symmetrically layering over the surface.

There are several common patterns that exhibit certain inherent characteristics. Additionally, these common patterns follow rules of construction. Knowing the rules can afford the designer the ability to alter the pattern within the constraints of material and construction.

Characteristics we are concerned with in this text are joinery methods, light behavior, constructability, water shedding, and thermal movement. These make up the first level of constraints.

Pattern systems must also relate to the surface they cover. Manufacturing constraints force many of the upper dimensional limitations on the panels that make up a surface. This condition of relative scale relates to the surface form in a cultural way. The modern age has helped develop the concept of sleek, unchanging surfaces, more machined than crafted; surfaces created from large blocks consistent in color and texture and devoid of discernable seams—endless. Patterns made of discernable elements, either distinct or subtle, can create poetry to the eye. The forces that constrain the surface patterns are born from the functional requirements. Not necessarily unique to metal, these constraints have dictated the patterning produced on the surface. Each of these constraints will be explored in depth. Common patterns used with metal and how they achieve the functional will be explained (see Table 4.2).

TABLE 4.2

Surface Patterns

Sheet Metal Surfacing Patterns
Staggered running bond—horizontal
Staggered running bond—vertical
Variation on running bond—angled
Grid pattern
Diamond pattern
Shingled "scale" pattern
Trapezoid pattern
"Gehry" pattern
Gored pattern
Triangle pattern

PATTERNS

Staggered Running Bond

Of all the patterns used in metal surfacing, the staggered running bond pattern, sometimes referred to as a modified "ashler" pattern, is one of the most consistently used. The pattern is derived from the stacking and coursing of rectangular forms. In California, some also refer to it as the "earthquake pattern," due to its similarity to those stair-stepping fracture cracks appearing in corners of walls after a strong earthquake. When used for block stacking, this pattern has inherent strength. Stacking one block directly on top of another, rather than offsetting the block, is unstable. Every child knows he or she can stack higher by offsetting the rows so the vertical seam does not align. By offsetting the vertical seam, the load is spread out across the surface. Localized collapses will be resisted and the load will be better distributed. Figures 4.2 A, B, and C are examples of the horizontal running bond pattern.

This structural benefit has minor significance as it relates to the pattern in metal. It is true that the overlapping plate elements that make the pattern are stronger when subjected to a negative load. They add some stiffness to the surface and interrupt the path, creating a zippering or toothed plate resistance to the applied load. Figure 4.3 depicts a horizontal running bond while Figure 4.4 indicates a staggering running bond. Note the vertical seam is offset from the middle.

The horizontal running bond is a common pattern used to create metal skins on vertical and horizontal surfaces both curved and planer. The horizontal seams are typically parallel and continuous, while the vertical seam is staggered and creates a broken vertical line. The horizontal seam is sometimes referred to as a "water line." It is a line set horizontally at a particular point on the surface, similar to the mark water would make if allowed to rise to that level. The distinction here is that if the surface sloped at different rates than adjacent surfaces, the line

FIGURE 4.2A. An example of horizontal running bond.

FIGURE 4.2B. Stainless steel at the Sebastian Café, Kemper Art Museum in Kansas City, Missouri. Designed by International Architects Atelier.

FIGURE 4.2C. Horizontal running bond applied on a corner.

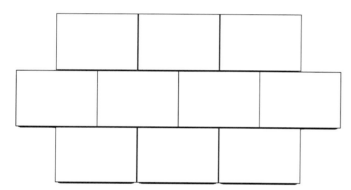

FIGURE 4.3. Horizontal running bond pattern.

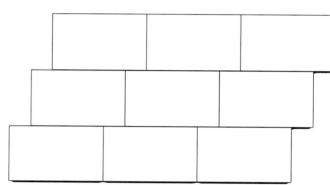

FIGURE 4.4. Staggered horizontal running bond pattern.

would still be at the same level. This would require the panels of various slopes to be manufactured to different sizes to keep the lines parallel.

The vertical seam is staggered. The junction is always a three-way joint. The vertical seam typically makes a perpendicular intersection with the horizontal seam. The stagger of the vertical joint breaks up the alignment of each panel and gives the appearance of a more monolithic surface.

This pattern is most common in thin sheet metal skins. Standard practice is to install one panel, then interlock and overlap the next panel to right. This continues level across the surface before a second row is overlapped and interlocked to the panels below. The vertical joint is staggered a particular amount to prevent a four-way junction from occurring. Four-way junctions accumulate several thicknesses of metal at one location, creating a gapping condition.

The vertical seam can stagger as much as 50 percent of the panel length or as little as a few centimeters. It is important that the vertical seams do not align. This breakup of the vertical line does not allow the viewer to concentrate on the accuracy of the alignment. The viewing eye does not move up along this joint line. Instead, the appearance is more horizontal; refer to Figure 4.5A. On lapping

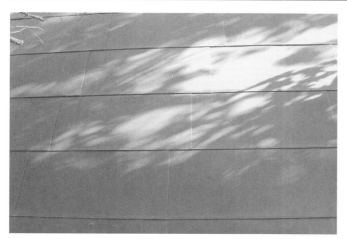

FIGURE 4.5A. Horizontal seam is more apparent.

FIGURE 4.5B. Vertical seam becomes apparent when viewed in one direction and in certain lighting conditions.

thin-gauge metal panels, the appearance changes on the viewing angle. When looking in the direction of the laps, they tend to conceal themselves, particularly on a dark surface. The surface appears banded.

On single-lock, lapped panels looking against the grain, the earthquake pattern shows itself with definition; see Figure 4.5B. This is because the rolled metal edge protrudes slightly from the surface due to the overlapping nature of the seam. Shadows are apparent, which can make the edge appear larger.

The symmetry in this system lies in its repetitive characteristic. Each vertical seam intersects the panel below at approximately the same offset. Each panel element within the body of the surface can interchange with any other panel. Each panel must lap over the adjacent panel in the same direction. Altering this will create a different appearance by accenting the overlap when viewed at a slight angle. Thus, all panels must run in the same direction. The darker the surface, the less the shadow lines play into this appearance.

On flush surfaces, with butt joints, there is no rolled edge, only the angle of view of the seam. The staggered joint breaks up the grid, and the pattern is tighter and more regular.

The horizontal dominates because the line is continuous and because the shadow produced by the overlap is more apparent. The broken vertical line separates the horizontal ribbon into panel units. The eye does not follow the staggering vertical seam, and thus it will not recognize a form in the pattern. Altering the color can change the priority and create stair-stepping patterns. The horizontal banding is concealed by the stronger contrasting color.

The lapping pattern provides a significant barrier to the environment, protecting the internal structures with multiple layers of material at the seam point. Nonoverlapping panel elements also provide significant protection to the interior, but weaknesses occur along the joint, particularly at the joint intersection.

Water control on exterior applications works well with the overlapping type of seam known as the single-lock seam; see Figure 4.6. On the single-lock seam, water cascades over the panel below. Blowing rains will track into the vertical seam, but again drain onto the face of the panel below. Known as a *shingling*

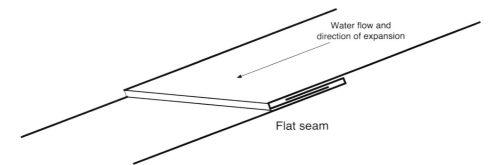

FIGURE 4.6. Flat lock seam.

effect, moisture is always brought back out onto the face of the panel below. The single-lock seam offers a barrier to moisture carried by the wind. The folded seam of the panel below offers a barrier to the incoming moisture, channeling it down onto the surface of the panel below. The horizontal seam functions in a similar manner. The return fold offers resistance to the blowing moisture, deflecting it back out to be removed by the force of gravity. The weakness lies at the junction of the horizontal to the vertical joint. On the surface, the panel above must lap over the intersection of two panels below.

When manufactured and installed correctly, only a small pinhole exists. Moisture with enough kinetic energy can enter this hole and arrive at the back side of the sheet. Under vertical applications, this hole is irrelevant. Very little, if any, moisture enters. Under low slope surfaces, sealing the small pinhole is necessary.

Running bond patterns made from nonoverlapping joints, commonly called *butt joints*, have similar issues with the control of moisture. On butt joints, water flows over the surface; however, it can track on the horizontal seam. When moisture hits the horizontal-to-vertical seam junction, moisture can enter if this seam is not closed or backed. It is important to take this moisture out of the vertical seam. Figure 4.7 indicates a vertical return that captures water and allows gravity to pull it downward and eventually out over the top of the panel below. The vertical seam should drain onto the top of the panel below, and the top of the panel should redirect the moisture to the face.

The horizontal running bond pattern construction is inherently strong. As loads are applied to the surface of one metal element, it is brought out to the edges where the metal is attached to the structure. The contribution of the adjoining panels is derived from the stiffening at the vertical seam. Generally, there is little contribution of stress from one panel to the next. The structure of the panel element is obtained by taking the load out at the perimeter.

Thermal changes are handled efficiently with the horizontal running bond. For the thin-skin system, the single-lock overlapping panel element, two sides are fixed with cleats back to the structure. They are created so that all expansion and contraction should proceed from these edges. As such, each panel expands or contracts over the panel below it and the panel beside it. No accumulation of stress develops. The thermal stress is relieved at each lapping element, like the

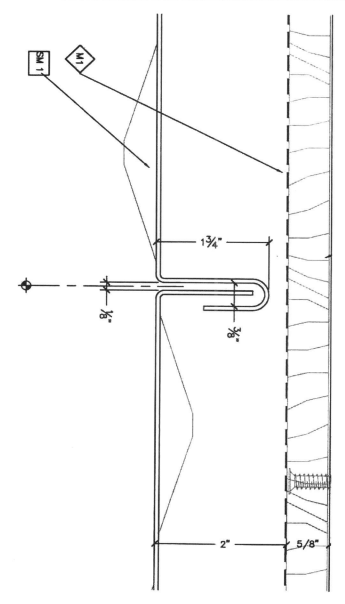

FIGURE 4.7. Inverted seam with return to catch and redirect moisture.

scales on a fish. Refer to Figure 4.8. Each panel is lapped over and interlocked into the panel below and to the side. The panel is pinned at the clips so all thermal movement is away or toward these fixed clip points.

Changes in dimension are taken up at the skin without stressing the internal structure. The key is to design and construct the joint so that stress, or the elongation that occurs when the metal expands, does not overwhelm it. For instance, if the panel expansion is calculated to be 0.06 inches, allow for this in the lap. If the panels are installed during the hottest period of the year, then allow for the skin to contract the maximum amount. Do not install the skin tight in the hottest period. When it contracts, it may overstress the surface and open the seam. An

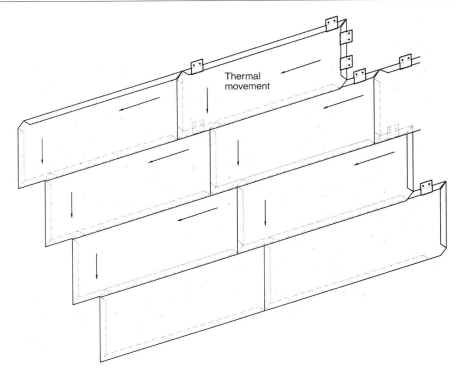

FIGURE 4.8. Direction of thermal movement away from or toward fixed clip locations.

enlargement of the seam is shown in Figure 4.9. All the expansion and contraction for the panel must be taken out at this seam.

The same goes for the coolest period: do not loosely assemble the skin elements. Doing so may allow the panel to expand far enough to disengage the interlocking single lock.

For nonoverlapping panels, the expansion and contraction must occur within the seam. Again, hard-fix two adjacent sides to allow the expansion and contraction to occur to the opposing side. The joint must be sufficient to take up thermal expansion. Fixing one major side will work as well, allowing expansion and contraction movement to occur away from this fixed edge.

Because the single-lock seam is manufactured from thin material, it requires a solid substrate directly behind the surface. Thick material does not form 180 degrees to develop the seam. The seam would be quite large and difficult to interlock on thick material because of the stiffness developed at the seam and the abundance of material at the intersections.

On thin, single-lock seam surfaces, care should be taken in the handling. Each panel has very low section properties because of the flatness. They can kink along the edge quite easily. This will increase the difficulty of installation and can read to the finish surface as a dent or buckle. When installed onto the solid backing, this surface performs well. Positive impacts are transferred to the support backup. Negative loads are taken up, along the perimeter of each panel element, and transferred to the structure behind.

For thicker panel systems the mechanical resilience is achieved in the stiffness and hardness of the material. Further stiffness can be imparted through the use of stiffeners or rigid backup material.

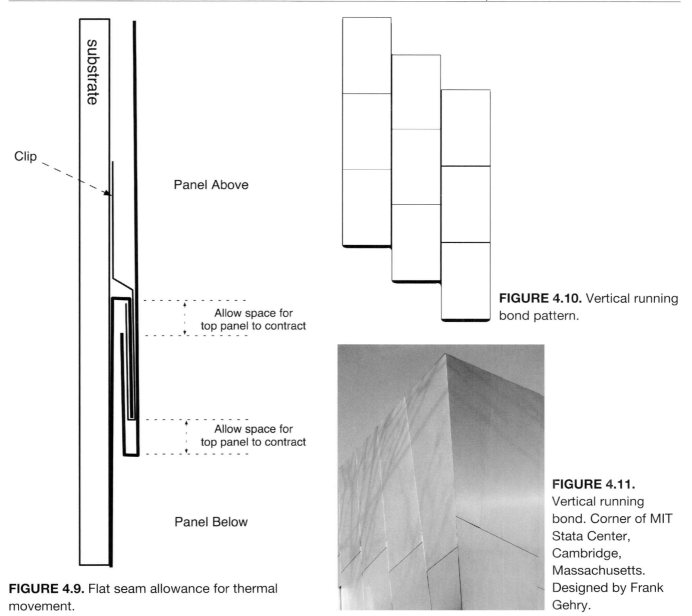

FIGURE 4.9. Flat seam allowance for thermal movement.

FIGURE 4.10. Vertical running bond pattern.

FIGURE 4.11. Vertical running bond. Corner of MIT Stata Center, Cambridge, Massachusetts. Designed by Frank Gehry.

This pattern, when installed correctly, will perform adequately for the life of the material. Stress buildup from thermal changes is relieved with each cycle and confined within a given panel element. Loading and unloading of the surface from dynamic forces of the environment are captured along the edge and then released.

Vertical Running Bond Pattern

The vertical running bond pattern is characterized by the vertical line becoming the dominant line. The pattern appears as vertical stripes with a horizontal seam, see Figures 4.10 and 4.11. One can modify the appearance by modifying the shape of the seam. For example, changing the vertical seam to a standing seam creates shadows along the seam. This tends to accentuate the appearance. Creating a standing seam at the horizontal will also create a shadow effect, but the offset of this seam reduces the dominance in regard to appearance.

The vertical running bond controls moisture in a different manner from the horizontal running bond pattern. Water tracks down the vertical seam from one panel to the next. The horizontal tracks water into the vertical seam. So it is very important to make sure this seam and the lap onto the next panel is handled very carefully to ensure moisture is not brought into the system. Figures 4.12A and 4.12B show a vertical running bond surface used on one of the MIT Stata Center structures designed by Frank Gehry.

Problems often occur when this pattern is used as a wall system. The challenge develops around openings, such as windows or doorways through these surfaces. Because the water is tracked down the vertical seam, it must be contained and directed out by the flashing at the interface with the opening; refer to Figure 4.13.

VERTICAL RUNNING BOND: ROOFS

The vertical running bond is used on many metal roofs. The typical standing seam with the staggered horizontal joint is developed from this pattern. The seams are continuous, running down the slope of the roof, and the horizontal is staggered across the roof. Moisture is tracked down the seam. The standing seam is generally the vertical seam on the roof, while the interlocking flat seam is the geometry of the transverse seam. Refer to Figures 4.14 and 4.15.

FIGURE 4.12A. Vertical running bond. MIT Stata Center.

FIGURE 4.12B. Vertical running bond. MIT Stata Center.

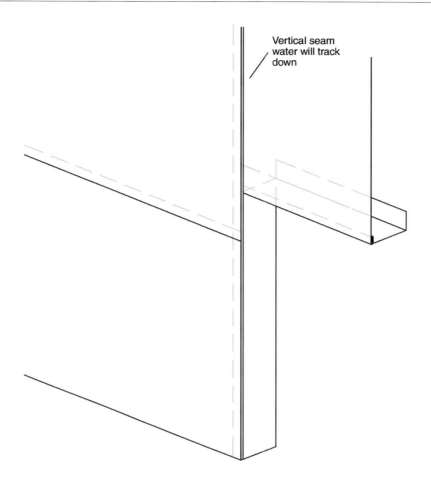

FIGURE 4.13. Openings through vertical running bond must address moisture in seam.

Batten seams of various configurations are also commonly used. The standing seam, in particular the batten seam, have bold expressions along what would be considered the vertical seam of the roof. This alters the appearance by creating a "striping" or linear appearance. A priority of patterns takes effect. The eye sees a bold expression and the corresponding shadow this expression makes. The staggered transverse or horizontal seam melts into the pattern. Similar to a wood floor, the staggered and offset transverse joint disappears, and the long, unbroken line of the wood edge dominates. Batten and standing seams make strong use of the priority of seam patterns. Other systems have similar effects.

Many attempts are made to use the flat seam on the sloping roof surface. Extreme care must be taken when detailing and assembling these panels to ensure moisture will not overwhelm the joint as it moves down the surface. As stated, with the horizontal running bond, the small pinhole at each corner should be sealed. With the flat seam, the designer and installer must understand channeling of the water along the continuous vertical line. Water will channel along this line and it will find entry points, if they exist.

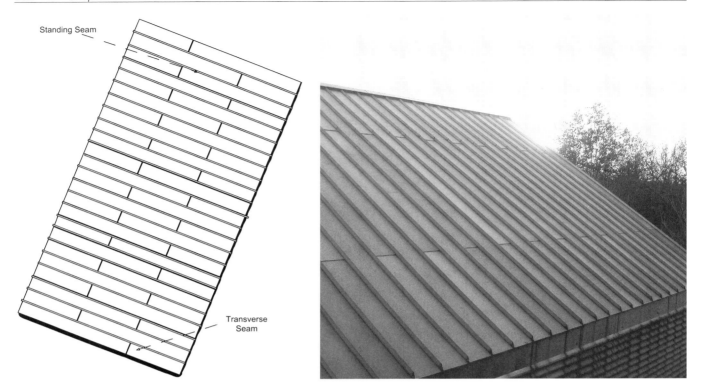

Standing Seam

Transverse Seam

FIGURE 4.14. Roof patterns made of metal sheet often are vertical running bond patterns.

FIGURE 4.15. Copper roof with vertical running bond.

Other seams are often used on the vertical to control this effect. The inverted seam, a proprietary system, controls this water flow. It recognizes that water will travel to the seam and allows it to enter into a continuous guttering channel. An inverted seam was used on the roof and walls of the Tacoma Art Museum designed by Antoine Predock (see Figure 4-16).

Functionally, the vertical running bond, when assembled correctly and with care around openings, will perform similar to the horizontal running bond. As mentioned, because the vertical pattern tends to track moisture, rather than shedding it like the horizontal pattern, it requires much more attention to detail when it is being fabricated and installed.

Resisting wind dynamics is essentially the same as the horizontal running bond, with one exception. The horizontal pattern is often made up of many smaller elements, whereas the vertical pattern often has long lengths before they are broken with the horizontal staggering seam. Because of this, the panel is typically narrow. Wide panels have fewer attachment points back to the structure per unit area, and thus are susceptible to greater loads along their seams. Surface deflections, known as oil canning, will be more prominent, but the structural capacity of the skin is much less.

Thermal changes are handled the same as on the horizontal running bond. When a standing or inverted seam is used along the vertical seam, expansion and contraction are limited, with some stress buildup. This is another reason why these patterns are typically narrow. The stress from thermal changes across a narrow sheet is drastically reduced in comparison to a wide sheet. Refer to Figure 4.17.

FIGURE 4.16. Inverted-seam stainless-steel roof and wall panels on the Tacoma Art Museum, Tacoma, Washington. Designed by Antoine Predock.

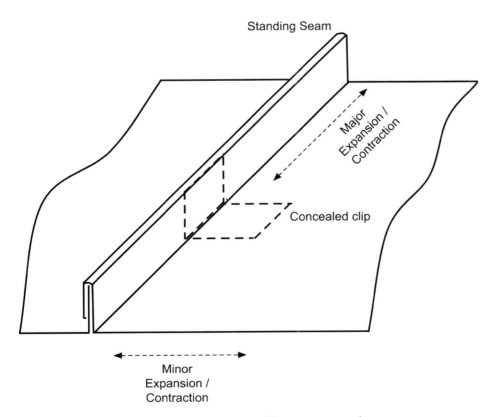

FIGURE 4.17. Thermal movement of standing seam panel.

For thicker material, material with enough section to create wide and long panels, the thermal changes must be handled within the seam. If lapped or interlocked, they must not accumulate stress across to the next panel. Similar to the running bond, they should relieve the stress at the joint opposite the side that is fixed.

Larger panels will require sufficient stiffness to transfer the dynamic wind loads to the structure without buckling or significant altering of the panel geometry. If under dynamic loading the connection at the seam undergoes changes in geometry as the face of the panel moves out of plane, eccentric loading of the clip or fastener may occur (see Chapter 3, Figure 3.12).

Variations in the Running Bond Pattern

There are several variations on the running bond pattern that involve breaking symmetry across the surface. The pattern may start out horizontal or vertical but then break and rotate to a different angle. Figure 4.18 shows an offsetting running bond pattern. Breaking of the pattern symmetry was used to skin the surface of the Bard College Theatre designed by Frank Gehry depicted in Figure 4.19.

All panel elements within a zone of geometry break must be set at the same angle. The symmetry of the panel element size and the offset remain unaltered,

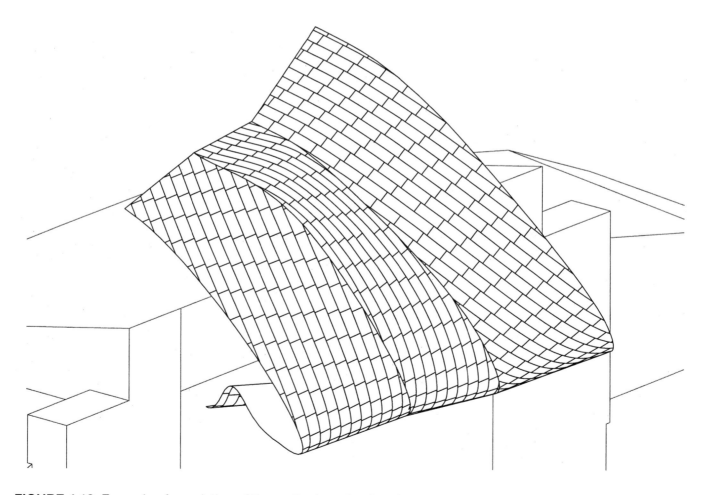

FIGURE 4.18. Example of a variation of the vertical running bond.

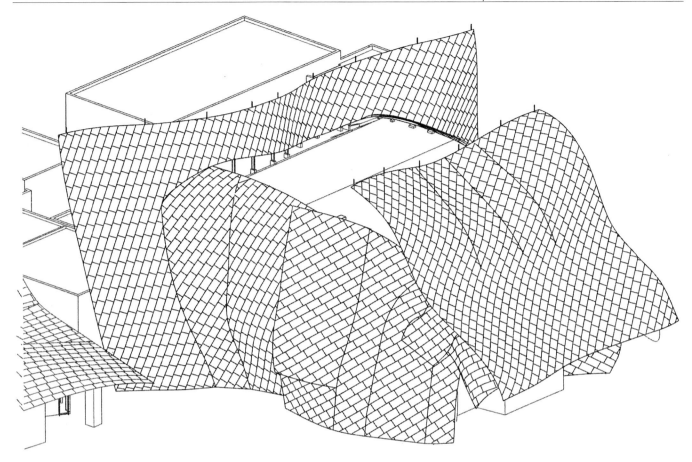

FIGURE 4.19. Example of a variation of the vertical running bond. Bard College, Annandale-on-Hudson, New York. Designed by Frank Gehry.

but the angle of the bands changes, and then changes again. At each change, a line occurs, which ends one pattern and starts another. Lapping direction is important on overlapping panels because the overlap line will appear different in certain light conditions. The seam will appear from one view and not be visible in the opposing view. Figure 4.20 shows a surface used on the Experience Music Project. The laps on the surface were generally running in one direction; however, certain laps as they roll into view show up more pronounced than others.

Grid Pattern

Unbroken vertical and horizontal joints characterize the grid pattern. Also known as the "stack bond," this pattern places one panel element on top of the next in a replicated symmetry. Refer to Figure 4.21.

The grid pattern creates four-way joints at the intersection of the horizontal and vertical seams. Refer to Figure 4.22. This four-way joint reduces the panel size tolerance to very tight limits. Small, even minute variations from one panel to the next are readily visible. The viewer's eye follows the edge of a smooth, flat surface to the corner where one panel meets the next. If this seam is tight, say, 1 mm to 2 mm in spacing, any minute deviation will appear.

FIGURE 4.20. Seams apparent in various lighting conditions. Experience Music Project, in Seattle, Washington. Designed by Frank Gehry.

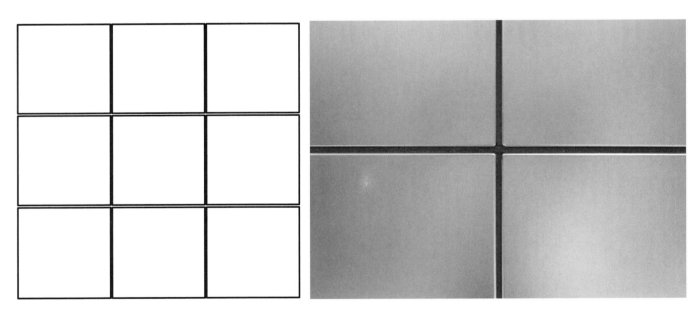

FIGURE 4.21. Grid pattern.

FIGURE 4.22. Grid pattern four-way joint.

From the fabrication viewpoint, the shear, brake (fold), and notching process must be exact, panel to panel. With thicker panels, the bend radius not starting at just the right point can complicate this. The bend and corner notch on thin panels must also be precisely placed panel to panel. The diagonal measurement for squareness must be held to a very tight tolerance. Deviations as little as 1 mm are visible with seams of less than 12 mm width.

If the panels are large, then expansion and contraction due to thermal effects can set the joint off as well. The panels may be manufactured near perfect dimensionally, but the thermal effects in variable degrees along the grain direction can make them expand or contract more in one direction than the other.

From the viewpoint of installation, shims are often used to set the joint line, with minor variations being taken out from one joint to the next. At what point the eye can distinguish the variations it is difficult to say. A 1-mm offset can be seen from a distance of 3 meters.

The more reflective the surface is, the more any deviation will be accentuated. A 1-mm difference can appear as a 2-mm joint.

It is suggested when designing a four-way joint to consider opening the gap between panels to a minimum of 3 mm. A tight joint of 1 mm or less will show minor deviations. A 3-mm joint will allow some tolerance in the fabrication and installation. Zero tolerance in any system of building construction is a disaster.

This grid pattern is best suited using the Rainscreen Principle and thicker metal skin. The four-way joint will track water both along the vertical and horizontal. Sealing this intersection is complex. It is possible to wet-seal it with silicone or other sealant material, but you face the inherent problems with wet seals and metal staining. Figure 4.23 shows staining around the sealant joints on white painted panels.

Gasketing can be complex with four-way joints. You can vulcanize the intersection of a horizontal to vertical, but with most gaskets the geometry changes, and thus the performance at the transition changes from vertical to horizontal. Double-wiper gasket designs effectively control moisture infiltration by taking the kinetic energy out of a blowing rainstorm. Another issue with gaskets is that they shrink. Thermally, gasket material moves differently from the metal and can shrink at different rates. This can open a seam in the gasket.

Thermal expansion and contraction of the metal surface can be handled with the seam of the grid pattern. Aesthetically, the changing alignment of the

FIGURE 4.23. Staining of adjoining surfaces from dirt collecting on sealant.

four-way joint may become apparent under extreme conditions. Since you must pin two adjacent sides, the expansion rate may be different, creating changes in the joint size.

Mechanical resilience is achieved by the material thickness. But this pattern does not work well with thin, lapping metal, so, typically, heavier folded material or sheared plates offer the stiffness to overcome most expected impacts. Figure 4.24 shows the large aluminum panels used on the Modern Art Museum of Fort Worth. The panels were 0.187-inch-thick (5-mm) aluminum. Stiffeners can be added on large surface elements to aid in keeping the shape. Inherently, there is no assistance obtained from the diaphragm interaction of one plate to another. Interlocking panels can achieve a level of support from adjoining panels, but usually this is ignored and each panel element is essentially on its own. Loads are taken to the perimeter and out at the seam or via applied stiffeners attached back to the structure. Figure 4.25 shows the attachment of a panel system occurring along the perimeter of the panel.

The Diamond Pattern

Another pattern used for centuries on metal domes is the diamond pattern. Refer to Figure 4.26. Typically manufactured in a similar manner to the thin-gauge running bond metal skins, this pattern is characterized by diagonal lines criss-crossing over the surface.

The shingling effect is not unlike the running bond patterns. Each panel overlaps the panel below. The uniqueness of this system is the way the offset of the laps occurs. On a typical diamond panel system, each horizontal row does not

FIGURE 4.24. Modern Art Museum of Fort Worth, Texas. The large panels are supported at the edge.

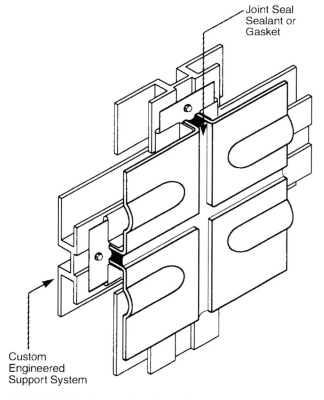

Joint Seal Sealant or Gasket

Custom Engineered Support System

FIGURE 4.25. Example of a grid pattern four-way joint.

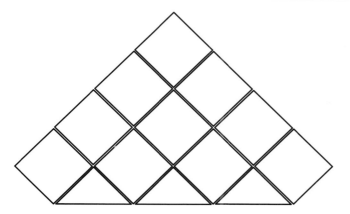

FIGURE 4.26. Diamond pattern.

interlock panel to panel; rather, it interlocks into and over the diamond panel in the previous row. The four-way offset with its layering of metal is reduced in appearance because the point at which this occurs is a local high point. This pattern usually occurs on curving or sloping surfaces. As such, each row above, with its local high point, rolls or falls back. Using this pattern on a vertical wall will show the four-way offset, and the shadowing will further accentuate this. Figure 4.27 shows an old gold leaf copper surface developed into a diamond pattern. The seams were hammered to flatten them down. Figure 4.28 shows a typical diamond pattern assembly and how the thermal movement will move from the fixed clip points.

On thicker material, the diamond pattern is either created by lapping one plate over the next without the single-lock seam or it is generated like the grid

FIGURE 4.27. Gold leaf over copper, in a diamond pattern. Note deterioration along the edge of this 50-year-old gold-leaf surface.

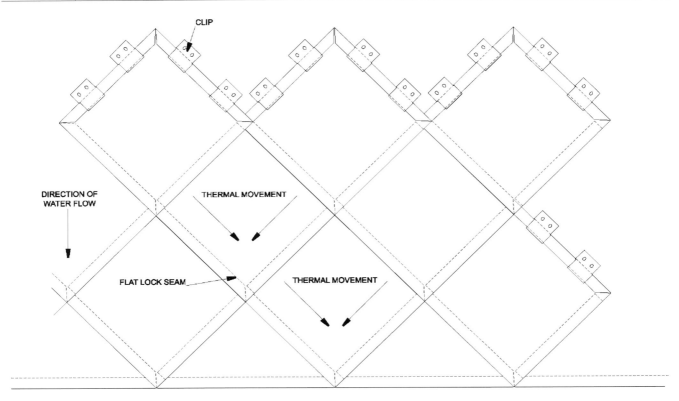

FIGURE 4.28. How a diamond pattern handles thermal movement.

pattern with reveals. This pattern in the single-lock, overlapping skin, is a very tight protective barrier. The lapping at the seam develops a sound impervious barrier to the ambient. Figure 4.29 shows a custom diamond pattern created from 1-inch-thick (25-mm) folded plates.

Moisture control is actually improved over the running bond patterns by placing the open hole or seam at the highest local point in the shingle. This hole is tucked up under the lap of two more sets of panels, where it can be sealed with sealant or a custom clip to deter moisture. The small pinhole is located in Figure 4.30.

The diamond pattern is inherently strong and utilizes the interlocking plates of the surrounding panels. Loading is taken out at the seam with the thin-skin single-lock system.

Dimensional changes of the panel elements caused by thermal effects are handled efficiently with the diamond pattern. The top edges of each panel are fixed, usually with clips; and the bottom edges interlock into the single-lock seam along the top edge of the row of panels below. Expansion and contraction are away and toward the clips, effectively sliding over the single lock of the panel element below.

Correctly installed, diamond pattern systems have shown centuries of performance due to the inherent strength and the reduction of stress maintained by the overlapping pattern.

FIGURE 4.29. Custom diamond pattern on the Tacoma Museum of Glass, Tacoma, Washington.

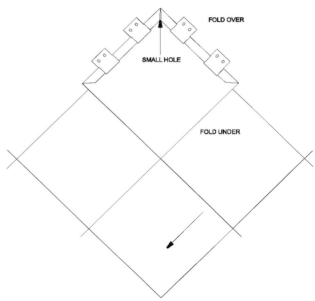

FIGURE 4.30. Hole position in a diamond pattern.

Shingled "Scale" Pattern

The shingled, or scale, pattern is a variation of the running bond pattern and the diamond pattern (see Figure 4.31). By offsetting the panel lap, you completely eliminate any continuous line and effectively remove the problem of minor deviations in the fabrication and installation tolerances that show if the dimensional control is not precise. The offsetting of the lap may pose issues with the installa-

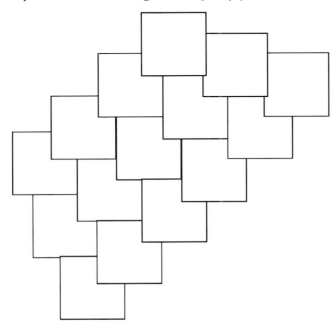

FIGURE 4.31. Shingled "scale" pattern.

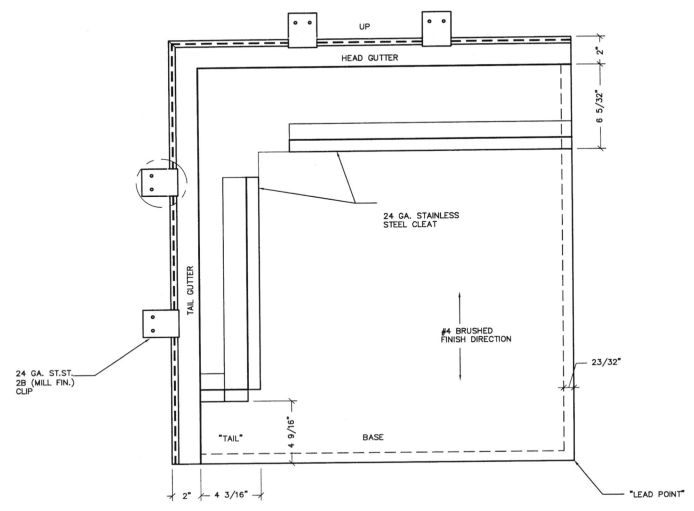

FIGURE 4.32. Example of the shingle "scale" panel used on Case Western.

tion layout process but the pattern is inherently flexible. Minor adjustments, if planned ahead, can be easily achieved in this pattern. Figure 4.32 shows a single panel. Figure 4.33 and 4.34 are of a set of panels. Figure 4.35 is a section through a lap showing the hierarchy of installation.

Each panel is a replica of the next with the exception of the edges. A very clear symmetry exists, but it follows rules that are not necessarily straightforward. This system works best with thin metal skins that can be lapped and interlocked. Straight or curved walls are irrelevant.

From an installation layout point, the correct location of the starting row of panels is critical. This is shown in Figure 4.34. On curved surfaces, further validation of where the rows of the pattern occur must be predicted and established on the under support surface. The installer must verify the location and adjust as necessary to maintain the pattern. If this does not occur, the pattern may begin to "unzip" itself as the angle of the surface changes.

When working with these alternative systems, it is necessary to apply an installation clip for precision alignment of each panel. There are rotational aspects to be controlled as one panel installs into the next. This is handled in the layout process.

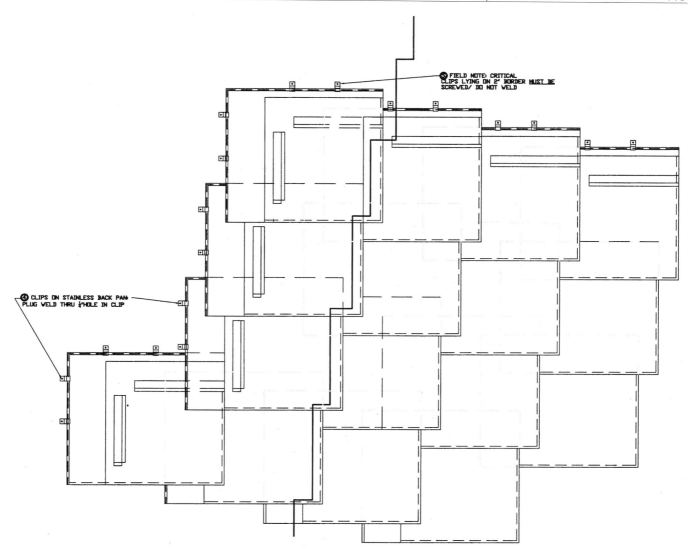

FIELD NOTE: CRITICAL
CLIPS LYING ON 2" BORDER MUST BE
SCREWED/ DO NOT WELD

CLIPS ON STAINLESS BACK PAN
PLUG WELD THRU ½"HOLE IN CLIP

FIGURE 4.33. Pattern generated from shingle "scale" panel on Case Western.

The lapping of the panels increases the overage at points where the running bond and diamond panel are most vulnerable. Thus this pattern achieves improved moisture control as water is shed over the surface. The added alignment clip also acts as a deterrent to moisture infiltration at the corner. The extended lap and added coverage would require a greater kinetic energy behind the water to push it behind the shingle.

Increased metal thicknesses can be utilized with these patterns because of the accentuation at the lap or because of fabrication processes that recess the surface. With the thicker metal held at the perimeter, similar to the diamond pattern, wind dynamics are resisted efficiently.

Thermal expansion and contraction of the panel elements is also similar to that of the running bond and diamond pattern. Each panel element expands from two edges over the top of the panel below and to the side. This effectively eliminates any buildup of stress from thermal changes and the dimensional changes they create in metal skins.

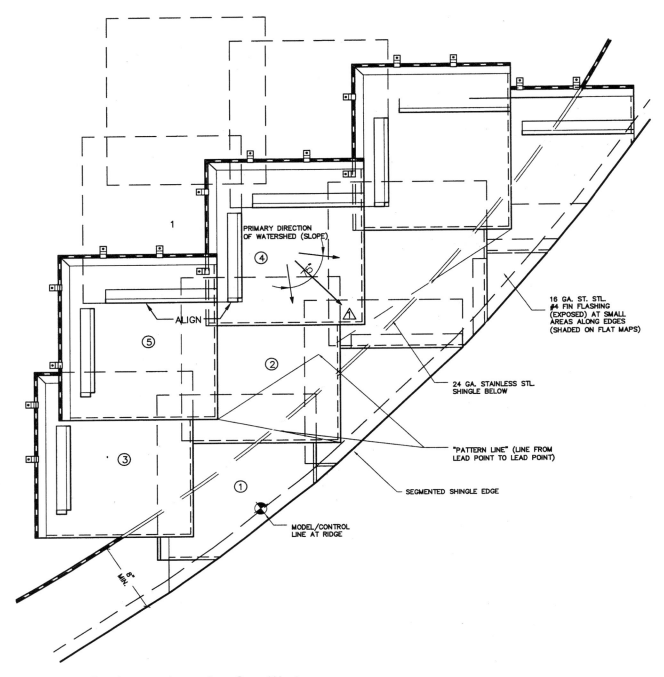

FIGURE 4.34. Starting panels used on Case Western.

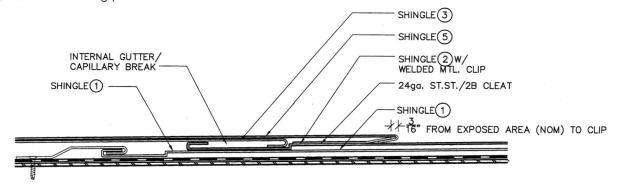

FIGURE 4.35. Overlapping condition of the shingled "scale" panel.

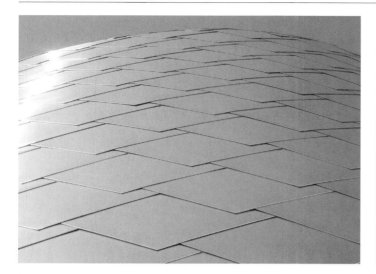

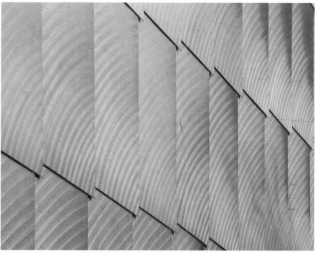

FIGURE 4.36. Weatherhead. Custom offset shingle pattern. Case Western University, Cleveland, Ohio. Designed by Frank Gehry.

FIGURE 4.37. New England Aquarium in Boston, Massachusetts, Custom offset shingle pattern. A custom radial polish was applied to the stainless steel. Designed by Swartz/Silver Architects.

As with the diamond pattern, the scale pattern should perform well over a long period of time. Special attention is necessary at the edges of the surface where the pattern terminates or changes to ensure that expansion and contraction is not restricted. Understanding the movement of the metal surfaces along these points will provide a very durable and long-lasting patterned surface. Figure 4.36 shows the finish work of the system detailed. Figure 4.37 is a slight variation on this theme.

There are other shingling patterns that do not generate a continuous line in either the horizontal or the vertical direction. They possess symmetry in repetitive form. They are installed in rows and have a staggered lapping that bisects the vertical symmetrical axis of the panel just below; see Figure 4.38. Generally, these are manufactured from stamping or pressing into molds, which, for economy, require a systematic approach. Any symmetry breaks require special consideration to avoid looking like a mistake.

Because of the imposed rules, they do not lend themselves well to complex geometries. Their small size allows for minor field adjustments on the surface but they require a certain bias to the horizon.

Shingles of this nature are fabricated in many different configurations and materials—from cast shinges such as those depicted in Figure 4.39 to formed shapes as those shown in Figure 4.40. They all operated under the same basic Rainscreen Principles.

The lapping hierarchy of the rows of panels controls moisture. Sometimes they engage into the panel row below, which improves the moisture control and alignment of the pattern. Typically, they simply shed moisture by using the constant of gravity on the flowing or blowing water.

Strength is achieved by increasing the section of each shingle element. Stamping or rolling the surface induces a thickness in the shingle form, which aids in the overall strength of the shingle.

FIGURE 4.38. Simple shingle panel.

FIGURE 4.39. Cast steel shingle covering for a subway entrance in New York City.

FIGURE 4.40. Tin shingle on dome of the Church at the Leaning Tower in Pisa, Italy.

Thermal stress is handled by the overlap. Each shingle is pinned at the top and allowed to expand over the shingle below. Because their size is relatively small, as compared to what is common in other running bond or diamond patterns, the dimensional changes will be minor.

Often they are nailed without clips. This leaves the long-term performance dependent on the quality and corrosion durability of the fastener. Therefore, it is recommended to use the highest-quality fastener that is most compatible with the materials being used. Perhaps even consider one or more levels of redundancy.

1. Museum of Science and Industry, Tampa, Florida. Designer: Antoine Predock. The blue stainless steel has a triangular rainscreen pattern.

2. Experience Music Project, Seattle, Washington. Designer: Frank Gehry. The "Sky Church" clad in red stainless steel, vertical running bond pattern intersecting with the blue painted aluminum skin of the "Veils" on Element 7.

3. Experience Music Project, Seattle, Washington. Designer: Frank Gehry. Element 5 is clad in gold glass-bead-blasted stainless steel. The pattern on the metal surface is assembled from trapezoidal metal sheets.

4. Experience Music Project, Seattle, Washington. Designer: Frank Gehry. Angel hair finish stainless steel. Note the curving fine edge of the canopy over the entry.

5. Experience Music Project. The red element is constructed of vertical running bond plates of interference red stainless steel. Oil canning visible from this view is generated from the stiffeners acting as heat sinks. At other views the surface appears flat.

6. Experience Music Project. The curving veils approach the monorail. ➤
The fine edge is constructed of glass-bead-blasted stainless steel.

7. Experience Music Project, Seattle, Washington. Designer: Frank Gehry. Interference red mirror stainless steel with a vertical running bond pattern.

8. Experience Music Project, Seattle, Washington. Designer: Frank Gehry. Under final construction. Some of the surfaces were left with the PVC protective coating on. Light is diffused as it strikes these surfaces, making them glow softly.

9. Experience Music Project, Seattle, Washington. ➤
Designer: Frank Gehry. The interface of panels to concrete is indicative of the extensive use of computer assistance on this project.

10. Robert Hoag Rawlings Library, Pueblo, Colorado. Designer: Antoine Predock. The metal surface is "dirty penny" darkened copper plates set in a vertical running bond. The panels are a pressure-equalized rainscreen.

11. Robert Hoag Rawlings Library. Note the lack of trim around the openings and corners. The surface was created to have all edges integral to the panels, thus creating the returns as a part of the surface and not applying bulky trim to the face.

12. Robert Hoag Rawlings Library. The variations in color add to the richness of the metal surface. Predock used the natural behavior of the materials to enhance the large regions of metal. These surfaces will continue to oxidize, but at a very slow rate. The expectations are for the surface to darken.

13. Super Highway Telecommunications Center, Gwachon, Korea. Designer: Space oh Associates. Zinc sphere enclosure is composed of 68,000 square meters of Rheinzink preweathered tiles.

14. MIT Stata Center, Cambridge, Massachusetts. Designer: Frank Gehry. The project in this photo is under construction. A metallic glow is generated by the angel hair stainless steel surface.

15. MIT Stata Center, Cambridge, Massachusetts. Designer: Frank Gehry. Running bond pattern applied over the curving surface. This surface is constructed of flat-seam, thin 0.7-mm sheets. Pattern and texture are distinctively different from the heavier 1.5-mm plates on the other surfaces.

16. MIT Stata Center, Cambridge, Massachusetts. Designer: Frank Gehry. Large element massing. Very smooth surface created by vertical running bond. Seams are somewhat invisible, as is the lack of flashing and trim. The windows appear to "punch out" of the surface.

17. The White Chapel at Rose-Hulman Institute of Technology, Terre Haute, Indiana. Designer: VOA Associates. Under construction. The reflectivity and the patterning are created by the flat-seam diamond panels.

18. The White Chapel at Rose-Hulman Institute of Technology, Terre Haute, Indiana. Designer: VOA Associates. Diamond pattern stainless-steel surface.

19. Shafran Planetarium at the Cleveland Museum of Natural History, Cleveland, Ohio. Designer: van Dijk Westlake Reed Leskowsky Architects. Metal surface constructed from panels set out in a grid pattern over a conical shape.

20. University of Iowa Laser Lab, Iowa City, Iowa. Designer: Frank Gehry. Clad with a #2D stainless-steel surface. The diffuse tone is created by vertical running bond panels.

21. Sheet Metal Workers 100th Anniversary project. Designer: ➤
Frank Gehry. A terne-coated stainless-steel surface is utilized.

22. 17th Street Causeway Project, Fort Lauderdale, Florida. Designer: the Florida Corp. of Engineers. This surface is created by a dull, shadow-finish stainless steel. The pewterlike appearance is created from coining minute offsets into the surface of a #2D stainless steel.

23. The Modern Art Museum, Fort Worth, Texas. Designer: Tadao Ando. This design utilized a pressure-equalized grid pattern panel.

24. St. Louis Museum of Science, St. Louis, Missouri. Designer: E. Verner Johnson Architects. This surface shows the characteristic patina of Monel. The standing seam develops a distinctive vertical-bias running bond pattern.

25. IBM World Headquarters, Armonk, New York. Designer: Kohn Pedersen Fox Architects. The surface is constructed of a pressure-equalized rainscreen. The joint utilizes a double gasket to make up a grid pattern across the surface.

26. The Richard B. Fisher Center for the Performing Arts at Bard College, Annandale-on-Hudson, New York. Designer: Frank Gehry. This surface is created by a horizontal running bond 1.6-mm-thick stainless-steel skin.

27. Kansas City Federal Court House, Kansas City, Missouri. Designer: Abend-Singleton Associates (now ASAI) and Ellerbe Becket Architects. This dull, shadow-finish stainless steel has very low reflectivity.

28. Tacoma Museum of Glass, Tacoma, Washington. Designer: Arthur Erickson Architects. This massive cone form is surfaced in a diamond pattern.

The Trapezoidal Pattern

This variation of the shingled, or scale, pattern is a plate that has two parallel sides, and one side, at least, cut to an angle; see Figure 4.41. The angle can change on each subsequent panel to create a unique and distinctive appearance. The length of the panels can also be altered to create variable patterns over a surface.

The patterns can run horizontally, vertically, or diagonally. The seams can be flat lock, inverted, simple lap, or a combination of seams. Laps should be positive-drained to keep moisture out. The panels can be thick plate or thin sheet metal. The joints will be dictated by the metal thickness.

FIGURE 4.41. Aluminum plate walls custom cut to emulate stone.

The Gehry Pattern

Creating an ever-changing, somewhat unique, pattern is difficult. On a large surface, it challenges the human tendency to symmetry and repetition.

On the Experience Music Project, completed in 2000 in Seattle, Washington, the renowned architect and artist, Frank Gehry, wanted the smooth, undulating surface to be made from lapping plates of thin metal. The metal plates themselves created a pattern with the seams. Seams were necessary because of the constraint imposed by the size of the sheet and the constructability of the form. Figure 4.42 is an image of the solid model used to define and create the seam that developed the surface of a portion of the project. The seams were to be different from anything of its scale or kind ever tried in metal. Conventional symmetric approaches were hammered into a bewildering complexity to mimic the sounds of rock 'n' roll. The metal had to have, in many instances, a dual curve to develop the intended form. To create the dual curve, a framework of custom cut and shaped aluminum frames were created into a panel. Figure 4.43 shows an image from the solid model that established the dual curving form. Almost organic in appearance, these frames support the final skin of metal that clad the Experience Music Project.

Metal sheets can absorb a slight degree of shaping before it buckles and warps. The edges of the metal sheet begin to crinkle as the dual curvature is induced. Thus the degree of the shape can be absorbed more effectively in several overlapping sheets, each with a degree of curvature, than a large sheet, much like the development of a curve from a series of small spline curves.

Each metal sheet, or skin, that developed the surface was cut from a rectangular sheet of production dimension. Each sheet was a trapezoid, rarely a parallelogram. Each trapezoid had a unique shape and bias on the building surface. The surface was generated from a digital model; the fabricator had to break the surface down to panels. Each panel occupied a specific space on the surface and

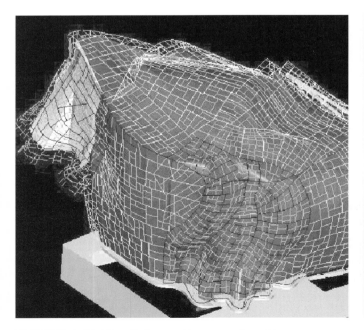

FIGURE 4.42. The Gehry pattern used on his Experience Music Project.

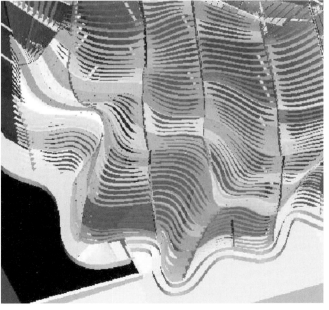

FIGURE 4.43. The panel support fin layout of the surface on the Experience Music Project.

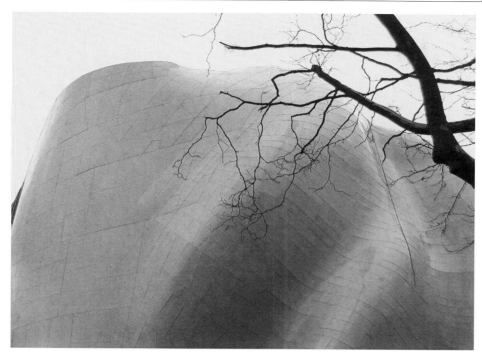

FIGURE 4.44. Flowing pattern on the "skirts" region of the Experience Music Project.

was made of several overlapping skins per panel. The end result was a fractured symmetry of interconnecting lines, interrupted by the occasional "peel" line. The peel line, as described by Craig Webb, one of Frank Gehry's chief designers, was a line that would be created if you were able to pull the skin back in one large section, like the skin of an orange.

To produce unique skins was difficult because, as one would set out to define the size of the sheet based on limits of the production sheet, curvature, and subsurface support location, one would subconsciously push you to a repeating pattern. It is just not a simple task to define unique patterns across an ever-changing surface devoid of flat planes and opposing corners—in particular, over a surface that covers 18,000 square meters.

A system of this nature with the ever-changing seam location and bias is difficult to waterproof. It can be constructed to protect the subsurface from radiation, physical impact, and wind-driven moisture, but water will still find a way in. It is very difficult to develop an ever-changing seam without utilizing a membrane or flexible seal; and even then, the possible breaches are enormous. Internal moisture control and venting is necessary to further protect the internal structures and fixtures.

Dimensional changes created from thermal loads on the metal are controlled within each skin element and then at the perimeter of each structural panel element. The thermal load would cause dimensional changes in the panel. Thus a tongue and groove system at the intersection was introduced. Figure 4.45 indicates this connection.

The overlapping skin elements that develop the visible pattern are such that the exposed fastener is placed into an embossed dish along the perimeter and

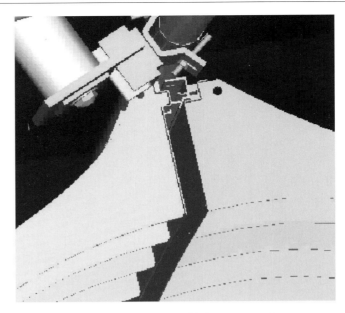

FIGURE 4.45. Panel-to-panel joint system to accommodate movement.

center of the skin. Similar to the skin on an airplane, the fasteners are located at finite distances from one another. The embossed recessed dish stiffens the skin at the fastener location. At the lap from one skin to the next, this embossed recess interlocks into a larger hole in the skin below. The larger hole allows the skin to expand and contract around the fixed point of the embossed recessed dish.

The skins are fixed to an aluminum frame. This frame will transfer the dynamic wind and pressure loads to the perimeter supports, but it must also

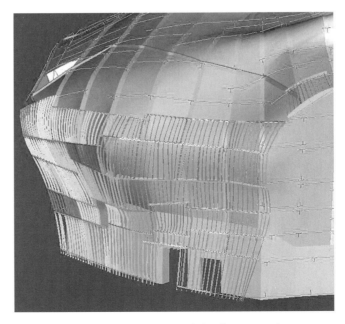

FIGURE 4.46. Digital image of the framework supporting the skin on the Experience Music Project.

relieve the stress created by dimensional changes in the thermal behavior of both the skin and itself.

What occurs along the sides of the panel, regardless of its particular bias, requires extensive dimensional control in the fabrication process. On the curved surfaces from one panel to the next, exactness must occur. The lap of one curved panel must be precisely that of the adjoining panel. If not, the seam will appear open and allow the panel element to be visible, which is not what the designer wanted.

To achieve this on Gehry's project, a digital model of the surface was created from the designer's model. The surface is actually a solid construct of digital information needed to define the intended surface. A relationship back to the structure was established to determine where the skin aluminum subframing would be able to transfer the dynamic loads imposed by the ambient. Once these points were established, the minimum size of the panel was defined. The aluminum frame, like the bones of a large vertebrate, would be shaped to precisely define the surface. Each frame member was unique in curvature, bias, and size. Figures 4.47A and 4.47B are of a panel set up in the shop. The panels were created by custom cutting frames, as described by the solid model, and then wrapped in thin sheet metal skin.

The shape of each panel was determined by a complex algorithm that took into consideration the surface at the particular location, the span from one attachment point to another, whether the intersection to the adjoining panel was an interlocking head or a floating jamb, the stress to overcome from the span, and the allowable clearance back to the underlayment. An engineer would review the computer-generated panel form to ensure two head conditions did not come together. A quick fit-up study was also performed digitally to ensure that the curvatures were established to match the designer's surface.

While this was occurring, another algorithm established the pattern. Guided by the designer's pattern layout, another engineer would place the pattern onto the surface containing the framing system. The pattern would be adjusted to

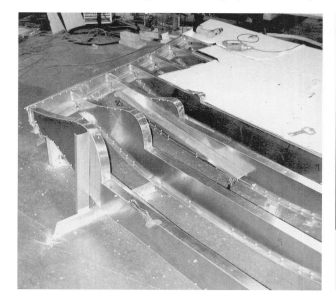

FIGURE 4.47A. Panel frame for the Experience Music Project in construction.

FIGURE 4.47B. Panel frame with outer skin applied.

meet the aluminum subframing, and the algorithm would place the embossed, recessed holes to match the framing.

Computer-controlled fabrication equipment would take the digital information and create the parts that would eventually be assembled into a panel. On the Experience Music Project, there were more than 3,300 unique panels with more than 20,000 uniquely patterned skins.

Gored Pattern

A simple pattern that is generated onto a constantly curving surface is referred to as a *gored pattern*. This process is similar to the way a pumpkin or a gourd develops a skin naturally to cover a unique curved surface. A pair of opposing poles is established, and lines are established between the poles on the curved surface. The lines fan out around the shape. These lines become the seam in the shape and establish the boundaries for the panel. Limitations are the production size of the sheet and the capability to induce a slight dual curvature in the metal.

A dual curved surface is one that has curvature in two directions, like the surface of a sphere or paraboloid. The curvature does not have to be the same and can vary from one location to another. A ruled surface is one that has curvature in a single direction, like the surface of a cone or cylinder. You can essentially place

FIGURE 4.48A. Pumpkins with gore pattern.

FIGURE 4.48B. Metal roof domes with gore pattern. Smithsonian Institution, Washington, DC.

a rule or straightedge on the surface and walk it around the surface. Like a cone it can be curved in one direction with a changing radius as you move down the length.

Gored surfaces are often limited by the dimension of the sheet that can be worked. If the size of the panel is excessive, additional seams running perpendicular to the polar seams are needed. This seam can be placed in a continuous line or, preferably, in the staggered format, to eliminate the four-way intersection. Using thin sheet metal, the polar seam can be a flat single-lock seam, a standing seam, batten seam, or inverted seam. The perpendicular seam can be a flat single interlock, a standing seam, batten, or single s type. If the surface is made from plates, the various plate joint assemblies can be utilized.

The changing radius of the surfaces on which these patterns are applied essentially go from a very low slope, almost horizontal at the pole, to near vertical at the equatorial region. Thus, controlling moisture out of the seam can be challenging. Generally, moisture is deflected at the longitudinal seams, with the upturned leg as the standing seam or batten seam. The inverted seam and flat seam control the moisture flow and direct it out at the bottom. Like the vertical running bond, moisture is tracked along the vertical seam. The transverse seam, when staggered, releases the stress buildup from thermal effects, similar to the horizontal seam in the running bond pattern.

The top of the gore pattern, where the surface is near horizontal, moisture control is the significant issue. This point is normally fixed, and expansion of the material goes away from the pole. Soldering or welding the joints can occur if this works for the design appearance.

The Triangle Pattern

The triangle pattern is often used on dual curved surfaces. A triangular shape intersecting other triangular shapes characterizes the pattern. The joint between the triangles is an open or a butt joint. Single-lock seams are not typically used because of the layering that would occur at the intersection of several triangles. A hierarchy is required to use the single-lock seam on a surface created from the triangular patterns.

One common pattern, the hexagon module, has six triangles coming together at any one point. Each triangle edge is curved to a particular radius. The triangular shape is less susceptible to local buckling of the thin skin. Shaping is performed on each edge separately, as if a cone shape is being developed over that edge. Depending on the severity of the curve, the metal develops the shape with little resistance. Often, simply curving an edge frame member and assembling with two other shaped edge frames will develop the shape. If the radii are large, the metal will lay over the frames without deforming. The sheet edges are cut straight, but when formed over the curved frame, they develop a curve that pulls away at the center. The joint between panels then varies, unless it is cut using other means than a straight shear.

On a spherical form, the triangles will have to change in dimension, depending on how they are applied to the surface. The surface should be clearly modeled to develop the various shapes required.

Banding

Creating horizontal or vertical banding on metal surfaces is accomplished by variations in color, reflectivity, or shadow. With any of the geometric patterns,

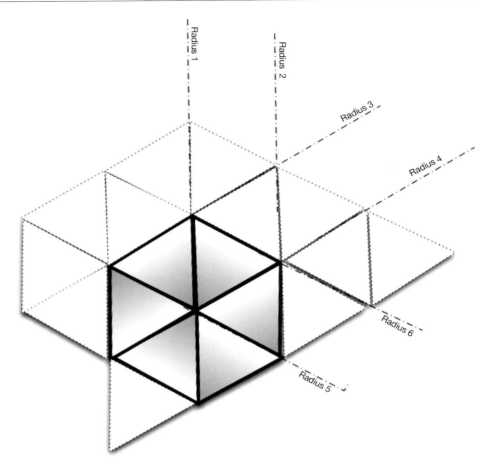

FIGURE 4.49. The triangle pattern.

altering color or reflectivity can create bold or subtle banding on the surface, as well as distinctive patterns. Creating reveals or offsets causes a contrast of shade that changes with light intensities.

Color changes in metals so far described can be achieved by application of paints or varnishes. These are somewhat temporary and do not involve metal surfacing. Color variations can also be achieved by using metals with different inherent colors. The challenge is when using metals with differing electro-potential (dissimilar) properties. Using metals that acquire color from light interference, such as stainless steel or titanium or anodized metal surfaces on aluminum, can be used without the concern for dissimilarity. Zinc as well can achieve various colors such as black and shades of gray. Panels manufactured from copper alloys can be mixed to create subtle changes in tone. Even as the patina develops, the alloying constituents create slightly differing colors. Table 4.3 describes the metals that can possess colors to create distinctive banding.

Changing the reflectivity by altering the surface finish can create distinctive banding effects. This is covered in more detail in Chapter 10. Stainless steel is well suited for creating contrasting surfaces because of its high reflective nature and its resistance to thick oxide development.

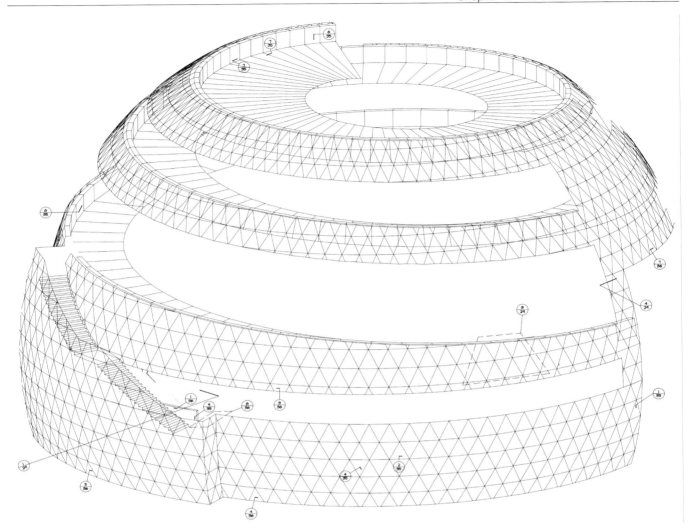

FIGURE 4.50. Triangle pattern used on the Tampa Museum of Science and Industry, Tampa, Florida. Designed by Antoine Predock.

TABLE 4.3

Metals That Can Develop Colors for Banding

Metals	Colors
Aluminum	Various anodized colors
Copper alloys	Subtle color differences from alloy to alloy
Stainless steel	Interference colors
Titanium	Interference colors
Zinc	Oxide colors

Horizontal and vertical reveals and offsets work to define a bias in the surface. Horizontal reveals give the illusion or add to the effect of length, as opposed to width. The opposite effect occurs with vertical banding. In addition, there is nothing to prevent horizontal banding of a surface. The challenges, for all approaches—perhaps more so for diagonal—is wrapping around the corners. Figure 4.51 depicts offsetting panels. This creates vertical shadow lines. This system was used on the Team Disney Building designed by Frank Gehry. Figure 4.52 is a detail of horizontal reveals taken around a corner.

On exterior surfaces, moisture will track in these reveals. As moisture cascades down a wall, various amounts will be pulled back by surface tension or be pushed by the energy from wind. As it collects, it will move through these reveals. Understanding the Rainscreen Principle is critical when designing using reveals and offsets.

There are an infinite number of ways to create a metal skin. However, the basic patterns generate from those listed. There is nothing to prevent the casting of plates or cutting of sheets to interconnecting fragments or a custom filigreed patchwork. All surfaces, though, must still create a boundary, a separation from one region to another.

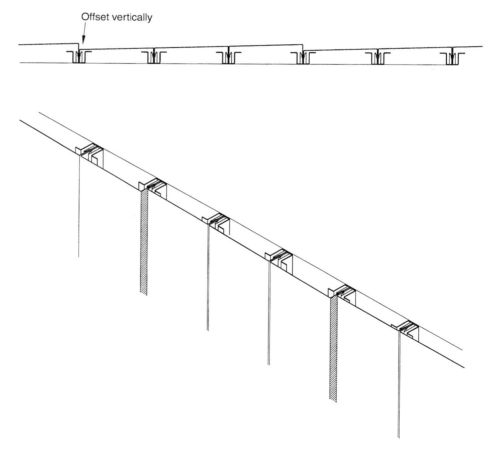

FIGURE 4.51. Example of vertical reveals.

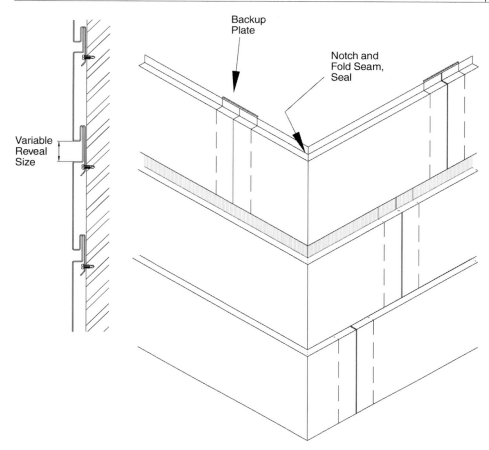

FIGURE 4.52. Example of horizontal reveals.

Moving in toward the surface, there are further ways of developing detail and patterning. The macroscale with its large visible definitions on the surface, the seams and joints between the elements that make up the surface, and the boundaries created by the edges define further the metal wrapping used to enhance our built environment.

CHAPTER 5
SURFACE TEXTURING: MACROSCALE

"I paint with shapes."
—ALEXANDER CALDER

The various patterns discussed in Chapter 4 involve the subdivision of a surface into various elements or panels. Functionally the subdivisions are necessary to accommodate the stress, movement, and constructability of a surface. Each element is bordered by a seam, edge, or transition that defines the local boundaries.

Within the boundaries of these finite elements, macroscale surface textures can be developed into a design. By macroscale, we mean a surface feature large enough to be seen from 3 meters. These include features that are not simply a texture, such as a surface embossing or polishing grit line, but features that actually protrude out from or into the surface that form an intrinsic design element on the surface.

Surface texturing by imparting relatively large features on the surface to provide detail and character involve moving (or removing) selective portions of the surface. Unlike etching or milling, whereby metal is removed, or embossing and coining, which deal with more microscale, surface texturing by macroscale shaping creates highly visible surface designs that add another dimension to the skin of an object (see Table 5.1).

There are various techniques involved but for the most part, macroscale embossing is a cold working process used on metal. The processes range from the very old techniques of hammering ductile metal by hand to modern techniques that move metal by explosive force into various die forms.

Creating three-dimensional forms by physically altering the surface is a unique art form. It is as old as metal itself. Gold and copper were some of the first metals, found in their pure form, that could be hammered thin into decorative objects. Moving metal in this way has roots in the art of Repoussé.

TABLE 5.1

Macroscale Surface Texturing

Macroscale Surface Texture	Constraints
Repoussé and chasing	Artistic, hand applied, to create unique and creative surfaces.
Mechanical hammering	Artistic, unique surface created by mechanical hammering.
Selective deep embossing	Artistic, unique surfacing or patterned grid surfacing. More production-oriented. Produced by machine. Various machine constraints.
Rib forming	Artistic or utility. Forming technique imposes depth constraints.
Wave form	Corrugated roll-forming constraints Brake forming depth and length constraints
Folded forms	Linear constraint. Must extend from one side to other of the sheet.

REPOUSSÉ AND CHASING

Repoussé is defined as moving the metal from the back. It involves the selective impacting of thin sheet metal with hammers and small-shaped forming tools called *punches*, which are rounded and flat. The punches come in a number of forms, often custom developed by the artisan. When the metal is struck with the tools or punches, yielding at the point of impact occurs and the metal shapes in the opposing direction.

Chasing refers to moving metal from the front side. Often, chasing work is performed on pitch beds. The pitch is moved into the recesses of the metal shape as it takes form, and thus provides support as further hammering occurs. Chasing generally occurs over a design sketched onto the surface of the metal.

The metal is stretched to varying degrees, depending on the ductility. Often the metal surface is worked from one side, then flipped and worked on the other. Repoussé, an art more than anything else, can achieve incredible designs on metal sheets. One artist or craftsperson on a single feature typically performs repoussé work. Copper, copper alloys, tin, aluminum, zinc, and gold are metals that are used by those who practice the art today. Repoussé is used on custom ornamental door surfaces, plates, wall coverings, and other small decorative surfaces of metal.

Once the metal surface has acquired the three-dimensional artistic design, it can be patinated to develop colors and hues. The recessed portions and the differential surface tempering that occur during the hammering process make for interesting, deep colors.

MECHANICAL HAMMERING

Born out of the repoussé art techniques, surface texturing by mechanical hammering can develop interesting custom surfaces. Again, hammering causes localized yielding of the metal. Covering an entire surface by selectively hammering can be an effort, but the result can be almost organic, like the shell of a large tortoise or the hide of a prehistoric beast. Refer to Figure 5.1.

The metal is often heated to remove work-hardening stresses that develop as the metal is hammered. Patinas or oxidizing processes are applied to enhance the surface. This can create a veinlike network of darker tones across the surface.

The mechanical hammering technique utilizes a rapid drop hammer device powered by a mechanical wheel. The speed and frequency of the drops are adjustable to accommodate the design and the worker. Surfacing elements are fed into the hammer and moved about to cover the surface. The part can be flipped to counter shaping that develops from one-side mechanical hammering.

The more ductile metals work the best, though stainless steel and steel can also be hammered, but with some difficulty. Copper, zinc, aluminum, and copper alloys are well suited for the mechanical hammering process.

Large surfaces will take time to produce. The smaller the hammering head, the more the part must be moved about to produce the hammered appearance. Thickness of sheets hammered in this fashion range from 0.016 inches (0.4 mm) to 0.06 inches (1.5 mm). Maximum thickness for steel or stainless steel is 0.024 inches (0.6 mm).

Hammering heads range in size from 0.25 inches (6 mm) to 3 inches (75 mm) in diameter. Larger hammering heads are possible but these take special equipment and require a very slow frequency of drop.

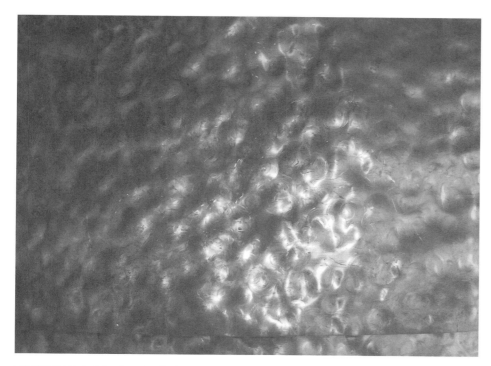

FIGURE 5.1. Mechanically hammered copper surface.

SELECTIVE DEEP EMBOSSING

A more rigid technique is selective deep embossing. Similar to stamping, the metal is passed through a set of dies to produce a deep texture by forcing isolated parts of the surface into recesses in one set of dies. The technique can be enhanced by application of Computer Numeric Controlled equipment, known by the acronym CNC, to position the dies anywhere across the surface. Producing textured patterns in this manner is limited mainly by the artistic ability of the designer; there are other physical limitations as well that will constrain this artistic ability (see Table 5.2).

Embossed bumps can be both inward and outward on a sheet. Refer to Figure 5.2. They can be one on top of another or they can be pierced through the metal to produce angle differences. Additionally, all these can be intermixed on a single sheet of material.

TABLE 5.2

Selective Deep Embossing

Constraints of Selective Deep Embossing
Depth is limited to 0.375 inches (9.5 mm), depending on thickness of metal.
Minimum spacing is restricted by a border around the die and the metal thickness.
Maximum size of any one embossed form is 6 inches (152 mm).
Tools and dies are created for a particular thickness of material.

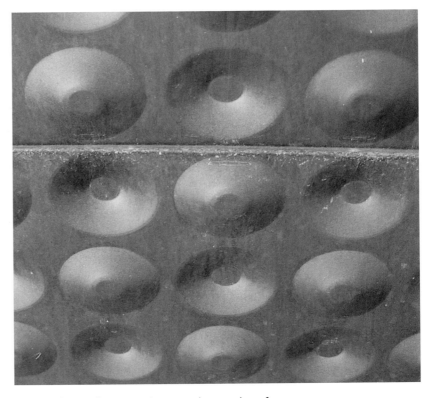

FIGURE 5.2. Custom deep-embossed surface.

Thicknesses up to 0.187 inches (3 mm) can be embossed. Embossed bumps are typically geometric shapes such as circles, squares, rectangles, or diamonds. Custom geometries can also be produced, and combining various geometric forms is possible as well. But because these are pushed by means of a tool and die, the geometry must fit within a circle of set diameter. Spacing of the embossed shapes requires an allowance for clearance of a holding die. The holding die fixes the sheet as the embossing tool pushes the metal into the metal die. The holding die is typically 0.375 inches to 0.5 inches (9 mm to 12 mm) out from the circle containing the die. Refer to Figures 5.3 and 5.4. Thus clearance requires the custom embossing to be no closer than this distance or you flatten the shapes previously pushed.

Edges of the bumps can be either hard, as if they were a metal plug cut out and applied to the surface, reference Figure 5.5, or they can be soft-edged, appearing as if they were simply rising out of or into the metal; refer to Figure 5.6. Altering the pressure and clearance of the tool and die creates this effect. Each tool and die is created for a particular thickness of metal. Changing the clearance allows the edge of the emboss to appear as if it were perpendicular to the surface or rolling softly up from the surface.

Proprietary methods can map images onto large façades by selectively embossing the surface. A design is created or a photograph is taken of a particular image. Next the image is converted to a raster pattern that relates to a controlling algorithm. Then the algorithm determines various spacing parameters, borders between elements, depth of emboss, and whether the emboss is inward or

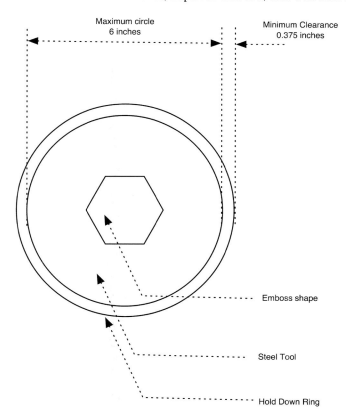

FIGURE 5.3. Maximum size and clearance requirements of a custom embossing tool.

FIGURE 5.4. Single-embossing tool for a turret machine.

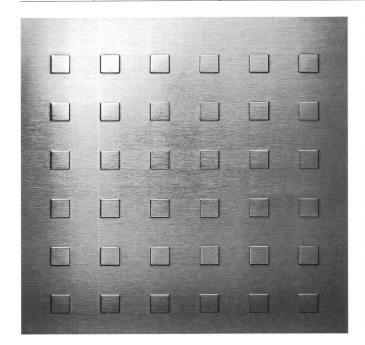

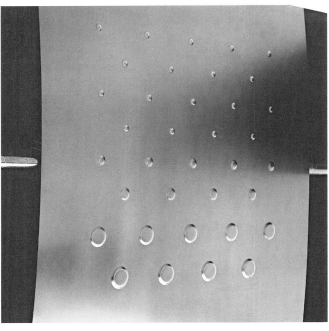

FIGURE 5.5. Hard-edged bump placed in a metal surface. Note the crispness of the bump edge.

FIGURE 5.6. Soft-edged bump placed in a metal surface. The edge is rounded.

outward. Finally, this is conveyed to computer-controlled equipment, which imparts the image into the metal surface elements. Images larger than 800 feet (240 meters) by 40 feet (12 meters) have been created in such a manner. The flexibility of selective deep embossing is enormous. Figure 5.7 shows a panel assembly used on the wall of the de Young Museum of Art in San Francisco. The

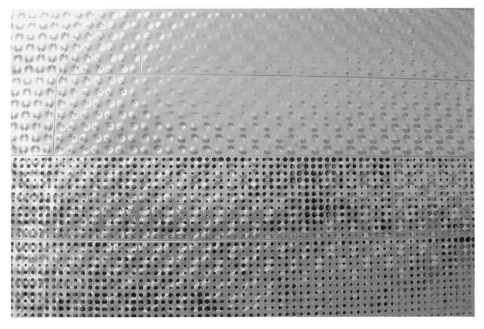

FIGURE 5.7. Custom-perforated and embossed design.

Museum designed by Herzog and de Meuron Architects used selective embossing to create the surface.

RIB FORM

Similar to the embossed bump is the rib shape. This surfacing feature is typically linear, but certain curved features can be imparted to a surface. They may be made to appear as if they grow out of the surface, beginning midsheet and terminating in the body of the sheet, or the ribs can span from seam to seam. Refer to Figure 5.8.

On large flat expanses, the rib feature can reduce oil canning by interrupting the stress in the thin flat diaphragm. Many premanufactured roof and wall panels utilize this characteristic in their products. By introducing a rib approximately of the dimension of a pencil running the length of their panel, they can capture the stresses in a surface and effectively reduce oil-canning appearance. The rib becomes an integral part of the roll-forming operation. It is created as a feature cut into the roll-forming rolls and, for the most part, cannot be eliminated without producing new rolls.

The rib feature can also be stamped or pressed into a thin surface, similar to the way a rib is placed in an automobile hood. They can be cast or milled if the metal surface is thick. CNC-pressing the rib into thin metal is also possible. This technique can even induce curves into the surface by essentially "rolling" the rib into the thin metal.

Ribs can be pressed into flat surfaces by press-brake operations. By using a press brake, the rib can be added to flat plates or produced as part of an assembly. The press brake offers tremendous flexibility in the rib size and location. Caution must be taken, however, when a cross brake must occur over a rib, because at the point of intersection, the rib will be flattened. Taking ribs around a bend will

FIGURE 5.8. Rib pushed into the metal surface.

require a miter, or allowing the rib to be flattened. If the choice is mitering, then a heavier thickness may be desired.

Curving of rib forms is possible. In effect, small ribs actually assist in the curving of plates. A sheet of metal with a rib or series of ribs passed through a set of plate rolls will stretch the rib form and induce a curve more evenly. Some flattening will occur on the rib, but only slightly.

Deep ribs that do not transverse the entire surface of the element induce differential pressures on the flat planes of the sheet. These differential pressures produce stresses in the thin metal, which will warp the surface element. Flattening processes such as stretching or reverse rolling through plate rolls can take some of this out, depending on the design of the rib and the metal. Stainless steel and titanium tend to warp more and are much more difficult to flatten. It is good practice to produce several test parts to determine the best method and appearance before proceeding on production runs.

WAVE FORM

Inducing waves into metal can be achieved in several ways. By waves, we mean any surface with curving features, which undulates inward and outward like the fold in a flag. Additionally, a "wave" is distinguished from a "fold" in that it is smooth and curvilinear as opposed to angular.

The simplest, most direct surface wave is the commercial corrugated form. Passing thin metal through roll-forming dies produces this form. Refer to Figure 5.9. Nearly all sheet forms of metal can be corrugated (see Table 5.3).

FIGURE 5.9. Vertical corrugated surfacing on the Gates Entry to the MIT Stata Center Project in Cambridge, Massachusetts.

TABLE 5.3

Standard Corrugated Depths

Standard Corrugated Depths: Aluminum, Steel, Stainless Steel
0.5 inches (12 mm)
0.87 inches (22 mm)
1.0 inch (25.4 mm)
1.5 inches (38 mm)
2.0 inches (50 mm)

Corrugations can also be pressed into the surface. This custom approach allows for more design flexibility. By pressing the waves into the surface, they can be spaced and altered in ways no roll former can approach. Where the roll-formed surface must follow precise dimensions, the press operation can space the curved corrugations out across the sheet, place them diagonally across the sheet, or myriad other possibilities. The depth, width, and bias of the corrugation can be altered during the brake-forming operation.

Casting of the rib forms from aluminum or copper alloys is another way to achieve this.[1]

FIGURE 5.10. Custom corrugated and perforated zinc panels.

---

[1] The rooftop lounge in the Peninsula Hotel in Kowloon, China, has a cast aluminum wall made to look like waves. Designed by Philip Stark, this fascinating wall appears to be flowing as a light source washes the wall. The light source is made of two (or more) lamps that alternate on and off. The effect is a wall of rippling waves.

FIGURE 5.11. "Wave" appearance created by selective polishing of the surface.

Again, like roll forming, the flexibility ends when the mold is created. You can only produce the shapes created on the mold.

Another method of creating the wave appearance is by polishing the surface with circular discs. Linear bands polished into the surface of a reflective material with small circular discs will produce the illusion of a three-dimensional wave. As discussed previously, the small grit lines will diffuse the reflected light. A series of altering grit lines creates the illusion of high and low wavelike features. Refer to Figure 5.11. This is actually a flat sheet of stainless steel with polished lines. The optical effect creates a feeling of a corrugated surface.

FOLDED FORMS

Folded forms are similar to waves and ribs in that they can be produced on a press brake in a number of different shapes. They must, however, travel the entire length or width of a sheet element. It is important to differentiate this form from a roll-formed wall panel by way of increased flexibility of design but with limited element size.

A folded form could be described as any shape you can create by creasing and folding a sheet of paper. A sheet of paper, like a sheet of metal, can be folded, flattened out, and refolded to produce shapes created from a series of offsetting planes. The folding adds significant section to the flat shape. Some folds can be curved, but because of the unbalanced section, curving is quite difficult to predict. Typically, folded forms interlock into adjoining elements or they are

FIGURE 5.12. Custom-shaped louver form with perforations.

FIGURE 5.13. Custom-shaped louver form sunscreen at the Children's Entrance of the de Young Museum of Art. Designed by Herzog and de Meuron.

stand-alone elements of a surface—stand-alone meaning their seams do not interlock to form a joint in the surface. See Figure 5.12 for a heavy copper folded plate form used as a shading louver. Figure 5.13 shows the louver installed.

FABRICATION TECHNIQUES

To produce these macro surfaces, specialized equipment is required. Perhaps more so, skilled labor is needed. Cold forming requires special control of the metal as it shapes. The CNC-controlled turret-style tooling is one flexible forming tooling device, as is a well-operated hydraulic or mechanical press. To achieve custom surfacing several specialized methods are available.

High-Velocity Forming
High-velocity forming is the supersonic movement of metal into a die. Basically, the metal is moved at such a high speed that work hardening of the metal does not occur. This phenomenon actually transforms the flat metal surface into a shaped surface matching a die. The die must be sufficient to accommodate the intense dynamic pressure without shattering, and the metal sheet must be of sufficient thickness to avoid necking down and tearing of the metal. Ductility is not a major concern because of the significant force involved. Titanium, stainless steel, aluminum, and steel can be formed using high-velocity methods.

The limitations, besides the very limited availability of such forming operations, is size of sheet or plates that can be formed. Thus, it is necessary to review with the forming operation what is possible.

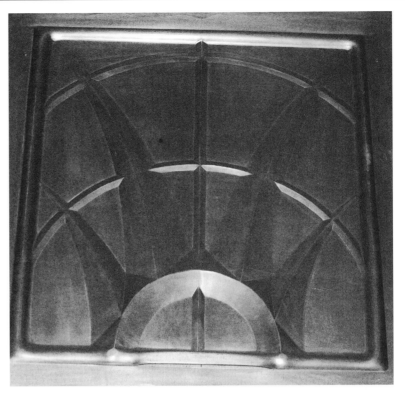

FIGURE 5.14. 1.5 meter by 1-meter explosion-formed panel.

EXPLOSION FORMING

Explosion forming is one form of high-velocity forming. In explosion forming, a die of sufficient strength is positioned behind a metal surface. An explosive charge is detonated, usually underwater. The detonation rapidly moves the metal around the die. The metal takes on the configuration of the die.

CAPACITOR DISCHARGE FORMING

Capacitor discharge forming, or electrical discharge forming, is another high-velocity forming method. This method involves passing a very high current discharge through a metal wire immersed in a bath of water. The wire vaporizes and the ensuing explosive force creates a pressure wave in the water bath, which pushes a metal sheet rapidly into a steel die. An incredible force is released by this method. The force is contained within the chamber of dies and water. The metal moves into the die at a speed in excess of 20,000 mph. At this near-instantaneous forming process, the metal does not undergo work hardening.

SUPERPLASTICITY

Superplastic forming is another method of shaping metal surfaces into intricate forms without developing cold working stress. It is not a high velocity forming method. This method involves heating the metal, usually aluminum or zinc, to the point at which the metal becomes plastic, which is just short of the melting point temperature. Hot compressed air is blown onto the metal and it forms over a steel die. The limitations, besides metal types, are size and cost of dies. Panel elements resulting from this forming method are very consistent, with no residual forming stresses. The panel assembly shown in Figure 5.15 was created by superplastic forming.

FIGURE 5.15. Superplastic-formed panels.

BLADDER PRESS FORMING

Bladder press forming is a process used by many aerospace companies. A bladder press involves placing the metal sheet over a low-profile die. The die is covered with a thick rubber sheet or bladder. A tremendous pressure, close to 40,000 psf, is slowly and uniformly applied to the bladder, causing the sheet to conform to the shape of the die. This forming method produces intricate shapes. Internal stresses can be present in the form but the tremendous pressure overwhelms most stresses that would cause the panel to warp. All sheet forms of metals can be formed in this manner. Die design is important to reduce tearing and necking of the part. Figure 5.16 shows stainless steel decorative panels with a small rib imprint created by bladder press forming.

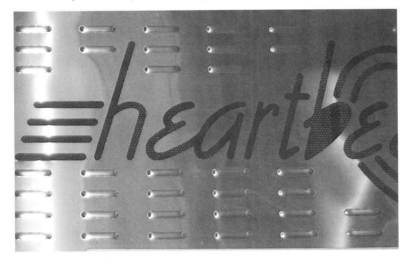

FIGURE 5.16. Bladder-press ribs into 14-gauge stainless steel.

As we move closer in, detail that defines the character of the metal surface becomes more and more evident. Seams break up the continuity both visually and functionally. Edges identify the borders of the surface. The performance of the seam and the appearance of the edges that make up a surface will galvanize the opinion of the observer. Special care should be exercised when dealing with seams, edges and transitions or all the surface embellishment will be without substance.

CHAPTER 6
SEAMS

" The devil is in the details."
—AUTHOR UNKNOWN

Smooth, flat plane, and curved surfaces can be produced from metal. But surfaces free of oil canning, smooth in appearance when viewed from various angles, and under different temperatures and lights are not common or simple to achieve. Such surfaces are made of finite units bounded by seams. Seams can be lapped, interlocked, or butted to create hairline joints, or they can be open to accentuate their appearance.

The seams that subdivide a surface, whether of metal, glass, or wood, exist because of limitations of material manufacture, stress, handling, or technical limitations of concealing the joint. They can also exist for aesthetic reasons. Seams are created to define patterns and are an intrinsic part of any surface.

Unlike human skin or the stretched surface of a balloon, metal surfaces must be created from smaller compact elements, or panels. In part, because the creation of such panels is from finite elements determined by the process of creating them, the seam on the surface defines a border from one element to another. It can develop a surface into a seemingly homogeneous layer where the seams all but disappear. An airplane or a ship is such an object, at once appearing as one large volume, but on close inspection is made of riveted or welded plates with lapping edges.

In nature, a leaf is made of a multitude of cells that each possesses a border. The border interacts with the next cell's border to form a structural diaphragm. The end result is one surface acting together to develop a form.

There are physical restraints characterized by all thin membranes. For example, human skin forms wrinkles and sags in areas of excess material or unsupported material. The same can occur with membranes of metal. Seams and joints are necessary to bridge across areas of excess or lack thereof. Seams take up the slack and reduce the effect of the thermal expansion. Where skin is pliable, stretching or wrinkling to accommodate, metal is not. It rips or buckles. Metal fatigues, it work-hardens, and can become brittle.

FIGURE 6.1. The intricate network of veins on the surface of a leaf.

CHARACTERISTICS OF SEAMS

There are basically three main reasons underlying the necessity of seams:

1. To accommodate the limitations of manufacture of the surface materials.
2. To reduce stress.
3. To account for physical limitations of the material making up the surface.

Metal surfaces, like most skins, are often required to keep moisture out or at least reduce the wind pressure carrying moisture into the system. The seam, because it is required to exist for the reasons given, must provide this function just as the unbroken surface of metal (see Table 6.1).

TABLE 6.1

Performance Requirements of a Seam

Performance Requirements of a Seam
Relieve stress buildup on the metal surface.
Control movement of the metal surface.
Control moisture on the surface.
Limit air infiltration through the surface.

Seams frequently need to restrict air movement as well as moisture. This is generally contrary to the very nature of a seam. They are gaps in the otherwise unbroken expanse. As a seam is a split, causing a breach in a surface, restricting the movement of air through the seam is a challenge. The solution is often left to thin flexible membranes placed behind or within the seam. Without a flexible material or seal connecting two adjoining plates, airtight conditions are not possible. Metal seaming cannot be made airtight and allow for movement without gasketing, sealant, or a flexible membrane. A tight folded seam, for all practical purposes, does restrict the movement of air to insignificant levels; but under relatively small differential pressures, air will move through the folded seam.

Thus a seam has to exist in a large surface because of limitations of manufacturing and material physics. The seam must perform as near as possible to that of the unbroken surface, and a seam must relieve stress buildup that occurs on a large expanse as thermal effects change the dimensions of the surface. Various seams used in sheet metal construction are shown in Figure 6.2 and described in Table 6.2.

TABLE 6.2

Various Sheet Metal Seams

Seam Number	Seam Description	Common Use
1	Flat-lock seam	Thin metal cladding.
2	Single-S seam	Thin metal cladding. Vertical or near vertical application.
3	Simple lap	Used with exposed fasteners or with other backup systems. Difficult to deter moisture.
4	Offset tongue and groove	Vertical applications. Good barrier. Can have capillary break as well.
5	Inverted standing seam	Vertical applications. Good barrier. Can have capillary break as well.
6	Recessed seam	Typically exposed fastener; vertical application. Sealant or tape often used to further moisture deterrence.
7	Standing seam	Horizontal or vertical application. Often double-locked for moisture deterrence. Thin cladding applications.
8	Double-lock standing seam	Thin metal cladding.
9	Spline	Vertical applications. Spline acts as a barrier. Exposed fasteners sometimes utilized.
10	Barrel	Used on thin, vertical, or horizontal applications. Can be developed into a curve.
11	Guttered interlock	Vertical and horizontal seam. Often used with a gasket to engage metal edges.
12	Inverted seam with drop/lock legs	Vertical or horizontal seam; heavy- or thin-gauge. Captures and gutters moisture out.
13	Butt joint with backup	Thicker sheet or plate. Vertical applications. Pieces are stud-welded to back side of plate.
14	Tongue and groove	Similar to numbers 2 and 4. Heavy plate often uses stud welding to attach interlocking extrusions.
15	Inverted seam	Vertical or horizontal. Thin or thick material. Internally guttered.

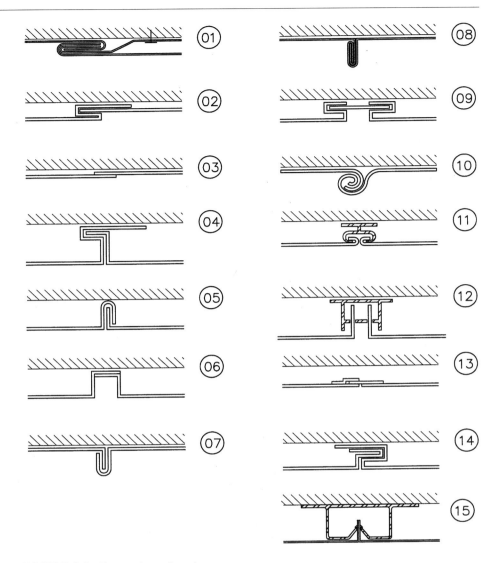

FIGURE 6.2. Examples of various seams.

LIMITATIONS OF MANUFACTURE

The seam provides an incremental approach to producing a surface. As with most other building materials—wood, stone, glass—the dimensional limitations posed by handling and production limit the practical size of the part. Even concrete continuously poured to create a slab must be segmented into panels, otherwise cracks will appear as dimensional changes occur in the slab.

With metals, the limit is in the form of production. The width limitation is dictated by the size of the sendzimir rolls used to reduce the thickness (see Table 6.3). As the cast block of metal is passed under pressure of the rolls, it spreads out and thins. This ribbon of metal is coiled and uncoiled as it passes under lightly polished cold working rolls, which further thin the metal. Thus, the first set of restraints comes at the mill where the metal sheet and plate are first developed. A large casting of copper, heated and ready to be rolled into thin sheet metal, is shown in Figure 6.3.

TABLE 6.3

Standard and Maximum Widths

Metal	Standard Width (inches)	Maximum Width (inches)
Aluminum	48	120
	60	
	72	
Copper	36	48
	39	
	48	
Copper alloys	48	48
Copper alloys—nickel silver	36	36
Lead	48	48
Monel	48	48
Steel	24	120
	36	
	48	
	60	
	72	
	96	
	120	
Stainless steel	36	96
	48	
	60	
Tin	36	36
Titanium	48	48
Zinc	39	39

STRESS RELIEF

At seams, structural continuity stops, and stresses accumulate or relax. Seams are a necessary feature for long-term performance and structural stability of all surfaces. Figure 6.4 shows an intersection of four panels on a horizontal running bond pattern. Each seam interlocks and overlaps. Thermal stress is taken out at these laps.

The seam in metal is where localized stress is relieved, or in some cases, accumulated. Often, a surface is designed to take the load imposed by wind dynamics and gravity out at the seam. Clips and attachment points back to the structure are conveniently located at the seam of many surfaces. This is because of several factors. As the surface is constructed, access is along the edges before the next incremental part is applied. Additionally, the edges usually are folded in some manner: a standing seam, a single-lock seam; all are folds at the edge. The

FIGURE 6.3. Casting of the initial blocks of copper.

FIGURE 6.4. Flat seam panel joint intersections.

folding provides an increase in cross section and thus stiffness, which better accommodates the stresses that accumulate at the attachment points.

Stress can be thermal or imposed. As the metal expands or contracts thermally, the seam becomes larger or smaller accordingly. As the metal is subjected to physical load, it moves. The movement occurs at the seam without transferring to the next sheet, plate, or form. Figure 6.5 diagrams how a flat seam panel system must expand and contract without restriction.

When the parts are joined, they move as a large unit. All connections and edges must move with the unit or stress will overwhelm the part. Each part should be pinned so that movement is controlled toward a joint. A bridge structure or a beam member has one side pinned, and the opposite side is allowed to move on a "roller" connection. Without this, it becomes an indeterminate structure with incalculable stress conditions.

Elongation occurs at the roller support side of a bridge. The expansion joint is integrated into the bridge surface at this side. The pinned side remains sta-

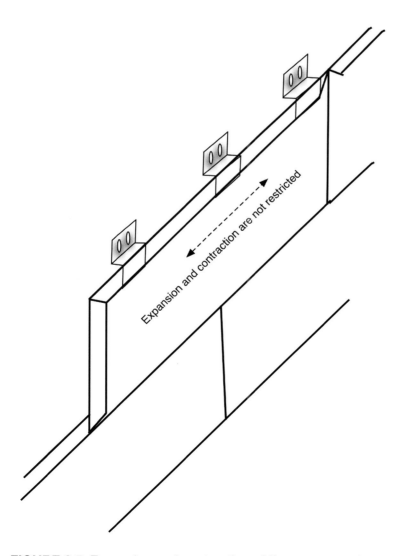

FIGURE 6.5. Expansion and contraction of flat-seam panels.

tionary at all times. This is the same for a metal plate or metal bar used as a load-transferring and load-bearing surface.

Movement in a metal surface can be outward as well. A curved surface, if pinned on all sides, moves in the direction of the curve when undergoing thermal expansion. Under physical load the metal may move opposite the curve and induce a deformation into the surface. Excessive stresses can develop if all sides are held. Overstress conditions from thermal expansion can build up at the points of connection if movement is restricted. A cylindrical water tank is welded as a unit, and expansion occurs across the entire radius outward. The thickness of the tank provides sufficient section, and the water in the tank reduces extreme thermal conditions.

Stress from Thermal Expansion and Contraction

The patterns created by the panel assembly of metal skins are produced by the propagation of the seam. The seam can be accented or concealed, flush or raised. Reduction of stress is accomplished by allowing adjacent panels or surfaces to expand or contract into or from the seam. This movement is generated from temperature changes experienced on the metal surface. For example, the flat-lock seam depicted in Figure 6.6 has the top of the lower panel, panel A, fixed in place by the clip. Thermal expansion of panel A is away from this fixing point. This point does not move or change its position. The opposite edge of the panel is similar to that indicated as panel B. The edge laps over and engages into the fixed edge of panel A. This engagement, however, floats in the plane of the wall. Thermal movement of the panel goes to this edge.

The panel, when warm, enlarges or expands slightly. This expansion goes to this edge and the panel slides over the panel below. The engagement of the edge must be sufficient enough to sustain the attachment. Otherwise, the edge would no longer be held back to the wall and would be subjected to wind loading.

Conversely, when the panel cools, it shrinks. If panel B were installed when hot and pulled tight into the single-lock seam of panel A, it could cause considerable stress to the joint when cooled. The joint may open from contraction of the metal. It is very important to allow for thermal movement in the seam. It is good practice to engage the panel, pull it snug, then relax it about 1.5 mm. This will allow it to both expand and contract freely.

All metal surfaces are going to thermally move, some metals to a lesser degree than others (see Table 6.4). Titanium has a very low coefficient of expansion, whereas aluminum and zinc are greater. Surfaces made from zinc, for example, must have seams that accommodate almost four times the thermal expansion as that of titanium.

It is suggested that all panels be fixed at two adjacent sides to allow thermal movement to occur away to the opposite side. A metal surface could also be fixed in the center along one edge, to allow expansion to occur to each edge. This would require careful design of the seam to accommodate the expansion of adjoining panels. As shown in Figure 6.7, sides opposite the fixed side must be free to move both away from the fixed point as it expands and toward the fixed point during contraction. The movement should be without restriction.

The fixing point must be rigid. If not, the panels will creep thermally, causing joints to tighten up in some regions and open up in others. When all edges of panels are not restricted, thermal cycles will move the panel to a new location until each cycle reaches some restriction.

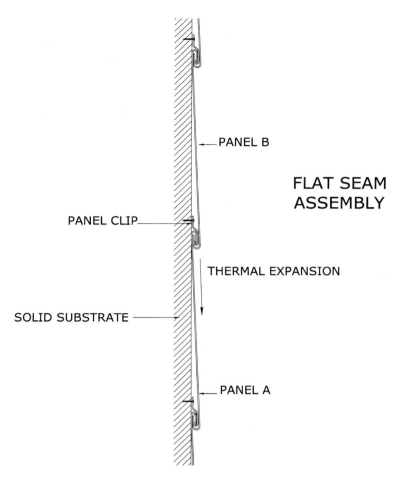

PANEL B

FLAT SEAM
ASSEMBLY

PANEL CLIP

THERMAL EXPANSION

SOLID SUBSTRATE

PANEL A

FIGURE 6.6. Expansion and contraction hierarchy of flat seam assemblies.

TABLE 6.4

Coefficient of Expansion

Metal /Alloy	Coefficient of Thermal Expansion (µin/in °C)	Expected Expansion (inches) of 120-inch Segment	Expected Expansion (mm) of a 3000-mm Segment
Zinc	32.5	0.15	3.81
Lead	29.3	0.13	3.30
Aluminum	23.6	0.11	2.79
Tin	23.0	0.10	2.54
Architectural bronze	20.9	0.10	2.54
Muntz brass	20.8	0.09	2.29
Yellow brass	20.3	0.09	2.29
Silicon bronze	18.0	0.08	2.03
Stainless steel	16.5	0.08	2.03
Gold	14.2	0.05	1.27
Monel	14.0	0.06	1.52
Iron/steel	11.7	0.05	1.27
Titanium	8.4	0.04	1.02

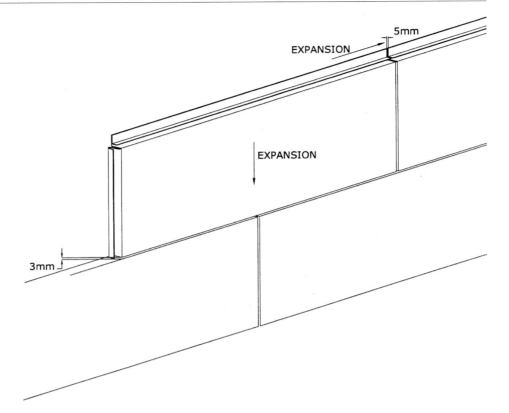

FIGURE 6.7. Thermal movement is toward and away from fixed points.

Do not construct the metal surface to require one panel to "push" an adjoining panel unless you intend on rigidly fixing them together into a single unit. Doing so will cause the panels to group up and possibly buckle in some areas as movement is confined.

PHYSICAL LIMITATIONS OF THE MATERIAL MAKING UP THE SURFACE

All surfaces, like everything else in the universe, are subject to the laws of physics. Thermal absorption, gravity, friction, elasticity, and inertia influence a surface and how it performs.

Columnar Effect

Large continuous surfaces, such as roof panels or wall panels, can experience a "columnar" effect as the expansion of the long length pushes against frictional forces that accumulate along the length. Consider, for example, a folded piece of paper several meters in length. The paper can be pushed along a smooth glass surface without deforming or buckling. But place the same paper on an asphalt surface and push it. The asphalt offers greater frictional forces, which resist the movement. The paper buckles because the frictional force between the paper surface and the asphalt surface overwhelms the shape and stiffness of the form. Make the paper form shorter and the frictional forces are reduced; the form moves without buckling. Even over the glass surface, there is a limit at which the friction between the glass and paper surfaces exceeds the strength of the paper form. If the frictional forces of moving it overcome the sectional strength of the surface, it will begin to show signs of buckling. The stiffness and cross section of the panel must be sufficient to supply the necessary force of moving under thermal expansion without overstressing or distorting itself. Like a column, individual elements that make up a surface must be able to support the loads imposed on it. Friction loads occur as the surface moves over the top of another surface. Gravity loads are defined by the dead weight of the surface. A wall surface, fixed at the base and required to expand upward, can experience loads that could exceed the cross-sectional strength.

One method of reducing these forces is to raise the panel off the surface of the supporting wall. This eliminates friction forces on the surface. It does, however, require a stiffer material. The seam is created in a deep section, which acts as a beam spanning between clips or connections. An alternative is to pin the surfaces at the top, allowing the expansion and contraction to go downward, thereby gaining the assistance of gravity. Figure 6.8 shows various standing seams that fix the metal panel to the substrate. The panel is supported from the standing seam clip. The standing seam gives the panel section properties to overcome resistance from the columnar effect.

On an open joint condition or one that has been sealed using a flexible sealant or gasket, the thermal movement of the panel is into the joint. The joint closes or opens as the thermal change in the metal causes the panel to increase or decrease in size. When the joint is tight and the panel is large, the geometry change of the panel can affect the joint appearance.

Oil Canning

Under temperature changes, the surface may show surface deflection characteristics commonly known as *oil canning*, a metaphorical term used to describe the

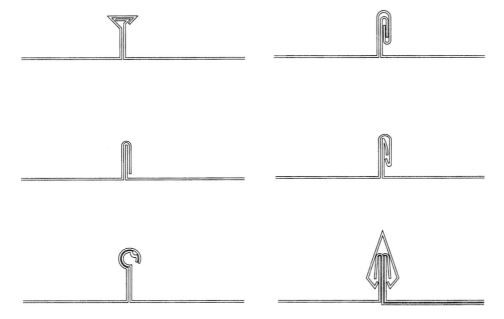

FIGURE 6.8. Various examples of standing seams.

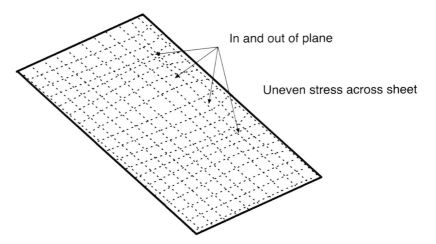

FIGURE 6.9. Uneven stress across a flat sheet.

characteristic of flat metal surfaces to show variations in relative reflectivity. These variations are caused by very slight undulations of the metal surface. See Figure 6.9. A surface of metal intended as a flat plain or a constant curvature can possess regions where relative variations exist or appear. These variations develop from differential stresses across the thin sheet of metal. Thin sheets are inherently unstable.

There are other factors that can lead to the occurrence of surface distortions known as oil canning (see Table 6.5). The process of making thin sheets at the mill—the reduction, coiling and uncoiling, and shearing processes—induce stresses into the thin sheet. These stresses are applied unevenly across the sheet or plate. Fabrication processes also induce stresses into the thin sheet. Fabrication equipment such as plate rolls, roll form equipment, and press brakes shape the metal by applying forces that must overcome the yield strength of the material. Such forming equipment will not apply the load evenly across the length of the metal surface.

To a lesser degree, additional factors, such as handling and shipping, also contribute. But probably the greatest influence are installation practices and design details. Installation practices that confine the edges of metal plates and

TABLE 6.5

Oil Canning Influences

Oil Canning Factors	Effect
Mill operations	Uneven stresses
Fabrication processes	Uneven stresses
Storage	Warping shape
Handling and shipping	Warping shape
Installation processes	Thermal movement not allowed for

FIGURE 6.10. Light oil canning on thin stainless-steel roof.

inhibit movement will create stress conditions that cannot be overcome by the stiffness of the metal surfaces. Movement is the result of thermal changes in the metal skin and physical loading of the surface from dynamic wind forces. These changes result in elongation in some areas and contraction in others. As the material enlarges, it can move in or out of the original position it was installed in.

Oil canning can be defined as uncontrolled distortion across a thin diaphragm. The thin diaphragm in this case is a metal surface. Thin is relative to the unsupported width of the sheet or plate; thus even with thick plates, oil canning can be present. The differential stress across the surface is induced into the metal sheet or plate during initial fabrication processes, subsequent final fabrication processes, and from handling and installation processes. To achieve flat surfaces, extreme care from beginning to end must be exercised. Figure 6.10 shows very slight oil canning in these large smooth panels created from the inverted seam system.

PREVENTING OIL CANNING

Preventing oil canning in a surface must begin with the selection and determination of the metal sheet or plate at the design and supply level (see Table 6.6). Use the appropriate thickness. The metal thickness will also affect and dictate the geometry of the seam.

There is a limitation to thickness, however. As you exceed 0.187 inches (4 mm) in thickness, for most metals, surface smoothness is limited. At these thicknesses, the metal surface is still greatly influenced by the hot rolling process. The hot rolling process leaves minute inclusions in the surface and can result in surface undulations from cooling of the plate out of the hot state. Cold rolling stretches the surface, elongating the grains and smoothing out the hot rolled surface defects.

TABLE 6.6

Mitigating Oil Canning before Fabrication

Source	Identification	Solution
Mill	Wave in plates	Cold rolling in pyramid rolls Stretching over block
Mill	Coil set—curvature along length	Stretcher leveling and tension leveling
Mill	Crossbow—curvature across width	Stretcher leveling and tension leveling
Mill	Edge wave in coil/sheet	Level and slit away the wave
Mill	Surface ghosting—coil splices, chatter, stop marks	Reject the portion where this occurs—it cannot be fixed.

Creating flat surfaces in metal can be a very difficult undertaking. Often the design requires a smooth surface, visually flat in appearance. The surface must be free of oil canning and so-called pillowing, both of which are visual surface-reflective distortions that are influenced by surface characteristics and inherent differential stress within the metal sheet or plate material. Thermal effects can also exacerbate the conditions.

Initial processes that need to be controlled begin at the mill, where the metal is initially cast. Regardless of the metal, the mill creates the initial alloying material and then rolls under pressure to the given thickness of the sheet or plate. The cast is a large plank of metal, generally several centimeters in thickness and close to a meter in width by several meters in length. As the metal is rolled under pressure to a thinner and thinner ribbon, the grains cool and elongate. The nature of the grain development across the metal creates local variations in stress across the metal plate. The thinner the sheet, the more passes under the pressure rolls. The rolls will have variations from the edges to the center created by structural properties of the roll. The center will not place the same pressure as the supported ends.

This ribbon of metal is rolled into a coil. Coiling of the metal also induces stresses into the metal. In this case, the stresses occur perpendicular to the grain. The length of time the metal is stored in this fashion will influence the nature of the material. The metal ribbon will often take on changes in the grain structure behavior.

BEGIN WITH FLAT SHEET MATERIAL

Flatness requirements of metal are necessary to achieve repeatable expectations in the finished product. Many products and processes of fabrication demand flatness as a criterion of acceptability and quality repeatability. New manufacturing processes operate on tighter tolerances and require the initial appearance to be flat, as do subsequent cutting and welding processes.

The flatness criterion takes effect at the initial coil and uncoiling process that all sheet material undergoes. Every metal sheet has characteristics induced from the initial casting and reducing processes. When the metal is cast, certain impurities remain within the alloy mix. These impurities are passed into the sheet when the cast billet is rolled thin under pressure. Each metal, when it cools, takes on a specific crystal structure. Metals are made of crystals. These crystals are rolled thin along the length of the sheet of material. These thin crystals are often referred to as the *fiber* of the metal, a metaphorical term used to describe the relationship of one portion of a sheet of metal with that of another portion. The fibers are stretched in different degrees across the sheet, and like the fibers in a matte they impart directional characteristics into the sheet of metal.

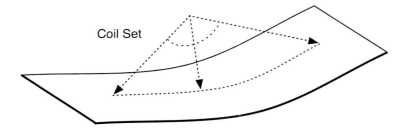

FIGURE 6.11. Coil set created by internal stress in coiled metal.

As the casting is rolled and pressed thin it becomes a long ribbon of metal with the fibers lining up in the length direction. When this ribbon is wound into a coil with a diameter small enough to create permanent curvature, the metal undergoes a permanent change called *coil set*. Refer to Figure 6.11. As the coil is unrolled, it will retain some of the curvature imparted by the roll. As the coil diameter decreases, the degree of coil set increases.

Uncoiling the ribbon of metal and cutting it into flat sheet lengths will result in small, curved sections with differential stress along the length of the sheet. The sheets may appear flat, but working with the sheet and the differential stress in the sheet will create difficulties in dimensional control. Oil canning conditions begin to appear before the product is even installed.

Along with coil set, another defect is often induced in the sheet of metal. *Canoe set* (also sometimes referred to as *crossbow*) is the surface-to-surface length differential that appears as curvature across the width. Refer to Figure 6.12. As the metal is recoiled on a small diameter arbor, the length of area will be less on the inside than on the outside. If the inside of the coil set is stretched along the length, it will shrink along the width.

Edge-wave is a problem in wide coils of metal. It results when the material along the edge of the coil is longer than the material in the center of the coil. Refer to Figure 6.13. Often on wide coils, the edges are trimmed. If you shear the sheet along the length, the outer edges will have longer material than the center. This defect makes it difficult to work with the material and will make it nearly impossible to create a flat surface.

All these conditions are the result of trapped stresses within the body of the material. Like hidden demons, they may not show themselves until subsequent processes or events occur. Even after the products are produced, changes in temperature can awaken these trapped demons and create undesirable surface undulations.

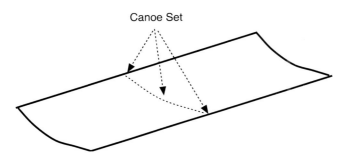

FIGURE 6.12. Canoe set created by internal stress from tight coiling of the metal.

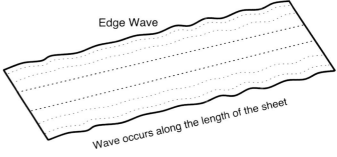

FIGURE 6.13. Edge wave created by internal stress from uneven pressure during coiling.

Often the problems lead to fabrication costs in the form of increased rejects or out-of-tolerance shapes. Stamping, bending, roll forming, and welding process are fabrication techniques that require stresses to be even and controlled. These processes can move the metal beyond its plastic range.[1] The metal can be elongated or compressed by stamping or bending processes that move certain areas of the surface more than others. Permanent shape change will occur, but often the internal stresses are trapped within the part.

The process to smooth out these sheets and eliminate the internal stresses trapped within the body of the material is called *leveling*. More specifically referred to as *stretcher leveling* or *tension leveling*, the sheet or coil of material is passed through a series of small rolls. To arrive at a truly leveled sheet surface, void of the internal stresses, the metal rolling must exceed the yield point in some or all parts of the material in order to permanently change the shape. If you merely bend the metal within its plastic range, it will spring back to the original shape once the forces are released. Bending past the yield point causes permanent changes in the material.

During this leveling process, the metal is passed through a sequence of alternating bending movements. One set of rolls bends the metal up, followed by a second set that bends the metal down; and again a set bends up followed by another set bending down. This alternate up-and-down bending of the metal over small-diameter rolls stretches the outer and inner surfaces of the metal sheet beyond the yield point. This process will stretch all the fiber from the outer edge to the center, including the neutral fiber, significantly beyond the yield point of the material. The end result is minimum, random, trapped internal stresses within the sheet of metal. Figure 6.14 shows an in-line leveling device used with sheet metal material.

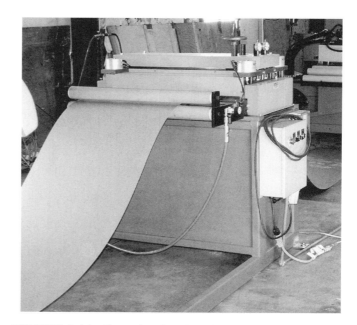

FIGURE 6.14. Stretcher leveling for thin sheet material.

---

[1] Plastic range refers to the stress/strain ratio graph. This is the area on the graph below the yield point of the metal. Metal can move within the plastic range without affecting change to its original shape characteristics.

This has to occur as the metal is taken off of the coil. It can, however, also be performed on individual sheets prior to subsequent fabrication processes. In roll-forming operations, this often occurs just after the coil spool and before the metal enters the first shaping roll. The more reflective the surface, the more even the slightest distortions will appear.

Sometimes these distortions are apparent in mirror surfaces, though they cannot be measured or felt. These are due to activities that occurred to the sheet or plate early in the hot-to-cold rolling process. Perhaps they are coil marks induced in the metal while the ribbon of metal is coiled and uncoiled. No amount of further polishing will eliminate these "ghost" effects. They usually are apparent only under certain viewing angles.

PILLOWING

"Pillowing" is similar to oil canning except that the former manifests in a more consistent distribution of stress across the surface. The term describes the intentional deformation of the surface. The center of the sheet or plate is set inward or outward of the edges, creating a smooth, but irregular, curve. The center of the sheet will be underdistorted by the confinement of the edges. Refer to Figure 6.15. The Frederick R. Weisman Museum of Art in Minneapolis, designed by Frank Gehry utilized "pillowing" sheets to develop the wrinkling effect.

FIGURE 6.15. Induced pillowing on the Frederick R. Weisman Museum of Art in Minneapolis, Minnesota.

The pillowing characteristic can be induced into thick sheets by rolling through pyramid rolls that apply pressure to the metal at different degrees across the surface. The stress distribution can also be such that the sheets can never be flattened entirely.

The best way to achieve the pillowing effect is to use nonleveled thin sheets of material, and form the panel into the configuration desired and pin the edges. The forming will create consistent stress points, causing the distortion to occur at roughly the same location on each sheet.

TECHNICAL LIMITATIONS OF FABRICATION AND HANDLING

The length limitation is dictated by manufacturing equipment and processes. Ignoring for now material physics, if roll forming is the process of creating the surface, then transportation and handling are the limitations. Many thin metal roofs, for example, are rolled at the construction site. Thus, the transportation process is overcome. Still, handling can be a difficult task as the team of individuals attempts to handle the limp "noodle" of metal into place.

In most plants, however, the fabrication equipment imposes limitations on metal sheets and plates (see Table 6.7). Shearing, curving, brake forming, punching, and presses all have limits imposed by physics, machine capacity, and floor space.

Brake forming, for example, involves the application of pressure to a linear die form. The die engages a metal sheet or plate of metal. The pressure forms the metal around the die, inducing a bend as the plastic limit is overcome. Pressure has to be distributed across a beam to induce a shape. These pressures may not be sufficient to evenly shape the metal. Thus, there are limits to the length of the die or press brake. These limits relate to the length of a piece of metal and to the thickness of the metal.

Larger sizes than those indicated in the table can be manufactured; typically, many smaller facilities do not possess the equipment or the knowledge to do so. Additionally, shipping and handling of thin sheets or large heavy sheets can be daunting. The ingenuity of many fabrication facilities can overcome the limitations of the equipment, but leveling, skidding, and handling of long sheets may pose the greater challenge.

TABLE 6.7

Dimensional Limits on Standard Fabrication Equipment

Process	Equipment used	Typical Length or Width Limitation
Folding	Press brake	3.5 meters length
Curving	Plate rolls	3.5 meters length
Punching, perforating	Turret	1.25 meters width
Shearing	Power shear	3.5 meters length
Cutting—plasma	Plasma table	3.5 meters length
Cutting—laser	Laser table	1.25 meters width
Cutting—waterjet	Waterjet table	1.25 meters width

Stiffeners

Application of stiffeners to the back, concealed surface of a sheet or plate will assist in flattening the surface and maintaining flatness. Stiffeners can be applied by using fusion studs or adhesives. Stiffeners work by adding section to the plate, thereby countering stress conditions within the plate themselves. Sometimes the surface is preshaped to control differential undulation of the flat plane, inducing a slight shape into the surface.

One less desirable aspect of stiffeners is that they can be thermal sinks. The stiffener will affect the temperature of the surrounding metal. On cool mornings you can read the stiffener locations behind the plates because moisture will collect at these cooler locations and form stripes on the surface. Additionally, copper, zinc, and, to a lesser degree, aluminum will oxidize at a different rate due to the temperature change and the moisture that condenses at these locations.

Stiffeners can also be more apparent as the sheet or plates thermally move. The stiffener restricts this movement, thus banding will occur from the in-plane, out-of-plane effect created by the localized oil canning.

Methods of attaching stiffeners to the back side of a metal surface are varied. Depending on the metal thickness, stiffeners can be attached by stud welding, adhesive, or high bond tape, or a combination. The minimum thickness that can receive a stiffener without reading through to the face side is 1.5 mm (14 gauge). Thinner metal sheet can receive stiffeners but they are more susceptible to visual read-through to the face side.

The approach to determine whether a surface needs to be flattened is to first manufacture a representative part from the metal intended. Then, install the panel element in the plane and manner similar to its intended final placement. Often, what appears when resting on a table in the plant may be different from that installed in its intended position. Review the surface visually and measure all noted distortions. Apply stiffeners to flatten the distortions, and view again, checking the dimensions to determine whether the stiffener succeeded in accomplishing a visually flat and smooth surface.

Laminating to Improve Flatness

Laminating the metal surface to rigid materials such as wood, honeycomb paper, honeycomb aluminum, or plastic can be a difficult prospect. It is better to consider tested composites with successful performance, particularly for long-term exterior requirements. The thermal and environmental exposures of such laminated products are severe. Metals move at different rates than the materials to which they are laminated, and this can shear adhesive bonds between the materials or induce thermal bend into the composite.

There are many composite materials available that have metal skins laminated to plastic cores, both solid and cellular; honeycomb cores of metal, plastic, and cardboard; and to a lesser degree, wood cores. These materials require a strong bond between the thin facing material and the core material. The core material provides strength and increases section. If thermal conditions are a possibility, both sides of the core must be laminated. Additionally, when both sides of the core material are clad with metal, the panel takes on structural capabilities. If the metal being laminated is not flat, or has internal stresses trapped within the body of the material, the lamination process will lock the stress until outside forces overwhelm the bond. The trapped stresses can work to shear the adhesive layer and the skin can delaminate.

When using an insulating material for the core, a phenomenon known as *thermal bow* can occur. A cold inner surface of metal and a hot outer surface can create differential expansion that will bow the panel. The insulating core isolates the two surfaces. Usually, a dark outer surface is needed to develop a temperature differential significant enough to create the bow effect.

WATER DETERRENCE

Water deterrence is a requirement of seams in surfaces used as exterior cladding. Most metal skins act as rainscreens. The metal surface sheds water without drawing water through the seam and behind the panel.

There are essentially five ways for water to appear on the interior surface of a structure. Each must be addressed to eliminate moisture occurrence.

- *Kinetic energy*: dynamic action of the wind
- *Gravity*: water flows downward, developing a pressure head
- *Capillary action*: surface tension between fluid and solid
- *Differential pressure*: suction action—lower interior pressure
- *Condensation*: moisture condensing on the interior surface

Wind can provide significant energy to droplets of moisture. We have all seen storms during which rain moves horizontally. The energy of this moisture can push it into seams and along seams. Wind-driven moisture can overcome significant barriers, splashing over returns and flashings.

To counter this energy force behind the moisture, there should be a physical deterrent to water infiltration. The lap, or interlocking edges of the panel-to-panel condition, must have a method of taking this energy out of the moisture. For example, a transverse seam on a roof appears highly susceptible to wind-driven energy. The first 180-degree hem abruptly stops moisture driven against this seam. Water may reach the second interlocking hem, but the first hem removed all the energy. The water then drains out at the edges over the top of the panel below.

Seams used on horizontal walls should also consist of joints that remove energy from moisture. Moisture driven by kinetic energy may breach the first barrier, but once the energy is removed, gravity sets in and pulls the moisture back out. Figure 6.16 shows a backup plate behind two thick plates of metal. If moisture infiltrates by capillary action into the seam it must continue around the plate to breach the wall. The backup plates should take all wind energy out, leaving capillary and pressure differential forces to be overcome.

Gravity, of course, keeps moisture moving downward once other pressures are removed. This can, in the case of wind-driven moisture, help. In other cases, gravity is the force that brings moisture into a surface. To overcome gravity, simply lap the systems to drain one over the other, and eliminate areas where water can collect and build up. Move moisture out and away in the most direct method available. Overlap panel surfaces in the direction of water flow. Create sloped drainage ledges that direct moisture out and away from reveals. Consider channeling structures that capture and direct the moisture down and back out exterior surfaces. Developing details that use gravity to pull moisture down and out as depicted in Figure 6.17 are excellent approaches.

One method of moisture entry into a structure is counterintuitive. Capillary action of a metal and liquid surface interface can pull water uphill. The phenom-

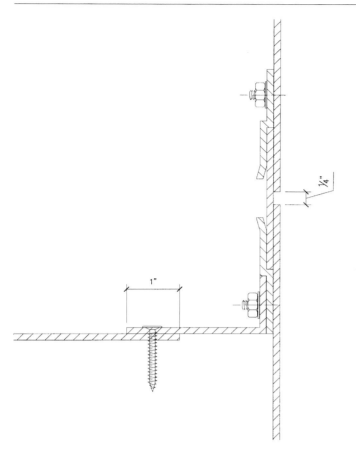

FIGURE 6.16. Horizontal interlocking seam with backup plate at the seam.

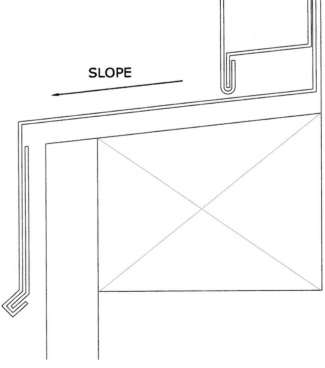

FIGURE 6.17. Sloping ledges allow gravity to assist in moving water out of a metal surface.

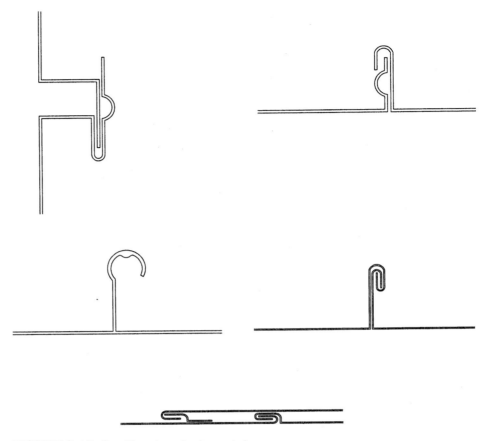

FIGURE 6.18. Capillary breaks in metal seams.

enon is attributed to the attraction of water molecules to a metal surface at close proximity. Capillary action will resist draining when the surface attraction overcomes gravitational forces. It is good practice to have a capillary break within metal-to-metal surfaces. Capillary breaks are simple enlargements of the metal surface. Creating the break allows the force of water tension to be lessened. As water moves through the gap, the space widens. This widening is like sucking water through a straw with a bulb in its length. Once water reaches the bulb, the force necessary to pull the moisture through the widened space goes way up. Thus, placing a bulb in the path allows gravitational forces to take over. Figure 6.18 shows various seams that incorporate capillary breaks within their design.

Sealants, gaskets, and other flexible substances can be designed into the seam as a physical block. Or seam geometry can be such that capillary action and negative pressures must overcome the force of gravity.

Differential pressure occurs when the atmosphere on one side of a surface is lower relative to the opposite side of the surface. This creates a force capable of pulling moisture on the high-pressure side into the low-pressure side. This can be coupled with kinetic energy, gravity, and capillary action to overwhelm surface seams and joints.

Many surfaces are tested for a pressure of 10 psf. This pressure corresponds to the force that 1.92 inches of water will impose on a surface (see Table 6.8). It is a comparative measure of pressure. The inches of water would correspond to how far water could travel vertically in a joint with the pressure differential of 10 psf.

TABLE 6.8

Corresponding Pressure and Inches of Water

Pressure (psf)	Corresponding Inches of Water
6.24	1.200
10	1.920
15	2.886

For example, if the design pressure head is 2 inches (50 mm), then moisture could travel vertically 2 inches within a seam. Thus, all flashings and returns within the seam must be greater than the 2 inches or the possibility of water infiltration exists.

Condensation occurs when warm moisture-laden air on the interior surface condenses on the cool surfaces of metal. Vapor barriers need to be established to keep this warm air from reaching the cool surfaces. Seams must not breach the vapor barrier. Figure 6.19 is an example where the cold regions on a wall may develop.

On most exterior wall surfaces, the vapor barrier should be located on the warm side. The point is to prevent moisture-laden warm air from reaching an area where the dew point temperature is met. The dew point temperature is where air becomes saturated with moisture and the moisture condenses as droplets of dew. If this occurs, water forms inside a surface.

As depicted in Figure 6.19, the dew point should always be located near the outside surface and well within the vapor barrier. Metal does not always cooperate, however. Metals are great thermal conductors with no real insulating value. Cold is drawn into the warm space via the metal-to-metal connections. Fasteners that enter the space, and seams that are in contact with backup surfaces, can develop cold zones that reach as low as the dew point temperature. Dew can form on these if warm air is allowed to come in contact with them.

The dew point temperature is determined by the saturation of moisture in the air. It does not need to be freezing for the dew point to be met. On days when

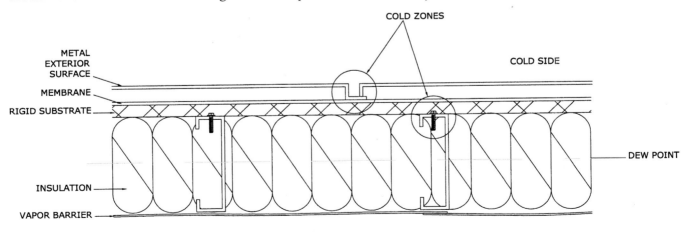

FIGURE 6.19. Potential cold zones on metal walls.

FIGURE 6.20. Condensation appearing on an uninsulated copper wall.

the humidity is very high, and on days when it is raining, the dew point temperature is raised. When this occurs, the cooler surfaces will attract and form moisture from the air.

LIMIT AIR INFILTRATION

Metal-to-metal connections alone are not sufficient to eliminate air movement. (The discussion on joint systems in Chapter 7 describes the use of gasketing and seals to create effective air barriers.) The metal-to-metal seam must be able to move and expand. Tight folds joining two metal plates greatly restrict air movement, but do not always accommodate the other requirements of a seam, such as thermal stress buildup. Metal-to-metal connections can remove the energy from the air but they will not be able to restrict the passage of air. This must be accomplished by the development of seals or the use of a barrier membrane.

CONCEALING THE SEAM

Darker metal surfaces conceal the seam or reduce its appearance by eliminating visible shadows and contrasting colors. Even lapped skins of dark, nonreflective metals will have less apparent seams. Butt joints that create hairline seams must somehow overcome the stress from thermal activity. Essentially, one could join the plates together to create a very large surface. The thermal movement could then be taken out at some defined region, such as an edge or plane change. The metal must be of sufficient stiffness to overcome the compressive stress generated by moving the mass to the joint. If the surface is curved, you can expect the movement of the surface to be in the direction of the curve.

The fixing mechanism must be designed and constructed to allow for this movement. The smooth, seamless look is a difficult appearance for large surfaces of metals. Eliminating seams or reducing their appearance to that of a thread poses challenges that counteract the physics and production limitations of the material.

A simple lap joint can make a surface appear seamless when viewed from a particular angle. Dark joint fillers or backing plates on dark surfaces will appear as a monolithic appearance when viewed from a distance.

Joining metal into large units, welding the seams, grinding, and final polishing the seams to achieve a massive monolithic surface requires precise and careful control of several variables. Shaped surfaces and curved surfaces can achieve large monolithic appearances somewhat more easily than large flat regions. The rougher the surface finish, the better. The higher the polish, the more visible the distortions created by welding and grinding. Figure 6.21 is an example of a shape created by forming and welding the edges of the stainless-steel form.

The steps necessary to make large monolithic surfaces with hidden seams begin with a near-perfect fit-up. Thick material, usually 0.08 inches (2 mm) or greater, is needed. The edges must be tight, and the finish surface plane must be even to the touch. Only the slightest of offsets can be felt. Separate the sheets and ease each joining edge by beveling back at a 45-degree angle. If a mirror finish is desired, bevel back only a maximum of 0.04 inches (1 mm).

FIGURE 6.21. Large curved column section with welded edge seams.

The two surfaces must be joined internally by welding or by an internal backup spline that is stud-welded to the base metal. The attachment must be sufficient to resist thermal movements induced during the final welding and finishing. Once fitted up, stitch-weld the face side together. Follow with rapid cooling to pull the heat away. Final weld is placed in the groove created by the 45-degree bevels. Use chill bars to cool the surface and draw the heat from welding out of the part. A fine weld, with very smooth edges, will achieve better results. It should appear as a thick pencil line, with no slag or splatter. The stainless-steel sculpture shown in Figure 6.22 was assembled in such a manner as described above.

The most difficult part of the process occurs next. Success is dependent on the even and clean removal of the weld down to the surface. On edges, you can block sand. On large expanses, consider covering the surface just to either side of the weld with heavy tape or even a piece of metal of 1-mm (0.04 inches) or less thickness. This limits the effect on the surface except at the weld. Use a thinner piece of metal or a tape on the next pass. The key is to take this down as finely as possible before you begin the final passes. If, when removing the metal back to

FIGURE 6.22. Large welded stainless-steel sculptural form.

the level of the surface, you overgrind the weld and create an indentation, it will be nearly impossible to repair. So take extreme care when you grind and polish down the weld.

Finish the weld down using finer and finer grit polishes. When the surface is even and level, look at it from various angles to determine if distortions from reflection are apparent. The area may need to be feathered slightly into the body of the part.

Finally, take it beyond the desired finish. If a mirror finish is desired, finish the surface polish with fine rouges. It may be necessary to finish the entire surface or at least blend to the balance of the surface.

Figure 6.23 is a very large intricate form assembled from large plates, welded and ground. The sculpture was designed by artist Shelly Bender.

FIGURE 6.23. Large plate sculpture made from welded stainless steel. Artist: Shelly Bender.

AESTHETIC CHALLENGES WITH SEAMS

The functional requirements of seams are necessary for any surface to adequately perform over time. Many of the requirements are necessary to meet aesthetic appearance needs, such as reduction of oil canning, reducing stress that can lead to deformation of the surface, and pillowing. Some additional challenges are listed in Table 6.9.

Dirt channeling occurs as a surface is washed over with rains. The moisture collects dirt and soot from other parts of the surface. When the dirt-laden moisture reaches a seam, not unlike a shoal in a stream, the dirt is deposited. These deposits change the reflectivity of the metal and show as surface discoloration.

Dirt channeling can be directed by design details such as extensions to produce drips and offsets that direct the moisture from the surface. Maintenance programs should be in place to clean the surface periodically, as you would a car. The more reflective the surface, the more this should be a requirement.

Alignment of the seams is a tolerance and quality control issue. As metals expand and contract, they may alter seam alignment, but the usual suspect is fabrication quality control or the tight tolerance requirement of the installation. Without an installation adjustment allowing for edges that develop the seam to be adjusted, the tolerance must be controlled in fabrication.

As the edges of an element are fabricated, slight deviations both in length and angle will throw off the alignment.

Visible seams demand that alignment be within 1 mm, (or 0.04 inches). This is a tight requirement and more objective than subjective, more dependent on perception and location. Quality control procedures that check the diagonal corner-to-corner dimension of a particular element should be determined and verified. Adjustments to the equipment should be made after reading the diagonal to take up angular differences or length dimension differences.

In all fabrication processes of surface elements, cutting and shearing the blank sizes is the first operation. Beginning with a blank that is not precisely cut and squared will lead to alignment issues in the finish surface. Most fabrication processes begin with an *origin line* on a blank and work from that. If the line is incorrect, all subsequent folding and bending will be incorrect. An accurately sheared or cut blank to very high tolerances on the order of 0.12 mm (0.005 inches) or better should be achieved. Most blanking and cutting tolerances are much more liberal, usually three times this amount. A qualified fabricator must recut to tolerance levels needed to achieve the quality alignment of the surface elements.

TABLE 6.9

Aesthetic Challenges with Seams

Challenge	Cause
Dirt channeling	Offsets that collect dirt and soot
Alignment	Tolerances of fabrication and installation
Shadowing	Wavering edge
Rounding	Fold is not sharp

Shadowing is related to the alignment of the seam. If the edges waver in and out as it overlaps another element, or if it does not align with the plane of the adjoining element, shadowing under certain light conditions can overemphasize the edge. This can also be introduced by pillowing that occurs along the edges caused by changes in dimension due to thermal changes. Typically, however, it is due to tolerance issues in fabrication.

This wavering aspect may be a product of the softness of the metal used, such as lead or thin copper. It can be a preferred appearance achieved by the soft undulation of the surface, or it can be introduced from the edge fold performed by the fabrication equipment.

Rounding of the edge happens with thick material or from equipment not powerful enough to shape the metal. Often, hand brakes are used to create custom elements in the field. Hand brakes have limitations in the forming of certain metals and certain thicknesses (see Table 6.10). Power-assisted equipment such as hydraulic shears and press brakes can overcome the plastic limits on most metals.

The edges created by power-assisted equipment are accurate and straight. Hand brakes lack the power to evenly distribute the forces across the edge. Field-formed edges often look rounded and less precise than shop-formed edges, and the seams these create are not as precise.

When placed next to or near power-formed seams, they will stand out and appear poorly crafted.

Aesthetic issues with surfaces tend to concentrate on seams, edges, and transitions. The eye defines the surface shape and dimension by these features. Thus, it should be these regions that receive the greatest amount of attention when developing surfaces of metal.

TABLE 6.10

Maximum Thicknesses to Consider Field Forming

Metal	Maximum Thickness to Be Formed Using Hand Equipment
Aluminum	0.032 inches
Copper	0.024 inches (16 ounces)
Copper alloys	0.024 inches
Iron/steels	0.024 inches (24 gauge)
Monel	0.024 inches
Stainless steel	0.019 inches (26 gauge)
Titanium	0.016 inches

CHAPTER 7
JOINT SYSTEMS: GASKETS, SEALS, AND INTERLOCKS

"Everything in the universe goes by indirection. There are no straight lines."

— RALPH WALDO EMERSON

The joint between metal elements is a critical aspect in the functional performance of a metal surface. The joint is a subset of the seam; specifically, it is the part of a seam that joins the two elements together. The joint assembles finite units into a larger interrelated surface, and often it must transfer the load from the surface back to the structure or to adjoining elements.

Moreover, the joint between elements of a surface exposed to the ambient often is called on to function as a restriction to air and moisture infiltration. As such, the joint must accommodate movement as the metal expands and contracts. The materials commonly used include flexible gaskets, sealants, and interlocking configurations of metal.

GASKETS

Flexible materials introduced to the seam must be able to expand and contract with the metal without splitting or opening. One such material commonly used is a gasket. Gaskets are often held in place via friction or by a groove interlock. They are extruded through dies to arrive at accurate shapes that can be interfaced with aluminum or formed steel configurations. The groove interlock can be seen in Figure 7.1. The aluminum extrusion and neoprene gasket are designed to fit together.

Gaskets work best in one-way relationships with metal. Intersections require special vulcanized moldings or adhesives. Gaskets often have reduced performance when bends are required. Gaskets also can "creep": as the metal they are attached to expands and contracts thermally, the gaskets also move, but at differing rates. They can bind and not return to their original position. If the gaskets are not held at the ends, they will "walk" along the groove. Furthermore,

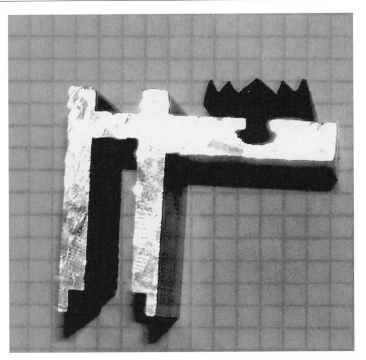

FIGURE 7.1. Aluminum-to-neoprene gasket assembly.

gaskets can, over time, with exposure to ultraviolet radiation, deteriorate to the point at which their performance is reduced, particularly the neoprene rubber gaskets. The material hardens, losing flexibility and with it the capability to provide a complete seal. Silicone gaskets have a better performance life and should be used whenever moisture penetration is critical and ultraviolet exposure occurs. Figures 7.2A and 7.2B are details from a glass to metal interface. Several bulb type silicone gaskets are placed to allow movement between the metal and glass assemblies. A wet seal is used at the perimeter of the glass.

Designs using wiper gaskets or bulb-shaped gaskets perform best and offer good shape-retention characteristics. Gaskets should be designed to block moisture from entering the seam; and in the event of entry, the gasket should remove the energy of the moisture. By reducing the energy of the moisture, gravity can take effect. The joint design should benefit from this and remove the water from the seam before it can infiltrate the wall. Double-gasketed seams can provide this feature. Refer to Figure 7.3A. A second gasket will restrict water passing the first gasket. Wind-driven moisture loses its energy as it passes the first gasket. The second gasket then captures the water and allows gravity to drain it out.

Other gaskets are used as compression seals. They are placed between two metal assemblies and compressed as the metal is joined. Refer to Figures 7.3B and 7.3C. The gaskets compress and seal the edges around the metal, preventing moisture from entering. Often they will have grooves on one side, which trap air as the gasket is compressed. This air is then held under pressure and resists moisture and air infiltration under the gasket.

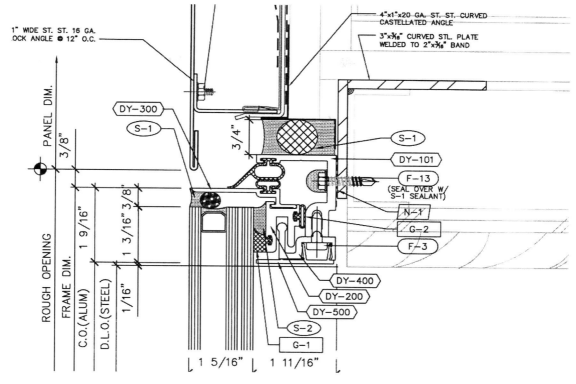

(A)

(B)

FIGURE 7.2A, B. Examples of metal-to-glass gasket and silicone seals.

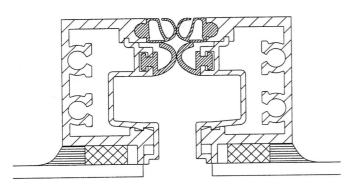

FIGURE 7.3A. Double-gasketed vertical joint.

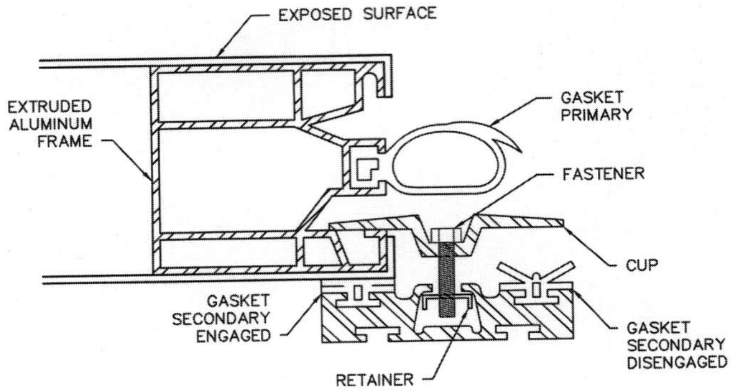

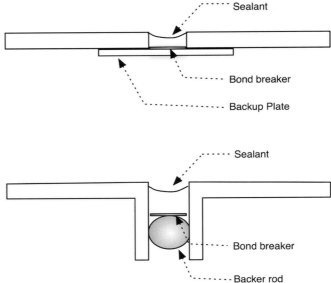

FIGURE 7.3B. Double gasket system—unengaged.

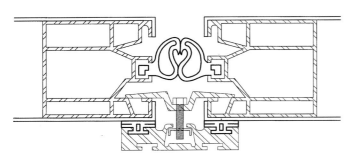

FIGURE 7.3C. Double gasket system—engaged.

FIGURE 7.3D. Sealant joints with bond breaker.

Gaskets are available in various densities called *durometer*[1]. Some are available in multiple durometers. It is critical to arrive at the proper density, to ensure the gasket has enough stiffness to hold its form yet still be flexible enough to maintain its resilience as it undergoes changes. When designing custom gaskets, various durometers can be extruded to test out the expected performance.

SEALANTS

A very common material used to join metal elements together is sealant. Sealants are elastomeric compounds that are delivered in a viscous form into the seam

---

[1] Durometer is the apparatus used to measure the hardness of rubbers and plastic. The testing is also known as the Rockwell Hardness Test. It essentially measures the resistance toward indentation and arrives at an empirical value. The value does not correlate with other properties or characteristics of the material being tested.

between two metal surfaces. Often referred to as *caulk*, sealant provides a flexible waterproof barrier along the seams on a surface. A typical sealant joint set between two metal elements is shown in Figure 7.23D. The first detail is of the edge of the metal and the second is when a backer rod is used.

Sealants have variable degrees of effectiveness when incorporated into sheet metal joints. Sealants offer flexibility; they can be joined around corners and eliminate joints in gaskets. Sealants also can provide for the three- and four-way joint intersection to create a continuous flexible membrane around the metal edges. Sealants can join dissimilar materials. Additionally, properly installed sealants can provide good air barriers.

Sealant applied into interlocking seams will develop barriers to moisture penetration and air infiltration. These joints conceal the sealant and offer protection from radiation; however, they make it difficult or impossible to inspect, repair, and rework. These sealants are usually factory-applied into the interlocking mechanism. Such sealants must stay partially fluid for long periods of time to enable the transport and storage of the material until they are installed.

Sealants can be messy and expensive. Typically, they are the first choice for repairing metal surfaces that have allowed moisture into the walls or roofs. Sealants, exposed on the surface, collect dirt and dust from the air. During rains, this dirt can be distributed to the metal surface adjacent to the sealant joint. With reflective metal surfaces and light-colored metal surfaces. this can be a major aesthetic issue.

There are various types of sealants, each offering different attributes. Some sealants are available in colors; others are limited to only a few colors (see Table 7.1). Silicones, as in gaskets, offer some of the best sealant types. Though difficult to apply, silicones provide long-term performance. Some silicone types offer high bonding strength and are used as joining compounds to fix metal to metal or glass to metal.

Proper sealant application requires the surface to be clean and dry. A wipedown of the joint with denatured alcohol prior to applying the sealant to remove fingerprints and light soils is standard practice. The use of bond breakers within the joint is a requirement of long-term performance. Bond breakers are

TABLE 7.1

Sealant Types

Sealant Type	Attributes	Disadvantages
Silicone	Excellent adhesion and long-term durability; excellent flexibility. Some have good structural attributes.	Limited colors. Requires more skill to apply. Difficult to clean.
Urethanes	Good adhesion, performance, and flexibility. Available in colors.	Difficult to clean. Color fades.
Acrylics	Good adhesion and performance. Available in colors.	Not as flexible. Loss of resiliency after several years of exposure.
Butyl	Inexpensive; easy to apply and clean. Available in colors.	Short life span. Loses flexibility.

tapes that provide a surface for the sealant but do not bond with it. The bond is made only to the face or edge of the opposing metal surfaces.

Most sealant manufacturers will perform adhesion tests to ensure their sealant can achieve sufficient bond to the metal surface. It is good practice to submit a sample of the metal and request adhesion tests from the manufacturer. It in turn will supply recommended procedures with the sealant selection.

DRY JOINT SYSTEMS

Dry joint systems are open joints, which allow water to enter between the panels but then gutter the water out of the system. Gasketed joints are essentially dry joint systems, but here they refer to metal joint systems without sealant and without gasketing. Consider the joint system shown in Figure 7.4. No sealant is used in either the vertical or horizontal joint.

Dry joints can be considered as rainscreens, that is, as surfaces that screen the structural surface from rains by reducing pressures that will allow the water to be driven back behind the panel. In essence, these systems "breathe." They allow air to the back side of the panel.

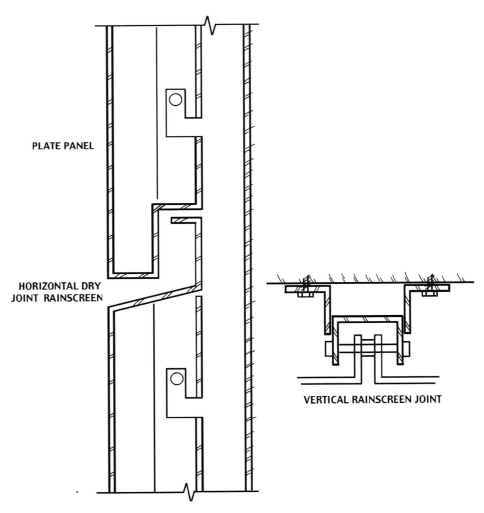

PLATE PANEL

HORIZONTAL DRY
JOINT RAINSCREEN

VERTICAL RAINSCREEN JOINT

FIGURE 7.4. Example of pin joint—pressure equalized system.

Dry joint systems are clean systems; they allow rain to pass freely over the surfaces without trapping dirt and soot. Washing patterns across the surface are not obstructed, and sealant does not collect dirt and redeposit it onto the face of the metal.

Dry joint systems are best developed with thicker materials. Thin panels can flutter as the pressures change, causing the fixing points to fatigue or disengage from geometry change.

On thin materials, interlocking joints are preferred. Such joints deter moisture from entering, and can be considered dry joints because of the lack of sealant at the joint. Interlocking joints are not airtight, but their geometry keeps them moisture-free by including a metal obstruction within the joint. This obstruction allows gravity to pull the moisture out of the joint.

Spline Type Joint

Spline joints provide a barrier to moisture and the kinetic energy behind the moisture. They offer a method of attachment to the supporting structure by fastening through the spline or by using the spline to conceal the fastener. The spline connection is a dry joint system, used mainly on flat plane surfaces. It can, however, be used as a backup, behind a wet (sealant) system where a bond breaker tape is placed over the spline. Spline joints do not restrict thermal expansion movement of the metal skin. They can be of contrasting colors to accent the joint or to match the surface metal color.

Surfaces held with spline joints are removable, by cutting them out. Reinstallation requires a modification using a clip and a false spline cover. Spline joints can occur on all sides or they can be coupled with other types of joint systems. The spline joint works best vertically, when used as a weather seam. A horizontal spline can trap and channel moisture into the wall. Refer to Figure 7.5.

Pin-Held System

The pin-held system, more commonly used in Europe, is best suited for wall cladding. This system is limited to heavy-gauge thickness materials because of the potential for rollover of the attachment leg. Another potential drawback of the pin-held system is the visual appearance of joint: the pin is visible through the joint—though it is recessed, and if dark will disappear into the shadow of the reveal. Also, it can be concealed by placing a folded metal channel over the reveal.

The pin-held system requires accurate layout of the pin location with that of the slots on the panels. The pins are spaced to match the slots and occur within a gutter channel. The gutter channel is anchored to the structure and spaced to receive the panel. The gutter channel catches moisture entering the joint and

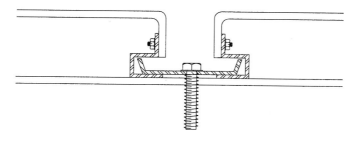

FIGURE 7.5. Example of spline joint—heavy thickness metal.

directs it to a place where it is removed from the wall. The pins must be of sufficient strength to overcome bending and shear loads. There also should be a method of fixing the panel against coming off the pins. Pinning one of the seams where expansion and contraction will not occur or installing a spacer that clips over the pins concealing them can accomplish fixing of the panel.

To eliminate rattling, a hard plastic ring is inserted around the pin. This can also be incorporated into the locking device to keep the panel from disengaging from the pins and aiding in the spacing of the panel elements. This pin-and-gutter system must run vertically and the panel must be able to rise up and drop down to engage on the pin. The panel will be dead-loaded on one of the pins, with expansion and contraction being away from this point. The capture slot at the pin must be designed to allow for the expansion without coming off the pin.

The pin-held joint is used on two opposite sides of a panel element, with the other seams being another form. The shingled rainscreen joint works well with this joint. Water running across the joint is drained into the gutter channels. An example of the pin-held joint is shown in Figure 7.4.

Drop-and-Lock Seam and Joint

The drop-and-lock seam and joint uses a series of integral connecting tabs to fix the metal surface to an internal channel. Moisture that breaches this dry joint system is captured or deflected by the internal gutter channel. The channel directs the water out at the base or into another trough, similar to the pin-held joint.

The drop-and-lock system can be used on either walls or roof surfaces, and has been shown to perform well in low slope conditions. It is a dry-joint system, but it can be augmented with a gasket or sealant. Similar to the pin-held joint, the integral tabs must be designed and located accurately to dead-load on one set of tabs and expand the opposite direction. The interlock of the taps must be sufficient to accommodate the maximum expected expansion of the surface without disengaging. As with the pin-held joint, the drop-and-lock system requires the panel to move up-in and then down for engagement. The drop-and-lock system is used on two opposing sides, with the other sides being another joint system, such as a flat seam or rainscreen shingle lap.

FOLDED/INTERLOCKING JOINTS

Folded and interlocking seams are commonly used on thin sheet metalwork. The folded seam is created in one of the following ways:

■ Mechanically folded in the field during installation from flat sheet or coil
■ Partial folded in the plant facility and finish-folded in the field
■ Folded entirely in the plant and interlocked in the field

Folded and interlocking seams have been in use by the sheet metal trade for centuries. This type of joint used on thin sheet metal surfaces will effectively shed water. The assembly of two metal skins creates an obstruction to moisture and wind while allowing the surface to thermally move. Properly constructed, they do not require sealant or gasketing.

Standing Seam and the Transverse Seam

The standing seam is a joint commonly used to interlock two thin metal panels. Used predominantly on roofs, the standing seam raises the joint between two

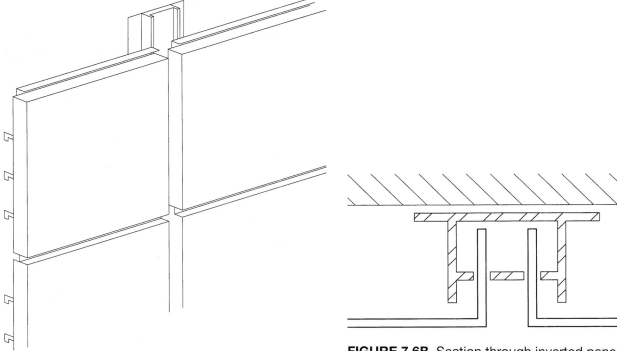

FIGURE 7.6A. Gutter at inverted panel joint.

FIGURE 7.6B. Section through inverted panel joint and gutter.

metal surfaces upward, off the surface where water will flow. This joint, as discussed in the section on vertical running bond patterns in Chapter 4, is the location where moisture will track. It forms the continuous line that directs water down a surface. If, in the case of a flat seam, it were to reside in the plane where moisture travels, water would accumulate. Thus, raising it off the surface drastically improves its performance. The standing seam can be curved along the length and, with difficulty, against the length. The surface must be stretched which will damage soft finishes and mar reflective ones. Figure 7.7 depicts several standing seam forms.

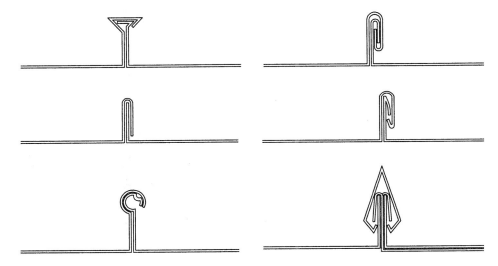

FIGURE 7.7. Various standing seam forms.

In contrast, the transverse, or horizontal, joint, which sets down on the surface, sheds water by the rainscreen shingle effect. On a standing-seam roof panel, the transverse seam is often assumed to be a potential problem, when in fact, if constructed correctly, it affords certain long-term benefits while keeping water outside the surface. Water does not track along this seam; rather, water cascades over the surface. The folded seam and the interlock effectively divert water back onto the surface. Figure 7.8 shows a detail of a transverse seam occurring between standing seams. The transverse seams are staggered from one panel to the next.

The transverse seam allows the roof to thermally move, thereby reducing stress in the roof pan. This prevents stress corrosion cracking behavior from developing. The seam is a single-lock seam and acts similar to that of the flat seam on a wall. There is some concern regarding the junction of the flat seam to the standing seam: because of its construction, two small pinholes exist where moisture can penetrate. Placement of silicone or solder or other sealant before applying the top sheet will close the hole and afford a watertight seam.

It's also important to note that a full cleat performs better than small, intermediate cleats. The full cleat, one that extends from standing seam to standing seam, offers further restriction to moisture. A simple test of both types will prove this out. Apply water to the seam using pressure. Pull the seam apart and examine the underlayment. The continuous cleat offers resistance. Small, intermediate clips allow paths for moisture.

A low-slope transverse seam, as shown in Figure 7.9, provides an additional enhancement. This seam incorporates an expansion chamber of sorts and effectively drops the pressure gradient driving the water into the seam, as well as a capillary break in the connection, while allowing expansion and contraction of

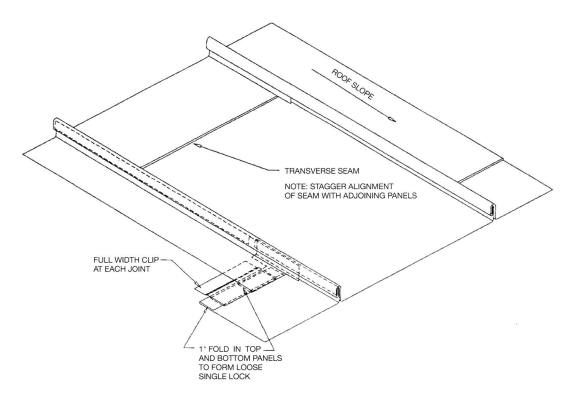

ROOF SLOPE

TRANSVERSE SEAM

NOTE: STAGGER ALIGNMENT
OF SEAM WITH ADJOINING PANELS

FULL WIDTH CLIP
AT EACH JOINT

1" FOLD IN TOP
AND BOTTOM PANELS
TO FORM LOOSE
SINGLE LOCK

FIGURE 7.8. Transverse and standing seam intersection.

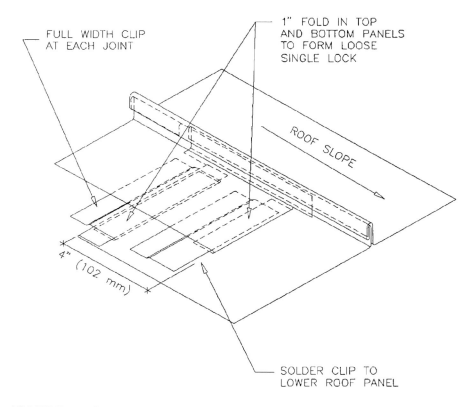

FIGURE 7.9. Cross section of low slope transverse seam assembly.

the surface. This type of seam operates well on the Rainscreen Principle. The low-slope seam has a capillary break, a physical restriction, and a single entry point with a chambered volume of air. Gravity takes over and drains the moisture out of the system.

FLAT-LOCK SEAM JOINT

The flat-lock seam is one of the more common sheet metal joining methods. It is simple to fabricate and install. The seam consists of 180-degree folds along the edge of a thin sheet of metal. Refer to Figure 7.10. Two adjoining sides fold to one face while the other two adjoining sides fold back. One sheet engages its fold into the fold of another sheet. A clip occurs in the seam and is concealed by the overlap. This seam is usually snug-fit but loosely engaged, allowing unrestricted movement.

The flat-lock seam curves easily in one direction. However, it is very difficult to curve the seam to any significant degree in the direction perpendicular to an edge. Surfaces constructed with the flat-lock seam expand and contract without overstressing. Expansion and contraction are always away from two fixed edges and over the panel to the side and below. To keep moisture out, they are most effective when installed on a sloping surface. The interlocking panels use the shingle effect, by constantly draining moisture over the next panel below. Flat-lock seam panel elements can be installed in any bias as long as the seam is positively drained. Flat-lock seam panels can be tapered, trapezoidal, diamond,

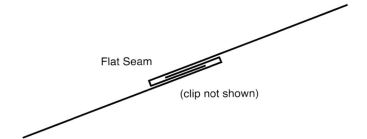

FIGURE 7.10. Cross section of typical flat-seam joint.

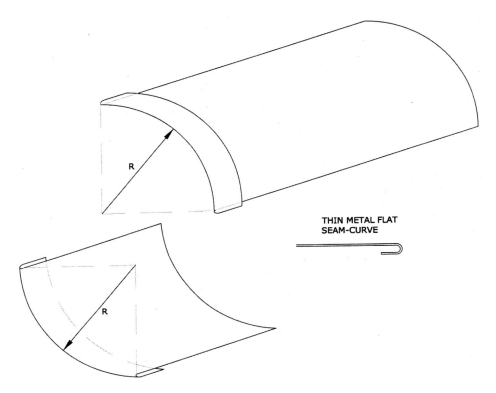

FIGURE 7.11. Curvature of flat-seam joint.

or triangular in form. It is one of the more versatile seams used in thin sheet metal construction. Figure 7.11 shows a flat lock seam curved parallel to the seam.

PITTSBURGH SEAM

The Pittsburgh seam is another sheet metal joint that has been in use for a very long time. Also known as a Pittsburgh lock seam, it requires a small edge of metal to be hammered down, effectively locking one sheet of metal into the other. Refer to Figure 7.12.

The Pittsburgh seam is used to join thin sheet metal together. The seam can be curved in one direction but not perpendicular to the seam. This type of joint is

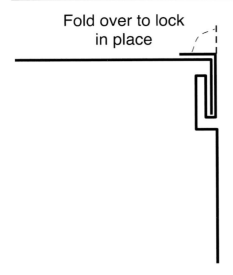

FIGURE 7.12. Pittsburgh seam assembly.

FIGURE 7.13. Pittsburgh seam on *The Boxes*, sculpture by Donald Judd.

used on sheet metal where the finish is not so critical. Galvanized steel, copper, and mill-finish aluminum all can be seamed using the Pittsburgh seam. Expansion across this joint does not occur. This is a tight joint, which interlocks two metal surfaces together. The joint is watertight under low pressure. Solder or sealant can seal the joint more thoroughly. Figure 7.13 shows the appearance of a finished seam assembly.

TONGUE-AND-GROOVE SEAMS

Tongue-and-groove seams develop smooth wall surfaces set at an even plane. They are common with roll-formed metal panels. The seam interlocks two edges of adjoining panels to create a very strong joint, and usually conceal a fastener or clip along one edge. The seam allows for limited movement and directs moisture that enters the gap at the joint along the seam. The independent slipping of the tongue and groove of adjoining elements provides expansion and contraction. Refer to Figure 7.14.

The tongue-and-groove joint does not interact well with right-angle seam intersections. Spline seams, simple overlaps, sealant joints can be used to develop the transverse joint intersecting the tongue-and-groove at right angles.

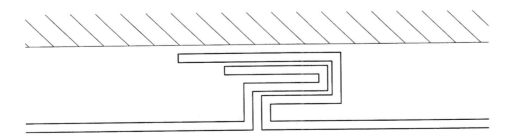

FIGURE 7.14. Example of tongue-and-groove seam.

Horizontal tongue-and-groove seams need special care to direct water out. Top-down installation can overcome this by placing the tongue section in position to direct water out. Layout of horizontal runs is required. Additionally, since the seam tends to track moisture, openings through the surface must be able to direct this moisture back out.

The tongue-and-groove seam performs well when used vertically, as the plank pattern this creates efficiently keeps moisture and air out, particularly when a gasket or sealant is introduced in the joint. Like all vertical seams, the joint offers a channel for moisture. It works well as long as penetrations are surrounded with flashing to direct the moisture out to the surface face.

Curving is accomplished by stretching the metal after fabrication. It can only be curved along the direction of the tongue-and-groove seam; it cannot be curved against the seam without collapsing the folds of the tongue and groove.

EXPOSED FASTENERS ALONG SEAMS

Exposing the fastener to create a pattern on the metal surface and to tightly fix the metal skin to the subframe, like that of an airplane skin, can create an appealing surface. Several challenges exist when doing this, however. Lapping of the metal to shed water can create variations such that two metal thicknesses are fixed to the subframe, followed by a sequence where three metal thicknesses must be fixed. This can create localized distortions at each panel. Additionally, the fastener itself must be designed with a shoulder to seat without overly compressing the metal sheet (the shoulder allows the fastener to engage tightly without dimpling the sheet). In addition, the fastener must be accurately set to

FIGURE 7.15. Exposed fasteners on the Bard College stainless-steel surface in Annandale-on-Hudson, New York.

prevent an angular seating of the head, further distorting the sheet around the fasteners. Or, instead of a shouldered fastener, a washer of special thickness can be used.

Dimpling and piercing the sheet where the fastener is to occur can effectively capture the distortion or puckering of the panel at the location where contact occurs. Expansion and contraction will also dimple, or warp, the metal between fastener points. Greater distance between fasteners will distort more than a tighter spacing. Tight spacing will reduce the amount of expansion and fix the surfaces together more tightly. Figure 7.15 is of the exterior surface of Bard College, designed by Frank Gehry. The panels are fixed to the substrate using exposed fasteners.

A gasket or seal is needed to help alleviate the capillary action of the lapping seam. A double seal or a finger-type gasket can reduce or eliminate capillary action. Without a seal, water can infiltrate this joint. The exposed fastener joint is more for appearance. Controlling moisture infiltration into the system is a difficult challenge, particularly where the slope is low. Figures 7.16 and 7.17 show exposed fastener assemblies.

WELDED AND SOLDERED SEAMS

Welding and soldering joints in metal are intended to be water- and airtight. A surface joined by welding is, for all intents and purposes, a single surface. Similar to a seamed and soldered surface, these surfaces and their connects must be designed so that expansion and contraction occur as a unit.

A discussion of welding techniques used on metal surfaces is beyond the scope of this book. Suffice to say, however, there are certain considerations all metal surfaces must undergo. Welding of architectural surfaces is an art unto itself. Architectural surfaces require removal of heat at the weld source to prevent warping of the surface plane.

Welding metal surfaces for architectural purposes should be performed on materials thicker than 1.5 mm (0.63 inches). Thinner materials can be welded, but the accompanying distortion may be too severe. Welding requires temperatures high enough to melt the metals being joined.

Soldering is best suited for thinner metals. Soldering involves the melting of a lead–tin or tin–antimony alloy and depositing it into a joint between two metal surfaces. The solder is deposited into a joint by capillary action. The molten metal is drawn up between the two surfaces. A flux is used as a wetting agent and to temporarily resist oxidation of the metals being soldered. Flux also helps in the uniform distribution of the solder between the metal surfaces. When this "filler metal" cools, it binds the two materials together and can effectively seal the joint from air and water infiltration (see Table 7.2).

Soldering, unlike welding, gets its strength from the seaming of the underlying metal. The solder itself is very weak and should not be used to transfer stress across the joint.

Brazing, sometimes referred to as silver solder or hard solder, is another method of joining certain metals. Brazing provides better strength and higher temperature resistance. It uses alloys that melt at a much higher temperature. The brazing procedure is essentially the same as for soldering.

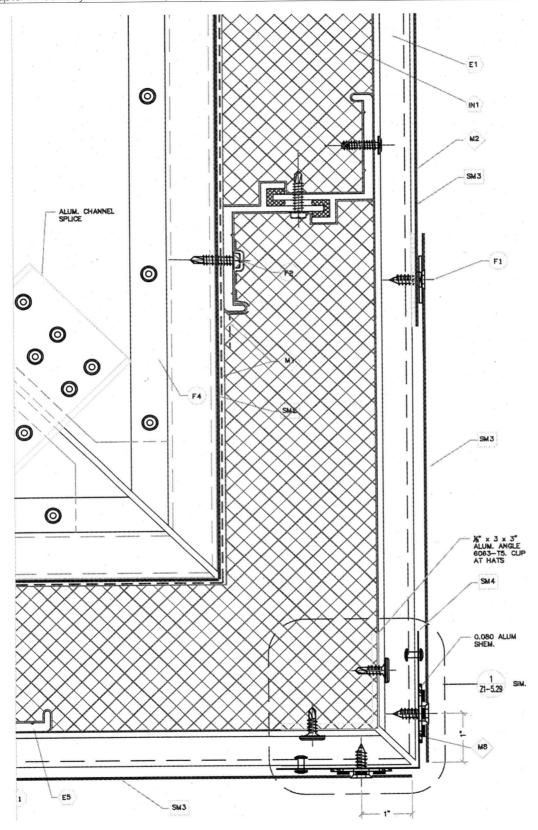

FIGURE 7.16. Example of exposed fastener lap seam.

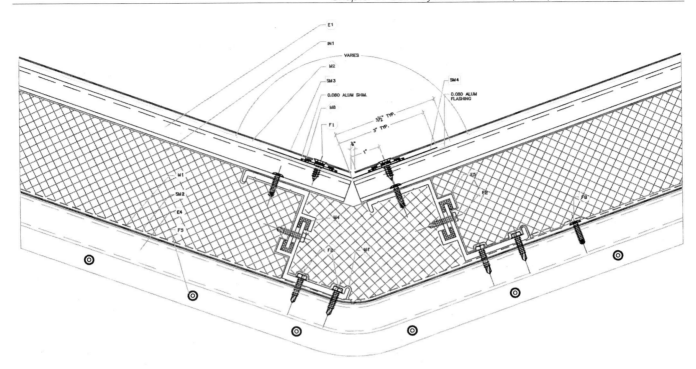

FIGURE 7.17. Exposed fastener assembly at symmetry break.

TABLE 7.2

Soldering Procedure

Steps Used to Produce a Good Solder Joint
1. Clean the surface to be soldered using a wire brush, sandpaper, or stainless-steel wool.
2. Cover the surfaces to be joined with a thin film of flux.
3. Assemble the metal to be joined.
4. Apply heat with a gas torch or iron.
5. When the metal surface is sufficiently hot, remove heat source.
6. Apply solder. It should melt on contact with the surface and deposit into the joint.
7. Neutralize all flux and rinse thoroughly.
8. Inspect for pinholes, seams, and cracks.
9. Rework if necessary to fill any suspect holes.

MAINTENANCE ISSUES WITH SEAMS IN METAL SURFACES

Seams direct moisture flow across the exterior metal surface. Building surfaces collect grime and airborne dirt, which will collect and concentrate during times of rain and dew runoff. The seam acts as a channeling point on the surface, which concentrates the grime and dirt at drips and edges. These concentrations stain the metal surface and raise aesthetic issues.

Periodic maintenance will eliminate and reduce the appearance of these stains. Most metal surfaces will self-clean to a point, as rainwater will wash the dirt from the metal surface. The smoother the surface, the more effective the self-cleansing operation. Coarse surfaces will hold the dirt and soot, making it necessary to augment the natural cleaning effects of rain.

To control the runoff, build in offsets and drip extensions to direct the water and break surface tension at the water-to-metal interface. This will eliminate a significant amount of dirt staining.

If the finish is a coarse or rough surface, plan for periodic washdowns of the surface. This will keep foreign matter from attaching to the surface, making their removal less difficult. Evaporation patterns on metal surfaces, particularly coarse surfaces, leave spots and dirt deposits behind. These should be rinsed occasionally to prevent any corrosive behavior from developing.

In colder climates, where salting of roads and sidewalks occur during and after icing conditions, it is very important to schedule a thorough washdown every spring. Deicing salts that become airborne and collect on metal surfaces will damage the surface finish of most metals, in particular stainless steel. On other metals such as copper alloys and weathering steel, deicing salts will create streaks and stains as they combine with the naturally developing oxides.

Not unlike the surface of a car, a periodic maintenance review and cleaning of the metal surface is recommended to keep the appearance and performance at their best. If corrosive materials are prevented from attaching themselves to metal surfaces, metal can be expected to last a very long time. Joints in the metal surface deserve special attention because of their tendency to collect and channel moisture from the surface. As such, deposits are concentrated more at these locations. Table 7.3 summarizes maintenance guidelines.

Like the hunters we once were, the eye moves over a surface with a consistent, homogeneous appearance searching for small disturbances. Seams and joints break up the surface into constructible packets and when regular in nature, the eye tends to ignore them. Subconsciously we always measure the extent of the surface that is before us. Our eye seeks the edges and transitions that make up the obstruction that confronts us.

TABLE 7.3

Maintenance Recommendations for Surface Seams and Joints

1. Schedule a rinse or wipedown of the surface.

2. Conduct an annual inspection of the seam and joint to ensure that gaskets, sealants, and fasteners are in place.

3. Remove debris that may collect in reveals.

4. Rinse road salts from metal surfaces at least once each spring.

5. Once every three to five years, thoroughly wash the surface with mild detergent and clean water.

CHAPTER 8
EDGES AND TRANSITIONS

"Borders . . . they prevent universal homogenization."

—TYLER VOLK, IN *Metapatterns*

On any surface, there is an apparent edge. Even the sphere of the Earth has an apparent "edge" where the sky intersects at the horizon. The edge can be a real transition to another surface or perceived as such by the viewer. The eye seeks out and follows the edges of a surface defining the boundary, the limits, that lie before it. The subconscious mind measures and evaluates the limitations confronting the view. The edges offer definition; they are the borders, a finite limit where one element ends and another begins.

This boundary can be a physical change or a change in color or contrast. Color change can be induced by pigments or by surface enhancements that alter light reflecting back to the viewer.

Correctly constructed edges are the defining details of a surface. Regardless of the quality of the finish, edges that are wavy and misaligned will have dramatic effects on the opinion of the quality of the surface.

LEVEL OF SHARPNESS

Metal surfaces takes on a level of sharpness, an appearance demanded by the nature of the material. The relative sharpness of the edges of metals varies. Depending on the type of metal and the form taken of the metal surface, the edge will appear either sharp and straight or undulant and soft. Some metals can be worked to produce a straight unwavering line, like the edge of a sword. Metals such as steel, stainless steel, aluminum, and titanium can be worked thin to produce strong unyielding edges free of any softening and undulation.

Low-reflective metals such as lead, copper, and zinc can have edges that appear gentle and pliable; and, depending on the scale, the edges can appear slightly wavy. Reinforced to increase their strength by adding shapes into the metal edge or forming the edge increases the strength and stiffness, improving

TABLE 8.1

Metal Edge Categories

Metals exhibiting a hard-edge appearance	Aluminum
	Brass
	Monel
	Steel
	Stainless steel
	Titanium
Metals exhibiting a soft-edge appearance	Copper
	Lead
	Zinc

the edge appearance. Edges of steel, stainless steel, brass, and titanium can appear precise, machined in appearance. These metals are stiffer and harder; hence the edges are sharper in both feel and appearance.

Creating surfaces from thin sheets will appear soft if the edges waver. Some of this is due to the oil canning, or surface deflection that occurs in the body of the sheet. Folding the edges of thin stainless steel or titanium and interlocking them into flat plates require the metal to raise off the surface slightly and then back down at the opposite edge. Because of the reflectivity of these surfaces, oil canning is more dramatic. Additionally, the edge has a softer appearance because it must also rise up slightly as one sheet joins the next.

FIGURE 8.1. Stainless-steel edge-to-glass interface. Bard College, Annandale-on-Hudson, New York.

Edges are defined by a contrast in color or a defined border. The border is a textural change or contrast. Edges can be established as a shadow created by an offset or protrusion from the surface. Shadows enlarge the apparent edge and offer a contrasting appearance against all but the darkest backgrounds. Figure 8.1 shows edgework of the metal system around a vertical window. The metal is made to appear as if it is "peeling away."

The edges are a transition from one metal surface boundary to another metal surface or to a different material altogether. They can also be termination points where the molecules that make up the surface create the final outpost to the ambient surroundings. Refer to Figure 8.2. Metal edges are defining the shape of the surface.

For metal surfaces the edge can occur in the form of individual panel seams creating patterns. The seam type and location can be solely an aesthetic decision or it can be influenced by the performance requirements of the surface or the limitations of the material form. Figure 8.3 is an image of flat seam joints coming together at a corner. The joint is even and relatively tight.

The edge can be a definition within the surface, describing changes in planes or transitions in material. Figures 8.4A and 8.4B are images of the intersection of the punched windows used on the MIT Stata Center designed by Frank Gehry. The joint and edge is crisp at the break in the window to wall interface. Typically, a seam is present at such a condition. These breaks in geometry of surfaces are visible because of the color, texture, or contrast differences between the two surfaces. They can also be apparent from the patterns that make up the surface. Breaking the symmetry by changing the pattern direction bias establishes an edge within a surface.

FIGURE 8.2. Gehry's Experience Music Project in Seattle, Washington. Stainless-steel edge defining the geometry of the surface.

FIGURE 8.3. Titanium edgework. Tight seam without flashing.

FIGURE 8.4A. Stainless-steel window box. Very clean edges and reveals.

FIGURE 8.4B. Close-up of the window box "punching" through the wall.

When edges are the outside extent of the viewable surface, they define the limits of the geometry. Smooth sleek surfaces usually end in smooth sleek lines created by the shaping of the metal. In contrast, poorly created edges take away from the overall surface appearance. Covers and bulky flashing can give a clunky look to a surface. Window and door trim can look applied and out of place. Offsetting plates that do not line up or that are inaccurately trimmed will attract the viewer's eye, explicitly detracting from the body of the surface.

Often, solutions to edges and transitions on metal surfaces involve applying covers of folded metal. The metal covers have no relationship to the overall pattern on the rest of the surface. This "Band-Aid" approach shows a lack of knowl-

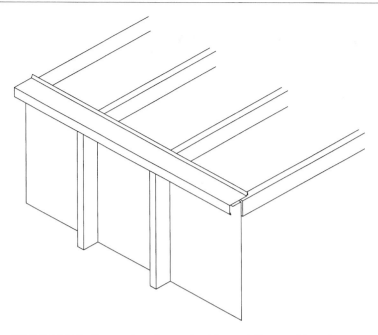

FIGURE 8.5. Example of a typical low-skill transition from one plane to the next.

edge and skill. It is generally the most economical solution; and if skill is lacking, it may be the only solution. The construction of these folded metal covers are such that water is kept out of exterior cladding surfaces by positive lapping. In other words, the folded covers perform a shingling effect, sometimes with sealant sandwiched between them. Refer to Figure 8.5. Flashings over the transitions are simple but not that attractive. Figure 8.6 shows cover plates installed over surface transitions. They take an interesting surface and make it "clunky" in appearance.

FIGURE 8.6. Cover plates, somewhat clumsy over the edge of the flat-seam panels. They appear out of place, more like a Band-Aid.

Some metal finishes have a directional nature to them. For example, satin-finish stainless steel has a finish running the length of the sheet. The finish is applied to the coil of metal as it is rolled out. Flashings around openings may have the finish running perpendicular to the balance of the metal surface. This will generate an entirely different appearance.

Metal is difficult to custom-fashion to degrees of accuracy the eye cannot discern. The reflective nature of most metal surfaces and the preciseness of metal edges show the least distortion. Skill and precision are the necessary virtues to achieving what is required. Unfortunately, the materials are very unforgiving. You cannot simply sand them down or add a filler to create the desired appearance.

The edges and transitions of a surface will either give the appearance of well-crafted elegance or cheap, hastily finished work. The edges and trim work on a surface are the most expensive and time-consuming part of the process. The results are, however, telling. Finely fitted and trimmed surfaces have a timeless appearance; they speak of quality. The lack of flashing covers as shown in Figure 8.7 requires a more precise construction and a better understanding of how the metal can be developed into a surface.

In creating surfaces from metal, the edges are often problematic because they are the most visible. Consider the various surface patterns discussed. Creating edges and transitions that possess the same moisture deterrence, the same flexibility, and the same appearance, without applying a patch or a cover, is usually the preferred result. The cost and skill level of the fabricator and installer are the limiting factors. Figure 8.8 shows the fit up of a custom fabricated ornament. The edges are welded and ground smooth. Figure 8.9 shows a metal-to-glass wall intersection. The edge of the metal is interlocked into an even flat seam, creating a clean line at the metal fold.

FIGURE 8.7 "Peel" breaks. Changing of surface symmetry.

FIGURE 8.8. Assembled decorative finial with welded edges.

FIGURE 8.9. Corner detail at glass window wall.

CORNERS

Bringing flat, thin sheets together at a corner is an art. A clean, smooth surface ending in a rough corner appearance will take away from the overall appearance. Geometry changes defined by two different sloped surfaces coming together can appear jagged where the seams do not come together in a smooth transition. Clunky, oversized flashings can make the finishwork appear cheap, like an oversized suit of clothes. Custom metal surfaces demand precise approaches to the final edgework.

For any of the running bond patterns, changes in plane can be handled in several ways. You can wrap the pattern around the edge or corner, which will involve showing the offset at the lapping edges of the individual sheets or plates. This requires laying out the pattern around the corner onto adjacent surfaces. One can start at the corner and work both directions, or fold the panels around a corner. Ensuring the seam does not occur at a corner is necessary to maintain a consistent appearance. Additionally, it is important to point out that the lap creates a shadow line, which will accentuate the vertical seam edge. If you start at the corner, the vertical seam will be visible on both planes when viewed from the corner. Figures 8.10A and 8.10B show a flat seam, horizontal running bond developed around a corner. No trim is apparent.

The pattern can also be absorbed into another seam. This will allow for a transitional break in the plane and will allow for change in angles of the seam. Additionally, by engulfing the pattern into another seam you "clean up" the edge by eliminating the visual nature of the offsets. This can also serve to control moisture at openings and ledges or eliminate sharp edges resulting from points at the transition. Figure 8.11 is a roof panel changing slope and direction. The panels are constructed to make the transition without trim or flashing covers.

Figure 8.12A shows a corner closure on a horizontal corrugated surface. The corrugations simply butt up to the vertical corner shape. Figure 8.12B is another version used to close off the corner of a horizontal corrugated surface.

Sheared or saw-cut edges that are not folded are considered unfinished. Unfinished edges of metal can be developed into a corner or transition by placing a backup behind the edge and offsetting the backup slightly. This backup metal shape is often referred to as a *spline*. The spline can be a folded plate of metal or a bar of metal held with clips. This commands the eye to follow the fold of the backup plate. It creates a slight reveal along the edge, but the result is better than

FIGURE 8.10A. Copper wrapping around corner.

FIGURE 8.10B. Horizontal running bond wrapping around corner.

FIGURE 8.11. Roof slope transition. Trim is concealed.

FIGURE 8.12A. Corrugated wall termination at corner. Trim is used, but not as a cover.

FIGURE 8.12B. Corrugated transition with inward-formed corner.

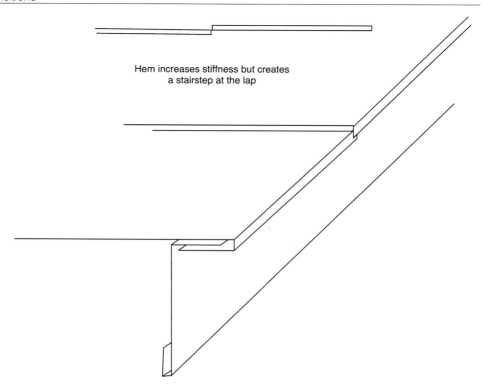

Hem increases stiffness but creates
a stairstep at the lap

FIGURE 8.13. Reinforced edge transition.

variations that occur when trying to align two edges of sheared metal. Figure 8.13 shows an assembled edge developed from thin flat seam material. The intersection of two panels will stair-step slightly at the lap.

If the edges "stair-step" or "saw-tooth" as they attach to the backup metal spline, the appearance will be compromised. Slight discrepancies can be accomplished by offsetting the edges slightly from the corner of the spline.

REVEAL AND OFFSET CORNERS

Reveals and offsets pose particular challenges with corner assemblies. Not only must they shed moisture as they fold around a corner, they must appear well constructed and resolute. The inexperienced or unskilled will approach corners with cover plates or other "Band-Aid" approaches to corners and transitions. It is easier to manufacture, but rather unpleasant and bulky in appearance.

On horizontal bands, the reveals must change direction at the corners. Outside corner reveals will require the sheet metal material to be notched, joined, and sealed to prevent moisture infiltration. Expansion and contraction must be away from the corner. The corner is a fixed point and all movement must be away from this edge.

CURVED EDGES

Edges that curve are formidable. Various seams can be developed into curves, few with ease. Depending on the direction of the curve, the metal may require stretching or even welding to achieve a smooth transition. Hemmed edges can be curved in one direction with little difficulty. The hem is performed by pressing a fold in a line or rolling a fold along a straight edge. Essentially, this creates two parallel lines, which will allow curving along a radius perpendicular to the parallel lines. The fold restricts curving in the direction along the parallel line. Partial stretching can be achieved to curve the edge slightly in the direction of the parallel lines. Stretching, however, usually scallops the edge slightly. Certain metals work better than others. Copper, aluminum, and steel can be stretched in this direction with some scalloping; stainless steel, to a lesser degree; titanium, not at all.

The backup spline works well on curved edges. The spline can be shaped by stretching the form or by notching out the edges. The notched edges are concealed by the lap-over of the metal plates. Notching the spline allows for the edge to undergo shaping and twisting in multiple directions. Even two dual curved surfaces can be brought together with a notched spline joint.

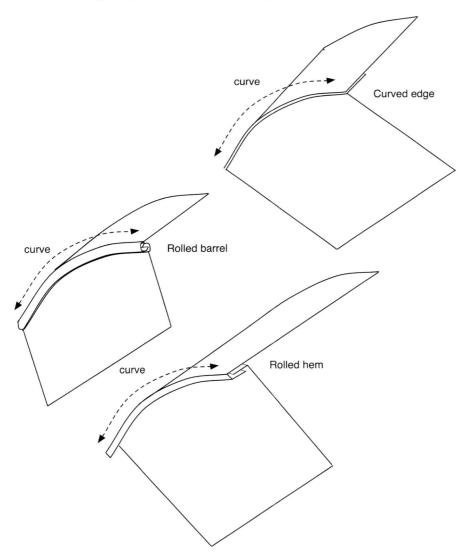

FIGURE 8.14. Curved edges.

SOFTENING AND EASING EDGES

In the case of thin sheet metal, unfinished edges can be sharp and pose a hazard. In the case of thicker sheet and plate, unfinished edges can have a rough appearance, as well as a sharp, hazardous edge. Shearing plates create a slightly rolled edge when they strike the surface of a sheet or plate of material. The roll is on the topside where the surface of the sheet meets the blade and goes downward toward the center of the sheet. On thick sheet and plate, the shearing action leaves a yield tear along the exposed surface of the edge around the center of the cross section. As the material yields, particularly with stainless steel, a very sharp overhanging extension of metal can be present. This overhang can be thin, uneven, and razor-sharp. Passing a file or a grinder along the edge will remove this edge and improve the appearance.

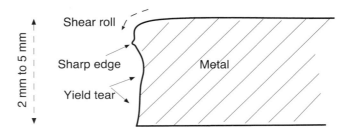

FIGURE 8.15. Section depicting sheared edge of thick metal sheet or plate.

TABLE 8.2

Cutting and Shearing

Cutting Method	Metal	Edge Quality
Shear	All sheet forms	Sharp microedges Microscopic roughness Thick materials roll down
Saw cutting	Plate and sheet forms of aluminum, copper alloys, and zinc Bar and tube forms of all metals	90-degree edge Rough edge, but not sharp
Laser cutting	Steel and stainless steels Titanium Zinc; and aluminum, to a lesser degree on special wavelength lasers Copper alloys (not currently practical)	90-degree edge Frosted appearance with a very slight heat zone
Waterjet cutting	All metals	90-degree edge Frosted appearance
Plasma cutting	Steel, stainless steel	Slight heat effect along edge of cut Some redressing the edge can be expected

On reflective surfaces, this rounding will make the joint between two sheets appear larger. Flipping the sheet over during the shearing process will flatten this edge and eliminate the rolldown on the exposed surface.

Saw cutting produces a square edge without the tearing that shearing produces. But saw cutting is slower and more time-consuming than shearing, and is best suited for aluminum, copper alloys, and zinc; it is impractical for stainless steel, steel, and titanium (see Table 8.2).

Laser cutting can produce an edge on steel and stainless steel that is very smooth. Lasers produce a fine line by heating the metal on a very localized basis. Heating is achieved by absorbing the wavelength to the point at which molecular bonds break down and the metal is vaporized. The edge is slightly frosted. Very little cleanup is necessary. But laser cutting is effective only with those metals that absorb the particular frequency of the laser being used. Aluminum does not cut well on certain lasers because of the absorption characteristics. Copper and copper alloys will not cut well on a laser due to the frequency and wavelength absorption.

Waterjet is an excellent method of cutting all architectural metals. Copper, lead, and titanium all can be cut with waterjet. Waterjet cutting utilizes a very high-pressure stream of water, often with abrasive added to improve cutting. Waterjet essentially saws a very fine edge of material as it passes across the metal surface. The edge produced is frosted in appearance. Little if any final cleanup is necessary. Refer to Figure 8.16.

Plasma cutting comes in various quality levels. Depending on the torch size and the gas pressure, fine cut lines requiring little to no cleanup can be accomplished. Figure 8.17 is a decorative screen cut from plasma by the artist Jesse Small. You can expect the edge to be slightly frosted with traces of burn on steel and stainless steel. Copper and aluminum tend to melt along the edge of contact, creating a rougher appearance. Refer to Figure 8.18. This image is of a copper edge cut with plasma.

FIGURE 8.16. Waterjet cut edge of thick aluminum plate.

FIGURE 8.17. Plasma-cut artistic screen wall, by artist Jesse Small.

FIGURE 8.18. Plasma-cut copper leaves.

V-CUT VERSUS BRAKE-FORMED EDGES

When a metal edge is created by press-brake forming, the typical fold is two times the thickness of the metal. Sometimes referred to as a *2-T radius bend*, this standard fold is rounded and smooth in appearance. Skilled press-brake operators have little problem consistently repeating the bending operation and achieving consistent parts.

On thicker sheet and plate, some inconsistencies can develop in the brake operation so that radius edges do not align from one part to the next. This can throw off alignment of panel edges and trim edges where one part aligns and comes into contact with another.

The rolled edge created by press-brake forming does not miter well. The rounded edge when brought together with another rounded edge at a corner will not match up completely, leaving a gap in the corner. Figure 8.19 shows a typical rounded bend when a 0.125 inch (3 mm) thickness sheet is folded. The bend radius is twice the thickness of the material, thus creating a rounded edge.

A technique known as V-cutting can reduce the misalignment behavior that can arise from the 2-T radius bending operation. V-cutting removes metal from the reverse side of the sheet by passing the sheet under cutting blades. The blades are accurately positioned both across the sheet and into the sheet. As the sheet passes below the cutting blade, a sliver of metal is removed, leaving a trough the shape of a "V" into the back surface of the sheet. When the sheet is formed by the press brake, the bend is significantly tighter. It is still a 2-T radius but the thickness has been appreciably reduced at the point of the bend. Thus, a tighter bend radius is achieved. Figure 8.20 shows the V-cut corners used on the Modern Art Museum in Fort Worth. The metal thickness was 0.187 inches (5 mm) yet the corner after V-cutting was very crisp.

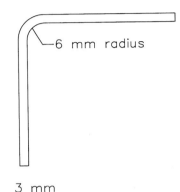

6 mm radius

3 mm

FIGURE 8.19. Brake-folded edge on thick material—2-T bend.

FIGURE 8.20. V-cut aluminum corner panel for the Modern Art Museum of Fort Worth, Texas.

The V-cutting process is more technically demanding and adds cost to the folding process; nevertheless, there are several benefits to V-cutting finish edges. The accuracy in setting the V-cut is usually to within 0.005 inches (0.127 mm). This precisely locates where the bend is to occur, whereas the press brake requires the matchup of a curving edge and is prone to slip slightly, even with an accurate back gauge. The V-cut allows for the development of miters. Once folded V-cut miter will match up to another with high accuracy.

THERMAL MOVEMENT ALONG EDGES

As surfaces undergo movement from thermal changes or structural loading, alignment of edges can be thrown off. If possible, the movement should be away from the edge or hidden within the edge. In other words, make the edges the fixed points and have the movement taken up in the body of the surface. What can occur is differential shifting, whereby one element of the edge moves differently from an adjoining element. This can materialize as a stair-stepping or saw-toothing along seams. If the prominent edges are fixed together to move as a unit, the offsetting of elements will not occur. However, the movement must be taken up somewhere else in the body of the surface.

For thicker metal surfaces, creating edges and transitions can involve more ingenious assemblies. Folding heavy plates around corners is a practical method for some systems. This effectively fixes the corner edge. The corners usually are subjected to more significant dynamic loading, thus attention to attachment points is an important requirement. Another approach may involve the offsetting of the corner, creating a reveal.

Many designs seek an appearance where the metal surface is intended to appear thicker. This can require a careful review of reveal joints as the corner wraps around soffits or overhang regions.

Transitions from one surface to another, whether the same material or another surfacing material, requires a clear understanding of movement and water control. Following the basic rules of creating rainscreen assemblies, as described in Chapter 5, is important for eliminating paths of moisture entry along edges.

The complexity created by edges and reveals can be daunting. Solid modeling of the surface can be performed to better evaluate where the edges and reveals travel, how they intersect other regions, and how they terminate. This way, the complexity of the seams and edges can be evaluated before the surface is manufactured and installed.

SHADOWS

The eye is drawn to contrast on a surface. Contrast can be created from the light and dark zones of shadows as they play across a surface. Shadows, like certain wavelengths of light, vary in intensity throughout the day. As an artist uses a charcoal pencil, shadows define the edges and seams that border a surface. Patterns are concealed until the outline of their edges is revealed by their shadow.

Overlapping plates, reveals, and surface relief that protrude from the body of a surface can create shadows. Overhangs that protrude out, sheltering the surface below from overhead light, generate shadows. The shadow is a volume of space shielded from the overhead light source. All surfaces and objects within that volume are shrouded in the cloak of the shadow. When a recess falls in shadow, color is removed. Reveals are dark in contrast to the surrounding surfaces. Using a reflective material in the reveal flashes as light strikes the reveal as if a light source were suddenly turned on.

When the light source is the sun, the shadow has a fuzzy, indistinct edge. When overcast, the entire sky becomes a light source, and shadows are muted. Artificial lighting can produce sharp transitions that play across a surface. Simple drip edges can create large extended shadows, which accentuate banding. Because most metals are more reflective, the shadow created appears darker and more contrasting.

A surface can take on a heavy banding appearance during certain daylight periods, then revert to an even level when the sunlight is more direct or the sky is overcast. Simple surfaces can become more complex and interesting in appearance. An example of this is the common corrugated metal surface. Refer to Figure 8.21.

Corrugated thin sheet metal has been around almost as long as flat sheet metal. Corrugating adds strength and stiffness to thin metal by developing a cross section with the characteristics of a beam.

Beyond the benefits of strength, corrugated surfaces produce a contrasting light and dark banding. This contrast is due to reflective surfaces along the outer curve and shadows in the recessed region of the corrugation. Even dark, diffused surfaces produce a contrasting banding when corrugated. Like a picket fence, the surface plane is defined in two dimensions; the contrast in color tones produces depth.

The banding forces the eye along the direction of the corrugations. Horizontal corrugations give the impression of a longer, more horizontal surface. The

FIGURE 8.21. Horizontal corrugated surface. Shadow effects can be striking.

viewer looks down the panel and the corrugations as the perspective broadens from the field of view. Vertical surfaces form a series of pipelike forms established by the bright outward curves and the contrasting dark, shadow regions. The banding creates symmetry across a surface that repeats in a very pleasing manner. There are a number of variations of corrugated surfaces available in most any metal that is rolled into sheet.

TRANSITION FROM METAL TO STONE, BRICK, CERAMIC, OR CONCRETE

When transitioning from a metal surface to one of stone, brick, ceramic, or concrete, both functional and aesthetic considerations must be established. Controlling moisture and air infiltration through the intersection is perhaps the primary concern. Functionally, the challenge is keeping the ambient behavior in sight while understanding the thermal, deflection, and seismic movements that will occur across such transitions (see Table 8.3).

The aesthetic challenge centers on how to create a reveal, flashing cover, or lapping condition that can accommodate the movements and keep moisture and air at bay, without looking out of place or temporary (see Table 8.4). Additionally, one must consider how the various dissimilar materials will interact when exposed to environmental conditions that are not always so pristine.

The transition should be designed and constructed to provide a very long-term maintenance-free life. Such transitions are very difficult to access, and even then are very difficult to rework. Consider a chimney flashing. Like most obscure flashings, they are intended to be problem-free for the life of the structure. Accessibility for rework and inspection is limited. Any rework will be problematic and expensive. Thus, it is best to deal with it the first time and account for all the potential issues.

To start with, consider the material. Use only stable, highly corrosive-resistant materials. Titanium, stainless steel, and copper offer long-term proven performance when coupled with concrete, mortar, and stone (see Table 8.5). Each of these metals has good fatigue resistance and can couple with other metals (except maybe copper) with little concern for dissimilar action.

TABLE 8.3

Functional Considerations of Transitioning from Metal

Moisture infiltration
Air infiltration
Long-term performance
Thermal movement
Seismic movement
Pressure loading

TABLE 8.4

Aesthetic Considerations of Transitioning from Metal

Reveal
Flashing overlap
Dissimilar materials

TABLE 8.5

Metal in Concealed Joints

Metal	Surface Metal Couple
Copper	Copper, copper alloys, lead-coated copper
Stainless steel	Stainless steel, zinc, aluminum, terne, galvanized steel, tin
Titanium	Titanium, stainless steel

To keep air infiltration at bay, use a flexible seal such as silicone, urethane, or synthetic rubber, in conjunction with a metal transition. The seal should be within the wall and protected from ultraviolet radiation. You can usually achieve adequate movement from such seals in two directions with restricted movement axially. Slip conditions that move axially more than once are difficult, if not unrealistic, particularly when air infiltration is of major concern. Generally what occurs is they move or slip axially on the first thermal cycles, then bind within the slipping mechanism.

Use a material that offers some axial elongation or develop a loose fit to allow for axial movements. Membranes can be sealed to one another to construct a miter and still create an impervious air barrier.

Covering the membrane with metal will extend the lifespan and provide water deterrence, leaving the air to the membrane. The metal covers require the development of slip joints or overlaps to accommodate movement. The challenge is to develop a joint or series of joints that allow movement in three directions without opening.

With concrete, stone, brick, and ceramic junctions, the metal must be able to deter moisture out to the exterior of the surface. Creating a thorough wall flashing is important. Moisture within walls can collect at the transitions where the material terminates. Control joints within these wall systems will channel moisture both on the face of the wall and within the wall to the transition. If a simple cover flashing is being used at these intersections, the recess control joint will pose a potential channel of entry behind the metal surface.

Creating a punched opening appearance—where the metal surface appears to be punching through the brick or concrete wall—achieves a stunning effect. The joint between the metal and brick or concrete should be a reveal of size to accommodate the tolerances of the materials and to produce a shadow line to enhance the punching effect. Depending on the scale, anywhere from 0.5 to 1.0 inches (12 to 25 mm) will suffice. Anything smaller than 0.5 inches (12 mm) will require special tolerance care in constructing brick and concrete. Metal can achieve it, but do not lose sight of thermal movement behaviors.

TRANSITIONS FROM METAL TO WOOD

Transitions from metal to wood surfaces are somewhat simpler because both materials are easier to work within tight tolerances (see Table 8.6). The difficulty lies in the air barrier aspects. To the degree that metal and sealants bond tightly to one another, the opposite occurs with wood and sealants. The joint needs to be designed with little dependence on sealants to keep moisture and air at bay.

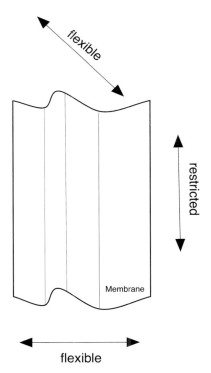

FIGURE 8.22. Flexible membranes can flex in two directions, but are restricted in the third direction.

TABLE 8.6

Metal-to-Wood Connections

Metals Little Affected by Wood Compounds
Titanium
Stainless steel
Lead
Lead-coated copper
Anodized aluminum (hardcoat)
Galvanized steel

Another challenge with wood is the effect it has on many metals. Some of the compounds that slowly leach out of wood can have damaging effects on certain metals. Some of these compounds prevent the oxide layer to grow on metals. Metals achieve long-term performance by developing a natural oxide layer that is relatively inert. Inhibiting the oxide layer from developing can expose the metal to erosion as well as pollution attack. The indication is a shiny streak on the surface of the metal. In reality, most woods are either dry or sealed so that any leaching is minimal and temporary, and thus the effect on metals is temporary.

Placement of neoprene or silicone gasket between metal and wood will also assist in improving the life of the connection as well as a seal. Wood undergoes dimensional changes over time and the connection to metal has to accommodate these changes.

Cladding over wood is common and requires a few precautionary steps. Separation of the two materials by felt paper is usually all that is necessary. The wood can breathe under felts, and the felts offer good moisture separation. For decades, many metal roofs were applied over felts on wood surfaces. Removal and inspection of many of these surfaces showed superior performance. Often, the concealed side of the metal appeared almost new. Some of this was due to the oxide inhibition of the leaching wood, but the environment of the underside when kept moisture-free is quite stable.

TRANSITION FROM METAL TO GLASS

Metal and glass work well together. Both materials offer smooth flat surfaces that accept sealants well. Both materials have tight predictable tolerances afforded by their consistent straight edges. Glass, being very inert, has no effect on the long-term performance of metal. Some metals can, however, leach their oxides onto glass. Lead, and to a lesser degree copper, develop compounds on their surfaces, which can redeposit onto the surface of glass, making it difficult to clean. Development of adequate drip edges will help alleviate this effect. Figure 8.23 shows various drip edges that utilize kicks to break moisture away from the surface or reveals that work to break surface tension.

Functionally, other than restricting moisture and air infiltration, thermal differences are of considerable importance when constructing metal-glass intersections. Glass has a very low expansion rate compared to most metals. Place-

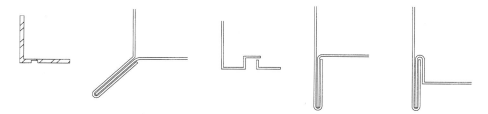

FIGURE 8.23. Edge transitions with surface tension break designs.

ment of metal directly in contact with glass will crack the glass; hence, expanding metal surfaces must be separated from direct contact with glass. Separation can be achieved by interfacing with a flexible gasket material or elastic sealant compounds. Allowing metal to come in contact with glass, particularly glass edges, will be disastrous. Glass requires flexible interfaces. If glass edges come in contact with fasteners or metal, edges will crack. Setting glass on rigid plastic or rubber blocks will cushion the edges of glass and take the dead-load weight of the glass. However, movement must be allowed at the opposing edges. If flashing over the glass edge with metal, sandwich a durable, flexible gasket or sealant between the metal and glass. Make certain, however, that the flexible material is fixed properly and maintained. These materials lack the useful lifespan provided by metal and glass materials. At some point in time they may loosen from thermal changes and simple deterioration, allowing the glass-to-metal contact.

The character of surfaces is influenced by how the designer and fabricator work the metal into a complete assembly. All the various fundamentals determine how the surface is perceived. Symmetry or broken symmetry, edges and transitions, and the way elements are joined to create a continuous surface affect the perception. These are what determine the way the surface interacts with the surrounding environment. Moving still closer from the macro-view to the micro-view further influences how a metal surface will appear and perform over time.

29. Cerner Corporation, North Kansas City, Missouri. Designer: Gould Evans Goodman Architects. Custom perforated in #4 satin finish stainless steel.

30. The Peter B. Lewis Building for the Weatherhead School of Management at Case Western Reserve University, Cleveland, Ohio. Designer: Frank Gehry. Viewed from a distance, the reflective, undulating surface glistens in the sunlight.

31. The Peter B. Lewis Building for the Weatherhead School of Management at Case Western Reserve University, Cleveland, Ohio. Designer: Frank Gehry. This reflective #4 satin finish surface is created by an offset diamond pattern.

32. The Peter B. Lewis Building for the Weatherhead School of Management at Case Western Reserve University, Cleveland, Ohio. Designer: Frank Gehry. The surface appears to roll over and cascade down from the roof.

33. Residential Tower, Chicago, Illinois. Designer: Lucien Lagrange & Associates. Preweathered zinc surface.

34. Apple Computer Flagship Store, the Grove, Los Angeles, California. Designer: Bohlin Cywinski Jackson. This grid pattern surface is a pressure-equalized rainscreen.

35. Rock and Roll Hall of Fame and Museum, Cleveland, Ohio. Designer: Pei Cobb Freed & Partners Architects LLP. The surface is constructed of a painted aluminum grid panel system.

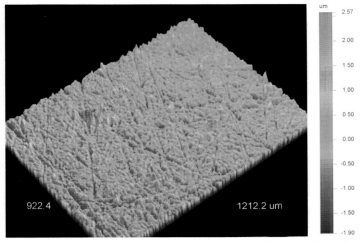

36. The microscopic three-dimensional display of the surface of angel hair finish stainless steel. Reading prepared from a Wyko NT1100 Optical Profiler.

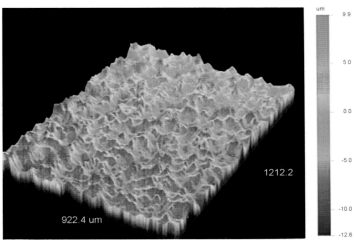

37. The microscopic three-dimensional display of the surface of glass-bead-blasted stainless steel. Reading prepared from a Wyko NT1100 Optical Profiler.

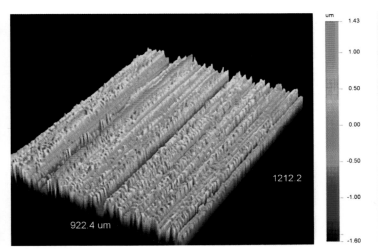

38. The microscopic three-dimensional display of the surface of No. 4 finish stainless steel. Reading prepared from a Wyko NT1100 Optical Profiler.

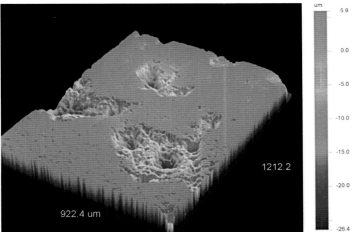

39. The microscopic three-dimensional display of the surface of shadow finish stainless steel. Reading prepared from a Wyko NT1100 Optical Profiler.

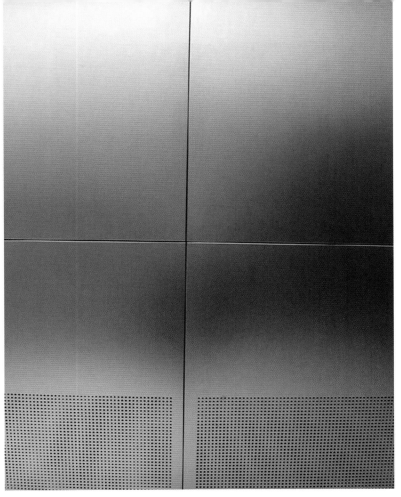

40. Apple Computer Flagship store, interior wall surface. Designer: Bohlin Cywinski Jackson. Four-way joint of a glass-bead-blasted stainless-steel perforated surface.

41. Topeka Library, Topeka Kansas. Designer: Michael Graves. Vertical running bond pattern.

42. Private residence. Designer: Marlon Blackwell Architects. Vertical running bond pattern used on weathering steel shingles. Image was taken six to eight weeks after exposure to the ambient.

43. Kansas City Board of Trade, Kansas City, Missouri. Designer: Joel Marquardt of the architectural firm of Gastinger Walker Harden Architects. The wall sculpture is created by hammered and preoxidized 1.5-mm-thick copper plates. The polished lower sections are coated with Incralac to maintain the bright appearance.

44. Tsing Yi Station, Hong Kong. Designer: Wong Tong Architects. Prepatinated copper roof. The roof edge folds over to create a clean, trimless appearance.

45. Tsing Yi Station, Hong Kong. Designer: Wong Tong Architects. Prepatinated copper roof. Running bond pattern on a double-lock standing seam.

46 Artwork by Shelly Bender. Cut and curved stainless-steel plate.

47. Artwork for Farmland Industry, Kansas City, Missouri. Designer: William Zahner. Ten-meter-tall, copper sculpture; darkened copper surface.

48. "Hope for Life" sculpture outside the Stowers Institute for Medical Research, Kansas City, Missouri. Designer: Larry Young. Stainless-steel plate with a custom coarse artistic grain applied.

49. Private residence, Minnesota. Designer: Meyer Scherer & Rockcastle. Copper roof with shaped ridge.

50. Water Tower Place Renovation, Chicago, Illinois. Designer: Wimberly Allison Tong & Goo. Dry joint assemblies manufactured from stainless steel. Diffuse texture linen finish and angel hair.

51. Private residence, Minnesota. Copper ridge rolls and curves along the length of the structure.

52. Nelson-Atkins Museum of Art parking facility, Kansas City, Missouri. Designer: Steven Holl. Perforated weathered steel around garage staircases. Moiré patterns created by overlaying one perforated surface over the other.

53. The de Young Museum of Art, San Francisco, California. Designer: Herzog and de Meuron. Light coming through the perforated ceiling panels at the entryway.

54. Millennium Park Band Shell Project, Chicago, Illinois. Designer: Frank Gehry. Structural panels shaped in aluminum installed on the steel frame.

55. Millennium Park Band Shell Project, Chicago, Illinois. Designer: Frank Gehry. Structural panels shaped in aluminum installed on the steel frame.

56. Millennium Park Band Shell Project, Chicago, Illinois. Designer: Frank Gehry. Structural panels shaped in aluminum installed on the steel frame.

57. Millennium Park Band Shell Project, Chicago, Illinois. Designer: Frank Gehry. Structural panels shaped in aluminum installed on the steel frame.

58. Pritzker Pavillion in Millennium Park, Chicago, Illinois. Designer: Frank Gehry. Large aluminum panels are clad with a surface of angel hair stainless steel.

59. Copper alloy 5-mm plate. The plate was acid-etched to create the initial design, followed by extensive hammering, oxidation, and highlighting.

60. Custom table created from curved glass-bead-blasted stainless-steel plate. Designer: Ellerbe Beckett Architects.

61. Selective plated nickel on brass to create an inlay appearance. The plate had an initial acid-etched design. After plating, the surface was oxidized.

62. de Young Museum of Art, San Francisco, California. Designer: Herzog and de Meuron Architects. Newly installed copper in the courtyard.

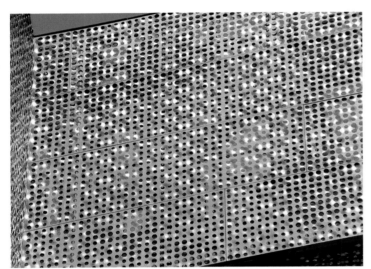

63. The de Young Museum of Art, San Francisco, California. Designer: Herzog and de Meuron. Custom embossed and perforated panels. Horizontal running bond pattern on the rainscreen panel element seams.

64. Titanium sculptural form in the Issey Miyake Flagship Store, Tribeca, New York. Designers: Frank Gehry and Gordon Kipping. This shape was digitally defined and attached to a formed steel skeleton. The surface is a soft, glass-bead-blasted titanium sheet.

PART III
THE TOUCH AND FABRIC

"A slumber did my spirit seal;
I had no human fears:
She seemed a thing that could not feel
The touch of earthly years."

—WILLIAM WORDSWORTH

As you approach within one meter, grit lines created by abrading the surface become apparent. Oxides appear now as clumps of color. Dirt, grime, and water spots are visible on the surface. Corrosion products stand out as adolescent blemishes on a background of smooth contours. You can run your hand across the surface and feel minute undulations. The color is not altered by shadowing or bright reflection. You see the fabric of the surface.

Even a slate floor of a consistent black color renders a subconscious interest in the texture of the stone. Lacking contrast the surface still fixes the mind to the intimacy of the unpredictable, yet similar, fractures that occur from slate to slate. A completely smooth slate surface, devoid of fractures and texture, would resemble perhaps glass or plastic. The fissures of the slate surface give it character and enhance the appearance. No two pieces of slate are exactly alike, but the similarity in the character of their surface variations make the floor appear homogeneous.

FIGURE III.1. Intricacies of a slate floor surface.

For metal the texture is developed from the interaction of the microscopic topography, the grains and their orientation, with surface alterations created by chemical, mechanical, and coating modifications. Like wood and stone, metal surfaces are not identical.[1] Cast and rolled thin, characteristics from plate to plate or sheet to sheet are very similar, but minor variations exist. In most applications, such variations are insignificant and invisible. In others, variations add character and provide a more natural, less machined character.

Two Metal Surface Categories

There are essentially two categories of surfaces available to metal (see Table III.1). First are surfaces that require for a particular effect additional mechanical or chemical preparations. Among these are satin- and mirror-finish stainless steels, prepatinated and statuary copper alloys,

---

[1] While working on the Sears Tower lobby renovation with the architect, John Albright, of DeStefano and Partners, we were involved with creating a strong and distinguishing texture of ground stainless steel. We had prepared over a period of several weeks a series of sample textures approximately 6 inches by 24 inches. These were prepared on stainless steel and were to be submitted for approval before we would make some 60,000 feet of the finish. On query about the adequacy of the samples, Mr. Albright stated, " I like some of them but not all." To my eye, at the time, they looked simply like hand-ground stainless steel. No two pieces matched because of the nature of the finish and the process. However, on further discussion with John Albright, he related, "I want the texture to be like that of the grain in fine wood. No two pieces are identical but you must feel that they came from the same tree."

TABLE III.1

Categories of Metal Surfaces

Metals that require additional preparations to their surfaces	Satin-finish stainless steels
	Mirror-finish stainless steels
	Prepatinated copper
	Statuary copper alloys
	Anodized aluminum
	Painted aluminum
	Painted steel
Metals whose surfaces are allowed to age naturally	2B stainless steel
	Copper
	Zinc
	Monel
	Weathering steel
	Uncoated galvanized steel
	Titanium
	Lead
	Tin-lead-coated metals
	Tin-zinc-coated metals
	Alclad aluminum

anodized aluminum, and, of course, painted aluminum and steel products. For the purpose of this discussion, however, painted metal is not considered. From a purist viewpoint, the metal is there simply to support the paint. The second category of surface comprises the naturally aging materials, allowed to combine with the variants the ambient surroundings present. Among these metals are copper, zinc, uncoated galvanized steel, alclad aluminum, weathering steel, titanium, monel, lead, tin–lead, and tin–zinc-coated metals. Often these are provided as-is from the mill. Granted, architectural or ornamental uses of these metals require some level of quality control.

There are a few finishes that fall in between these two categories. Zinc, for instance, is often preweathered to develop a darkened tone but then allowed to continue natural aging. The expectations are an even, dark gray-blue appearance. Prepatinated copper is another material that is expected to further weather but at a very slow, somewhat predictable way.

In general, though, the metal surfaces that require additional preparations are usually intended to weather very slowly, if at all. The processes in the beginning should predicate the end appearance. There is still a margin of surface variations to be controlled and understood.

Surface Treatments to Metals

For the metals that require some additional application or treatment, there are three main categories of surface alteration. Many of these methods can be combined to develop more elaborate surfaces, or they can be stand-alone measures. Figure III.2 is a comprehensive list of processes performed on the surface of metal to enhance the interplay with the environment and light.

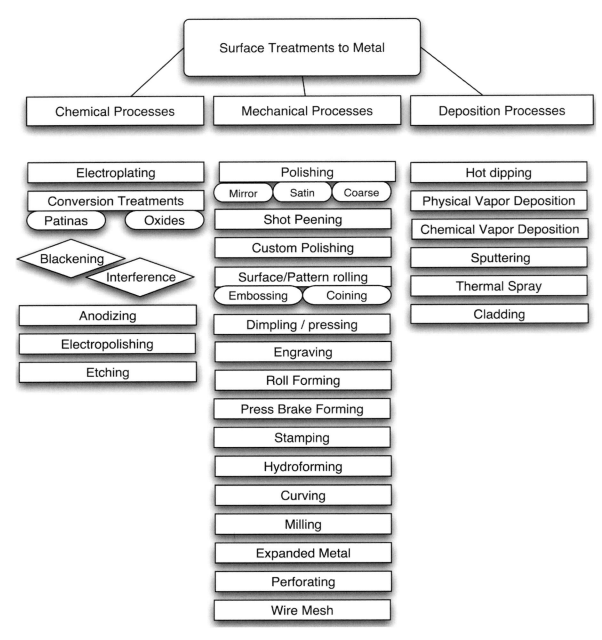

Figure III.2. Processes performed on the surface of metal to enhance the interplay with the environment and light.

Chemical treatments approach a metal's surface on a very intimate level. Molecular interaction occurs with the metal surface. The intention is to influence the metal surface by causing it to join up with other compounds and develop molecular bonds, or break bonds in the case of electropolishing and etching.

Many chemical treatments interface with the surface on an aesthetic level, forcing the molecules on the surface to join with other substances and form compounds that resist change. They achieve this by developing a layer on the surface that is stable, unreactive; that is, a layer that resembles what nature develops over time.

Some chemical treatments go beyond what would naturally develop and create surfaces possessing oxides, several thicknesses greater than normal. These are accomplished by subjecting the metal to electrical currents and controlled baths of strong oxidizing agents. The surfaces are more corrosion-resistant and possess attractive colors unlike the natural appearance of the metal.

The mechanical treatments performed on metals are more invasive. They work the metal surface to create a microscopic topography that adds dimension to the appearance. The surface of the metal is altered, moved around, or removed to create surface character that interacts with light or gives shape to the metal. There are many mechanical processes and they can be combined with chemical and deposition processes.

Mechanical processes should leave the surface of the metal with similar corrosion behavior. When performed correctly, they can provide surface textures that are free of contamination and unaltered by stress or heat buildup.

Deposition processes involve applying one metal onto another. All deposition processes involve two metals. Regardless of the surface texture, the deposition process applies a very thin layer of metal onto the surface of another metal. It is performed in such a manner that a metallurgical bond is developed between the two metals. Because the layer is so thin, surface characteristics of the base metal translate through. However, with deposition processes, the surface appearance is that of the deposited metal. Metals are applied to the surface by deposition to enhance the properties of the base material. The deposited metal acts as a barrier, protecting the base metal. They also enhance the appearance by adding color or surface attributes such as hardness.

When choosing a metal, you compare the various aspects of color, gloss, reflectivity, and texture. Such a subjective process requires a close comparison of the various surface finish forms. There are techniques to better quantify the appearance parameters to ensure some level of consistency. Close analysis of the surface can disclose much about the initial appearance of the metal, but it also can provide information to predict how the metal will change.

All metals change with time. There is no stopping it; you can only slow the process. Often, as the metal ages, it encounters various compounds that influence aging. Some of the compounds encountered can lead to a disappointing performance if they are allowed to remain on the surface. If identified early on, corrective measures may be put in place to thwart the effects. The hope is always to age gracefully and predictably.

CHAPTER 9
CHEMICAL PROCESSES TO ENHANCE METAL SURFACES

"Nothing exists except atoms and empty space: everything else is opinion."

—DEMOCRITUS (460BC–370BC), Greek Philosopher

Chemical processing methods to enhance the metal surface are common (see Table 9.1). Chemical processes are distinguished from other surface treatments by noncontact modifications to the metal. The surface interacts on a molecular level to create compounds or ions that either are removed from the surface by dissolution into an aqueous solution or are developed onto the surface by interaction with other compounds.

Many everyday materials have metals that have undergone some level of chemical processing. Most of the processes develop durable surfaces that enhance the original metal in color, corrosion protection, and surface texture. The following is a discussion of these processes and how they affect various metals.

TABLE 9.1

Chemical Processes to Enhance Metal Surfaces

Electroplating
Conversion treatments—patinas
Conversion treatments—interference coloring
Conversion treatments—anodizing
Electropolishing
Etching

ELECTROPLATING

Electroplating is a chemical process in which objects are immersed in an aqueous bath while a low-voltage direct current is applied to the object. The object to be plated receives a negative charge and is referred to as the *cathode*. Another metal, also immersed in the same solution, is given a positive charge. This metal is known as a *sacrificial anode*. Some of the positively charged metal goes into solution as charged metal ions. A very thin layer of these metal ions is evenly deposited on the surface of the cathode metal. The deposited metal forms a very thin metallic coating on the surface of the target cathode.

Electrodeposition is another term used to describe electroplating processes. Several common methods are used in electroplating, but each is essentially the same process of removing ions from a solution and depositing them on another surface (see Table 9.2).

Of the various methods, selective electroplating is especially intriguing for ornamental work. Selective electroplating involves masking off sections of a material and plating the exposed areas. The method uses a wand-type applicator, which when moistened in solutions containing the metal ions, plates them to the exposed portion of the base metal. The appearance of metal inlays of one metal into another can be achieved (see Table 9.3). Designs and highlights are also possible across the surface of a metal.

Plated surfaces are durable if they are prepared correctly. As with all chemical processes, the base metal must be thoroughly cleaned of all oils, greases, and oxides. Roughening of the surfaces is not required; however, having a slight grain will provide "tooth," to allow the plating material to better key into the surface.

Protecting the surface with clear lacquers or other clear films is necessary on a few of the plated metals to resist tarnish. The plated metal surface will act the same way as the metal would in other uses. Copper plating will oxidize just as a copper sheet surface would.

CONVERSION TREATMENTS

Conversion treatments are surface treatments that develop or convert the surface of a metal into a mineral form or oxidation form of the metal. The surface develops a thin adherent layer of the metal oxide or metal compound, not unlike what would develop over time. That said, some conversion treatments take the surface beyond what would ever be expected to occur in nature. The interference coloring processes used on stainless steel or titanium or the oxidation process of anodizing all go well beyond what would occur naturally.

TABLE 9.2

Electroplating Methods

Rack plating—small parts, sheets, fabricated parts
Selective plating—plating on selected areas
Barrel plating—small parts, rotating barrel
Continuous plating—sheet and strip

TABLE 9.3

Metals That Can Be Plated onto Other Metals

Cadmium	Nickel
Chromium	Platinum
Copper	Silver
Gold	Tin
Lead	Zinc

Patina is defined as a surface change due to age. The colloquialism refers to the oxide that appears on any metal after exposure to the atmosphere or to processes of conversion. The average layperson can easily recognize the patina of an old, weathered, beautiful green copper roof. The green appearance emulates quality and something out of the past like few other surfaces. We seek to copy these natural phenomena by using faux patinas applied to steel or even wood.

Natural-forming copper patinas are the result of the metal combining with various elements in the ambient. Such elements combine with the copper and form colorful patinas of green, blue-green, and gray-green. These compounds are the equilibrium form of the metal on this earth. Creating them quickly is more art than science. However, a brilliant Swiss scientist, Dr. Hans Laubi, created a green patina that is very similar to that which arrives naturally to copper when exposed to atmosphere.

Ironically, hindering natural patina growth in North America and Europe today is the improved quality of the air, at least as far as sulfur is concerned. Copper and the beautiful green patina characterized on the surfaces of decades-old copper take much longer to produce now, and perhaps never will.

Our view of patinas on copper, lead, and terne are forever changed. The original view was generated when compounds existed in the atmosphere, mainly compounds of sulfur from combustion of coal. Since these have been reduced, those green patinas on copper and the dark gray tones on lead and terne coatings are no long quickly created by atmospheric exposure.

Patinas, which are compounds close to the mineral forms of the elements, can, however, be developed artificially. Several commercially available patinas are offered for different metals and innumerable custom patinas. Table 9.4 lists the patinas of various metals.

TABLE 9.4

Patinas on Various Metals

Metal	Patina	Color
Aluminum	Aluminum selinide	Black
Aluminum	Aluminum oxide Aluminum selinide	Gray
Copper	Copper oxide	Brown
Copper	Copper oxide	Black
Copper	Copper chloride	Green-blue
Copper	Copper sulfate	Green
Copper	Copper ferrite	Golden brown
Lead	Lead oxide	Dark brown
Lead	Lead oxide	Red (usually not desired)
Lead	Lead carbonate	Whitish gray (usually not desired)
Monel (Cu/Ni)	Copper oxide Nickel oxide	Brownish green
Weathering steel	Ferrous hydroxide	Orange-brown
Zinc	Zinc carbonate	Blue-gray

To develop the conversion coating, the first, and most important, step is to clean the surface. Removal of oil, oxides, scale, grease, and even fingerprints is very important. Simply mechanical grinding and polishing will not do; chemically etching the surface to remove the oxide layer is mandatory. For every metal there are several surface deoxidizers that work to remove the outer oxide layer. Copper, for example, can be surface-treated with 60 percent phosphoric acid to remove the oxide surface. You must follow all recommended safety precautions when using acids. Phosphoric, combined with a mild surface abrasion, will provide a surface ready to react with various chemical agents. Time between preparation and application must be kept to a minimum. Once the surface is clean, it is very receptive to oxidizing agents and compounds that will produce remarkable colors.

INTERFERENCE COLORS

Interference coloring of metal is created by the interplay of light with the dual surfaces of the metal and its transparent oxide. However, the oxides must be of sufficient thickness to create interference conditions with the reflecting light.

Transparent oxides occur on nearly all metals at some time in their development. Metals such as copper and lead develop thin, clear oxides, which eventually combine with compounds in the atmosphere that develop colored oxide forms that are no longer transparent. Initially, however, the clear surface oxides develop and interference colors can be apparent as light interplays with the dual surfaces . Copper can appear black, red, purple, and yellow when the initial oxide develops. Lead can have almost a rainbow-colored sheen on first exposures to the air. These interference colors disappear as the oxide film thickens and becomes less transparent.

Other metals require additional chemical and electrochemical treatments to establish colors. Metals such as stainless steel and titanium will rapidly develop a clear oxide layer when exposed to the air. The development is almost instantaneous. This oxide layer is very thin and does not support the development of light interference behavior. Thickening the clear oxide layer is necessary in developing the interference effects. Exposing the metal surfaces to strong oxidizers does this.

The Phenomenon of Light Interference
The phenomenon of light interference occur on metals, which can develop thin, transparent films. The thin films are consistent in thickness and are very stable. Essentially, light reflecting off of the base metal surface undergoes a phase reversal. Light reflecting off of the oxide to the air interface surface has the same phase as the incident light.

If the film is thin, the two reflections will come back with opposite, but aligned, phases and will interfere with one another. This type of interference is known as *destructive interference*, and the surface will appear black. Refer to Figure 9.1. However, if the film has a thickness of $\lambda/4$ (a quarter of a wavelength), then the wave that reflects from the base metal surface will have its phase altered by a half cycle since it has traveled a quarter in and a quarter out of the film. Thus, it will be in phase with the light reflecting off of the air/oxide interface surface. This is known as *constructive interference*. It is often associated with a bright fringe of light. Refer to Figure 9.2.

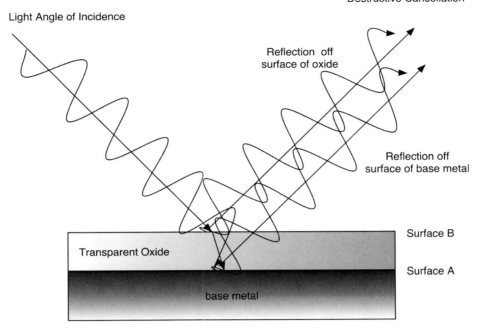

FIGURE 9.1. Diagram of destructive cancellation phenomenon.

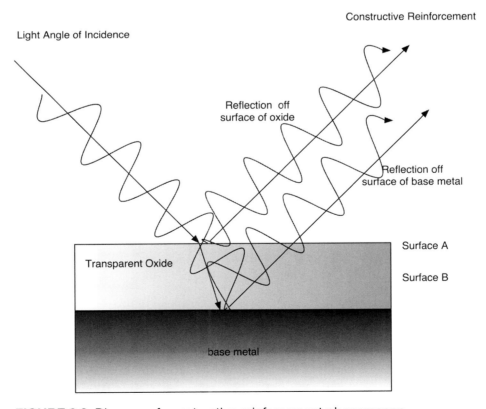

FIGURE 9.2. Diagram of constructive reinforcement phenomenon.

The colors produced from light interference are not mixable. You cannot, for example, "add" more gold to blue to lighten it. The process of achieving color is not the same as for dyes and pigments. We are so used to being able to add a little more of one pigment to another in order to match colors or develop complementary colors. Light interference achieves a color in an entirely different manner from that of pigments, dyes, and coatings. It would be like asking the sky to be a different blue color. The wavelengths that correspond to colors are immutable. Light interference causes a shift in wavelength perceived by the eye by cancellation of portions of the light wave and by reinforcing other portions. The laws of physics preclude adjusting the wave for the benefit of a color match.

An interesting phenomenon of light interference colors is the angle-of-view effect. The thicker films, when viewed from different angles, can have differing colors. For example, green-interference stainless steel, when viewed from a distance, appears green across the surface. As you approach, the angle of view changes. As the view angle increases, you look through a different thickness of oxide and the color appears red, gold, or even blue, yet the surface in front of you appears green.

For stainless steel, the base metal finish affects the colors that can be generated (see Table 9.5). Mirror finishes reflect deep metallic colors. Satin finishes such as a No.4, Angel Hair, or glass bead produce colors that are softer, diffused in reflection. To develop the interference colors on stainless steel, the sheets are cleaned and dipped into a heated bath of chromic and oxalic acid. After a predetermined period of time, a thickened layer of chromium oxide develops on the surface.

Because the oxide layer is identical to the natural-forming chromium oxide, except that it is thicker, it can be expected to last a very long time. It is resistant to ultraviolet radiation, meaning it will not fade; there is really nothing to fade or decompose in the way of added dyes or films.

The oxide layer as an extension of the stainless-steel surface can be formed, pierced, and shaped without damage. It will, however, scratch. Once scratched it will not "heal" itself to the original thickness. The color of the scratch will be apparent as the natural silver color of stainless steel. Thus, use interference-coated stainless steel in places where it will not be subject to abrasion.

Titanium can develop interference colors as well (see Table 9.6). In the 1950s, it was found that by applying a low voltage to the titanium surface while it was immersed in an electrolytic bath, the titanium oxide on the surface would thicken. After a certain span of time, colors appeared evenly across the surface. The colors are created by the phenomenon of light interference. This phenomenon

TABLE 9.5

Interference Colors on Stainless Steel

Bronze	Red
Blue	Green
Gold	Black

TABLE 9.6

Interference Colors on Titanium

Very light gold tone	Purple with gold tones
Pale gold	Blue-purple
Gold	Dark blue
Dark gold	Medium blue
Dark gold with purple tones	Pale blue

also works on the other reactive metals. Besides titanium, there are five other metals considered as reactive. Niobium is one of those, used extensively in jewelry. The reactive metals are very strong, electronegative metals; they are poor conductors of electricity. As the electrical current is applied, a thicker oxide grows within the conductive electrolyte. The oxide is clear and thin, and it performs well as an interference film on the titanium. A specific voltage will consistently yield the same oxide thickness and thus the same interference color.

With a constant voltage, different intensities of the same color can be produced as the titanium is immersed in the conductive fluid. Increase the voltage, and different colors are obtained. As with stainless steel, the color is generated from light interference with a clear, thickened oxide film. There are no applied films or impregnated dyes to decay from exposure to ultraviolet radiation.

The film is hard and durable, but when scratched, it will not redevelop to the thickness necessary to create light interference. The scratch will appear as the natural titanium color.

Sheets with interference color can be shaped and formed without damage to the oxide. As with stainless steel, consider using interference colored metal in locations where abrasion is not likely.

ANODIZING

The oxide layer is produced by immersion of aluminum into acid solutions, usually sulfuric acid. A current is developed, with the aluminum sheet acting as the anode with the acid solution of the electrolyte, and the immersion tank or some other material acting as the cathode. The thickness of the aluminum oxide is linearly related to the voltage applied. Refer to Figure 9.3.

The process of anodizing requires several basic steps. First the metal is cleaned and etched to remove foreign particles and oxides from the surface. This pretreatment process is performed in a bath of sodium hydroxide. (Etching produces a course surface that quickly and severely fingerprints, thus care in handling after etching is extremely important.) The sodium hydroxide etch produces the tex-

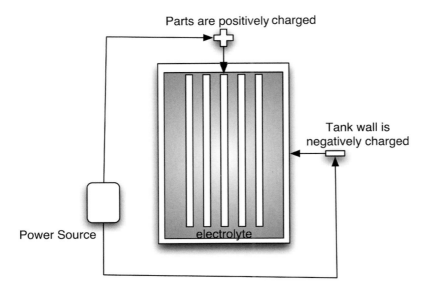

FIGURE 9.3. Basic anodizing process.

ture of the final anodized surface for most applications. The most common of the etched surfaces is the medium matte surface. Etching results in the removal of a layer of aluminum and leaves the surface receptive to further treatments.

The anodic oxidation process develops a dual structure. Over an amorphous layer of aluminum oxide grows a crystalline layer. The crystalline layer has a hexagonal cell structure with a columnar pore extending from the surface inward, normal to the base metal. Refer to Figure 9.4. As the crystalline layer develops, about half the aluminum consumed in the oxidation process passes into the electrolyte solution while the balance is retained as oxide in the hexagonal coating.

The clear anodized aluminum oxide coating developed using the sulfuric acid process creates a surface that is essentially the mineral bohmite. The clear oxide coating created by the anodizing process has a thermal conductivity 10 percent that of the base metal. The oxide surface has a coefficient of linear expansion only 20 percent of the base metal. They will develop small microcracks when stretched or bent. When heated above 80°C, small cracks will form. Under normal circumstances, the oxide layer is brittle in thicknesses greater than 0.05 μm. Table 9.7 delineates these characteristics.

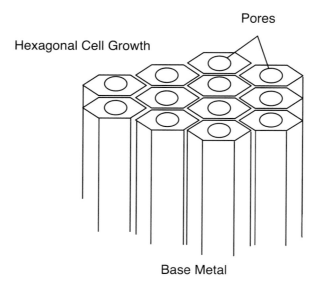

FIGURE 9.4. Diagram of hexagonal pore growth on an anodized surface.

TABLE 9.7

Characteristics of Anodized Aluminum Coatings

Thermal conductivity	10% of base aluminum material
Coefficient of linear expansion	20% of base aluminum material
Hardness—typical anodized film	200 to 300 HV
Hardness—hardcoat	350 to 550 HV
Reflective index	1.59 to 1.62

Aluminum is available in basically three forms—rolled, extruded, or cast—all of which can be anodized. Rolled would include all sheet and plate goods. Extruded includes bars, rods, and tubing, as well as custom shapes.

Pure aluminum is not in common use due to its softness. Adding small amounts of various alloying elements create structural, appearance, and performance characteristics (see Table 9.8). Adding from 1 to 2 percent of Cu, Mg, Fe, and Si can change the behavior and coloring characteristics of the metal. Of the alloys used in architectural processes, 6063-T5 or 6063-T52 is common for surface quality and anodizing consistency.

Methods of Anodizing

The sulfuric acid anodizing process creates a clear and transparent coating. The longer the exposure time, the thicker the coating, until a maximum thickness of 40 μm is achieved. If there is silicon, iron, or manganese present, grayness in the clear coating develops. The gray color deepens as the thickness of the clear anodizing proceeds.

There are several methods of anodizing aluminum to achieve color (see Table 9.9). Each method offers advantages and disadvantages depending on

TABLE 9.8

Anodizing Behavior of Aluminum Alloys

Aluminum Alloy Series	Major Alloying Constituent	Anodizing Quality	Brightness and Gloss
1000 series	99% pure	Excellent	Very good
2000 series	Copper	Poor	Fair
3000 series	Manganese	Very good	Fair
4000 series	Silicon	Good	Poor
5000 series	Magnesium	Very good	Good
6000 series	Silicon and magnesium	Very good	Fair

TABLE 9.9

Anodizing Methods

Method	Basic Process	Advantages	Performance
Dye dipping	Fill pores with organic dyes	Numerous color choices. Excellent color match	Poor lightfastness; use for interiors only
Inorganic salts	Fill pores with metal salts	Limited color Good color match	Stable; exterior use acceptable
Alloy coloring	Alloying constituents create color	A4043 best to produce gray	Color uniformity a problem. Not commonly used
Organic acid anodizing	Organic acids create color tones in alloy	Several colors are possible	Limited to bronze and ambers
Electrolytic metal coloring	Deposition of metal particles into pores	Good colorfastness	Color limitations, but decent match potential

intended use. In general, the idea is to produce a consistent repeatable color and finish that will last for the service life of the part.

ELECTROPOLISHING

Electropolishing, when performed correctly, provides a surface with very high uniformity and good luster. The process involves placing a metal surface, whether a formed part, casting, or a sheet of metal, into an electrolytic solution. A direct current is maintained between the part, which is the anode, and another conductor. As the current is passed through the part, high points, low conductive particles, and other foreign matter are removed. The surface is left with a high luster and uniformly bright finish. Under microscopic inspection, the surface is featureless, void of small scratches that often accompany the mechanically polished surfaces.

There are several types of solutions used to develop the electrolyte used to electropolish various metals. Each involves strong acids or oxidizing agents, which demand care and control. Handling of these chemicals is best done by persons with proper expertise and knowledge of disposal procedures.

Most metals can be successfully electropolished (see Table 9.10). The resulting finish is more corrosion-resistant, and more homogeneous. Stainless-steel surfaces that undergo electropolishing are left with a surface enriched with chromium. This improves the corrosion resistance of the metal.

Electropolishing is well suited for producing a bright, reflective surface on the softer metals, though soft metals such as zinc, copper, and aluminum are difficult to polish mechanically. Additionally, various shaped and fabricated parts and cast forms can be successfully electropolished. But on formed shapes and cast parts, it is difficult, if not impossible, to achieve an even mechanical polish.

ETCHING

Chemical etching processes, which have been around since the time of alchemy, are today reaching new levels of potential since the advent of semiconductor manufacturing. Historically, alchemists knew certain metals could be dissolved in various fluids. Designs were placed on metal surfaces, and the chemicals—strong acids—would be applied to the surfaces. Foaming and fizzing would occur; and when the chemicals were rinsed away, a surface pattern would remain. Early etching of metal was performed for decorative purposes on swords

TABLE 9.10

Commonly Electropolished Metals

Aluminum	Stainless steel
Copper alloys	Tin
Gold	Titanium
Monel	Zinc
Silver	

in both the Middle East and Asia millennia ago. The metal surface would have some design painted onto the surface with wax or animal grease.

The process today is similar. A resist of a light-sensitive polymer is applied over the very clean surface of the metal. A design is produced as a negative and applied to a glass plate. The plate is placed over the light-sensitive resist and exposed to a powerful light. The part of the resist concealed by the design is shaded, while the part exposed undergoes a reaction, with the light allowing it to be rinsed away. The result is a resist in the form of the art design. The exposed regions of metal are presented to a strong acid (see Table 9.11). The acid acts on the metal to dissolve the surface a layer at a time. With each application more metal is removed.

Etching of metal surfaces can produce very attractive designs. A much slower production process, etching involves the selective removal of metal by dissolution. Sometimes referred to as *chemical milling* when large, deep portions of metal are removed, the etching process can produce very fine and accurate designs without creating stress in the metal substrate.

TABLE 9.11

Etching Compounds for Various Metals

Metal	Etching Agent
Aluminum	Hydrochloric acid
Copper	Ferric chloride
Steel/stainless steel	Ferric chloride
Titanium	Hydrofluoric acid
Gold	Aqua regia

FIGURE 9.5. Etched brass floor plate, 48 inches in diameter.

Once the resist has been applied correctly, the metal sheet or part is passed through a chamber that sprays the etching fluid onto the surface. Often the finish surface of the metal is facing downward and the etching fluid is sprayed toward it. Gravity pulls the fluid down, along with small amounts of metal that have been dissolved. This occurs for several minutes depending on the depth of the etching. To avoid undercutting the resist, the spray should be normal to the surface to the greatest extent possible.

Etching uses very powerful chemicals in a controlled chamber. The surface is cleaned both before the process and during the removal of the resist. Before removal of the resist, the etched portion can be filled with paint to highlight the recessed portion. Once the resist is removed, further decorative treatments can be performed on the metal surface: highlighting by polishing the top surface, oxidization processes—just about any process that typically is performed on a nonetched sheet.

All metals can be etched. On a decorative level, steel, stainless steel, copper alloys, and, to a lesser degree, magnesium and titanium are metals that receive chemical etching well. Etching, or in actuality, chemical milling, is performed on aluminum for industrial and aerospace purposes. Rarely is an entire surface etched, although attempts to etch the entire surface of stainless steel to achieve a specific finish characteristic have been performed with some success. What occurs when large areas are etched is mottling or streaking. This is due to impurities in the metal, which redeposit on the surface. Called *smutting*, this blackish-looking film is difficult to remove and equally difficult to control. Another issue is the initial porosity of the surface. The oxide layer, which usually protects the metal, is totally removed. The resulting surface holds fingerprint oils and other foreign materials.

Chemical processes go right to the molecular level of a surface. These methods can produce aesthetic and performance enhancement to surfaces created from metals. They result in a uniform alteration of the metal, generally without affecting internal stress or other physical properties. This is opposed to mechanical processes, which do affect internal stresses within the metal as they alter the surface by physically moving the metal under force.

CHAPTER 10
MECHANICAL PROCESSES

"The first edge is made with the blunt whetstone."

—JOHN LYLY

The twentieth century presented various mechanical processes to metals. These processes were developed mainly for the "new metals," metals that would hold their appearance and not develop surface oxides. Buffing and polishing were performed on various metals to shine them, but the satin polishes were less common until stainless steel and aluminum were developed.

The mechanical finishes are an important feature used in architectural and ornamental applications. Essentially, all metals produced at the mill undergo some aspect of mechanical processing. Mechanical processes are defined as those that physically impart a surface or shape to metal (see Table 10.1). There is a physical connection and transfer of energy from one surface to another to produce a finish or surface more refined than what is provided at the mill.

For the discussion on surfaces, alterations to the surface topography in order to induce specific reflective behaviors are described. The finishing techniques can be applied to nearly all forms of metal, plate, sheet, bar, tube, structural shapes, and castings. Dimpling methods, such as embossing and coining, as well as perforations, expanded metal, and the forming operations are limited to sheet and some plate forms. Wire mesh can be developed from both wire and thin strips of metal interwoven into sheets.

MIRROR, SATIN, AND GROUND FINISHES

Today, the mirror-polished, satin, and ground finishes are used to accentuate the surfaces of various metals, which typically include those metals that do not develop thick-colored oxides or metals that are prevented from developing oxides by application of clear coatings (see Table 10.2).

Polishing processes are performed on all forms of metal. The processes vary depending on the form, whether sheet, bar stock, or casting, but the resulting sur-

TABLE 10.1

Mechanical Processes Performed on Metal Surfaces

Mirror finishing	Roll forming
Satin finishing	Press-brake forming
Ground finishing	Stamping
Glass bead finishes	Hydroforming
Shot peening	Pyramid rolling
Custom polishing—multidirectional	Stretch forming
Embossing	Milling
Coining	Expanded metal
Dimpling/pressing	Perforated metal
Engraving	Wire mesh

TABLE 10.2

Mirror, Satin, and Ground Finishes on Metals

Metal	Finish	Comments
Aluminum	Mirror polish	Needs protection
Aluminum	Satin polish-directional	Needs protection
Aluminum	Satin polish-angel hair	Needs protection
Copper alloys	Mirror polish	Needs protection
Copper alloys	Satin finish	Needs protection
Copper alloys	Ground	Needs protection
Iron	Angel hair	Needs protection
Iron	Ground	Needs protection
Stainless steel	Mirror finish	No additional protection
Stainless steel	Satin finish	No additional protection
Stainless steel	Angel hair finish	No additional protection
Stainless steel	Ground	No additional protection
Titanium	Light angel hair	No additional protection
Zinc	Satin finish	Needs protection
Zinc	Ground	Needs protection

face finishes are similar in appearance. Various polishing grits are used to produce the polish. These grits can be matched in belts, discs, pads, and other surface-polishing media. The major difference lies in controlling the angular aspect. For sheets, plates, bars, and tube forms of metal, the polish can be linear, usually down the length of the object. Cast objects may not facilitate this directional aspect and require matching grits with pads. However, the change in angle will change the apparent color because of the way light reflects off the surface.

Mirror Polishing

Buffing the surface with fine polishing wheels typically produces mirror finishes. Mirror finishes, also known as *specular finishes*, are the result of smooth, very fine grain surfaces, free of oxides.

Mirror specular surfaces are possible on coil material from the mill source. The mill uses high polished rolls when the metal is cold rolled and reduced in thickness. The high polished rolls impart a very smooth surface on the metal. The mill forms are known as "as fabricated" finishes and are available only on thin, cold rolled metal sheet. Sheet material of the heavier thickness is not as bright and reflective as thinner sheet. This is because the number of cold rolling passes performed is limited on the thicker sheet material.

Specular mirror surfaces produced by buffing wheels and rouges are performed on the as-fabricated mill surfaces provided on sheet, plate, bar, or tube forms. They are also produced on fabricated, spun, and cast parts.

It is important that the surface be clean of oxides, weld discoloration, and abrasions or weld splatter. If the fabricated surface can be electropolished prior to polishing, results will be improved. Polishing will not remove heavy grit lines or gouges in the surface. These must be removed by sanding with media, particularly the very fine grit media.

The characteristics of specular polished finishes are an even luster where the angle of incidence equals closely the angle of reflection (see Table 10.3). You could say an image is reflected clearly; however, this corresponds more to mirror specular. Detail is recognized in the reflected surface on mirror specular surfaces. For specular surfaces, the image is not necessarily easily discernable; light hitting the surface and reflecting back to the eye is seen as a bright disc shape.

On many metal surfaces, slight distortions can often be seen on the surface. The distortions are visual; they cannot be determined by passing your hand over

TABLE 10.3

Specular Finishes on Various Metals

Metal	Reflective Designation	Metal Form
Aluminum	Specular Mirror specular	Sheet, plate, bar, tube, castings, mill-as-fabricated in most forms
Copper	Specular Mirror specular	Sheet, plate, bar, tube, castings, mill-as fabricated in sheet form
Copper alloys	Specular Mirror Specular	Sheet, plate, bar, tube, castings, mill-as-fabricated in sheet, plate, bar, tubing
Stainless steel	No. 9	Sheet
Stainless steel	Super No. 8	Sheet
Stainless steel	No. 8	Sheet, plate, bar, tube
Stainless steel	No. 7	Sheet, plate, bar, tube
Stainless steel	No. 2BA	Mill sheet
Stainless steel	Mirror specular	Castings, fabricated parts
Tin	Specular	Sheet, tube, bar, mill-as-fabricated
Zinc	Specular	Mill-as-fabricated

the surface. These are dislocations within the metal that reflect light differently from surrounding surfaces. It's as if they are just under the surface of the metal, but no amount of polishing will remove them. Dislocations are minute impurities that are in the initial casting. As the casting is rolled thinner, these become stretched out. These imperfections are more apparent on thicker sheet and plate. Thin sheet stretches these imperfections into a line, hence they become far less apparent.

Satin Polish

Fine grit lines or scratches on the metal surface characterize the satin polish finishes. The grit lines are applied by passing an abrasive over the surface of the metal (see Table 10.4). Abrasives plow the surface of a metal and turn grooves without removing significant amounts of material.

Satin finishes are distinguished by whether the grit lines form a directional reflective surface or the surface is nondirectional. Directional finishes are applied to coil, sheet, and plate, as well as bar and tube. The surface is passed below a rotating polishing wheel or belt, which imparts linear scratches along the length of the sheet. For tubing the finish can be applied along the length or around the circumference. Both are considered directional finishes. Application of the directional finishes produces even and consistent grit lines. The reflectivity should be similar, without light and dark hazing from uneven grit depth. There may be, however, occurrences where surface oil or grease has streaked sections of the polished surface.

Grit size is considered the size of the sieve used to size the abrasive media. There are several common grit sizes used. The smaller the grit value, the coarser the finish produced.

The nondirectional satin finishes known as Angel hair and vibration, as well as other similar somewhat proprietary finishes, are produced by a fine grit sanding disc or abrasive pad moved in a circular manner over the surface of the metal. The result is a finish with little if any directionality to it. There are numerous variations of the process. Applying it over the surface of a cast or assembled metal product is not difficult. Blending the surface to match other parts is also possible. The process requires the careful match of the polishing grit and a device with a similar arc radius to that used to apply the finish. Figure 10.1 shows two brass surfaces welded together. The weld is taken down and the finish is applied to blend the two surfaces together.

The nondirectional finish should be consistent in appearance. Across any part of the metal surface, thousands of extremely small scratches radiate from a

TABLE 10.4

Satin Polishes on Metals

Metal	Finish Designation	Metal Form
Aluminum	Satin finish—100 to 150 grit	Sheet, plate, bar, tubing
Copper alloys	Satin finish—100 to 150 grit	Sheet, plate, bar, tubing
Monel, nickel	Satin finish—120 to 150 grit	Sheet
Stainless steel	Satin finishes, No.3 100 grit, No.4 120 to 150 grit, Hairline 180 grit	Sheet, plate, bar, tubing

FIGURE 10.1 Angel hair applied over welded corner.

central bright circle. Each tiny scratch reflects the light at right angles to the plane of incidence. Each scratch spreads the light at right angles to the tangent of its arc direction at any given point. Because of this, the circular scratch is only visible to the observer in this plane. Move around and the circle of light moves with the observer.

Ground Finishes

Ground surfaces are coarse, multidirectional finishes applied by the heavy grit discs. The discs address the surface of the metal at a slight angle at high-revolution speeds. Only a small section of the disc meets the surface of the metal at any one moment. The applicator brushes the surface quickly. The process simply touches the metal surface to create a small irregular patch of ground surface. Keeping the grinding disc on the metal surface longer can produce larger "ribbons" of the grinding finish. Figures 10.2A, B, and C are of various surfaces that have received the ground finish. Each is slightly different. Figure 10.2A is of a large stainless steel sculptural shape. The finish is applied to the final welded form. Figure 10.2B is of panels finished with a ground texture and assembled on a canopy. Figure 10.2C shows the ground finish as an accent for other stainless steel finishes.

The ground finish is an artistic process, best produced by hand, although it can be mechanized. The key is similar to patterning processes. If some level of rhythm is not achieved, the surface can look sloppy and unplanned. The various angles produced by the disc striking the surface will cause a glitter effect on the surface. As the observer's viewpoint changes, light reflects off various patches in strong contrast.

When working with the ground finish, produce samples and record the rhythm that works best for the particular surface. For formed parts and cast parts

FIGURE 10.2A. Ground finish on a stainless-steel sculpture.

FIGURE 10.2B. Ground finish on building entryway.

FIGURE 10.2C. Sears Tower (Chicago, Illinois) interior ornamental surface. Ground finish applied at insets.

with tight shapes, smaller "brushstrokes" will give better results. When producing large fabricated parts with significant expanses of flat areas, consider producing the finish on flat sheets, then fabricate and assemble the shape and fill in to complete the finish.

When creating this finish, use new discs dedicated only to the metal being work on. Problems often occur on stainless steel when grinding discs used previously on steel are used on stainless, causing contamination of the stainless-steel surface. The same will happen to copper and copper alloy surface and aluminum surfaces. Minute steel particles can become imbedded into the surface causing un-repairable damage to the base metal.

Metals that receive the ground surfacing well include:

■ Stainless steel

■ Copper alloys

■ Aluminum

■ Steel (clear-coated)

Polishing or abrading processes impart their own nuances to the metal surface. Wear on the polishing disc or belts will produce unique surfaces subject to the time of application. Multiple belts and discs can assist in blending the surfaces and allow for repeat production of the particular polish. But the polish is not exactly the same over every metal surface. Understanding and controlling the variations is critical when it is important to appear alike. If the technique used to apply the finish changes from deterioration of the process or time and direction of application, or if the atmospheric environment has changed during the processing, the appearance of the surface can be altered significantly. Understanding how to control and define these variables is an important concept in achieving predictable surface textures.

Creating a very coarse ground finish has some drawbacks in terms of long-term corrosion inhibition. Abrasive gouges create grooves without removing the metal entirely. This can occur with very hard but worn abrasive discs, belts, or wheels. The worn abrasive particles are dragged across the surface and can leave thin "tongues" of metal. These tongues are minute bits of metal turned over at the groove edge. The surface has a smeared look to it. This can, if exposed to the environment, create crevice corrosion cells when moisture and corroding substances, such as chlorides, are trapped below the metal tongues.

Care for and Concerns about Abraded Finishes

Abraded finishes produce grooves and gouges into the metal surface by passing the hard abrasive material across the surface. The abrasive medium used on metal is aluminum oxide or silicon carbide. Some proprietary pad material are synthetics with specific levels of fineness and hardness. They are available in various equivalent grit sizes.

Each abrasive creates the fine linear and radial textures on metal. As the abrasive wears, they become dull and can rip microscopic tongues of metal that curl back on the surface. These are defects and alter slightly the finish on the metal. They also can become regions where crevice corrosion can become fixed on the metal surface.

Another concern is frictional heat on the metal surface. This is partly due to worn-out abrasives, but is more inclined to be the product of excessive speed and pressure of the pads against the sheet, which can discolor the metal surface.

Process controls are essential for finishes generated from surface abrasion techniques. Perhaps the greatest detriment to abraded surfaces occurs when process controls do not restrict the use of tools and pads to specific metals. These postmill operations require stringent controls for the use of the equipment, as contamination of polishing and abrading equipment and the transfer to other metals can be significant. You cannot, for example, use the same tools on stainless steel that you use on steel and expect to achieve a passive stainless surface. The tools contaminate the surface of the stainless steel with iron particles. The passivity is now altered, for all intents and purposes, for the life of the metal.

Glass Bead Finish

The glass bead finish is a nondirectional satin finish applied by the kinetic impact of small glass spheres onto the surface of a metal. The glass bead itself is distinguished by its spherical form. Several sizes are available, each of which can create subtle differences on the finish (see Table 10.5).

The impact of the glass to the metal surface creates a small indentation. The indentations are rounded, and they tend to overlap. This overlapping crater produces light-scattering behavior, effectively diffusing the reflectivity. Figure 10.3 shows three different grit sizes of glass bead finishes layered over one another.

The process can be applied to any metal form, sheet, bar, or casting. Note that this is not a cleaning process. If the surface of the metal has dirt, scratches,

TABLE 10.5

Glass Bead Sizes*

Mesh Size	Grit Size	Micron Range
20 to 30	25	840–590
25–45	35	710–350
30–50	40	590–297
35–60	48	500–250
40–70	55	420–210
50–80	65	297–177
60–100	80	250–149
70–140	105	210–105
100–200	150	149–74
140–270	205	105–53
170–325	248	88–44
270–1000	635	53–10
325—very fine	700	44—very fine

*Bold are typically used.

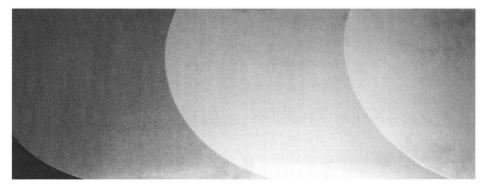

FIGURE 10.3. Various glass-bead surfaces. (Courtesy of Rimex Metals.)

or even fingerprints, glass-bead blasting will not remove these. On the contrary, it will fix the grease or fingerprint into the surface, making it impossible to remove.

The process involves feeding glass beads from a hopper into a high-pressure stream of clean, dry air. The outlet sprays the beads at high speed onto the surface of the metal. The glass beads that impact on the surface can shatter. The shattered beads are removed in a separator, and the spherical beads are recycled back into the hopper. The process seems simple, but to achieve a consistent, nonmottled surface requires further controls (see Table 10.6).

The process works well on stainless steel, titanium, aluminum, and brass. On stainless steel, the finish is bright but diffuse, almost crystalline in appearance. Glass bead finish stainless steel is characterized by a soft, grainy reflection. Direct light reflecting off the surface is diffused by the multitude of small overlapping impact craters made by the glass beads. The surface appears bright and deep in full sunlight. On cloudy days, it takes on the appearance of pewter. Low sun makes it glow purple and reddish silver. Because of the reflectivity of stainless, it is far more sensitive to minor variations in the blasting process. Careful control of the glass bead application is critical to eliminate hazing and mottling in the reflection.

On titanium, the surface created by glass-bead blasting is matte in appearance. Bead blasting effectively removes the glossy sheen apparent on cold rolled titanium sheet, leaving a soft grainy appearance. On aluminum, glass-bead blasting creates a dense thin layer at the surface. The appearance is a white, slightly mottled surface that readily fingerprints. Following the blasting process, clear-anodizing the surface will produce an attractive, even appearance that takes on a blue-silver color tone in bright sunlight. The appearance is deeper than that of clear-anodized over specular-finish aluminum.

TABLE 10.6

Glass-Bead Blasting Variables to Control and Monitor

Variable to Control	Effect
Base metal quality	Good specular and clean surface is necessary,
Base metal consistency	To match, you must use metal from the same casting.
Base metal temper	Surface hardness must be matched from sheet to sheet; otherwise, the impact craters produced by the beads will vary.
Bead size	Must be consistent and free of shards and foreign materials.
Surface of metal	Must be as clean as possible, free of all scratches and fingerprints.
Process of blasting	Develop a sequential travel path to ensure all surfaces receive the same amount of texturing.
Compressed air	Dry: must have oil- and water-free supply of air; otherwise, watermarking will occur.
Pressure	Establish the correct pressure to achieve the desired results. Altering the pressure will produce a mottled surface.
Flattening (for sheets)	The process will shape the metal. Blasting the reverse side is required. Leveling also is an option.
Postcleanup and handling	The surface is delicate. Remove all dust by blasting with clean air. Use gloves to handle the material. It fingerprints easily when newly blasted.

Shot Peening

Shot peening differs from glass-bead blasting in that, in lieu of glass, small spheres of metal are used, usually of stainless steel. Steel shot should only be used on steel parts. The stainless-steel shot can carry tremendous energy to the surface of the sheet. Shot peening imparts a relatively shallow layer of the surface into compression. This helps reduce tensile stresses in the metal by increasing the residual compressive stresses, which also resists fatigue and corrosion. Shot peening stainless will harden the surface as well.

The texture is coarser than that developed via glass-bead blasting. A slight burnishing of the surface also occurs, which produces a somewhat brighter tone to the metal. Significant shaping also occurs. Back blasting will help return the flatness, but the process greatly increases the surface hardness, making further forming operations difficult. Shot peening on castings, pipe, and bar will work adequately with little to no shaping. As with glass-bead blasting, the surface should be clean. Unlike glass bead, shot peening does remove small amounts of metal from the surface. It can, depending on the hardness of the shot, leave metal on the surface. Thus, steel shot used on stainless steel will leave small particles of steel on the surface. These particles can corrode, damaging the stainless-steel surface and rendering the surface nonpassive.

Custom Polishing: Changing Textures and Direction

Decorative effects can be created by selectively applying the satin finishes or mixing satin finish with other reflective finishes. Alternating the finish direction from one angle to another creates decorative surfaces that utilize the point reflection behavior of light. Figure 10.4 shows a large reflective stainless-steel plate custom polished with concentric circles.

FIGURE 10.4. Custom radial polishing on stainless steel.

These finishes scatter the light effectively and at very subtle levels. The scattered light is polarized and appears with different intensities based on the angle of view. Observed from one direction, one surface will appear brighter than an adjacent surface. Both surfaces may have precisely the same finish, with the exception that one surface is applied at a different bias. By applying a satin finish at angles to one another, light reflecting back to the observer arrives with different intensities. The effect is startling, but can be layered to develop fascinating surfaces that appear and then disappear depending on the angle of view.

Including portions that maintain the mirror surface intermixed with the satin finish produces localized contrasting appearances. Other finishes, such as glass bead or adding color by interference methods, enhance the appearance even further. Figures 10.5A and B show selective polishing creations by Rimex Metals of England. Figure 10.5B shows the subtle artwork that appears under certain reflective angles.

FIGURE 10.5A. Custom selective polishing on stainless steel. (Courtesy of Rimex Metals.)

FIGURE 10.5B. Designs in selective polish are visible at different angles. (Courtesy of Rimex Metals.)

EMBOSSING USING PATTERN ROLLS

Embossing using pattern rolls is an economical process, assuming a manufacturer already is in possession of a set of rolls. Names like "stucco embossed," "canvas," and "leathergrain" allude to the nature of the appearance.

Thin metal sheet or a ribbon of metal from a coil is passed through two pattern rolls. The patterns on each roll are positives and negatives of each other. The thin metal exceeds its plastic limit and permanently deforms to match the pattern on the rolls. The pattern produced on one side of the sheet is essentially the negative pattern of the opposite side. The rolls are massive and require precise machinery to impart the texture correctly and consistently. The capital expense of a set of rolls is significant, thus the limitations on the various textures available.

Embossing using pattern rolls typically covers the entire sheet from edge to edge. The embossing surface is stiffer than an unembossed sheet. The plastic deformations across the surface slightly work-harden the metal, but it also stress relieves the surface. Thinner gauges can be used when the surface is embossed. The surface deformations are small, ranging from 0.125 inches (3 mm) across to as large as 0.375 inches (10 mm). The overall height out of plane of the surface is typically not more than 0.125 inches (3 mm) and usually much less. The lightness of the surface disturbance is such that forming operations can still be performed. Embossed sheets are cut in shears, roll formed, brake formed, and stamped, with little effect on the surface patterns. Refer to Figure 10.6 for a few examples of embossed sheet metal surfaces.

Viewed from a distance, embossed surfaces induced by pattern rolls produce a smooth, flat-looking surface. On polished or reflective metal surfaces, the small indentations and outward protrusions effectively scatter the light. The result is a

FIGURE 10.6. Various embossed metals. (Courtesy of Rimex Metals.)

monolithic appearance with reduced oil-canning tendencies. The texture is not readily apparent when viewed at a distance.

Embossing using patterning rolls can be performed on any sheet metal material. Textures produced by this method have directionality to them. Certain embossing patterns have a subtle directional nature to them, whereas others are more definite.

COINING

Coining is a similar process to embossing in that a pattern is imparted only to one side of the metal. This technique uses very high pressure to induce the texture into the sheet. Coining produces fine textures with names like "linen," "shadow," and "moonbeam." The process requires the use of a sendzimir roll, which induces a tremendous pressure on the metal, pressure so great that the metal thins from the pressure. Placing a light, patterning roll onto the sendzimir imparts the texture into the top surface of the metal during the final pass. The opposite side of the metal does not receive a pattern. The texture produced is very fine. The upsetting of the surface is less than a millimeter across and only fractions of a millimeter in depth. The pattern occurs across the entire surface of the sheet. The back side of the sheet is smooth. Some stress relief occurs, but nothing near that of embossing with pattern rolls.

Similar to embossing, the coining process does not affect the metal's capability to be sheared, formed, or stamped. The disruption of the surface does not take the metal beyond its plastic region, but the process does provide a flatter, more stable sheet of metal, so some stress relief must be occurring.

Additionally, the process of coining is a relatively economical process with limitations similar to embossing. The capital cost of the roll is not as significant as that of embossing rolls; that said, the equipment needed to apply the pressure, the sendzimir rolling mill, costs more than a small building. The finishes are produced at the rolling mill as a special architectural or ornamental run. It is not standard production finishing. The pattern roll is inserted into the sendsimir mill only infrequently and only for large orders.

This means coining is subject to large quantities or to quantities being stocked.

Textures induced into the metal via coining processes influence light reflectivity of the surface. The textures are, in most cases, deeper than surfaces developed from mechanical processes induced via polishing or grinding belts, but less than that of embossing. Figure 10.7 shows the very light texture produced by coining the surface.

The color and reflectivity of the surface is highly influenced by the reflectivity of the base metal. Coining is induced onto the sheet at the mill, thus the base finish is always a mill finish. For stainless steel, this offers essentially two forms of coined surfaces: one that is dull or low reflective, and one that is bright or medium to high in reflectivity. For aluminum, the surface is placed on medium to high reflective surfaces, followed by some form of postfinishing such as anodizing, which dulls the surface down, or brightening, to create a higher reflective surface.

Copper alloys are rarely embossed, but typically the mill cold rolled finish surfaces are textured. Generally, coining or embossing the surface can texture

FIGURE 10.7. Lightly coined stainless steel. (Courtesy of Rimex Metals.)

any metal in sheet form. The process seams well suited for stainless steel, steel, and aluminum. Titanium and zinc also have been embossed; but in the case of titanium, the surface hardness resists good patterning.

With both coined and embossed textures, postprocesses can be performed to enhance the appearance. Chemical processes such as anodizing on aluminum, patination on copper alloys, and interference coloring on stainless steel can be performed. Prepainted steel and aluminum sheet are often embossed to improve the flatness. Light embossing, such as "stucco" embossing, is a common surface texture used on prepainted metals. The embossing flattens the sheet and evens the stresses prior to roll-forming operations. This reduces rejects and virtually eliminates edge wave on the coil of metal.

Mechanical processes can be performed on the embossed and coin sheets to enhance their appearance. Passing an embossed sheet through a surface-polishing machine will induce a polish to the tops or high points of the embossed pattern. This creates a contrasting reflectivity of polished surfaces in a pattern over another pattern. The effect, known as *highlighting,* is performed on painted and interference-colored stainless steel to further the contrasting color effect.

Table 10.7 lists the metals that are commonly embossed or coined.

DIMPLING/PRESSING

Embossing can also be performed selectively using programmed tooling. This technique imparts very decorative surface designs or textures. This form of embossing involves a much larger-scale surface deformation process. There are several processes that can produce surface textures considerably larger than embossing or coining on rolls (see Table 10.8).

TABLE 10.7

Metals Commonly Embossed or Coined

Metal	Mill Finish Available	Description of Reflection after Coining
Stainless steel	2D	Low reflectivity
Stainless steel	2B	Medium reflectivity
Stainless steel	2BA—bright annealed	High reflectivity
Aluminum	M12—nonspecular	Medium reflectivity
Aluminum	M11—specular	High reflectivity
Copper	Cold rolled	Medium to high reflectivity

TABLE 10.8

Production Speed and Cost for Various Processes

Process	Speed of Production	Cost
Embossing on pattern rolls	Fast	Low
Coining on pattern rolls	Fast	Low
Dimpling—CNC	Slow	Moderate to high
Hydroforming	Medium	High
Etching	Slow	High
Repoussé	Very slow	Very high

One process involves stamping the metal surface selectively to the point of plastic deformation. Passing a sheet of metal through a computer-controlled press can create unique designs across the surface. The designs are input via a digital link into the machine, which interprets the location of the deformation across the surface of the sheet. The embossing can be deep, as much as 0.60 inches to 0.078 inches (15 to 20 mm). The embossing can vary depending on the nature of the design. Refer to Figure 10.8.

Embossing in this manner is limited to sheets, whereas pattern-rolling processes can be performed on coil stock material. Another significant drawback to this form of patterning is that the stress induced into the surface is uneven and difficult to predict. The result often is a curved or warped sheet that will require other processes to flatten it.

ENGRAVING

Engraving selectively removes metal from the surface. A special cutting-head stylus passes over the metal surface and removes small amounts of material. The path is repeated until the desired depth is achieved. There are directional aspects

FIGURE 10.8. Custom-embossed copper panels.

to engraving. The tooling works best when moving in a linear direction. There are engraving wheels, which can scribe a surface to a radius. Figure 10.9 is a logo engraved into nickel–silver alloy material.

Roll Forming

Roll forming is a process by which metal is shaped by consecutive rolls. A sheet of metal is passed between a series of matching rolls. The metal undergoes plastic

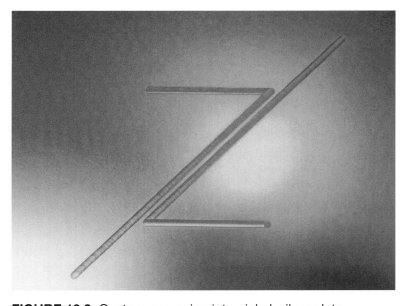

FIGURE 10.9. Custom engraving into nickel–silver plate.

deformation as it conforms to the shape of the rolls. As it moves to the next set of rolls, called a *station*, further deformation occurs and the metal form is permanently altered. Roll forming produces shape along the length of a sheet or plate of material. In other words, the cross section at any point of a finished roll-formed element along the length is consistent. This is similar with an extruded part.

Roll forming equipment is expensive. The process economizes by virtue of the rapid shaping the metal undergoes, but the capital cost is high and must be allocated over a significant amount of surface. The available shapes and dies limit the design to some degree. Typically, the cross section of a roll-formed element is in the 1-inch (25.4 mm) to 3-inch (75 mm) range. Deeper cross sections are possible on large equipment. Because a typical roll former has from 12 to 20 stations, the cost involved in producing a series of custom rolls is high. Additionally, setup aspects of roll-forming equipment require a significant amount of material to be produced. It is not a method for producing small-quantity runs, nor is it an effective way of producing small elements. Figure 10.10 shows a roll forming system.

Roll-forming shapes are always linear; they span in one direction. Sheet in coil form is what the roll-forming equipment uses. Typically, the thickness of metal used is between 0.024 inches (0.6 mm) and 0.063 inches (1 mm). Figure 10.11 shows examples of cross sectional shapes that can be roll-formed.

PRESS-BRAKE FORMING

Press-brake forming is more flexible as far as linear cross sections. Press braking offers the flexibility of creating small runs of special shapes and small sizes. Thicker materials can be formed by hydraulic press equipment. On some hydraulic presses, steel plates as thick as 1.0 inch (25.4 mm) can be formed. Typical press brakes operate on materials from 0.019 inches (0.06 mm) to 0.187 inches (3 mm).

The brake-forming process is more labor- and time-consuming than roll forming, and thus more costly. Additionally, there are limits in the brake-forming

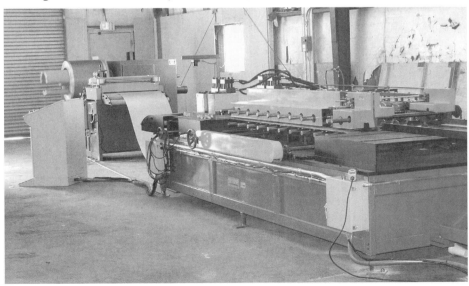

FIGURE 10.10. Roll-forming station.

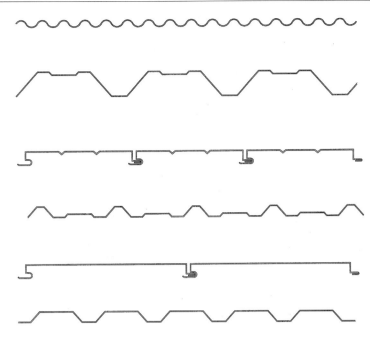

FIGURE 10.11. Example of roll-formed profiles.

equipment, which consist of maximum length and tonnage needed to form certain shapes.

Skilled press-brake operators can form shapes from sheet and plate material that taper and curve from one end to the other and even along the length. Press brakes, like roll forming, impart a linear direction to the element being shaped. Again, though, a skilled press operator can create shapes from the linear application of a die to alter the linear effect.

Forming metal with a press brake occurs when a metal sheet or plate is passed between two companion dies. The dies shape the metal through plastic deformation to a predicted shape. The plastic limit is achieved as the metal yields under the pressure of the dies. The metal folds up in response to the pressure. Refer to Figure 10.12 for an end view of a press-forming process.

Press brakes are used to develop many of the seams and joints depicted in this book. The press is a mainstay in the metal fabrication industry. The approach to forming metal using press brakes has not changed for a century, although improvements such as CNC controls and flexible and multiple shaping dies have increased the value of a press brake.

The finish of the metal is little affected by the press-brake operation, although some slight frosting may be visible at the bend point. This is more apparent on mirror finish and colored stainless steels. Anodic finishes and some thick aluminum sheets will show minute microcracking at the bends.

STAMPING

Stamping is a rapid forming process that pushes metal sheet and plate under high pressure into a rigid die or form. Like roll forming, the dies are expensive and small runs are impractical.

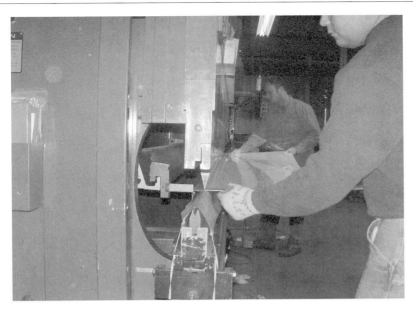

FIGURE 10.12. Press-forming operation.

In stamping operations, the metal is stretched into a particular shape. Some deformation and thinning may occur. The dies must be engineered to allow the metal to move into the particular form. All stamping operations offer this service. Refer to Figure 10.13. This decorative copper antefix was stamped from carved wooden dies.

FIGURE 10.13. Ornamental copper stamping.

Stamping is similar to press-brake forming in that tremendous pressure is brought to bear on the sheet, plate, or bar material. Large presses capable of shaping steel plates and sheets as large as 60 inches by 144 inches (1530 mm by 3660 mm) are available. These massive presses are used in industrial applications where a large, repetitive shape is pushed out.

The surface finish of the metal can be slightly altered during stamping processes. The metal around the bends typically frosts over slightly as the grains are being stretched. Special oils and slip-sheets can be used to allow the surface to move as it is pushed or pulled into a die. These slip-sheets prevent friction buildup that might lead to tearing the part.

Stamping is not suitable for anodic finishes on aluminum and on some thick aluminum sheets. Proper die design is necessary to eliminate tearing at the corners and edges, as well as waves. as the metal is pulled into the corners.

HYDROFORMING

Another process that creates more regular patterns on the surface is hydroforming. The patterns are produced on a die, usually a thick steel plate. Patterns are essentially holes cut into the thick plate; then a sheet of metal is placed over the plate and subjected to tremendous hydraulic pressures. The pressure pushes the metal against the plate, and where the holes have been placed, the metal sheet stretches into the hole and undergoes plastic deformation. When the sheet is removed, a pattern of smooth indentations occurs on the surface. The patterns can be regular or irregular. The metal sheet stretches into the holes neatly without generating differing stresses. The result is a flat sheet of metal with a pattern of smooth, rounded impressions.

The process can be repeated to create sheets of the same pattern over and over, or the sheet can be shifted to create a different pattern in relation to the sheet edges. The embossed surface using this method allows for a maximum deformation from the surface of approximately 0.125 inches (3 mm).

Pyramid Rolling

Plate forming on pyramid rolls produces a curved smooth surface. The process involves passing a sheet or plate through a stack of rolls. The rolls induce a mild stress into the metal and shape the surface into a curve. The curve is adjustable. Passing metal plates through pyramid rolls can develop various radii. The curvature can vary from one end of the sheet to the other by adjusting the pressure. The surface produced is a ruled surface, which is defined as one where you can place a straightedge on the surface so that all points on the line touch. This is opposed to a dual curved surface, where the straightedge would ride up off the surface.

Each metal will curve slightly differently because of the varying stresses in the sheet. All sheet and plate material can be curved using plate rolls. With clean rolls, the surface of the sheet or plate is not altered. Thus, any finish can be passed through the pyramid rolls without concern for altering the surface.

Plate rolls can also be used to flatten surfaces. Passing a curved or warped sheet through the rolls from one side to the other will take out internal stress, causing the warping behavior. A hot rolled sheet with surface warping can be passed through a set of pyramid rolls and curved so that the outer surface is to the outside of the curvature, thus stretching the outer face. Then when flipped and passed through a second time, the warping and surface deflection will be removed.

With skill, an operator can create curved surfaces from ribbed and formed flat panels. Using rubber spacers, hard plastic spacers, and shim spacers, intricate shapes can be curved using plate rolls. Cone shapes can be produced using pyramid rolls. They comprise a ruled surface. Cylinder form surfaces are the most common. Minimum diameter is usually around 4 inches (100 mm) greater than the roll diameter.

Small dual or compound curvatures can be created using plate rolls. This is achieved by wrapping the rolls to induce more pressure in one area than another. The compound curvature is very slight in one direction.

Stretch Forming

Stretch-forming operations take metal forms, tubes, plates, sheets, and even formed parts, and pull them over a die shape. The ends of the part to be curved are held, and a large curved die is brought into the part. Simple curves can be achieved rapidly and without damage to the material. The finish on mirror surfaces can be altered slightly, and the ends of the part will sometimes have grip marks.

All metals can be stretch formed. Depending on the operator's skill level, nearly all metals and metal shapes can be curved using modern stretch-forming equipment. Tubes, pipes, and even I-beam sections can be curved.

Milling

Milling creates surfaces by removing material selectively from the surface. Several types of milling are used in architectural and ornamental work. Chemical milling sprays dissolve acids on the face of the metal. Where the metal is not protected with masking or other restricting material, the metal is removed.

Typically, milling is performed on a milling machine that passes a rapidly spinning tool over the surface of the metal. The spinning tool selectively removes small shards of metal. Large and small, thin or thick plates can be milled. Decorative designs are possible, but limited in scope.

EXPANDED METAL, PERFORATED METAL, AND METAL MESH

Piercing holes through metal sheet and plate is a simple process. Unlike other materials, metals are well suited to be punched or pierced. There are two main types of pierced metal: expanded and perforated.

Expanded Metal

Piercing the sheet of material and stretching it over a die to create openings in the surface produces expanded metal. Expanded metal can be flattened or raised to produce a slight lip at each penetration, not unlike a cheese grater.

Expanded metal is an inexpensive screening material that can be developed into mesh, like screens or large panels. Refer to Figure 10.14. The openings, due to the forming method, take on a diamond appearance. Various metals can be expanded in this manner—steel, stainless steel, copper, titanium, essentially all metals that come in sheet form. The process is usually performed on thin sheet material with a maximum thickness of 0.060 inches (1.5 mm). Perforated metal, on the other hand, is a more engineered, design material.

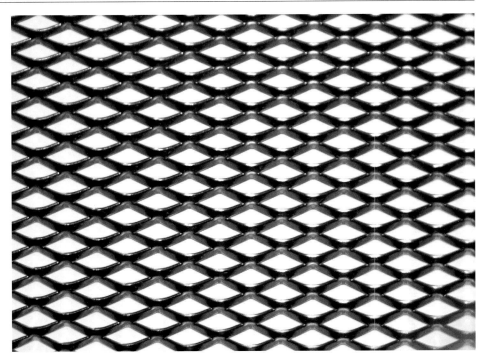

FIGURE 10.14. Expanded titanium mesh.

Perforated Metal

Perforated is the description given to a body of metal surfaces that have been pierced or cut with the purpose of removing portions of the body of the sheet. Perforated metal is available in a vast array of hole sizes, shapes, and grids. Perforations can be just about any shape and size opening through metal. Patterns can be staggered, grid, random, or custom. Numerous standard holes and hole sizes are available. Figure 10.15 depicts two standard patterns, staggered grid and straight grid with round holes.

From an economic point of view, perforated metal can be produced similar to expanded metal on a large gang-punching machine. An entire series of rows across the width of a sheet can be created at one time. This method limits the flexibility but keeps the cost down. Gang punching can also be performed on selected portions of the sheet to limit the area of transparency.

Custom perforation is also possible. Custom perforation offers the designer tremendous flexibility. Holes can be pierced any place on the sheet and in any configuration imaginable. The surface takes on a textural quality and an intriguing pattern as light passes through. Custom perforation requires the use of CNC machines that punch or cut a hole in a specific predetermined location.

Perforated metal creates a textural appearance on surfaces. From a distance, perforated metal surfaces look slightly darker. Refer to Figure 10.17. The holes do not reflect light back to the viewer so they tend to darken the overall surface appearance. When light from behind is allowed to show through, they tend to lighten the surface appearance.

Perforated metal can perform as a sound suppression surface, reducing noise and echo. Perforated metal surfaces also can be sound-transparent,

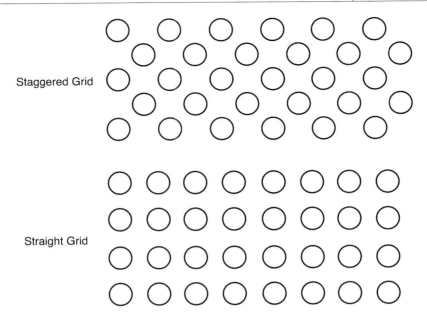

FIGURE 10.15. Standard perforated patterns—staggered and straight grids.

FIGURE 10.16. Custom perforation over glass curtainwall.

FIGURE 10.17. Custom perforated stainless wall.

allowing sound frequencies to pass through them and into another sound-absorbing material. Or perforated metal can act as a "tuned acoustic absorber." Depending on the hole size and spacing, various frequencies pass through the holes into the surface behind without reflecting back.

In the first instance, when perforated metal acts as a transparent acoustic cover, the amount of free area would need to be maximized. Refer to Figure 10.18. Sound-absorbing insulation material must be placed directly behind the surface to capture the sound frequencies. For example, one inch of glass-fiber insulation will absorb high-frequency sounds effectively, but other frequencies are not so readily absorbed. Increasing the glass fiber to six inches and the absorbed becomes very efficient, approaching 99 percent of all incident noise energy.

When the metal surface is being used as a tuned resonance absorber, sound is absorbed in a narrow range of frequencies. Refer to Figure 10.19. By considering the thickness of the perforated metal, openness of the perforated sheet, and distance back to an acoustic absorbing material, the frequency to be absorbed can be determined.

Additionally, perforated metals can be designed to suppress other wavelengths and frequencies. Perforated metals can inhibit microwaves, radio waves, and other electromagnetic waves.

PERFORATED METALS AND LIGHT

Perforated metals allow light to pass through and reflect on other surfaces, creating shadows and patterns. The effects of light passing through perforated metal surfaces creates patterns that match that of the metal but elongated by the angle of light and altered by light-bending effects. Figures 10.20A and B are of a "flame" form created from perforated metal. The form is illuminated from the inside.

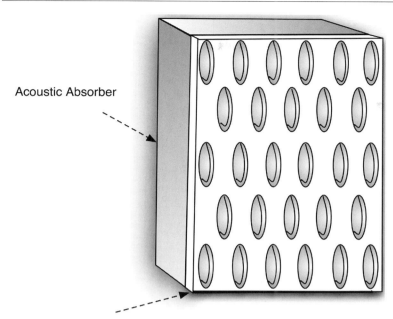

Acoustic Absorber

Perforated Metal Surface- Transparent to sound waves

FIGURE 10.18. Perforated metal considered as a transparent acoustic cover.

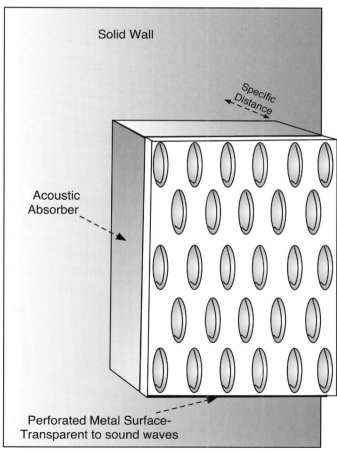

Solid Wall

Specific Distance

Acoustic Absorber

Perforated Metal Surface- Transparent to sound waves

FIGURE 10.19. Perforated metal used as a tuned resonance absorber.

FIGURE 10.20A. Perforated flame form.

FIGURE 10.20B. Peak of perforated flame form.

The interaction of the perforated metal surface with light can be one of the more intriguing and beautiful behaviors observed with metal. The effects are dimensional, not simply the interplay of light with a single surface but with multiple surfaces. Moiré pattern effects develop when one perforated surface is positioned over another perforated surface. Moiré patterns are created when two semitransparent patterned surfaces are positioned over the top of one another. The image formed on the retina at one instant is superimposed over the image previously formed. Your eyes constantly scan the surface, and the effect of the one image over the other gives the illusion of movement. On round holes, the patterns are round and radiate as you walk about the surface.

Another intriguing effect occurs with light passing through perforated metal surfaces onto another surface. Light interference causes light and dark fringes to appear. Refer to Figure 10.21. At the dark regions, the perforated holes appear as a light contrast, while on the light bands, the perforated holes are fuzzy and less defined. This is due to interference from one opening to the next. Different effects are generated from different patterns. Refer to Figure 10.22.

Perforated metal surfaces can appear as solid surfaces during daylight times and can be beacons, internally illuminated at night. Depending on the pattern and hole spacing, perforated metal can appear as a solid illumination; or if the perforations are more irregular, the surface can take on a motif as the light creates strong contrasts. When back-illuminated, the metal becomes dark, regardless of the color and reflectivity.

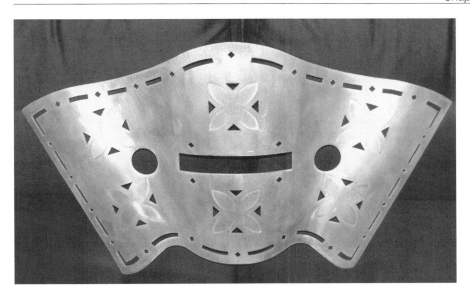

FIGURE 10.21. Custom waterjet-cut perforated light sconce.

Viewing through perforated surfaces is affected by the size of the perforated hole and the spacing. If the surface is pierced with many regular small holes, and the open area is in the 40-percent range or better, the surface acts more as a screen. Your eyes focus on the brighter regions, which are the regions on the other side of the perforated metal. If the perforations are fewer and the open area is less than 40 percent, your eyes tend to focus on the metal. The metal surface dominates.

If the holes are large, 1 inch (25 mm) in diameter or greater, it depends on how close you stand to the surface. At close proximity, say 6 feet (2 meters) and less away from the wall, your eyes tend to focus on a single hole or a few closely spaced large holes. As you move back, the perforated wall takes on the appearance of a large diaphanous screen.

Mixing small holes and large holes on the same surface can produce disturbing effects as you attempt to look through the surface. Your eyes have difficulty focusing. As your eyes constantly scan the surface, they go from the distant view through the large hole back to the surface created on the small perforation. The effect is not comfortable. This occurs when you are standing close to the perforated surface.

Wire Meshes

Woven wire meshes create intriguing surfaces that reflect light and allow light to pass through them in unique ways. Wire meshes are made of stainless steel, aluminum, and copper alloys, sometimes combinations. Wire surfaces can be bright or dull. The tops can be polished to highlight and brighten a portion of the surface. Wire meshes can be woven with various-diameter wires to enhance the surface texture further.

Wire mesh surfaces are best viewed in close proximity during daylight. The detail of the surface is visible. When backlit or when light is washed over the surface of perforated metal at night, interesting textural effects created by light and dark contrast can be produced.

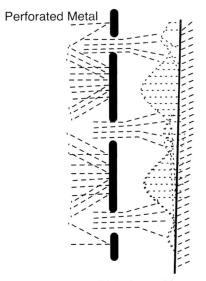

Perforated Metal

Light intensities vary
Banding occurs between
perforation rows

FIGURE 10.22. Light passing through perforated metal creates light bands of varying intensities.

Wire mesh surfaces when viewed from a distance of several meters lose much of their textural character; they appear flatter. Figure 10.23 shows various examples of wire meshes.

Wire meshes can be formed in various shapes. They are generally fixed at the edges and draped. Forming them can be difficult because of the differential pull each wire of the mesh experiences. This causes the surface to want to warp. They can be rolled and hung. Their weight, coupled with the openness of the surface, allows for adequate wind resistance. They work best in a tensile form because they lack rigidity when in compression. Figures 10.24 and 10.25 depict large stainless steel mesh panels used to create the exterior walls on the Forum for Contemporary Arts in St. Louis, designed by Allied Works Architects.

There are a multitude of mechanical processes that can be used on metal. Currently limited by the physical restraints of the machines or the artistic ability of the applicator of the finish, you can expect the number and variety of finishes to increase in the future. The mechanical finishes sit well between the chemical processes and deposition process used to enhance the surface appearance of metals. Many of the finishes can be combined to produce stunningly beautiful surfaces unlike any seen before.

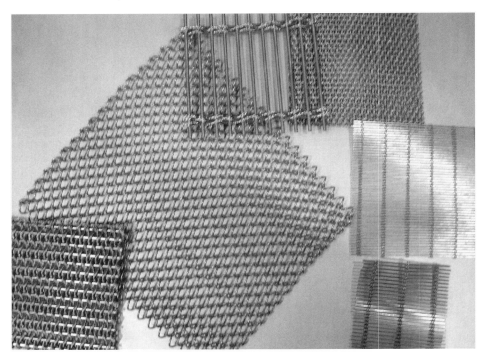

FIGURE 10.23. Various wire meshes.

FIGURE 10.24. Wire mesh panel joint.

FIGURE 10.25. Wire mesh panels on the Forum for Contemporary Arts, St. Louis. Designed by Allied Works.

CHAPTER 11
DEPOSITION PROCESSES

"Man's mind, stretched by a new idea, never goes back to its original dimensions."

—OLIVER WENDELL HOLMES

Deposition processes are techniques whereby one metal is applied to the surface of another metal. The interaction, unlike electroplating, which involves chemical transformations, creates a strong, metallurgical bond between the metals. Deposition processes involve relatively new techniques as compared to the very old hot-dipping processes, whereby lead–tin alloys are coated onto steel plates (see Table 11.1). Many of these techniques are more widely used in other industries, such as semiconductor manufacture, industrial manufacture, and aerospace. The introduction to the architectural and ornamental marketplace is in its infancy.

TABLE 11.1

Deposition Processes Used on Metals

Hot dipping
Physical vapor deposition
Chemical vapor deposition
Sputtering
Plasma arc spray
Wire flame spray
Powder flame spray
Electric arc spray
High-velocity oxyfuel
Cladding

Some of the techniques hold promise for creating unique surface colors and behavior attributes. Vapor deposition processes that thinly apply metals such as titanium onto the surface of stainless steel introduce unique colors previously unavailable. The processes of deposition hold significant promise to the future of metal surfaces.

HOT DIPPING

Hot dipping is the process by which one metal is submerged into a molten bath of another metal with a lower melting point. The most common hot-dipping process is hot-dipped galvanizing. Ubiquitous products made from galvanized steel are indicative of the low-cost, high-value benefit of the hot-dipping process. Hot-dipped galvanizing involves immersion of a sheet, plate, or form of steel into a molten bath of zinc. This economical method puts a continuous, unbroken zinc coating over the entire exposed surface of the metal. The expected service life of a steel fabrication in corrosive environments is benefited by the galvanic protection afforded by the zinc coating. Expected service life is directly proportional to the zinc coating thickness.

The hot-dipping process creates a metallurgical bond between the zinc coating and the steel or iron substrate. When the steel sheet or fabricated part is dipped into the molten bath, a thin high-purity layer of zinc develops on the outside, with transition alloy zones developing at the interface of the base metal surface and this pure zinc. Refer to Figure 11.1. This interface layer is a mix of zinc and iron with a progression of greater zinc concentration to almost 100 percent pure zinc at the surface.

Galvanized steel coatings have a characteristic spangle. The rapid cooling of the zinc creates the spangle. The zinc forms large crystals with defined boundaries. The largest spangle can be an interesting mosaic of unique crystal forms ranging from 0.08 inches to 0.40 inches (2 to 10 mm) across. Their appearance and form cannot be controlled and the development of the crystals other than their range of size cannot be predicted.

FIGURE 11.1. Transition layers of hot-dipped galvanized steel.

New galvanized sheet is reflective. The spangles appear as contrasting silver-gray tones. Each crystal, as it forms, has minute lines set at a bias to the neighboring crystal. The lines are the initial dendrites that form to create the crystal lattice. They are not visible with the naked eye. The microscopic lines reflect light at different angles. Light striking the surface is reflected and scattered by the fine lines, creating the appearance of color differences. As the surface weathers, tiny eruptions of zinc oxide and carbonates develop. The surface loses much of its reflective sheen because this microscopic rough surface absorbs and diffuses much of the light. The spangle is still apparent but subdued by the gray, flat reflectivity.

Various levels of spangle are available, from very small, tight crystals to the large crystal spangles. Today, in the United States, the large spangle is more difficult to come by in continuous hot rolled sheet material. A tighter, smaller spangle is more readily available in the United States. Lead, in small quantities, is needed in the molten zinc bath to produce the larger spangle. More often today, antimony is substituted for lead in the galvanizing bath. Additionally, in the continuous hot-dipping process, small amounts of aluminum are also added. The result is a brighter, more reflective finish.

The lead is a significant factor in creating the large spangle. Dispersed in the molten bath of zinc, the lead is a catalyst in forming the crystals on the surface. Lead is tightly controlled in the hot-dipping bath used on larger steel surfaces. The lead affects the surface tension of the molten zinc. It promotes uniform coating formation across the steel surface.

Hot-dipped galvanizing is common on exposed structural shapes used to support anything from handrails to screen walls. It can be exposed to the environment or it can be used as finish surfaces on interior fabricated parts. Hot-dip galvanizing is easily applied to large fabricated steel assemblies. The parts can be welded, cleaned, and hot dipped to create a consistent surface with a predictable appearance.

For exterior assemblies, it is good practice to coat the inside of hollow steel shapes as well as the outside surfaces. To accomplish this, molten zinc must be able to enter the hollow section. This may require a bleed-down hole of sufficient size placed into an end plate. Just as with any closed or semiclosed volume, when submerged, air must escape before fluid can enter. The bottom of base plates should be coated, as should other joining plates and the inside of bolt holes. The hot-dipping process tolerates surface inconsistencies and defects in the steel. Best results are still obtained from clean steel surfaces.

There are several standard coating thicknesses or weights available with hot-dipped galvanizing. For sheets and thin plates, the common galvanized surface is a G90 coating. For heavy structural shapes, hot dipped after fabrication, it is recommended to use the A123 coating designation, which equates thickness of steel with required zinc thickness.

The designations are given as representative weights per unit area. However, there is a peculiar practice when qualifying thicknesses of galvanizing obtained from continuous hot dipping and that obtained with postfabrication hot dipping. With sheet and plate coated by the continuous hot-dipping process, the designation used is the same as that for posthot-dipping processes. The thickness of coating on the surface, however, is different. The continuous process is based on average coating of zinc applied per unit of area—both sides, whereas hot dipping after fabrication is based on the thickness of a coating measured on one side. For example, a G90 coating classification on sheet equates to a thickness of 19 μm per side for a total coating of 38 μm, whereas for a structural shape, G90 coating classification requires a thickness of 38 μm on all exposed surfaces.

Galvanized steel specifications to use for the various processes are shown in Table 11.2.

The postfabricated process immerses shapes into molten baths of zinc. The baths can be as large as 60 feet (20 meters), so that large sections can be constructed and processed at one time. The molten metal is maintained at a temperature range of 445° to 465°C. The longer the parts are immersed, the greater the coating thickness of zinc. Typically, steel parts are immersed from one to five minutes. Some shaping can occur as stresses within the fabricated parts are relieved from the high temperature of the molten baths.

Other metals and alloys of metals are also applied by the hot-dipping method (see Table 11.4). Besides zinc, metals such as aluminum, lead, and tin, and combinations of zinc–tin, lead–tin, and zinc–aluminum are hot-dip-applied to the surfaces of steel, stainless steel, and copper.

Each coating offers different attributes to the base metal being coated. From an appearance standpoint, hot-dipped aluminum coatings are bright and are good heat reflectors. Lead coatings are darker. Initially, they possess a glossy appearance that on extended exposure to the ambient give way to a dark, flat, gray-black appearance (see Table 11.5).

TABLE 11.2

Galvanized Steel Specifications

Postfabricated hot-dip galvanized steel	ASTM A90, ASTM A123, ASTM A153
Continuous hot-dip galvanized steel process	ASTM A525
Metallizing	CSA G189, BS 2569

TABLE 11.3

Coating Thicknesses for Galvanized Steel

Coating Designation	Minimum (oz/sf)	Minimum (g/sm)
G235	2.35	7.20
G210	2.10	6.40
G185	1.85	5.60
G165	1.65	5.00
G140	1.40	4.30
G115	1.15	3.50
G90	0.90	2.80
G60	0.60	1.80
G30	0.30	0.90
G01	No minimum	No minimum

TABLE 11.4

Hot-Dip Metal Coatings

Base Metal	Coating Metal
Steel	Zinc
	Tin
	Aluminum
	Lead
	Terne (Lead–tin)
	Aluminum–zinc
Stainless steel	Zinc–tin
	Terne (Lead–tin)
Copper	Zinc–tin
	Tin
	Lead

TABLE 11.5

Changes in Coating from Initial Exposure to Aged Exposure

Coating	Initial Appearance	Aged Appearance
Aluminum	Bright, diffused reflectivity; white color hue with a small tight spangle	Reflectivity drops off slightly over time.
Tin	Bright, silver-gray color; fine grain, little to no spangle	Slowly tarnishes; loses reflectivity.
Aluminum–zinc	Medium spangle; bright diffuse reflective surface; whitish gray in color	Reflectivity gives way as slight tarnish develops on the surface.
Zinc (galvanized)	Medium spangle, bright appearance; silver-gray in color	Dulls down to a nonreflective gray tone.
Terne	Glossy gray color; reflective sheen on the surface	Dulls down to a dark gray color.
Lead	Glossy dark gray tone	Dark gray-black, low reflective surface.

VAPOR DEPOSITION PROCESSES

There are several methods classified as vapor deposition, including chemical vapor deposition, physical vapor deposition, sputtering, and ion implantation. Vapor deposition is the process by which simple evaporation and condensation of a metal in high vacuum occurs on the surface of another metal. The result is a surface with a thin, bright coating of metal.

Chemical and physical vapor deposition processes differ in that the former uses chemical compounds to form the deposited surface and the latter uses a metal itself. Thus, for most architectural uses, physical vapor deposition is the process used.

Physical Vapor Deposition

In physical vapor deposition, an "arc evaporation process" is used on the alloy metal to form highly charged metal ions in plasma. The plasma is mixed with nitrogen or other inert gas. The positively charged plasma is attracted to a negatively charged surface. Ion by ion the vaporized metal is deposited to the sheet, forming a thin film uniformly across the surface.

Measuring the electrical potential passing through the deposited metal film controls the thickness of the film. Various interference hues can be developed by the deposition of the vaporized metal. Measuring the thickness will establish the color and allow repetition for large-scale production.

Titanium is commonly applied, using the vapor deposition process but other metals can be as well. For large exterior architectural applications, however, titanium is almost exclusively used. Vapor deposition colorizing involves coating metal ion, as shown in Table 11.6.

The base metal used for many decorative applications is stainless steel. The surface of the stainless steel can be finished in any number of ways, mirror, satin, Angel hair, glass bead, or even ground finishes. The result is a very attractive surface with distinctive color (see Table 11.7).

Sputtering

Sputtering is a physical vapor deposition process in which a metal is vaporized and ejected at low temperature at a surface. Sputtering is a dry-coating vapor deposition process. The vaporized metal is applied in a plasma stream under vacuum pressure. A sealed vacuum chamber is brought under high vacuum as a small amount of argon gas is introduced into the chamber. A high voltage is applied between a stainless-steel surface, which is made the anode, and a cathode. The cathode, in the case of architectural and ornamental objects, is ceramic material such as titanium nitride or titanium carbide. The cathode glows under the high voltage, and a plasma state is created. The argon molecules collide against the cathode and disperse atoms of the cathode material. The atoms, in a

TABLE 11.6

Metals Applied Using Vapor Deposition

Base Metal	Coated Metal
Stainless steel, steel	Aluminum
	Cadmium
	Chromium
	Cobalt
	Copper
	Gold
	Hafnium
	Iron
	Lead
	Molybdenum
	Nickel
	Silver
	Titanium
	Tungsten
	Zinc
	Zirconium

TABLE 11.7

Interference Colors

Black
Bronze
Yellow
Gold
Rose gold
Platinum
Smoke gray

TABLE 11.8

Colors Produced by Sputtering TiN or TiC on Stainless Steel

Gold
Yellow-gold
Charcoal black
Bronze
Purple-red
Silvery yellow
Pink
Soft gray

charged vapor form, condense on the surface of the stainless steel. The result is a very uniform, thin coating with high abrasion resistance.

Just about any material can be applied using sputtering (see Table 11.8). The energy used to apply the vaporized metal is sufficient to make a good bond on the targeted surface. Additionally, all surface textures of stainless steel can receive the thin 0.3 μm coating. Sputtering can be applied to mirror, satin, glass bead, Angel hair, etched, coined, and embossed finishes and textures.

For all vapor deposition processes, the substrate to be coated must be thoroughly cleaned of all foreign surface particles. It may also be necessary to heat the metal to ensure it is dry and to force out all trapped gases within the surface pores.

THERMAL-SPRAY SURFACES

There are several methods in common use for applying metals to the surface of other metals using extremely high-localized temperatures and high-velocity gases. These methods are called *thermal-spray*. Thermal-spray surfaces are thick film coatings produced by various techniques, which use either powder or wire form of metals. Reference Figure 11.2.

Thermal-spray techniques include plasma spray, wire flame spray, powder flame spay, electric arc spray, and high-velocity oxyfuel (see Table 11.9). Each method involves applying molten or semimolten metal onto another surface, usually metal, but other base surfaces are used as well. The molten material travels at extremely high speeds from a custom nozzle device. They are sprayed onto a cool surface of the base material. Upon hitting the surface, they rapidly cool and solidify into what are called "splats." These splats form a coating of metal approximately 10 to 500 microns thick. The performance of thermal-spray coatings rely heavily on the successful application of various, sometimes complex, parameters.

For each of these processes, it is critical to have clean base metal surfaces. Abrading the surface is often desirable to improve the adhesion. Abrading the surface of the base metal provides a tooth to aid the thermal-spray metal in keying into the surface. Grinding and shot blasting are also common methods of preparing the surface. However, shot blast alone is usually not sufficient in achieving the necessary roughness needed to properly key a thermally applied coating. Shot blasting coupled with roughening the surface with a grinder, partic-

TABLE 11.9

Thermal Spray Techniques

Plasma arc spray
Wire flame spray
Powder flame spray
Electric arc spray
High-velocity oxyfuel

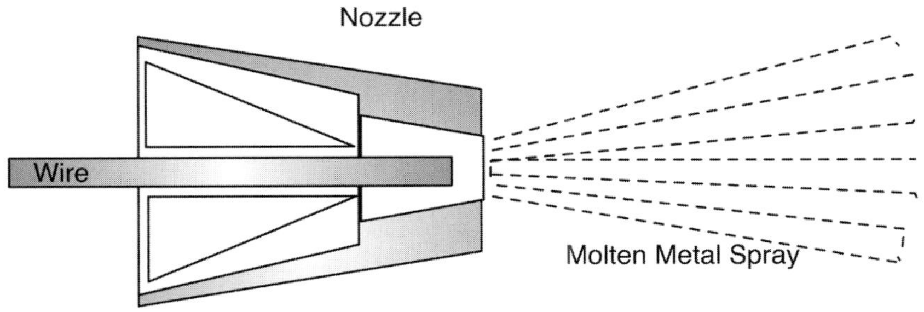

FIGURE 11.2. Diagram of flame-spray apparatus.

ularly grooves and seams, will provide a sufficient surface to key in the thermal spray material.

Thermal spray coatings are rough and usually require some postfinishing to achieve a good surface appearance. Postfinishing by grinding, planing, shot blasting, and sanding will produce a smoother, more pleasing surface. Computer-controlled (CNC) milling will produce very accurate surfaces on both flat and shaped surfaces.

Plasma Arc Spray

Plasma arc spray uses a plasma-forming gas such as nitrogen or argon. The plasma-forming gas is both the heat source and the propellant source for the molten metal. The plasma arc is created when a high-voltage arc is struck between an anode and a cathode within the gun, ionizing the gas. Metal in powdered form is fed into this ionized stream of hot gas and projected at high speed onto another surface. The result is a very dense coating of the once-powdered metal. The thickness is from 0.05 inches to 0.10 inches (1.25 mm to 2.5 mm). The density is close to that of the wrought metal.

The finish surface created is very coarse. Oxides will develop on the surfaces, similar to that of the wrought forms. Shaping occurs when the process is applied to thin sheets. This distortion is created by the impact of the metal to the surface more so than the thermal transfer that occurs as the metal solidifies.

Wire Flame Spray

Wire flame spray applies coatings of any metal available in wire form and that has a melting point below the temperature of the combustion flame. Also known as *metallizing*, the wire flame process involves melting wire in a combustion flame and atomizing by a blast of compressed air. The compressed air shoots the molten metal onto the base metal surface, similar to spray painting. This process is a good low-cost applicator of thermal spray metal. It is the more widely used thermal spray process. Used particularly for corrosion protection by applying zinc or aluminum; other metals can also be wire sprayed onto various substrates.

Powder Flame Spray

Powder flame spray is similar to wire flame spray. Simply, a powdered form of the metal is fed into the flame. Both the powder and the flame spray methods produce good dense surfaces with medium permeability (see Table 11.10).

Electric Arc Spray

Electric arc spray processes feed two wires into a special nozzle. The wires each carry a powerful electrical current, which creates an arc, melting the wires. Compressed air atomizes the molten metal and propels it to the surface of the base metal. This process produces a relatively porous surface but can cover a large area rapidly. The surface is very rough, but it can be burnished afterward to soften the coating.

High Velocity Oxyfuel

High-velocity oxyfuel (HVOC) is an industrial process that involves high-velocity combustion of mixtures of oxygen and fuel to heat and propel partially melted powders of metal at very high velocities. This essentially embeds the molten metal into the base metal. The process is so rapid that little or no oxidation occurs

TABLE 11.10

Common Flame Spray Metals

Zinc
Aluminum

on the deposited metal parts. Very fine particles can be used to build up thick, very hard, impervious coatings.

CLADDING

Cladding is joining one metal to another by applying intense pressure. Usually, two sheets are rolled together. The process can be done either hot or cold. If done cold, it is followed with a heat treatment step to better complete the interface.

Cladding one metal to another is utilized more in industrial applications. Steel clad with nickel is used for some ship hulls. High-purity aluminum is clad over other alloys of aluminum to improve corrosion resistance. The outer skins of airplanes are made of this cladding, also known as alclad. Alclad is achieved by hot dipping aluminum alloy in baths of pure aluminum or spraying sheets or plates with molten pure aluminum. The sheet is then passed through pinch rolls to better bond the two surfaces together.

Silver, gold, and platinum are clad to steel, copper, or aluminum to produce chemical-resistant surfaces. Clad materials have the same color and appearance as the wrought forms of the material. Strength of clad metals is derived from the base metal. The clad metal does not provide any meaningful strength character to the combined material.

Another method of cladding one metal onto another is explosion forming. This process involves placing two or more plates of metal next to one another in a large wooden fixture and surrounding the metal with high explosives in such a way that the explosive force wave actually joints the metals together. Figure 11.3 is a section of a nickel plate approximately 1 inch (25 mm) thick explosion bonded to a 0.25 inch (6 mm) thick copper plate.

FIGURE 11.3. Nickel-clad plate joined to copper plate by explosion-forming process.

The resulting bond is a metallurgical bond. The cross section at the seam between the two metals looks like a series of small waves that essentially zip the two different metals together. This process is predominantly used to create large plates for naval ships. One plate offers the protective layer while the other plate allows welding or stiffness. Plates of copper, for example, can be clad to plates of steel or stainless steel to provide an antifouling behavior to the hulls of ships. The process has only been explored for architectural and ornamental use.

Cladding of copper to stainless-steel sheets has been used infrequently as a roofing and sheet metal flashing material. The stainless-steel sheet provides strength to the copper while reducing the amount of copper needed.

These processes range from the old, simple dipping process of galvanizing to the more technological vapor deposition processes. They have all had success in the realm of architectural metal surfaces. They can be combined with chemical and mechanical processes to further enhance the surface of the metal.

Chemical, mechanical and deposition treatments are enhancements to the micro-surface of the metal. They help change the way light interacts and produces color and reflectivity. To understand the nature of the material you begin to work with, the alloying attributes, will further assist in achieving a particular surface—as well as how the material should be treated and handled.

CHAPTER 12
VARIABLES INVOLVED WITH CREATING METAL SURFACING

"Our life is frittered away by detail... Simplify... Simplify."

—THOREAU

Metal surfaces are derived from certain constraints introduced at the time of manufacture of the base material. Whether it is plate, sheet, tubing, or rod, base manufacturing processes impart characteristics in the basic metallurgy that influence the surface behavior and performance of the metal. Additional constraints develop as the metal is processed further. Polishing, forming, welding, and assembling processes leave attributes on the surface of metals, attributes that have long-term effects on the performance of the metal.

As with the fabric patterns of woven rugs, the constraints of the medium will play a structural part in the creation of the texture. Dyes applied to the fabric flow in direction of the threads. The threads themselves must crisscross other threads. The constraints in the process influence the pattern produced on the finish product.

Clouds developing in the atmosphere, or ice crystals forming on a tree, each develop out of a consistent natural constraint, but the constraint itself does not necessarily limit the infinite possibilities; it just confines them within a path.

Metals used in design are created initially from hot, molten liquid. This molten liquid solidifies into crystals. The crystals have predetermined geometries defined by the relationship of their atoms with the atoms of the other compounds alloyed with them. This relationship determines certain metallurgic characteristics unique to the alloy combinations. Subsequent quenching and cold working processes can further alter these characteristics. These crystals form into lattices, which make up the grain of the metal. The grain can have a direction. The grain can be stretched into long, thin fiberlike shapes or they can be tight angular polygons. Like the thread in a cloth, the grain in the metal influences the finishing and forming characteristics of the metal sheet, plate, wrought, cast, and extruded forms. The initial grain and its subsequent cold working, quenching, and annealing form impart significant character to the metal. This is character that will remain with the metal until it is melted back down or disintegrates into dust.

The grains are distinguished by the grain boundary that separates them from one another. This boundary is the point of general corrosive attack. The early stages of oxide growth occur at the boundaries of the grains.

The texture created on the surface of the metal should look as if it was born of the same "mother," but perfect replications in nature are not typical. They may be born of the same mother, that is, the original casting, but early experiences in life will shape their appearance and behavior. Impurities in the initial alloying components, the conditions of the reducing rolls used to thin the slab of metal, the atmosphere during annealing, and the conditions of storage can all influence the newly produced metal—and this before it meets the shaping fabricator and the final end use. Apparently, it's not just our children who are influenced and shaped by their early environment.

Certain of these characteristics are metal-specific (see Table 12.1). That is, the processes currently used in the manufacture of the specific metal are influential in the surface quality and performance. Other characteristics are important with all metals used in architecture, and controlling their influence on the surface quality is possible and more predictable (see Table 12.2). These will be discussed

TABLE 12.1

Metal-Specific Variables

Variable	Ability to Control	Effect on performance	Influenced By
Alloying constituents	High, via specifications	Significant—color, formability, corrosion inhibition, strength	Mill, at time of casting
Annealing process	High, via specifications	Color, formability, finish	Mill, at time of cold rolling
Tempering	High, via specifications	Formability, impact resistance, strength	Mill, at time of cold rolling
Surface defects (inclusions)	Medium, via inspection	Appearance—shows as small pits or small lines	Mill—pickling and cold rolling

TABLE 12.2

Variables That Influence All Metal Types

Variable	Ability to Control	Effect on Performance	Influenced By
Storage	Medium, via inspection	Imparts defects such as coil set, oxidation	Storage facility
Fabrication	High, via specification	Significant—oil canning, flatness, mars, scratches, dents	Fabrication facilities knowledge and abilities
Handling	Medium, via inspection and planning	Significant—oil canning, mars, fish eyes, scratches	Packaging, site, installation company's ability
Installation	Medium, via prequalification and inspection	Significant—oil canning, thermal binding, denting, fish eyes, other	Installation company and site inspection

as they relate to metal forms in general and are simply guidelines in achieving improved results of metal forms.

ALLOYING CONSTITUENTS

During the initial processes of developing the alloy, various impurities can be detrimental to the long-term performance of the metal. Impurities are unavoidable in commercial production of metals. They are present in the ore and are introduced in the recycling process.

Mills can remove some impurities by adding compounds to the molten metal that will readily combine with certain impurities and precipitate out of the molten mixture. Mills work to a particular range dictated by the industry standard established for that metal.

The objective is to tighten this range when possible and affordable. Table 12.3 indicates certain components that should be kept to a minimum in order to improve performance.

By controlling these impurities in the alloying process when the metal is initially cast, improved performance will be achieved. Many of these impurities fall within allowable alloy tolerances. Thus, if you leave it up to the commercial standards, you can expect to receive anything within the range. It is recommended you consult the mill that develops the initial casting. Often corrections and adjustments can be made to improve on the quality of the cast metal. These adjustments must be specified. Industry standards often allow variations that can reduce the alloy's capability to achieve the desired end results.

Impurities added to various metal elements will improve certain characteristics (see Tables 12.4 and 12.5). For example, aluminum in its pure form is very soft and ductile. The addition of small amounts of other elements such as magnesium or silicon greatly improve the strength. The trade-off usually is small reduction in corrosion resistance.

Other metals, such as steel, which is iron with the addition of very small amounts of carbon, have good strength and workability due to the addition of carbon. Add now chromium and small amounts of nickel, and the steel has corrosion-resistant characteristics superior to the pure iron form. Add copper to the

TABLE 12.3

Alloying Constituents to Control

Metal	Alloy Constituent to Control	Reasons
Aluminum	Silicon	Streaking, corrosion resistance
Copper	Phosphorus	Corrosion resistance
Stainless steel	Sulfur	Corrosion resistance
Stainless steel	Carbon	When welding, low carbon content is desirable to prevent chromium carbide development.
Titanium	Carbon	Titanium carbides will discolor the annealed metal.
Zinc	Sulfur	Brittleness

TABLE 12.4

Wrought Aluminum Designation

AA Designation	UNS Designation[a]	Major Alloying Element
1xxx	A91xxx	99% purity—unalloyed
2xxx	A92xxx	Copper
3xxx	A93xxx	Manganese
4xxx	A93xxx	Silicon
5xxx	A95xxx	Magnesium
6xxx	A96xxx	Magnesium and silicon
7xxx	A97xxx	Zinc
8xxx	A98xxx	Other elements

[a]UNS stands for the Unified Numbering System established for metals and alloys.

TABLE 12.5

Cast Aluminum Designation

AA Designation	UNS Designation	Major Alloying Element
1xx.x	A01xxx	99% purity—unalloyed
2xx.x	A02xxx	Copper
3xx.x	A03xxx	Silicon with copper or magnesium
4xx.x	A04xxx	Silicon
5xx.x	A05xxx	Magnesium
7xx.x	A07xxx	Zinc
8xx.x	A08xxx	Tin
9xx.x	A09xxx	Other elements

steel and it weathers to a beautiful orange-red color. Zinc, another commercially pure metal, has trace amounts of titanium to give it better strength and formability.

For all metals used in architecture, various alloying elements are needed for improved performance (see Table 12.6). Other trace elements have more detrimental effects.

ANNEALING AND TEMPERING

Every metal, when cast and rolled or extruded into its usable form, undergoes a buildup in stress. As discussed earlier, the crystal lattice of the metal is formed when the metal is cast. This lattice or grain is then stretched and shaped from subsequent cold and hot working processes. Tempering, heat treatments, and

TABLE 12.6

Alloying Constituents for Various Metals

Base Metal	Alloying Element	Attribute
Aluminum	Copper	Improve strength
Aluminum	Manganese	Improve ductility
Aluminum	Silicon	Lower melting point
Aluminum	Magnesium	Improve finish
Copper	Tin	Color, lower melting point
Copper	Zinc	Color, strength
Gold	Silver	Color, strength
Gold	Copper	Color, strength
Iron	Carbon	Improved ductility and strength
Iron	Chromium	Improved corrosion resistance
Iron	Nickel	Improved corrosion resistance and hardness
Lead	Tin	Hardness, color
Nickel	Copper	Workability, color
Tin	Antimony	Workability
Zinc	Titanium	Workability

cold rolling do little to modify the base color of the metal, but the processes do change ductile characteristics and the ability to further finish the surfaces. Degrees of cold rolling will modify the reflectivity of most metal surfaces by reducing the roughness of the surface. The cold rolling process elongates the grains while tempering makes the grain size more uniform. Tempering is a heat treatment process performed on all metal forms.

The uniformity of the grain size is important to controlling the color and appearance of the metal part. Differences in color will develop when the surface is polished, anodized, or interference-colored. The differences are due to several variables, which are very difficult and expensive to control.

INCLUSIONS AND OTHER SURFACE DEFECTS

There are no clear universal standards for defining the quality of architectural quality sheet, bar stock, or extrusion surface. Whether the metal is aluminum, copper alloy, or cold rolled steel, the level of surface quality as defined as "architectural quality" is not defined by any industry standard.

Keep in mind, many of the finishes specified by the designer are already in a finished state awaiting fabrication. Stainless steel with a #4 satin or mirror finish, embossed surface, or coined surface is usually provided finished to the fabrication facility. These materials should meet a level of quality established by samples submitted. It is the sheet, bar stock, and casting that undergo post-fabrication processes that must begin with a prime surface quality. This is in the interest of both the designer and the fabricator. From the fabricator standpoint, it is going to make the job of achieving the finish surface easier and more cost-effective. From the designer viewpoint, the end product will be of superior quality and of higher consistency.

There are some specific specifications, which when met by the original material supplier, should lead to improved surface quality. From a general standpoint, specify the surface of the metal to be "architectural quality." This general description is interpreted as requiring the surface to be superior "commercial quality," which can be all over the board. Simply put, it means whatever the supplier is able to sell. It does not matter whether the finish product is going to be mirror polished and incorporated into an art form or used as a form for concrete. If you buy it, then it is "commercial quality."

"Architectural quality" means the material is intended to be utilized to produce something that will be visible and will be graded on its appearance. Thus, one company's architectural quality may be another company's rejects. There are certain defects that are unacceptable as architectural quality (see Table 12.7).

For the variety of end processes, different requirements are necessary. Consider decorative plating requirements on tube material. Tube stock is manufactured from steel sheet, which is available in different commercial qualities. The surface quality "standard" is developed over time within the industry as a standard of acceptable measure (see Table 12.8). The quality is defined by the average roughness, Ra.

Ra is the arithmetic average of readings taken from a profilometer. The lower the number, the smoother the surface. If a flat sheet has significant roughness, the shaping of a tube will increase the width of the valleys in the sheet. This makes the plating process more difficult and increases the cost to achieve good quality. It is better to begin with good-quality surfaces when producing acceptable finish products.

For solid bar material, the issues are similar. There is no universal surface quality standard. Solid material created at the mill by hot rolling, extruding, or sawing is provided as-is. The mill usually sends the solid bar in bulk to various storage facilities that warehouse the materials and then distribute to the market-

TABLE 12.7

Unacceptable Surface Defects in Sheet Metal

Coil stops
Chatter
Edge wave
Scratches, gouges
Dents, dings, impressions
Surface oxides
Surface mars (coining streaks)
Canoe set, crossbow, coil set
Die lines on visible surface of extrusions/bar
Excessive orange peel
Roughness above Ra 50

TABLE 12.8

Surface Quality of Cold Rolled Steel Sheet

Plating Quality	Roughness	Finishing Required for Smooth Plating
Commercial bright finish	0 to 10 *Ra*	Little to no buffing required
Commercial plating quality	10 to 25 *Ra*	Additional polishing and buffing
Light matte finish	25 to 45 *Ra*	Significant polishing required

place. The demand for most solid material is industrial in nature and the surface quality is not of great concern. Scratches, orange peel, mars, and discolored regions are normal (see Table 12.9). If higher quality is needed, then the solid bar will need to be ordered from specialty distribution facilities that provide finish quality. You can expect to pay significantly more per length of the finished or partially finished material.

Surface of Castings

Cast surfaces can have a roughened texture induced by the mold used. Many cast objects are developed in sand molds, which impart a surface that is grainy and rough. Various grains of sand can be used to improve this surface, and postfinishing process can also be performed. When castings are first removed from the molds, they will have a layer of oxides, sand, and scale sticking to the surface. This layer is removed by blasting with such media as hydroblasting with water, sand, steel, and stainless-steel shot blasting, or by acid pickling. Cutting and grinding must also remove the gates and risers stems used to feed the metal

TABLE 12.9

Various Surface Defects and Their Cause

Surface Defect	Possible Cause	Solution
Streaking in anodized surface of aluminum	Impurities in the alloy cast	Special-order casting. Shave off top 30% where impurities accumulate.
Pits in aluminum casting	Outgassing of the aluminum during the casting process	Improve quality control at cast facility. Recast parts.
Pitting in copper alloy; extrusions when mirror polished	Impurities in the alloy	Will not polish out. Fill with welds and repolish or satin-polish the surface to hide. These are in the metal.
Streaks in the copper alloy sheet	Oxides rolled into the surface at the mill	Very difficult to remove. Replace material.
Pits or elongated small scratches in stainless-steel plate	Hot rolling stretches out the surface inclusions	These are in the metal and cannot be polished out.
Streaks and deep ridges in flat extruded aluminum or brass surfaces	Extrusion die has rough edges	Polish out the die surface, with particular emphasis on the visible faces.
"Orange peel" on plated surfaces	Coarse base metal	Polish out the surface and replate.

FIGURE 12.1. Cast aluminum with outgassing surface imperfections.

into the mold. If the resulting finish is to be the "as cast" grainy look, then one should design the risers and gates to occur off the exposed face of the cast metal.

In cast forms of metal, voids and air pockets will pose the greatest problems with the quality of the final product. Outgassing from the interior of the casting can cause spalling of the surface. Refer to Figure 12.1. This may require filling by adding weld material into the space. Again, this can damage the "as cast" appearance. In such instances, you might consider a heavy stainless-steel shot finish or a honed plasma finish. These resemble the "as cast" texture.

Other casting methods such as lost wax investment casting, ceramic shell, and die casting provide a smoother surface. Still, some level of surface preparation is necessary to remove the oxides and investment remnants that remain on the surface.

Surfaces of Structural Shapes

Often it is desirable to use hot rolled products in various assemblies such as handrail supports, stairways, and exposed beams and columns. Sometimes the structural shape is a sculptural part of a finished assembly. Continuous casting into special cross-sectional shapes that are then hot rolled into structural sections produces both steel and stainless steel.

On hot rolled plate, shapes, tubing, and bar stock, inclusions take on the form of small scratches or pits on the surface. The more the surface is polished, the more the pits appear. These are common in large plate materials of brass and stainless steel. They develop into the metal at the mill and cannot be eliminated simply by grinding and polishing. Figure 12.2 is a stainless steel structural T-shape. The mill surface is grainy and dull in appearance.

For steel, the surface of hot rolled structural shapes is often coated with an oxide-inhibiting oil or paint. Little care is shown for the surface finish. Scratches, abrasions, mars, and oxides are often on the surface. Because these are not typi-

FIGURE 12.2. Structural T-shape created from hot
rolled and shot-blasted stainless-steel shape.

cally considered architectural quality, it is very difficult to get ideal finish surfaces without postprocessing to some degree.

There are various methods for preparing the surface of steel in order to arrive at an acceptable finish. These preparations are used on the steel prior to the application of the final finish. The final finish may be paint or galvanizing. The processes have a wide range in cost as well as quality. The specific requirements are defined by the Society for Protective Coatings and are described as Surface Preparation Specifications for Steel (see Table 12.10).

Using the designations established by Society for Protected Coatings will arrive at a suitable surface for finishing. One might review samples of the various designations, particularly if the intention is to have a rough "steel" appearance. Removing the rust and loose scale, then coating with a clear paint finish will arrive at this appearance. Using an oxide inhibitor in the paint will assist in preventing under-film oxidation.

When working with steel, cleaning the surface of all oxides by blasting or grinding leaves the surface receptive to attack from any sort of oxidizing agent. If the intention is to leave the steel appearance as-is, you must immediately coat it with an oxidation inhibitor. Handling the receptive steel surface will generate fingerprints below a clear lacquer surface. The more humid the ambient conditions, the more rapid small rust spots will appear. Consider heating the surface to evaporate all excess moisture prior to application of the finish clear coating.

If galvanizing of the steel is the intention, then one of the less costly surface preparations can be considered. Galvanize coatings have a level of roughness that will conceal many minor imperfections. However, gloss paints, even with thick primers, will show surface imperfections such as scale. The paint must have a sound surface to adhere to. It is wise to consider samples to determine the appropriate base surface.

TABLE 12.10

Surface Preparation Specifications for Steel

SSPC Designation	Description
SP1 Solvent Cleaning	Minimal preparation of steel. Remove oils, grease, dirt, and other contaminants. Perform surface cleaning with solvent, vapor, alkali, or steam.
SP2 Hand Tool Cleaning	Remove all loose rust, mill scale, and paint by hand chipping, sanding, and wire brushing
SP3 Power Tool Cleaning	Remove all loose rust, mill scale, and paint by power tool chipping, sanding, grinding, and wire brushing.
SP5 White Metal Blast Cleaning	Remove all visible rust, scale, and foreign matter by blast cleaning using sand, grit, or shot.
SP6 Commercial Blast Cleaning	Remove visible rust, scale, and foreign matter by blast cleaning using sand, grit, or shot. Cleaning is performed until at least two-thirds of the surface is free of foreign material.
SP7 Brush-Off Blast Cleaning	Remove all visible rust, scale, and foreign matter by blast cleaning using sand, grit, or shot, except tightly adhering residues of scale and rust. Expose numerous, evenly spaced bare metal surface spots.
SP8 Pickling	Completely remove rust and scale by acid, duplex, or electrolytic pickling.
SP10 Near-White Blast Cleaning	Blast-clean the surface until 95% of the area is free of all visible foreign matter, rust, and scale.
SP11 Power Tool Cleaning to Bare Metal	Remove all visible rust, scale, and foreign matter by power tool.

Stainless-steel structural members have a more refined surface. Stainless-steel shapes must be pickled and blasted with stainless-steel shot to remove all surface oxide and slag; otherwise they will corrode. The surface may still have mars and a few scratches depending on how they are stored. Typically, they arrive from the mill with a smooth, clean, grainy surface.

Satin and other high-polish finishes will require significant postfinishing. Angel hair finishing is somewhat easier. To achieve a finish surface capable of passing close scrutiny, much work will have to be performed.

The extrusion process is used to produce aluminum and copper alloy structural shapes. Refer to Figure 12.3. The surface is much smoother than hot rolled structural steel surfaces. The extrusion process is more costly, and the end product is usually visible and expected to be of high quality. They must be packaged and shipped in the highest quality containers. Usually stored inside, aluminum and copper alloy material should be expected to have superior finishes requiring little if any postfinishing work.

Aluminum and copper alloy extrusions do have several production issues to overcome. To begin with, the hot metal is pushed through a steel die. The die imparts a cross section onto the hot metal as it is forced through the opening. The extrusion is cooled under tension as it is brought out of the die. As it exits the die, it wants to sag slightly, so the opposite end is pulled, putting the extruded material in tension.

Residual die marks are unavoidable as the hot metal is pushed through the dies. If the dies have any minor imperfections, these will be imparted all along the length of the extrusion. If they are significant, the die must be further polished before continuing the extrusion process.

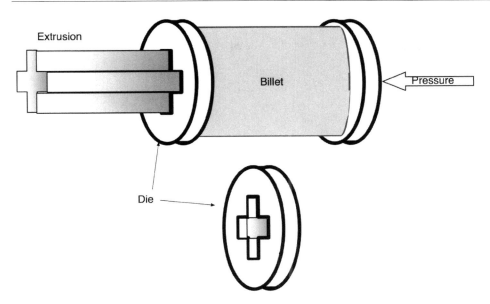

FIGURE 12.3. Diagram of extrusion process.

MILLED SURFACES

Milling of metal surfaces achieves very fine tolerances and produces a "machined" appearance, which has very smooth and reflective surfaces with fine ridges produced by the scalping of the mill tool. Refer to Figures 12.4A and B. These are shapes milled from solid stainless steel bars. A mill takes off successive levels of metal, a sliver at a time, to a predetermined point. Under most circumstances, it is not feasible to remove material from large surfaces. Generally milling by end or side mills is performed on smaller parts of an assembly.

Aluminum, copper alloys, steel, stainless steel, and zinc can all be milled. Milling is performed on Computer Numeric Control (CNC) equipment. The stock material must be fixtured in the machine. A rapidly spinning cutting tool is brought to bear down on the metal stock. At the same time, lubricating cutting fluid is applied liberally to the surface to keep temperatures down as small slivers or chips of metal are rapidly removed.

STORAGE CONCERN

Storage of metal, both in the raw stages and in the fabricated goods stage, must be performed in a controlled environment (see Table 12.11). Most metals, if allowed to get wet, will develop an adherent dark stain, which is very difficult to remove. Store metal in dry, well-ventilated spaces.

Upon receiving metal goods, it is recommended that a close inspection be performed to uncover issues that may be initially concealed. Check the crate the material arrives in for signs of mishandling or improper storage. Check for wetness within the crate. If found wet, immediately dry the material. If the metal is cold, allow it to warm slowly. Moving cold metal into a heated workspace will cause condensation to form on the surface, which could lead to staining. Figure 12.5 shows water stains on galvanized steel surfaces. The white stain is zinc oxide and zinc hydroxide that has developed on the galvanized surface.

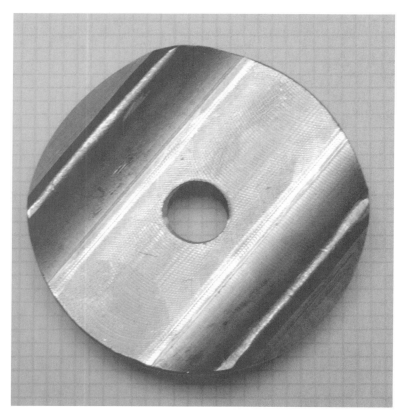

FIGURE 12.4A. Milled stainless-steel bearing plate.

FIGURE 12.4B. Milled stainless-steel knuckle arm.

TABLE 12.11

Storage Concerns

Metal	Storage Issues	Corrective Measures
Aluminum—mill finish	Water stains	Water will create dark stains that are difficult to remove.
Aluminum—anodized	Scratches	Polish out; but reanodizing will result in different color tone.
Aluminum	Age hardening	Long-term storage will age-harden the metal, making it brittle.
Copper	Water staining	Water will create mottled stains that cannot be easily cleaned. Allow it to weather out, or scrap it.
Copper alloys	Water staining	Remove with phosphoric acid and repolish.
Copper alloys	Oxides	Remove with phosphoric acid and repolish.
Steel	Rust	Use a commercial rust remover and refinish.
Zinc-coated steel	White stains	Difficult to remove, as it is created by water on surface.
Stainless steel—mirror or satin finishes	Scratches	Refinish.
Stainless steel—rolled or #2 finishes	Scratches	Scrap—cannot be repaired
Titanium	Scratches	Scrap—cannot be repaired
Zinc	Water stains	If unweathered, use a commercial cleaner.
Zinc	Scratches	If unweathered, polish out.
Zinc—weathered	Stains or scratches	Scrap—cannot be repaired.

FIGURE 12.5. Severely water-stained galvanized steel.

Many metal sheet and plate materials are provided with a protective film. Many of these films are adhered with a low-tack adhesive that can harden and adhere to the metal surface after the plastic coating is removed. Often, paper interleave is better as temporary protection prior to fabrication. This allows for inspection of the finish surface before forming operations. The material will need a final protective coating after fabrication.

FABRICATION

Improper fabrication technique results in surface defects on architectural metal products. Often, surface defects are unwittingly transferred to the metal surface (see Table 12.12). Some practices can permanently damage and influence the long-term performance of the metal. Fabrication facilities often work various forms of metal on the same equipment. Dies get worn and damaged. Fabrication practices also are often dependent on the skill of workers. Processes and techniques vary sometimes, to the detriment of the quality of the metal surface.

Fabrication facilities must exercise caution when working with steel and iron, not because these are susceptible to contamination but because they can contaminate other metals in the facility. Steel particles can be transferred to surfaces via grinding equipment, polishing equipment, even worktables. Steel particles embedded in copper alloy surfaces, aluminum surfaces, and stainless-steel surfaces will rapidly corrode when exposed to the atmosphere. Steel particles can also scratch softer materials such as aluminum and copper.

Steel dies should be protected with various special membranes when forming soft metals. This protects against scratching and marring, but does not

TABLE 12.12

Fabrication Defects

Defect	Fabrication Cause	Remedy
Crazing on anodized aluminum	Inflexible anodized coating	Post-anodize. Fill microcracks with enamel.
Small reflective mars on the edges of fold	Damaged die; segmented die.	Refinish dies. Use thick protective cover on die.
Surface scratches	Iron filings; rough working surfaces	Clean preparation tables.
Iron particles that contaminate surfaces	Nondedicated equipment; dust and grinding spray onto other surfaces	Dedicate equipment. Use good fabrication practices.
Indentations at corners of folds in sheet metal panels	Overbending at the break	Use better brake operation process.
Corrosion around welds of stainless steel	Welds not passivated; chromium carbide precipitation at the surface	Passivate by selective electropolish. Use low-carbon alloys.

protect from damaged dies. Often the dies used on press brakes are assembled from smaller sections. If the form being shaped is larger than one of the die sections, it must span over the splice. On reflective surfaces, the location of this splice, just as the location of mars and dents on the die, can translate through onto the finish metal surface. Even a length of masking tape can translate onto the surface when the pressure of forming dies or stamping dies impart their forming pressures on the metal.[1]

HANDLING

Keeping the surface of finished and in-process goods clean and free of contamination from iron particles, wet concrete, moisture, and other foreign matter is critical to ensure success. The transport of finish goods should be addressed as well, to ensure finish materials are protected from road salts, diesel fumes, and other hazards of open transport. Steel banding and loose crating will scratch most metal surfaces and dent some of the thinner products. Handling to and from a fabrication facility is critical to achieving sound results in finish delivered product.

Thin and soft sheets such as copper and aluminum will flex and kink if overstressed during handling. Care should be exercised when handling architectural products. Soft metals will also scratch more easily if dragged over harder surfaces such as steel or concrete. When sawing or cutting soft metals, be certain the fine particles created are not left on the surface, as these can also scratch the surface during handling. Use gloves whenever possible. Handling unfinished aluminum,

---

[1] While fabricating the reflective satin-finish stainless steel for Gehry's Weatherhead roof surface, a piece of tape was applied to the blanks before forming. The tape was a direction arrow applied by a roller on the decoil line to ensure we always processed the metal in the same bias as it came from the coil. The stamping process went over the tape. When we constructed a mockup we noticed a small imperfection in the same place on every panel. When we inspected the die, we found nothing to indicate the cause. It was not until we processed a few more that we noticed the mark occurred where the thin tape was over the surface.

copper, copper alloys, and, to a lesser degree, zinc, with bare hands can transfer acid moisture to the surface. These often are not removed in the cleaning processes and will appear afterward as fingerprints or handprints on finish surfaces.

A special note of caution is necessary when it comes to preparing for delivery and handling of steel products, galvanized steel, and weathering steel intended for use as architectural cladding. Often, workers do not consider these materials as finish goods; they do not perceive their architectural appeal, hence associate them with mundane industrial surfaces. When this happens, they do not handle the material with care. Other objects may be stacked on the surface, and unwanted scratches and stains are imparted to the finish material. Workers should be advised, "This surface is precious; handle with care." It is also good practice to cover the surface. As with finished concrete, workers are often not appreciative of a utilitarian material being used as an architectural surfacing.

Proper packaging of the finish products for delivery to the project is one of the most important steps. Simple oversights can lead to the destruction of very expensive work. The product must arrive at the job site undamaged, with the finish it had when it left the fabrication shop.

Some packaging materials will damage and corrode metal surfaces. Packaging that absorbs water can hold moisture against the surface of the metal and stain it. Some polystyrene used to package finish parts will scratch the surface. Polystyrene also can scratch the interference color on stainless steel and the anodized surface of aluminum and copper surfaces. Instead, it is better to use soft foam closed-cell wraps that do not absorb moisture. Acid free paper wraps can be placed next to aluminum, zinc and galvanized surfaces prior to the final packing. Avoid the use of tapes on the metal surface facing. Adhesives can transfer through to the metal surface.

Steel banding should never be allowed to come in contact with finish metal products. Separate with wood or foam spacers. Steel banding will not only scratch the material but will also impart steel particles into the surfaces, which can rust when exposed. Use foam spacers that do not outgas from closed cell deterioration. Use dry wood and always separate from contact to the metal surface.

When using protective films such as polyethylene or other proprietary films be certain all air bubbles have been smoothed out. Trapped air and creases in plastic film will translate to many metal surfaces as light 'ghosting' stains. Additionally, the wrong adhesive can create maintenance headaches if it remains on the metal after the film is removed.

Electrostatic films work well on many metals. Using low tack adhesives on the film is highly recommended. Do not allow the film to remain on the metal for significant lengths of time. If used outdoors, consider a UV resistant film. Even then, do not leave the film on for extended lengths of time.

INSTALLATION

Next to fabrication processes, installation processes are among the more important criteria to achieving long-term performance to a metal surface.

As discussed earlier, expansion and contraction of the metal panels that create the surface mosaic are critical to proper installation. The storage on the site, the handling of the product during installation, and the exposures of other surface materials are variables that need to be addressed in the installation process.

The finish surface should be delivered from the factory, well protected. The protective film or wrapping should remain in place long enough to allow the surrounding work to occur without jeopardizing the finish. All the care and concern taken from the casting of the metal through the fabrication process, the storage process, and the delivery can be for naught when a mishandled tool is run over the finish surface of the metal.

The installation crew should review instructions on the care, handing, and installation of the finish metal work. An understanding by those who, in the end, are responsible for achieving the finish work is critical for success.

CHAPTER 13
ANALYSIS OF SURFACE APPEARANCE PROPERTIES

"The details vanish in the bird's-eye view; but so does the bird's-eye view vanish in the details."

—WILLIAM JAMES

The human eye incorporates several parameters in determining the visual characteristics of a surface. The eye is very sensitive to small differences in appearances. In particular, subtle changes are easily distinguished when viewing flat, planer surfaces. These are changes in texture. Most textures on metals are created by microscopic alterations to the surface, alterations that press into or cut into the metal. Some textures develop from the microscopic oxide growth on the metal surface. The oxide growth can be benign, a desirable surface film that provides protection to the underlying element. Or the oxide can be a malignant form, an attack on the grain boundaries on the metal surface. The oxide from such occurrences is created by chemical agents alighting on and reacting with the metal, usually with the presence of moisture.

The human eye also can detect subtle changes in color. Surface properties that determine how the eye perceives relative differences in appearance are gloss, surface roughness, and color. For most occurrences, these are subjective evaluations. Whether a surface is the same color or texture as an adjoining surface can be influenced by several factors, including ambient light, angle of view, surrounding colors, and surrounding reflections.

With metals, the subjective influences are considerable. The reflective nature of many metal surfaces and the development of thin oxide films and textures mechanically applied can have significant effects on any subjective evaluation. For instance, if two samples are from the same sheet, and one receives a texture while the other does not, the colors perceived will be different. Texturing fractures the reflection off the surface and scatters the light. As such, it often lightens dark surfaces and darkens light surfaces. Apply a directional texture on two samples and rotate one 90 degrees and the color will appear different. Take the same two samples and offset one at a very slight angle difference and the surfaces will appear in different colors.

COMPARING TWO METAL SURFACES

There are several objective approaches available to examine the color and tone of metal surfaces. These approaches examine and quantify the gloss, surface roughness, and color. If any one of these three characteristics is different between two surfaces, in full light conditions, they will not match in appearance.

Color

Color measurement is established by determining three numerical quantities based on the 1976 CIE System.[1] The first of these measurements is the lightness scale, L, which runs from dark black, 0, to bright white, 100 (see Table 13.1). The second measurement obtained is the red–green vector, **a**. Positive denotes red tint, 0 denotes neutral gray, and negative denotes green tint.

The third measurement used is the yellow–blue vector, **b**. Positive denotes yellow tint, 0 denotes neutral gray, and negative denotes blue tint.

Color measurements are taken with a colorimeter. For metals, use two colorimeters with different illumination techniques. For the first, use a colorimeter that takes diffused illumination of the surface and examines the color of the light reflected normal to the surface. This will be influenced by the light-scattering behavior of the surface texture. The second analysis should be made using a colorimeter with an illumination by a collimated beam of light introduced at an angle of 45 degrees to the surface and at normal to the surface.

When comparing two surfaces examined with this technique, the algorithm, which establishes the level of color difference, is as follows:

$$\Delta E_{ab} = \sqrt{(L_2 - L_1)^2 + (\mathbf{a}_1 - \mathbf{a}_2)^2 + (\mathbf{b}_1 - \mathbf{b}_2)^2}$$

▓ If $\Delta E < 1$, the eye cannot distinguish a difference in the color.

▓ If $\Delta E > 1$, the surfaces will appear as a different color. The greater the value, the greater the difference in appearance.

TABLE 13.1

Lightness Scale

Lightness Scale	L	0	to	100
Red–green vector	**a**	+	0	–
Yellow–blue vector	**b**	+	0	–

---

[1] CIE is the Commission Internationale de l'Eclairage, also known as International Commission of Illumination. The CIE System is a chromaticity diagram, which allows color samples to be described mathematically and to represent the dominant wavelength.

Gloss

Gloss is defined as "specular reflectivity of the surface." Gloss is the result of microscopic irregularities on the surface of the metal. Terms such as "mirror finish," "satin finish," and "dull finish" are descriptions of the apparent gloss. Specular polished surfaces are mirrorlike surfaces that reflect light back to the viewer in the form of intense localized glare if the light source is positioned at an angle of incidence to the viewer.[2] The color, regardless of the metal surface color, appears white because this is the most intense reflection. When light hits the surface at an acute angle, it is concentrated and intensified by the concentration. Until the angle of reflection is altered to change the concentration, the view is blinding white.

Mirror stainless steel, bright annealed stainless steel, natural finish, or color interference, specular polished aluminum, polished brass and copper surfaces, even mill-finish copper alloy surfaces can reflect light at intense levels, which can be painful to view in bright light at the angle of incidence.[3]

Curving the surface to create a convex reflection will not reduce the intensity because of the point-by-point reflection away from the angle of incidence. Creating a concave surface will intensify the reflection to the point at which viewing the surface can cause damage to the eye. It also has been noted that concave mirror surfaces set out of doors create hyperbolic mirrors. When the sun strikes them just right, the sun's energy is concentrated and magnified. Leaves and debris in the line of reflection have been known to ignite. On a simple undulating mill aluminum surface, the concave portion of the panel has been seen to increase the temperature at a specific point in the reflection by as much as 20 degrees.

Polishing metal with fine grit lines can soften the reflectivity by introducing light-scattering behaviors. That said, the high reflective nature of metal is maintained and can be used to create contrasting outlines and patterns on the surface. Altering the reflectivity of the surface creates relative light and dark regions. It is possible to alter the reflectivity by modifying the surface finish so that one section reflects light differently. Changing finishes by altering polish grits or by altering directional grains in the metal will produce differences in reflectivity. Slightly altering the angle of one sheet or panel in relation to another will also produce differences in reflectivity. When planned, this can create an interesting mosaic effect. When unplanned, the result is disturbing. The effect of minor out-of-plane surfaces can be fleeting. When viewed up close, the surface matches and appears consistent. As the angle of view changes or the distance increases, the differences in reflection can make the surface appear patchy and quilted.

Figures 13.1A and B show a diffused-finish stainless-steel surface as seen in differing light. All material was taken from the same coil of metal. Each shingle, because of the overlapping seam, is set at a similar reflective angle to the viewer. A couple of the shingles in the field, however, are at slightly different angles. At this angle of view, the two shingles appear different. But when the metal shingles were installed, the installation crew could not see the difference; from their viewpoint it was not apparent. Something in the seam manufacture or in the installation created a slightly different installation angle.

---

[2] Angle of incidence is defined as the angle between the incident ray and the normal to the surface.
[3] Angle of reflection is defined as the angle between the reflected ray and the normal to the surface.

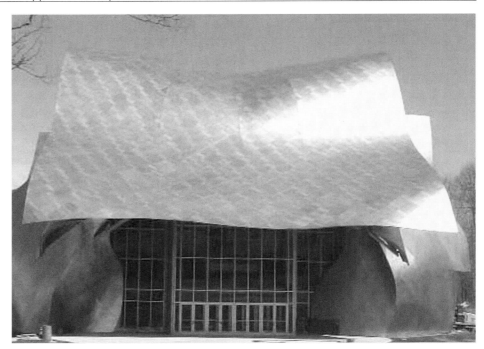

FIGURE 13.1A. Angel hair stainless steel in bright sunlight. Bard College, Annandale-on-Hudson, New York.

FIGURE 13.1B. Bard College. Angel hair stainless steel in overcast sky.

FIGURE 13.2. Barrel-vault ceiling created by altering the finish direction. St. Joseph, Missouri. Designed by SFS Architects.

Similarly, directional aspects of finishes can be used to create altering reflections on the metal surface. The purposeful alteration of the surface can enhance the finish appearance. The project shown in Figure 13.2 utilized panels of directional satin-finish stainless steel set at an alternating bias. Each panel was installed with the linear polish set on a perpendicular bias to the adjoining panel. The effect enhances the curved barrel vault and actually breaks up any panel-to-panel imperfections. When unplanned, this creates significant appearance defects. All sheet metals have a grain direction, which is imparted to the metal surface when it is rolled thin at the mill.

Considering how light interacts with the surfaces of materials, it can be said that the basic fiber of a material produces what the eye perceives as gloss. Light hitting a material is partially absorbed and partially reflected. If the light is scattered at the microscopic level, the reflection is muted. Consider paper or fabric. Light hitting the surface is partially absorbed; some passes through and a portion is reflected. The fine texture of the fibers scatters the light, making the surface appear flat. Glossy paper or fabric has a smoother fiber surface, and light hitting the surface has a greater component reflected. Scattering is minimized. Coatings such as paint and lacquers smooth and level out the microscopic hills and valleys between the fibers and grains. This provides the surface with a glossy, almost wet look.

Metal surfaces are smoother and less fractured by fiber or grains. They absorb light only to the first layer of molecules. Lacquering may provide a wetted look, but generally lacquering or clear coating will not enhance the reflective appearance. Clean, smooth surfaces provide the most metallic appearance.

Surface roughness is a measure of the texture of the metal. Moving out from the grains of the metal, surface roughness measurements consider the imparted disruption of the surface via mechanical or chemical means. These include the hot and cold rolling processes and pickling processes the surface of the metal initially undergoes.

Surface roughness characterized by fine, small grit lines will scatter reflected light. This is the macroscopic level. Light hits the surface from a single direction on a point-by-point basis. The roughness of the surface reflects the light back from various points at different angles. The light reflection is scattered and the image reflected back is indiscernible. Color will be maintained but muted, with reflected edges softened and distorted. Surface roughness is considered as "visual perception of large-scale irregularities." This is more a macroscopic evaluation of the surface beyond the effects of the various metal grains, and is more in tune with the topography of the metal surface itself.

MICROSCOPIC EVALUATION

Using a high-powered industrial microscope capable of being positioned anywhere on a surface, subjective observations can be made. With a 60× microscope, depth and direction of surface grit lines and grains can be evaluated. Contaminants can be seen, along with scratches, large microcrevices, and other surface defects. A high-powered microscope is adequate for visual comparison of samples and finishes. Lighting the surface from an angle will aid in the detection and comparison. Using polarized light will also aid in evaluation of the surface.

MEASURING SURFACE ROUGHNESS

Average Roughness

One measure of surface roughness is *Ra*, which is the arithmetic average roughness taken by six readings over various regions of a metal surface. The readings are taken by passing a profilometer over the surface. The profilometer is a diamond-tipped stylus capable of reading very minute ridges and valleys on a surface. *Ra* is measured in micrometers or microinches (0.000001 inches). The smaller the value of *Ra*, the fewer extreme irregularities found on a surface; thus, a reading of *Ra* 10 is smoother than a reading of *Ra* 30. Since the measurement is also linear in nature, a reading of 30 indicates the surface irregularities measured are three times as great as those measured to a *Ra* of 10.

For comparison, a fine No. 4 finish produced by 150-grit sanding belt on stainless steel has a *Ra* in the 10 to 25 range. A No. 2B finish surface may read in with a *Ra* in the 0 to 10 range. The average roughness measuring technique is two-dimensional; it takes the average of the highs and lows encountered. This technique of measuring a metal surface roughness is in wide use. It does not, however, capture significant changes in height, finish bias, or symmetry, all of which play a part in the finish appearance of a metal surface. Average roughness is a single line reading or spot reading across the surface, and does not necessarily reflect the appearance the surface will impart.

Optical Profiling

Significant advances have been made in measuring conditions that affect attributes of metal surfaces. Techniques such as optical profiling provide a three-dimensional visual of the surface and establish parameters that enable a more thorough evaluation of the surface character.

Optical profiling is a method of taking three-dimensional measurements to determine certain characteristics that influence surface appearance. This profiling method is a noncontact measurement of surface roughness characteristics involving reading a surface with an interferometric optical device. Optical profiling uses the interference of two light beams from a white light source to measure surface profile characteristics not possible with other instruments.

The information obtained using an Optical Profiler is a set of parameters that correlate to certain aspects of the roughness character of a metal surface. Three-dimensional measurements are taken of a surface, from a very small square. Then the local, minute topography is analyzed to accurately map out the terrain.

Two sets of parameters are developed from readings taken. Additionally, relationship algorithms take the information and determine further surface characteristics. The first set of parameters, *R*-parameters, are similar to those developed for the two-dimensional profilometers that simply provide up-and-down readings across a straight line (see Table 13.2).

For three-dimensional optical profile devices, additional parameters are examined beyond the *R*-parameters. These are called the *S*-parameters, and they establish an array of information (see Table 13.3). The *S*-parameters provide

TABLE 13.2

R-Parameter Readings

R-Parameter	Definition	Application
Ra	The average roughness, similar to two-dimensional readings, except it encompasses a plane versus a line of points.	Detects general variations in overall profile variations in and out of the mean plane.
Rq	The root mean square average between the height/depth deviations and the mean surface as taken over the area examined.	Also known as RMS, this reading represents the standard deviation of the profile heights and depths.
Rp, Rv	Maximum peak and maximum valley of the surface.	Visually, this can provide information on the "depth" of the finish appearance (author's evaluation).
Rt	Maximum difference between the highest and lowest readings.	Describes the overall roughness.
Rsk	Skewness. Measure of the asymmetry of the profile. Negative values indicate a predominance of valleys. Positive values represent a predominance of peaks.	Determines porosity of surface.
Rku	Kurtosis. A measure of the distribution of spikes above and below the mean plane.	Spiky surfaces $Rku > 3$; bumpy surfaces $Rku < 3$. $Rku = 3$ represents a random surface.

TABLE 13.3

S-Parameters

Parameters to Measure	Description
Amplitude	Overall height of local features
Spatial	Frequency of local features
Hybrid	Combination of height and frequency
Functional	Relationship of surface to performance such as machining and surface behaviors

TABLE 13.4

Relative Surface Roughness: Typical Metal Surfaces

Relative Roughness of Various Surfaces (From smooth to rough)
Super No. 8 mirror-finish stainless steel
No. 8 mirror stainless steel
Specular- (mirror-) polished brass
No. 2BA—bright annealed stainless steel
Specular- (mirror-) polished aluminum
Titanium—fully annealed, nonglass bead
No. 2B finish stainless steel
Mill specular copper
Angel Hair-finish stainless steel
No. 4 finish stainless steel
No. 2D finish stainless steel
Shadow finish stainless steel
Anodized aluminum
Glass bead stainless steel
Weathered zinc
Galvanized steel (G90)—medium spangle
Oxidized copper

roughness, spatial, and hybrid information on a three-dimensional surface (see Table 13.4).

A representative test performed on four samples of stainless steel, each with a different finish, produced the results shown in Table 13.5. These metals are each shown in the color insert of this book, along with the analytical image as seen by the Optical Profiler. The first sample is alloy 316 stainless steel with a Shadow™ finish, which is produced by coining a light pattern into the surface of the stainless by rolling the metal under very high pressure. The base metal provided from the mill was a No. 2D. The mill then produces the shadow finish by running the ribbon

TABLE 13.5

Optical Profile Tests on Four Samples of Stainless Steel

Finish	Ra	Rq	Rt	Rv	Rp	Rsk	Rku
Shadow	3.33	4.78	34.02	−27.74	6.28	Negative	>3
Glass bead	2.01	2.52	21.87	−11.78	10.09	Positive	3
No. 4 finish	0.35	0.44	3.14	−1.89	1.25	Negative	>3
Angel Hair	0.23	0.37	6.75	−1.62	5.12	Positive	>3

of metal under a patterned sendzimir roll. The patterned roll pushes into the No. 2D finish with extreme force, creating a dull, decorative surface.

The second sample is a glass-bead-finish stainless steel. It was produced by blasting the surface of a No. 7 polish stainless steel with a medium-grit glass bead at 40 psf. The stainless steel is alloy 304. Glass beads impact the stainless-steel surface and impart microscopic, overlapping impact craters on it.

The third sample is the No. 4 finish stainless steel. This surface is a conventional high-quality No.2B mill finish sheet that has the satin No. 4 finish applied by passing a continuous coil under a belt sander with a 150-grit abrasive. The alloy is 304. This common finish is similar to the ubiquitous satin-finish stainless-steel surfacing used on everything from kitchen sinks to column covers.

The angel hair finish is the forth sample analyzed. It was applied over a No. 2B mill finish sheet using a rotating 60-grit abrasive pad. The alloy used was 316 stainless.

The readings were taken from a noncontact Wyko NT1100 Optical Profiler capable of measuring step heights from 100 angstroms to 1000 microns. This state-of-the-art Wyko Optical Profiler is is manufactured by Veeco Metrology. Each sample was measured with a 5× magnification, which profiles a 0.9 mm by 1.2 mm area with a lateral spatial interval of 3.29 microns.

The results indicate the "shadow" finish to be the overall roughest of the four finishes tested. It also has the lowest reflectivity of the four finishes. Because the finish is coined, which is a one-sided embossing operation, you would expect the depth into the surface to be significant, as indicated by the negative Rv and the negative Rsk. The large Rt, the maximum vertical distance between the highest and lowest point, along with the large average Rv value indicates a relatively consistent indentation. This should correlate to a consistent finish appearance when viewed from different angles.

The glass bead surface has significant roughness, but it is interesting to note the distribution is random, as described by the Rku of 3. The Rsk is positive, but only slightly. The average reading came to 0.12, as compared to the No. 4 at −0.338 or the angel hair of 3.10. This would indicate an equal distribution of relative peaks and valleys across the surface. This would also correlate to a finish that reflects light the same from differing viewpoints.

The No. 4 finish is a smooth finish. The linear scratches that characterize the No.4 finish are very consistent. The Rt readings across the surface were in a very short range. The Rku was only slightly greater than 3. This would indicate the texture is relatively consistent across the surface. The negative Rsk indicates the scratches are into the surface without significant rising to create the linear ridges. Essentially, a No. 4 is not a series of microscopic ridges but a series of linear valleys.

The "angel hair" finish is the smoothest of the surfaces, with a *Ra* of 0.23 on the sample examined. It is interesting to note, however, that the angel hair surface has occasional peaks not clearly indicated on the *Rp* average. There was one reading of 11.5, which comes from a 5-μm peak extending out from the mean plane. This occurs occasionally across the microsurface of the metal, and might explain the sparkle that is seen on the surface of "angel hair" when viewed in certain lights.

The Optical Profiler provides significantly more information about the surface of metal than simple *Ra* readings from a stylus. Characteristics such as *Rp* combined with *Rsk* indicate that the outward distribution of the occasional peak can produce a sparkle. The inward texture as indicated by the negative *Rsk* would indicate a duller surface.

SURFACE ROUGHNESS CHARACTERISTICS

Metals have varying surface roughness characteristics imparted to them by the nature of their particular grain and by mechanical and chemical processes applied to them. Consider the tarnish that develops on silver or copper utensils. It is apparent because the surface has lost its luster. The surface on feel and inspection is rougher. Applying a chemical cleaner with a mild abrasive will return the surface to the original luster. It does this by dissolving the metal oxide that created the tarnish.

The metal surface seeks out the oxides and hydroxides from air and forms new compounds on the surface. These oxides sometimes combine with sulfur, carbon, and chlorine from the air. The compounds that form are natural compounds. They emulate the minerals found in nature. Using a microscope one can discern small patches of these compounds. The patches are rough and extend out from the surface. They form across the surface, and as distance between them diminishes, the appearance of the surface is altered. Polishing compounds remove these patches by light abrasion and some dissolution.

SURFACE CHEMICAL ANALYSIS: SPECTROSCOPY

Metal surfaces on occasion come in contact with substances that cause some unforeseen effect while interacting with the atoms along the external interface. The effect may be indicative of discoloration, staining, or surface pitting. To determine what may be deposited and creating the undesirable reaction on the surface, special analysis needs to be performed. One method commonly used is *photoelectron spectroscopy*.

There are several forms of photo electron spectroscopy, all of which essentially work on the same principle. In all atoms, the electrons occupy certain energy levels. With solid surfaces, there are energy levels that are involved with bonding one atom to the next. However, in such bonds, electrons can occupy a range of energy levels, known as *bands*. By selectively bombarding the surface of a metal with various energy sources and reading the photoelectrons emitted from

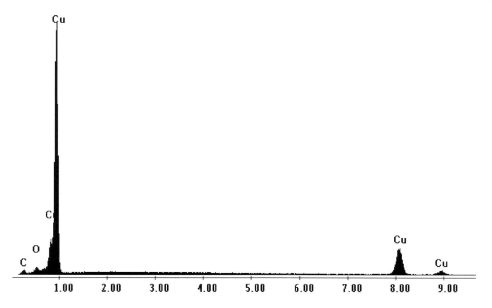

FIGURE 13.3. Example of a reading from a spectroscopy surface analysis.

the surface at different angles, the energy of the electrons can be determined; this is known as *band mapping*.

This analysis pinpoints very minute surface conditions of materials, and by atomic analysis can determine what the various element components are on the surface. It does this by bombarding selected locations on a surface with an energy source and reading the response. Every element has its own signature response. The response is an energy release that is compared to theoretical averages to determine what precisely is the particular element makeup on the surface.

If a surface has a contamination or visual alteration that needs to be examined, then taking a spectroscopic analysis using a photoelectron spectroscope will determine which elements are at the particular location. Refer to Figure 13.3 for an example of a surface reading using spectroscopy. The readings are taken from a very small localized part of a surface. Quantitative indications of the

TABLE 13.6

Various Tools of Surface Evaluation

Analysis	Information	Relative Cost
Human eye	Color differences, reflective differences	Inexpensive
Microscopic analysis	Grain direction, grit intensity, and depth Surface contaminants, oxides, oils Surface roughness	Inexpensive
Roughness Measurement—*Ra*	Average linear reading of highs and lows encountered	Inexpensive
Optical profiling	Accurate microscopic surface topography	Moderate
Scanning electron microscope	Grain boundaries, surface contaminants, microcrevices	Moderate
Photoelectron spectroscopy	Elemental makeup of various surface components and contaminants	Moderate to high

amount of a particular element can be obtained by taking several readings of a general location. This can tell whether chlorides, sulfides, or other contaminants are present on the surface. The photoelectron spectroscope can provide information on the type of oxide and the components of the oxide. An evaluation can then be made on the cause of the contamination, hence how to proceed with any corrective action or cleaning procedure.

Another common method used in the evaluation of metal surfaces is the *scanning electron microscope* (SEM). A scanning electron microscope acts similar to a conventional optical microscope but with significantly more power. Using such a device, chloride deposits within a corrosion cell pit of stainless steel can be observed. In addition, the SEM can be equipped to perform elemental microanalysis on the surface. This will provide information on the type of contaminants on the surface and whether oxide is on the surface; but, unlike photoelectron spectroscopy, it cannot determine the type of oxide.

All of these approaches are available to examine the surface differences on metal that cause changes in appearance and reflectivity. Microscopic compounds that can be potentially damaging to the long-term performance of surfaces can be identified. In the hands of an expert, these tools can provide a wealth of information to be used on the long-term expectations of metal surfaces (see Table 13.6).

CHAPTER 14
THE AGING OF THE SURFACE

> *"Though I look old, yet I am strong and lusty;*
> *For in my youth I never did apply*
> *Hot and rebellious liquors in my blood."*
>
> —WILLIAM SHAKESPEARE
> *As You Like It,* Act II, Scene 3

Metals are exposed to differing environmental conditions throughout their useful life. Metals used in one part of the country can be subjected to exposures entirely different from those of similar metals in other parts of the country. Simply put, normal expectations of how a metal will age can differ by the environment to which it is exposed, in particular, the first several weeks. The first few weeks of exposure can be critical for the natural development of the protective oxide layer on a metal surface. Figure 14.1 shows various metals and the typical expectations of aging under normal exposures.

Copper alloys, for example, exposed to a polluted industrial environment with significant levels of sulfide contaminants rapidly develop an oxide layer that thickens at a steady rate. However, if copper is first exposed to a milder atmosphere where a thin film of cuprite (copper oxide) forms, and then is exposed to the polluted environment, a much slower rate of oxidation will follow. The cuprite layer effectively protects the copper surface from attack by pollutants.[1]

Metals can be placed into two distinct categories: Category A, those that visually transform over time as they take on other compounds to develop new surface characteristics (see Table 14.1), and Category B, those metals that essen-

---

[1] In the book, *Copper and Bronze in Art* (Leidheiser 1979), David A. Scott states, "Laboratory experiments demonstrate that if copper is first exposed to an atmosphere containing small amounts of hydrogen sulfide and is then removed from it, the copper will continue to corrode at an acceleration rate. If, however, the copper is first exposed to pure air so that a thin film of cuprite forms, it will not tarnish if then exposed to air containing some hydrogen sulfide."

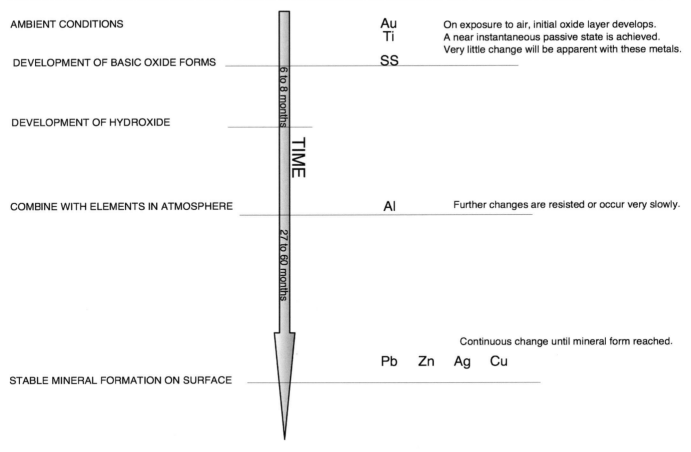

FIGURE 14.1. Changes metals undergo over time.

tially remain visually unchanged (see Table 14.2). The first category imposes a time parameter on the surface. The challenge to the designer using such changing metal surfaces is to be confident in predicting the eventual appearance. The challenge presented by the second metal surface category, for all intents and purposes, is to maintain its appearance with little change, for its useful life.

Every metal exposed to the ambient develops an oxide layer along the interface of the metal to the atmosphere. The growth of these oxides varies from metal

TABLE 14.1

Category A Metals: Those That Visually Transform over Time

Aluminum—natural uncoated
Copper
Copper alloys—brass and bronze
Lead
Monel (nickel-copper)
Weathering steel
Zinc

TABLE 14.2

Category B Metals: Those That Change Little over Time

Aluminum—anodized
Copper alloys—prepatinated darkened
Gold
Stainless steel
Titanium

to metal and with the type of exposure to which the surface of the metal is presented. The nature of the surface has a part in the development of the oxide on the metal surface. Mirror-reflective surfaces develop oxides at slower rates because the polished surface sheds moisture and contaminants more effectively than coarser surfaces.

Moisture and airborne contaminants accelerate the generation of oxides by acting as reactive agents. Moisture aids in the development of metal ions, charged particles that readily combine with oxygen, carbon dioxide, and other reactive substances such as chlorides and sulfides.

EXPECTATIONS OF CATEGORY A METALS

For most metals, the first category rules. The surface gloss will change on exposure to air as oxidation of the metal surface occurs. As oxide layers grow, the reflective level will be altered. The oxide layers inhibit light reflection in two ways. The oxide is rougher and scatters light. Oxides will allow some light to pass through and absorb certain wavelengths. For instance, dark oxides will effectively absorb the infrared wavelengths and convert them to heat. But, in general, a dulling effect occurs. Visually these metals can change in color and texture as they combine with natural components in the surrounding environment.

The incoming beam of light striking a metal surface will interact with the surface of a solid material in one of two ways. If the surface is very smooth, a specular reflection occurs. This happens with newly exposed metals such as copper. The visible light is reflected off the surface. If, however, the surface is rough from a layer of oxide, a diffused reflection occurs; light is scattered. Diffused reflection acquires some of the color of the object because it penetrates slightly into the object.

Light Striking an object = Light scattered + Light reflected
+ Light absorbed + Light transmitted

Light reflected from an oxidized, weathered metal surface is considerably less than that from a polished, newly exposed surface because of the roughness of the oxide on the surface. A larger amount is absorbed and some of this is converted to heat. Some may also be reemitted as fluorescence, adding to a metallic luster, even with a weathered surface. Copper, for instance, as it first begins to oxidize, can have various compounds present on the surface depending on the environment exposure. Various colors from dirty black to yellows and orange interference colors can be present in the initial weeks of exposure, particularly in humid environments. On close examination of the surface, small bright spots of color created by fluorescence can be apparent.

As the surface of metal ages, the oxides mainly grow outward. The oxides take on mineral forms. As more and more stable mineral forms develop, the oxidation process slows down considerably. Some inward oxidation occurs with some metals where stronger galvanic cells develop around grain boundaries. This is not a uniform behavior, but more spotty. The corrosion behavior is known as *pitting*. This is a common phenomenon of most metals as they age, particularly in industrial and marine environments.

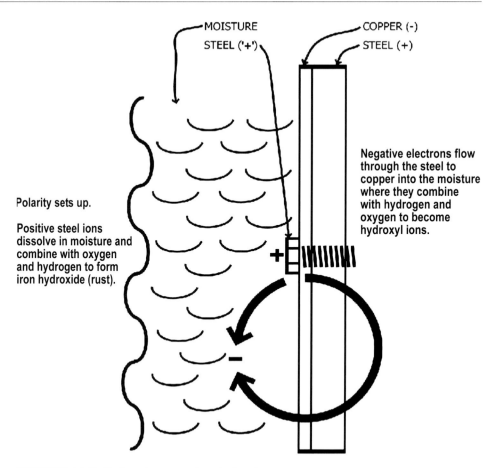

FIGURE 14.2. Galvanic corrosion behavior.

Oxygen and moisture are the main aging components of metal. See Figure 14.2. In the presence of water, microscopic corrosion cells develop on the surface of all metals. These corrosion cells occur because of differences and impurities on the surface. Oxides and hydroxides develop across the surface as oxygen combines with the free ions on the metal surface. The absorbed radiation helps break down some of the weaker molecular bonds, but surface atoms on all metals seek oxygen.

Other compounds also present in the atmosphere, such as carbon, sulfur, and chlorine, join in forming thicker patinas on this first category of metals. Elevated ozone concentrations, in combination with other substances such as sulfur and chlorine can affect the oxidation on the surface of metals. In industrial environments, sulfur and carbon dioxide, as well as soot, play a major role in the development of the patinas on metals. Seacoast environments are more subject to chlorine. However, in many northern climates, the extensive use of deicing salts can place high concentrations of chlorides in close proximity to metal surfaces. Rural exposures offer a more benign environment to most metals. Lead and terne would be the exceptions, at least aesthetically. These lead-based surfaces need more corrosive environments to develop their characteristic surface patinas. In rural exposures, red lead oxide and lead carbonate develop. The red lead color is streaky and looks more like rust on steel, whereas the lead carbonate appears somewhat chalky.

Aluminum

Aluminum in the uncoated, unanodized natural state is usually provided with an embossed texture. Whether embossed or smooth, aluminum when first installed is very bright and metallic silver in appearance. As exposure to the environment progresses, the brightness begins to fade. Humid industrial and coastal atmospheres accelerate the oxidation process. Small blotches begin to appear. On close examination, these are grayish black, fuzzy growths. Severe exposures, those close to the sea or in significantly polluted environments, will show these surface oxides much more rapidly, in a matter of weeks. In rural environments, these will not appear for 10 or more years, particularly if the surfaces receive periodic rains.

If the environment is a concern, consider alclad coatings. These pure aluminum coatings are bright in appearance and resist corrosive effects much better and for a much longer period of time.

Copper and Copper Alloys

Copper and copper alloys are perhaps the most visually changeable of all the metals. The expectation is that new copper exposed to the atmosphere will develop an even brown cupric oxide (Cu_2O) in a matter of weeks, then darken and eventually arrive at an even consistent green patina. In reality, what happens between the "new" shiny look of copper and the even green patina is a highly capricious path.

Copper immediately begins to seek out oxygen. If the environment is dry, the process is slow. If the environment is moist, the process is rapid. Initially, the surface can become very spotty, with differing colors of oxide appearing across the surface. These different colors can range from browns and blacks to yellows, oranges, reds, and dark purples.

In seacoast exposures the dark browns with a slight green tint can be visible, as well as the dark spots, though the dark spotting is rare. This form is the mineral tenorite and is somewhat unstable. It can look particularly undesirable when it appears over the more reflective copper background. It will soon give way to a hydroxide version of copper such as cuprous oxide or trihidroxychlorinated copper compound. This intermediate stage is characterized by various colors intermixed with the spotting, colors such as maroon, red, dark yellows, and deep purples. This period of time, when the copper can appear somewhat abhorrent, can be expected to last several weeks.

After several months of exposure, the copper surface should develop a darker brown tone lacking the coppery luster but still having some metallic aspects intermixed. Interference colors should be prolific, particularly the dark purples, yellows, and dark reds. With each month of exposure the spottiness recedes, still apparent on close examination but not the dominating color variations. After approximately two to three years, the surface develops a rich brown. Rural environments may still possess slight purplish tones going to rich browns. The copper surface will continue to darken and develop a rich brown tone.

If the installation is coastal or heavy industrial, a different twist will occur. The copper may go significantly darker, with tints of green showing in approximately three years. In such environments, it is likely you will see the green becoming more and more apparent. At about seven to ten years in coastal climates, the green will continue to intensify, developing the mineral form paratacamite. The color is a pale green to bluish green.

In urban-industrial zones, copper sulfur develops. This develops more slowly off of a dark copper background. The mineral form of this oxide is bronchatite. It can eventually develop into a pale to medium dark green color. The color will be even and consistent, but on close examination, streaks and dark blotches will be apparent. Soot and other contaminants will intermix with the copper sulfate surface. On all these surfaces, bright coppery streaks appear intermittently where moisture is trapped and leaches out onto the surface.

For copper alloys, the conditions are essentially the same. Cast copper alloys often have slightly coarser surfaces and collect contaminants quicker. The surfaces also tend to go darker more quickly. (Prepatinated and darkened copper alloys are discussed under the second category of metals since these components essentially are intended to remain unchanged.)

Lead

Lead when first installed rapidly develops a sheen that gives it a wetted look. Interference colors of blue, purple, and gold are visible. Soon, after several weeks of exposure, the lead loses its gloss and begins to appear dark and gray. Upon further exposure, the gray darkens further to an almost gray-black appearance. This will occur anywhere from one to three years. Some light streaking is apparent where moisture collects and drains back out onto the surface.

Monel

Monel when newly installed is almost indistinguishable from stainless steel. The high nickel content gives it the look and feel of the iron-chromium-nickel alloy, and when given a polish has similar reflective characteristics. Depending on the severity of the environment, whether urban-industrial or seacoast, the metal will slowly develop a thin patina with very slight brownish green tones.

This patina grows slowly. Eventually, after approximately 10 to 12 years, the surface takes on a duller, dark brown-green tone. No longer resembling stainless steel, the unique color acknowledges the other component in the monel alloy mix, copper. So whereas nickel controls the appearance in the early years, copper and its oxides control the appearance of the later years.

Weathering Steel

Weathering steel installed in the raw unweathered form looks like dark carbon steel, often with some rust around the edges. As the metal surface comes in contact with moist humid air or water, spotty surface rust develops. With each passing day, the rust becomes more uniform across the surface, particularly if rain is washing the wall. Eventually, usually after one to two months, the surface is entirely covered with a very light red-orange oxide. Surfaces receiving the runoff turn rust-colored as loose particles wash down off the surface.

After several more months, the surface oxide continues to develop, usually with an occasional black spot or streak from soot and contaminants that have reacted to the surface corrosion.

After a couple of years, the weathering steel appears dark red to brown. Further staining is reduced as the oxide becomes more adherent and dense on the surface of the metal.

Zinc

Zinc is often provided in a preweathered form. The preweathered surface is dull blue-gray or greenish gray in tone. The grain appearance is very definite. The grain runs in the length direction. As the zinc weathers, the surface darkens and turns more blue-gray in appearance.

Further aging occurs as the zinc surface turns a medium gray appearance, with little change in appearance beyond an even gray to blue-gray color.

EXPECTATIONS OF CATEGORY B METALS

The metals that remain virtually unchanged over time are highly resistant to their environment. The surfaces can be considered highly ordered. They have an indistinguishable surface oxide layer at the interface to the ambient. This oxide layer is like glass, in that it refuses to interact with the effects of radiation, moisture, and atmospheric compounds such as sulfur and chlorine. With the exception of gold and patinas on copper alloys, these metals are of the most recent time of humans. Many of these metals should maintain their appearance with only an occasional cleaning to remove soot and contaminants from the surface.

Anodized Aluminum

Anodized aluminum has tighter time limitations than most of the others in the list in Table 14.2. When first installed and for the next several months, no visual changes in the finish will be apparent. After the first year, the surface may pick up some light airborne soot deposits that can be removed easily with a simple washdown of the surface. On the hard coat, thick-anodized surfaces, little fading will be apparent for the first five to seven years. After this, you can expect some lightening of the color due to ultraviolet light and general oxidation of the surface. Keeping the surface cleaned will help eliminate soot and other particles that may affect the surface.

On mineral impregnated anodized surfaces, those that are provided with colors from red, blue, purples, golds, and yellows, expect to see considerable fading after eight to ten years.

Copper—Prepatinated and Darkened

Prepatinated copper surfaces and statuary copper alloy surfaces can be expected to appear as first installed for several years. Patinated copper in particular will achieve a darkening or thickening of the green patina, but generally require little to no maintenance for many years. Statuary finishes on copper alloys can be expected to darken and show perhaps some green patina surfaces after many years, but will not change all that significantly.

What often happens, however, is some level of deterioration. Sound patina coatings should last several decades. Some streaking may occur initially where the patination did not take hold. Often, some of the coating abrades from the surface due to wind and rain. Bright copper spots are signs of the patina never really catching hold. If this occurs, standard practice is to reapply some of the patina solution and allow it to redevelop. One needs to be certain the spot is clean and free of oils or other contaminants that might have been the cause for the rejection of the surface oxide in the first place.

On statuary finishes, the color will go dark, whether a light statuary or medium statuary is applied. Wear will occur at points on the surface that are frequently handled and rubbed. These may brighten, then tarnish and develop a slight green to black tint. Statuary surfaces can be stripped and refinished to return them to the original color if they darken too much or if they are to look as newly finished bronze surfaces.

For both the patina and statuary surfaces, often a coating of oxide-inhibiting lacquer is applied—lightly on patina surfaces in an attempt to help bond the patina to the surface, more heavily on the statuary surfaces.

If patina surfaces are to be refinished for whatever reason, water blast or walnut shell blasting is often used to take off the old surface and prepare it for a new application of patina solution.

Gold

Gold leaf when first installed is very bright and lustrous. With very little maintenance the properly installed gold leaf surface will continue this appearance for decades. First deterioration begins to appear around the edges of the leaf, not from the gold oxidizing or prematurely deteriorating, but from the material to which the leaf is applied. The base material, usually copper alloy, deteriorates between the joints of the gold leaf. This leads to the eventual flaking and thinning along the edges. From a distance the leaf surface appears less bright and reflective.

Once the surface begins to deteriorate, there is little that can be done to stop it. The solution is to clean off all edges of gold leaf and refinish the base material that is showing weathering. Sanding and light blasting with glass or walnut shells, followed by a wipedown with a good solvent or mild acid, can be considered. The surface is then repassivated with benzotrianozole or other antioxidant. Reseal the surface and reapply the leafing.

On plated surfaces, a similar deterioration can occur starting around the edges. Plated surfaces will not last as long as other coatings, such as leaf, because they are very thin and can have microcracks, which allow moisture to the base material. Plated surfaces will need to be cleaned. Sanding helps restate a surface "tooth" to add in the keying of a new plate coating.

Stainless Steel

Among all modern metals, stainless steel is used with the intention that it will remain the same in appearance almost indefinitely. If maintained, the surface will last a very long time. If not, stainless steel will develop a spotty appearance as it ages. Stainless steel, exposed to the atmosphere, will eventually develop an oxide on the surface. The oxide is a very light reddish brown. This will occur in marine environments and heavy industrial environments after several decades, sooner if not maintained.

In environments where road salting is prevalent, spots will appear on stainless-steel surfaces. If not cleaned, the spots will proliferate. The spots are dark in contrast to the lighter, more reflective surrounding surface. These are small pits in the surface. The dark color is due to the dissolution of iron from the stainless steel and the redeposit of iron oxide on the surface around the pit. If this is allowed to continue, eventually the entire surface will be covered with the dark stains. This development can be generated from the presence of chlorides or other halogens accessing the surface of stainless steel.

The rougher the stainless-steel surface, the more cleaning can be expected because of the significant amount of airborne particles that will collect. Simple periodic washing of the surface each spring augmented by natural rainstorms will keep stainless-steel surfaces lasting a long time.

Titanium

Titanium is a very inert material; very few natural environments will affect it. The surface after mill processes rapidly develops a thin oxide layer that resists most other influences. Sulfur, chlorines, and carbon dioxide do not faze the surfaces of titanium. Short of an occasional cleaning to remove soot and foreign particles from the surface, little else has to be done to maintain its appearance.

Table 14.3 describes what can be expected of various metal surfaces exposed to the typical environments—environments that have moderate levels of moisture and combustion products. Table 14.4 describes how long before you would expect to see oxidation behaviors appear on the surface of various metals.

RESTORATION POTENTIAL

Restoration involves an in-depth evaluation of the extent and nature of the transformed metal surface. Specifically, the question is, will restoring the metal involve cleaning, surface oxide removal, or more intensive surface repair and selective replacement? Restoration may also require the restoration of patinas on the surface. An understanding of the surface temperament is critical.

TABLE 14.3

Changes in Metal Surface from Typical Exposures

Metal	Initial Oxidation	Prolonged Oxidation
Aluminum	Small fuzzy gray patches	Uniform gray with some darker patches
Copper	Brown oxide; streaky with gold tones	Brown uniform color with green tint
Copper alloys—commercial bronze, red brasses	Brown to yellow-brown; streaky surface	Deep dark brown color
Copper alloys—architectural bronze, muntz brass	Brown to dark brown streaks and spots	Deep dark brown with blackish streaks
Gold	Little change	Loss of reflectivity around edges
Lead	Streaky surface with interference colors	Dark even gray with some white streaks; sometimes red stains
Monel	Loss of reflectivity	Green-brown even patina or gray-green patina
Nickel	Gray spotty tarnish	Gray-green patina
Weathering steel	Orange-brown streaky patina	Dark reddish brown color over the surface
Stainless steel	Small reddish spots if exposed to contaminants	Very light, transparent reddish haze.
Tin	Light tarnish spots	Even tarnish over surface
Titanium	Indiscernible	Formation of titanium carbide below oxide in presence of acid rain environments
Zinc	Darken tarnish; initially spotty oxide	Even zinc carbonate or chlorinated hydroxide; dark gray color

TABLE 14.4

Various Metals and Expected Time Until Surface Oxides Become Visible

Metal	Surface Finish	Arid Environment	Moist Environment
Aluminum	Alclad	5 to 10 years	2 to 5 years
Aluminum	Specular	5 years	6 to 12 months
Aluminum	Coarse	2 to 5 years	3 to 6 months
Aluminum	Anodized—clear	10 to 15 years	7 to 10 years
Aluminum	Color—mineral	10 to 15 years	7 to 10 years
Copper	Cold rolled	12 to 18 months	3 to 6 months
Copper	Prepatinated	Very little change	Very little change
Copper	Predarkened	10 to 15 years	5 to 10 years
Copper	Blackened	Unknown	15 to 20 years
Brass	Mirror polished	3 to 6 months	1 to 3 months
Lead	Mill	1 to 2 years	6 to 12 months
Monel	Specular	5 to 10 years	1 to 2 years
Steel	Mill	3 to 6 months	Several days
Stainless steel—300 series	Mirror	100 years plus	50 to 70 years
Stainless steel—400 series	Mirror	10 years plus	1 to 2 years
Weathering steel	Mill	3 to 6 months	Several days
Tin	Mill specular	2 to 5 years	6 to 12 months
Titanium	Mill	Unknown	Unknown
Zinc	Mill specular	5 to 10 years	2 to 5 years
Zinc	Preweathered	15 to 20 years	10 to 15 years
Zinc coating	Galvanized	5 to 10 years	2 to 5 years

If simply cleaning the surface is the intent, then it is important to establish the following: means of access to the surface, whether the surface has a protective coating or patina that may become damaged from the exercise, and how the cleaning method used will need to be collected and disposed of. Best practice is to test an area and evaluate the results. Find a small accessible region, apply the cleaning solution, and utilize a brush if necessary. Closely examine the surface to determine if more stringent methods need to be utilized.

Start with the simplest approach, which is enumerated in Table 14.5 and discussed more fully in the following paragraphs. A mild, biodegradable detergent used with hot water applied with pressure can remove most soot and grime from a metal surface. Adhesive residue left from protective films will be removed, as will loose lacquer coatings, with this sort of mild detergent pressure wash. At the same time, patinas of copper, zinc, and weathering steel will not be affected. Gilded work can be approached in a similar manner, but reduce the pressure significantly and avoid using coarse brushes.

TABLE 14.5

Steps in Restoration Process

1. Clean with mild, biodegradable detergent. Use hot fluid and pressure.

2. Inspect seams and note all tears and buckles. Repair and reinspect every few months.

3. Identify all major soot deposit zones. Note and thoroughly clean them. Take corrective measures.

4. Inspect gaskets and seals. Rework and replace all broken seals.

5. Identify all corrosion cells. Determine cause. Clean per specific metal requirements.

With the surface cleaned of soot and dirt films, examine the seams and joints of the surface. Note any tears or buckles, as these are indications of possible overstress conditions. If the tears are allowing moisture to enter the surface, then repair them. Note their position and reinspect them every three to six months for a year. This should put them through a thermal cycle. If the tear returns, it is most likely endemic; something must be binding the surface and overstressing the region. In this case, contact an engineer and review both the thermal movement of the surface and the structural loads imposed on the surface in light of the tear or buckle.

With the clean surface, inspect, where you can, the gaskets and seals to ensure they are still functioning correctly. Repair any gaskets that have loosened or become torn. Remove all old sealant and replace it. When inspecting sealant, be sure the seal has simply pulled away from shrinkage and not because of a lack of bond breaker.

When inspecting the surface, note all locations where soot and dirt are collecting and developing adherent stains. These often still appear as surface films or smears and can discolor reflective surfaces. Pressure washing may only remove the top layers. These regions should be thoroughly scrubbed to remove the film and dirt. Address the condition by adding deflectors, if possible, to move the moisture, which carries the dirt. If this is impractical, consider cleaning these areas more frequently.

Inspections should identify corrosion cells that may be developing on the surface. Corrective measures must be based on the specific metal making up the surface. Corrosion cells appear as discolorations on the surface of the material. Table 14.6 represents the visual corrosion particles that appear on the surface for various metals.

To restore the reflective character, it is necessary to first remove the oxides and resmooth where the oxides leave localized indentations into the microscopic surface. Oxides develop around grain boundaries and removal will take away some of the metal. Polishing evens out the surface and restores the metallic nature until the metal oxide reestablishes itself and the process returns.

The tenacity of oxides to the base metal varies from metal to metal and the length of time the oxides have been developing. Think of the common experience of having to polish silver that has tarnished from years of sitting in storage. This oxide develops out of a relatively stable and dry environment. When fingerprints

TABLE 14.6

Table of Visual Corrosion Products

Metal Type	Visual Corrosion	Cause
Aluminum	Fuzzy dark gray spots, usually on tops of ledges	Water setting on surface
Aluminum	Black stains	Setting water
Copper	Bright copper appearance on dark background	Erosion of oxide; sealant leaching on the surface
Copper	Rust stains	Steel particles
Copper alloys	Black spots with pitting	Dezincification
Gold	Edges fraying/discoloration	Metal below gold deteriorating
Iron/steel	Red rust; powdery edges	Moisture attack
Galvanized steel	White stains and blotches	Moisture attack
Lead	White or red streaks	Formation of lead carbonate or red lead oxide
Stainless steel	Dark reddish spots	Free iron on surface
Stainless steel	Reddish blotches and spots	Chloride attack on surface
Zinc	White/gray fuzzy spots and streaks	Moisture attack
Zinc	Perforation/disintegration	Moisture attack from underside
Titanium	Darkish appearance, dull reflectivity	Titanium carbide formation

are encountered, the level of effort put into the polishing must increase dramatically. The acidic, moist deposit left by handling the silver surface develops a deeper oxide that actually etches into the surface.

Once a surface has oxidized, it is more prone to redevelop the oxide after it has been cleaned. Removing rust, iron oxide, from steel can be done with many standard rust removers. The rust will return quicker to the spot if left unprotected.

Oxides on metals are always combinations of other substances. Two of the more prevalent substances that combine with oxygen and the metal surface are sulfur and carbon, common substances in the atmosphere. These develop, respectively, into sulfates and carbonates, which become highly adherent and stable compounds when formed with metal. The oxide form often is insoluble in water and thus difficult to remove. The insoluble form is what occurs in nature and closely emulates the mineral form. This is the patina referred to that develops on a metal surface exposed to the atmosphere. In the prevalent atmosphere of today's environment, other elements are also in supply. These elements will develop on the surface of metal and, in combination with the metal, create substances on the surface layer of exterior metals. These are chlorides and chlorates; and, particularly on the coasts, silicates and phosphates are becoming more common as well.

Removal of Surface Oxides and Patinas

On occasion a patina surface of copper will become contaminated from corrosion particles of steel. The steel corrosion particles emerge from the decay of steel members in close proximity to the surface. The appearance is rust streaks. The

TABLE 14.7

Mechanical Methods of Cleaning Heavy Surface Oxides

Mechanical Cleaning Method	Comment
Glass shot peening—40 psf	Removes heavy oxides. Textures the surface slightly. Can warp metal.
Walnut shell peening	Removes oxides and grime without surface alterations.
Sodium bicarbonate	Removes oxides without damage to the metal surface.
Plastic media (Several varieties and densities are available.)	Removes oxides with little to no damage to the metal.
Water—medium-high pressure of 1000 to 7000 psi	Removes and cleans surface without damage to the metal and reduces dust.

rust will not harm the copper but it does make for a rather unattractive surface. The remedy is to remove the rust, but to do so requires the removal of the patina.

Sometimes unwanted oxides find their way onto the surface of metals (see Table 14.7). The oxides appear as streaks or stains; or paint in the form of overspray may be on the metal surface. The surface needs to be returned back to the original, unoxidized metal.

Chemical treatments can strip the surface of oxides and paint, but often the hazards posed by such chemicals in the environment present a challenge. On small surfaces, chemical treatments will work well. Test a similar surface to determine the dwell time or use the chemical treatment sparingly to dissolve unwanted oxides.

Electrochemical treatments are excellent methods of cleaning oxides from surfaces. This process can be performed in an electropolishing bath, or better still as selective electropolishing. The caution is to keep from "burning" the surface. This occurs more with metals that are not as efficient electric conductors.

On large surfaces, mechanical means can be considered to clean the oxides and other unwanted deposits from the surface. Again, it is wise to test a section to determine the best approach. Some surfaces may require selective removal of large foreign particles that adhere tenaciously to a surface before the overall mechanical approach.

Glass bead is rarely used on large exterior objects because of the dust created and the change to the metal surface. In controlled environments and relatively small surfaces, glass beads can be effectively utilized. You can refine the bead spray nozzle and carefully and selectively remove tight and adherent oxides. Glass bead does not remove oils, fingerprints, and soils, because the impacting tends to fix the soils into the metal surface. When restoring the patina, the surface created by bead blasting aids in producing a "tooth" into the metal, which will aid in the development of the repatination process.

The use of other abrasives is discouraged. Other than the environmental hazards of abrasives such as sand and silicon carbide, they can damage and possibly contaminate the surface.

Walnut shell peening is often considered for use on large surfaces. With the exception of the dust generated, walnut shell cleaning is an excellent choice for removing oxides from the surface of metals. Walnut shells do not damage the surface of even soft metals, and the waste is biodegradable.

Like walnut shells, sodium bicarbonate is also biodegradable. This white powder can be washed away with water. Sodium bicarbonate does not harm the metal, but it is not as effective on thicker oxides.

Plastic media created from recycled material work well on oxide removal. Soft media leave a slight film that can interfere with prepatination. The waste must be collected, so using them on large exterior surfaces can be expensive.

Water blasting is an effective way of removing tenacious oxides from the surface of metals. Used in two forms, medium pressure (1000 psi) and ultra-high pressure (30,000 psi), this process can rapidly strip a metal surface of loose sealant, oxides, and patinas. Dust is minimized with this stripping process; however, professionals should perform the process, as the high-pressure flow is loud and dangerous. The ultra-high pressure can actually pierce thinned metal.

With all surfaces, arriving at a method of cleaning and maintaining the appearance is critical for the long term. Metals, as with most other materials, need some degree of care. Even the steel plates on a tank need to have some cleaning to keep them operational. Metals are a natural material and as such are constantly interacting with the surroundings. With a better understanding, the unpredictable can be identified and adjusted.

Metals are a unique material, possessing properties no other material can approach. Working knowledge of metal is as old as civilization. What will be interesting is how humankind expands this knowledge into the future.

APPENDIX A
RELATIVE COST
COMPARISONS

The relative cost of one metal versus another is often a mystery. The graphs shown here are intended as guidelines to assist in the evaluation of metal and metal finishes based on cost.

The relative cost of one metal versus another, evaluated on cost per unit of surface area and similar thickness, is depicted in Figure A.1. Additional processes

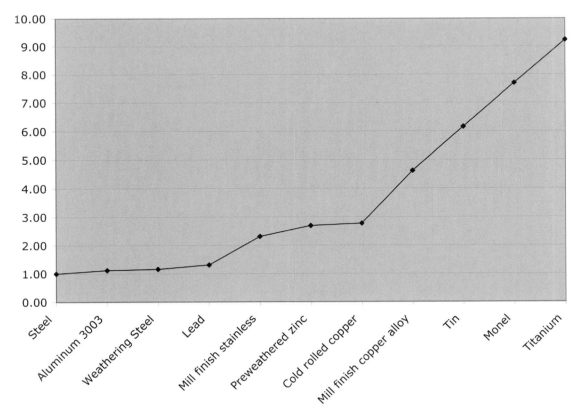

Figure A.1. Relative cost of various sheet metals of similar thickness.

must be undertaken, such as finish, fabrication, and possibly postfinishing, delivery, and installation. All are costs that can vary depending on the metal.

Additionally, market factors play a significant role. Copper, for example, can range in value to below preweathered zinc, depending on the metals supply and demand. This represents the cost of a sheet of metal delivered to the floor of a fabricator.

Note that Figure A.1 refers to metals provided from the mill without secondary finishes applied. The quality from the mill should always be architectural quality. Commercial quality standards are rarely to the levels needed for good architectural or ornamental work. Moreover, one mill's commercial quality may be another mill's architectural quality; therefore it is always advisable to acquire metal samples that represent the quality a mill can provide.

For the various metals used to create architectural surfaces, different thicknesses are required to achieve different textures and systems. You will rarely see heavy thicknesses used as roof surfacing. Similarly, you will not see thin material used as pressure-equalized, un-backed rainscreens.

Some metals offer better stiffness than others when used as a surfacing material. Stainless steel and titanium are stiffer metals than copper and zinc, for example. Furthermore, you should never use weathering steel less than 0.05 inches in thickness.

As stated before, these relative comparisons do not take in consideration the fluctations in market supply and demand. Figure A.2 delineates the relative differences between the various metals if used as a metal roof surface over a solid underlayment or as a flat-seam running bond surface.

For thicker metals surfaces, such as pressure-equalized rainscreen walls, column wraps, or other large surfaces, Figure A.3 offers some relative compari-

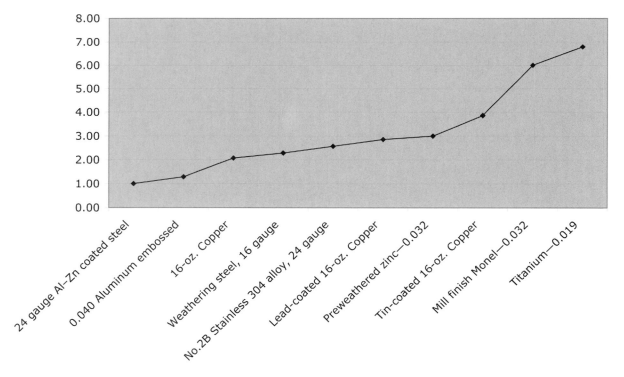

Figure A.2. Relative cost of thin metal cladding.

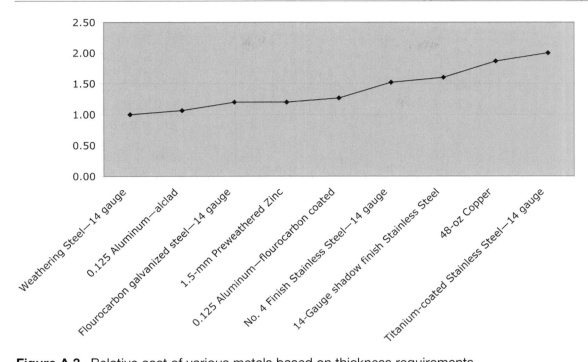

Figure A.3. Relative cost of various metals based on thickness requirements.

sons of various metals. Metals such as titanium are often coated over other metals such as stainless steel by physical vapor deposition processes. Other metals such as steel are typically galvanized, then coated with a high-quality paint system.

In practice, each metal must be taken, finished, shaped, packaged, and delivered to the location where it is to be installed. Certain metals are more difficult to work with and finish. Titanium and stainless steel, for example, require more elaborate equipment and higher skin to work than, say, aluminum or even copper. Thus, these costs are introduced into the surface when you create and install the surface elements.

Figure A.4 considers the typical cost of the added processes. Note that there are expected fluctuations by region and market conditions. Many of the metals' base prices will fluctuate from year to year as the market supply and demand rises and falls.

Note that some regions of the country have levels of expertise that will influence the final installed cost of one metal versus another. Titanium, for example, does not cost 25 percent more than monel of similar thickness; the skill necessary to work with titanium is not that much different than working with monel. However, currently, the knowledge of the material will have some influence on the final installed price. Titanium cannot be refinished if scratched, for instance, so a larger contingency may be reflected in the price.

In discussing the various finishes and how they affect the ultimate cost of the metal, Figures A.5, A.6, A.7, and A.8 provide relative comparisons of respective costs. Each metal has its own specific range of finishes, so they are reviewed individually. Many of these finishes can be applied over others, such as anodizing over glass-bead-blast aluminum, therefore the relative cost is not additive, but it is higher than glass bead alone.

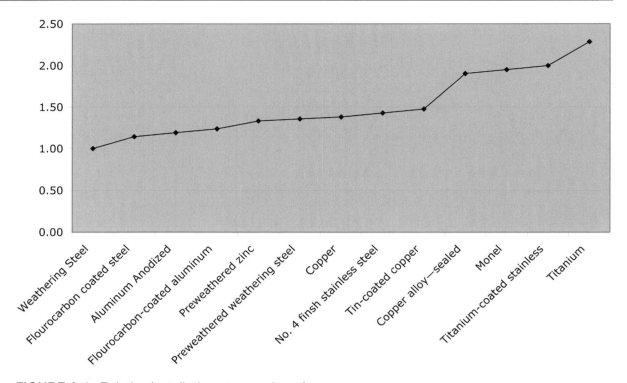

FIGURE A.4. Relative installed cost per unit surface area.

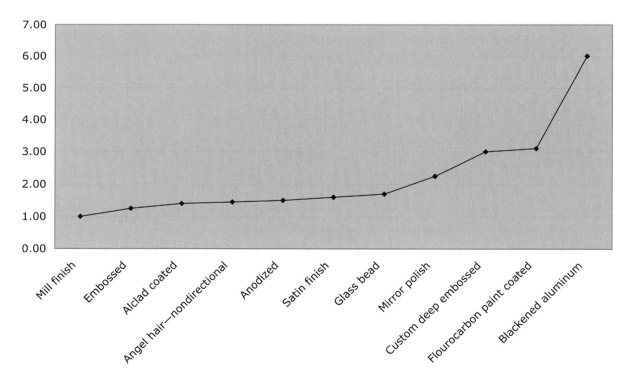

FIGURE A.5. Relative cost of various aluminum finishes.

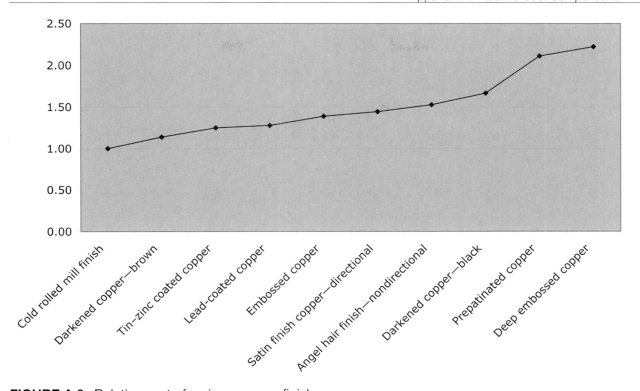

FIGURE A.6. Relative cost of various copper finishes.

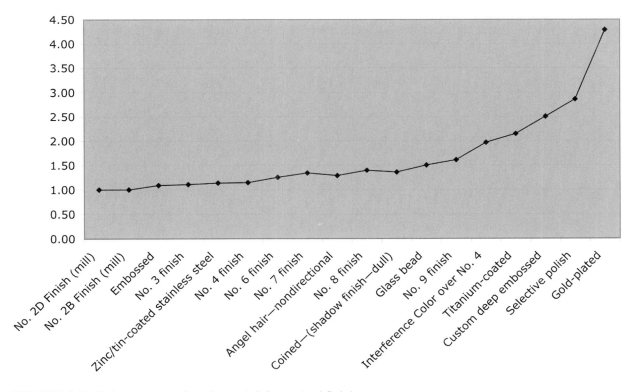

FIGURE A.7. Relative cost of various stainless steel finishes.

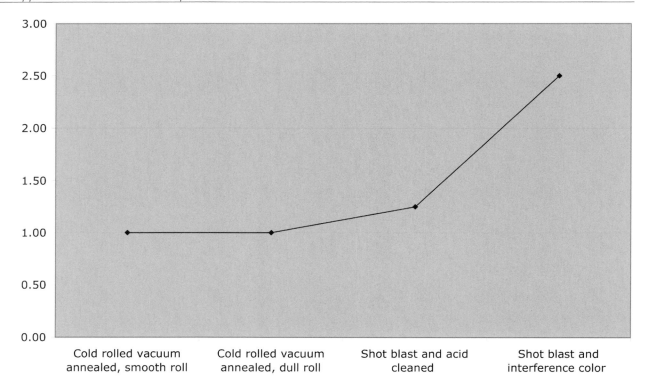

FIGURE A.8. Relative cost of various titanium finishes.

It is important to point out that these relative values do not take into account labor to fabricate or installation costs. These costs are dependent on the surface and how accessible it is.

Often, on projects still in the design stage, it is beneficial to have an idea of comparative costs. However, comparative costs do not usually account for the maintenance, long-term performance, or weathering characteristics of the metal. These factors, as well as others, must be included to arrive at a true, albeit subjective, conclusion as to which metal is best suited for a particular surface.

Figure A.9 compares metals with various finishes. The caveats to this are, one, that the price at any given time may fluctuate based on supply and demand, and, two, the relative values do not take into account fabrication, installation, skill, maintenance, long-term performance, or weathering characteristics.

Obviously, this graph does not compare all the finishes available, just a representative few. Other custom finishes are at the high end, while more ubiquitous finishes are near the low end.

All the materials represent metals that should have a useful life span in excess of 30 years. Titanium, for example, is often considered a 100-year metal; and copper and zinc have applications that existed longer than that. Stainless steel and aluminum, if maintained, are expected to reach this length of life span, but they have not been in use long enough to know for sure.

Galvanized, aluminum–zinc-coated steels were left off because of their shorter expected life span. As with painted material, the service life could be the aesthetic appeal of the pigment in the paint rather than the metal. Depending on the paint finish, painted aluminum would fall somewhere in the middle, with the more expensive, three-coat finishes falling on the right side of the graph.

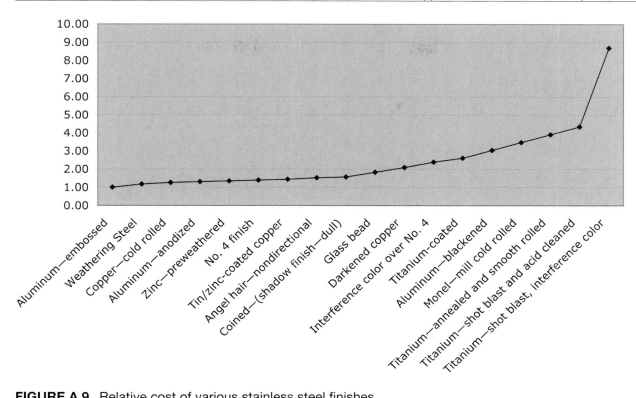

FIGURE A.9. Relative cost of various stainless steel finishes.

APPENDIX B
FINISH DESIGNATIONS

Sheet Form of Metal	Mill Finishes	Secondary Finishes
Aluminum	Unspecified Nonspecular Specular	Mirror finish Satin finish—directional; fine, medium, coarse Glass bead Angel hair—nondirectional Embossed Anodized Blackened
Copper	Unspecified Cold rolled Prepatinated Predarkened	Mirror finish Satin finish—directional; fine, medium, coarse Glass bead Angel hair—nondirectional Embossed Blackened
Copper alloys	Unspecified Specular	Mirror finish Satin finish—directional Glass bead Angel hair—nondirectional Embossed
Gold	Foil Leaf	Not applicable
Iron	Hot rolled Cold rolled	Not applicable
Lead	Mill finish	Not applicable

Sheet Form of Metal	Mill Finishes	Secondary Finishes
Monel	Cold rolled finish	Mirror finish Satin finish—directional Glass bead Angel hair—nondirectional
Steel	Hot rolled Cold rolled	Satin finish—directional Glass bead Steel shot Angel hair—nondirectional
Stainless steel	Hot rolled and pickled (HRAP) No. 2D No. 2B No. 2BA Shadow Coined	No. 9 mirror No. 8 mirror No. 7 No. 6—directional No. 4—directional No. 3—directional Angel hair—nondirectional Glass bead Embossed Interference-colored
Tin	Cold rolled	Specular Fine satin Angel hair
Titanium	Cold rolled, vacuum annealed, cold rolled on smooth finishing rolls Cold rolled, vacuum annealed, cold rolled on rough finishing rolls Shot blast and acid cleaned	Interference-colored
Zinc	Cold rolled Preweathered Preweathered, blackened Preweathered, gray	Satin finish—fine, medium, and coarse Angel hair—nondirectional finish

Extruded Form	Mill Finishes	Secondary Finishes
Aluminum	As fabricated Architectural surface quality	Mirror finish Satin finish—directional; fine, medium, coarse Glass bead Angel hair
Copper	As fabricated Architectural surface quality	Mirror finish Satin finish—directional; fine, medium, coarse Angel hair—nondirectional Glass bead
Copper alloys	As fabricated Architectural surface quality	Mirror finish Satin finish—directional; fine, medium, coarse Angel hair—nondirectional Glass bead
Lead	As fabricated	Not applicable
Stainless steel	As fabricated, pickled As fabricated, pickled and shot blast	Specular polished Satin finish—directional; fine, medium, coarse Angel hair—nondirectional Glass bead
Zinc	As fabricated	Preweathered

GLOSSARY

Ablation

The removal of a material from a surface by the application of energy.

Ambient

An environment that surrounds and contacts a surface.

American Society of Testing Materials (ASTM)

The organization that sets standards for testing, evaluating, and manufacturing materials in the United States.

Amorphous

Noncrystalline. Refers to a form or material that is not comprised of crystals.

Angstrom

Å, AU. A measuring unit mainly of light wavelength, but also considered as 1×10^{-9} millimeters.

Anisotropic

Exhibiting different properties along an axis in different directions.

Annealing

A process by which metal is heated to a temperature above the *critical* temperature. It is then slowly cooled at a controlled rate until it reaches room temperature. This allows the work-hardened grain structure to recrystallize into new grain structures, free of stress. These grain structures impart a more soft and ductile character to the metal.

Anode

The positive pole of an electrolytic cell. The anode is the electrode where oxidation reactions occur. Anodizing aluminum, for example, makes the aluminum sheet the positive pole when it is immersed in the sulfuric acid bath. The aluminum sheet develops aluminum oxide on the surface.

Artificially aged

An accelerated aging process, as opposed to a natural aging of metal. Achieved by heating a metal above room temperature for a defined period of time.

Benzotriazole (BTA)

A tarnish-inhibiting compound used on copper alloys to inhibit surface oxidation.

Bitumen

Asphaltum or pitch. A term for various sticky, black hydrocarbon materials.

Blanket deposition

Deposition of a material over the entire surface.

Brazing

Welding process that uses a filler metal applied at high temperature between two closely spaced metals. The process is similar to soldering except that the filler is usually an alloy variation of the two metals, and the temperature is much greater. The melting point of the filler metal is below that of the two metals being joined. The filler metal is fed between the two metals by means of capillary action.

Bright annealing

Annealing in a controlled atmosphere to inhibit the discoloration of the bright surface.

British Standards (BS)

The organization that sets standards for testing, evaluating, and manufacturing materials in Britain.

Capillary action

The force by which a liquid in contact with a tight surface-to-surface space or hole intrudes by means of surface tension.

Carnauba wax

A hard wax taken from the carnauba palm.

Case hardening

Surface heat treatment process used to produce a hard, wear-resistant surface on metal. Methods of surface hardening include carburization, cyaniding, nitriding, flame hardening, and electroinduction hardening.

Cathode

The negative electrode of an electrolytic cell. As opposed to the anode side of an electrolytic cell where oxidation occurs, the cathode undergoes a reduction reaction.

Chasing

Term used to describe the moving of a metal surface.

Chatter

A surface defect on sheet metal created by the unstable tooling or polishing belts.

Cladding
A layer of metal that is metallurgically bonded to another metal.

Coefficient of thermal expansion
Change in unit length corresponding to a change in temperature.

Coining
A cold process in which a metal surface is squeezed against a pattern die to impart the negative of the pattern into one side of the surface.

Cold work
The manipulation of a metal beyond its plastic limit while at room temperature. Usually refers to strain-hardening behavior of the metal as it is worked at room temperature.

Crazing
A microfracturing of the outer oxide layer of a metal surface.

Creep
Change in dimension of a substance over time while under load.

Deposition
The general description for the application of a metal onto another material surface, whereby a molecular bond is made between the metal surfacing material and the base material.

Dielectric
Materials that do not conduct electricity.

Diffused reflectance
Reflection of light over a range of angles relative to a particular incident angle.

Dual curvature
A surface that curves in two different planes, such as a sphere or hyperbolic paraboloid. Placing a straight edge on the surface will at no point settle onto the surface.

Electrode
Conductor through which a current enters or leaves an electrolytic cell.

Electrolyte
Current conductive solution between two electrodes.

Electroplating
Deposition of metal films from solution on other metals.

Etching
Process of chemical and/or electrolytic removal of material.

Evaporative deposition
Condensing a thin film of a material on a substrate, under a vacuum.

Fatigue
Failure of a structure caused by repeated stress over a period of time.

Gilding
The application of a thin layer of gold leaf or powder to a surface.

Grain
An individual crystal.

Grain boundary
Microstructure of metals. Grain boundaries are narrow zones between one crystal orientation and that of another.

High-velocity forming
A group of processes that rapidly move metal into forming dies.

Incralac
Trade name for a clear acrylic lacquer developed by the International Copper Research Association. The lacquer contains benzotriazole.

Lattice
A definite atomic structure corresponding to the crystallographic orientation of the atoms.

Litharge
Lead oxide (PbO).

Metallization
The act of adding metal to a substrate.

Passivation
Formation of an insulating or protective layer directly over the metal surface to protect the surface from contaminates, moisture, and further oxidation. Renders the surface unreactive.

Patina
The coloration of the surface of a metal by development of various oxide components either naturally or artificially.

Physical vapor deposition (PVD)
Ballistic transportation of evaporated material to the substrate surface under a high-vacuum environment. Pure metallic film formed by vaporizing solid or alloy metal under vacuum utilizing an arc evaporation process. The resulting highly charged metal ions form a plasma when mixed with nitrogen or other inert gases. This plasma is attracted to the base metal, which is negatively charged. Ion by ion, a thin metallic film uniformly grows on the surface to a predetermined thickness.

Pickling
Cleaning of oxides from the metal surface by acid baths or washes.

Precipitation hardening
The process of age hardening, which occurs quite rapidly in the first few days after casting, then much slower over the next several weeks.

Pressure equalized
A wall system whereby the inside pressure on the surface of the wall is allowed to balance with that of the exterior side of the wall.

Rainscreen

A surface that efficiently sheds moisture by removal of the force propelling it, and allowing gravity to pull the moisture down and to the exterior side of the surface.

Roughness

Microscopic peak-to-valley distances of surface protrusions and depressions, measured in angstroms.

Ruled surface

A surface capable of having a straightedge passed tightly across it without rising off the surface.

Running bond

A pattern of elements that create a series of parallel seams with offsetting perpendicular seams.

Sinter

To heat without melting.

Solder

A low melting-point alloy that can wet copper, conduct current, and mechanically join two parts. Usually an alloy of lead–tin.

Solution heat treatment

Heating a metal alloy to a temperature above the *transformation* temperature. The metal is then rapidly cooled by air or by quenching in water or oil. After a short period of time, the alloy begin to increase in hardness and strength. This increase in hardness can continue for days.

Strain-harden

An increase in hardness and strength due to plastic deformation of the metal while undergoing cold working processes.

Tarnish

A thin oxide layer that develops on a metal surface.

Temper

The hardness and strength of a metal produced by cold working and thermal treatments.

Temper designations

Heat treatment designations for aluminum alloys. These include:

F: As fabricated

O: Annealed, softest temper

H: Strain hardened

H2: Strain hardened and partially annealed

H3: Strain hardened and stabilized

W: Solution heat treatment

T1: Solution heat treatment; naturally aged

T6: Solution heat treatment; artificially aged

T9: Solution heat treatment; artificially aged and cold worked

Terne

The name given to a group of lead–tin alloys applied to steel or stainless-steel sheet.

Thermal spray

A group of processes that apply one metal to another by creating a localized high-energy spray of molten metal onto a cold surface of a base metal.

Toothing

Microscopic indentations in metal surfaces to increase the interface surface and to produce a keying effect of a layer or coating of one metal with another metal or compound.

Tripoli

A fine abrasive consisting of mostly fine silica with small amounts of aluminum oxide and iron oxide.

Verdigris

Pigment derived from copper acetate.

Yield

The occurrence of plastic deformation in a metal.

Yield point

The first stress in a material, typically less than the maximum attainable stress where an increase in strain occurs. A transition from plastic to elastic deformation of the material.

BIBLIOGRAPHY

Agricola, G. 1956. *De Re Metallica*. New York: Dover Publications.

ALCOA. 1973. *Forming of Aluminum*. Pittsburgh, PA.

American Iron and Steel Institute. 1979. *Sheet Steel*. Steel Products Manual. Washington, DC.

American Society of Metals, 1989. *Metals Handbook*. Metals Park, OH.

———American Society of Metals. 1983. *Metals Reference Book,* 2nd ed. Metals Park, OH.

———1998. *Metallurgy for the Non-Metallurgist*. Materials Park, OH.

Beranger, G., Henry, G., Sanz, G., and Sollac Group. 1996. *The Book of Steel*. Paris, France: Lavoisier Publishing.

CASTI. 1998. *The Metals Redbook—Nonferrous Metals,* 2nd ed. Edmonton, Canada: CASTI Publications.

Deutsches Kupfer-Institut. 1987. *Kupfur Im Hochbau*. Berlin.

Drayman-Weisser, T. 2000. *Gilded Metals-History, Technology and Conservation*. London: Archetype Publications, Ltd.

Edwards, J. 1996. *Coating and Surface Treatment Systems for Metals*. Stevenage, Hertfordshire, England: Finishing Publications Ltd.

Feneau, C. 2002. *Non-Ferrous Metals*. New York: Unicore.

Frankel, F., and Whitesides, G. 1997. *On the Surface of Things*. San Francisco: Chronicle Books.

Frohlich, B., and Schulenburg, S. 2003. *Metal Architecture Design and Construction*. Basel, Switzerland: Birkhauser.

Goethe, J. 1840. *Theory of Colours*. Cambridge, MA: MIT Press.

Grilli, E., Blanco, F., Notarcola, S., Sbrana, A., and Zanini, A. 2002. *Unknown Nobleness*. Roma, Italy: SMI Group.

Hughes, R., and Rowe, M. 1991. *The Colouring, Bronzing, and Patination of Metals*. New York: Watson-Guptill Publications.

Hullman, H. 2003. *Naturally Oxidizing Metal Surfaces—Environmental Effects of Copper and Zinc in Building Applications.* Stuttgart: Fraunhofer IRB Verlag.

Hurst, Steve. 1996. *Metal Casting.* London: Intermediate Technology Publications, Ltd.

Ishii, M. 1996. Discoloration of Titanium in Atmospheric Environment. *The effect of micro surface-morphology on spatial distribution of specular glossiness of architectural titanium sheets.* Tokyo: Nippon Steel Corp.

Kipper, P. 1995. *Patinas for Silicon Bronze.* Loveland, CO.: Loveland Press.

Kodas, T., and Hampden-Smith, M. 1994. *The Chemistry of Metal CVD.* New York: VCH Verlagsgesellschaft mbH and VCH Publishers Inc.

Lamphier, L., and Spence, T. 1994. "How Fabrication Affects Finish." *Tube and Pipe Quarterly.*

LeBlank, R., and Smith, K. 1992. *Gold Leaf Techniques.* Cincinnati, OH: ST Publications.

Lynch, D., and Livingston, W., 2001. *Color and Light in Nature,* 2nd ed. Cambridge, MA: Cambridge University Press.

McCreight, T., and Bsullak, N. 2001. *Color on Metal.* Madison, WI: GUILD Publishing.

Minnaert, M. 1954. *The Nature of Light and Colour in the Open Air.* New York: Dover Publications

Nassau, K. 1983. *The Physics and Chemistry of Color.* New York: John Wiley & Sons, Inc.

National Association of Architectural Metal Manufacturers. 1976. *Metal Finishes Manual.* Oak Park, IL.

National Association of Sheet Metal Contractors. 1929. *Standard Practice in Sheet Metal Work.* Pittsburgh, PA.

Nichols, S. 2001. *Aluminum by Design.* Pittsburgh, PA: Carnegie Museum of Art.

Rossing, T. and Chiaverina, C. 1999. *Light Science.* New York: Springer-Verlag New York, Inc.

Scott, D. 2002. *Copper and Bronze in Art.* Los Angeles: Getty Publications.

SMACNA. 2003, *Architectural Sheet Metal Manual,* 6th ed. Chantilly, VA.

Stewart, I. 1995. *Nature's Numbers.* New York: Basic Books.

Wade, D. 2003. *Li: Dynamic Form in Nature.* New York: Walker and Company.

Webb, M. 2000. *Lacquer Technology and Conservation.* Oxford, England: Butterworth-Heinemann.

Young, Ronald D. 1994. *Contemporary Patination.* Escondido, CA: Sculpt-Nouveau.

INDEX